The Nile Tributaries of Abyssinia

AND

The Sword Hunters
Of the Hamran Arabs

THE NILE TRIBUTARIES OF ABYSSINIA

AND

THE SWORD HUNTERS OF THE HAMRAN ARABS

SIR SAMUEL W. BAKER, M.A., F.R.G.S.

Rockville, Maryland
2008

The Nile Tributaries of Abyssinia and the Sword Hunters of the Hamran Arabs by Sir Samuel W. Baker, M.A., F.R.G.S. in its current format, copyright © Arc Manor 2008. This book, in whole or in part, may not be copied or reproduced in its current format by any means, electronic, mechanical or otherwise without the permission of the publisher.

The original text has been reformatted for clarity and to fit this edition.

Arc Manor, Arc Manor Classic Reprints, Manor Classics, TARK Classic Fiction and the Arc Manor logo are trademarks or registered trademarks of Arc Manor Publishers, Rockville, Maryland. All other trademarks are properties of their respective owners.

This book is presented as is, without any warranties (implied or otherwise) as to the accuracy of the production, text or translation. The publisher does not take responsibility for any typesetting, formatting, translation or other errors which may have occurred during the production of this book.

ISBN: 978-1-60450-125-4

Arc Manor
P. O. Box 10339
Rockville, MD 20849-0339
www.ArcManor.com
Printed in the United States of America/United Kingdom

I dedicate this book,
With special permission,

TO HIS ROYAL HIGHNESS ALBERT EDWARD,
PRINCE OF WALES,

As the first of England's Royal race
Who has sailed upon the waters of the Nile;
The lake sources of which mighty river are honoured
By the names of his August parents.

Contents

Preface	9
Above the Cataract.	11
Chapter II (Untitled)	25
Wild Asses of the Desert.	40
Route from Cassala to Souakim.	49
The Storm.	59
Sheik Achmet Abou Sinn.	70
The Departure.	81
The Plagues of Egypt.	93
Form a Raft With the Sponging Bath.	118
A Few Notes at Ehetilla.	131
The Ford.	145
Old Neptune Joins the Party.	165
The Lions Find the Buffalo.	176
A Foreboding of Evil.	189
Antelopes on the Settite.	204

ABOU DO IS GREEDY.	220
WE REACH THE ROYAN.	233
A CAMEL FALLS, AND DIES.	252
SEND A PARTY TO RECONNOITRE.	262
ARRIVAL AT METEMMA, OR GALLABAT.	272
FERTILITY OF THE COUNTRY ON THE BANKS OF THE RAHAD.	284
WE LEAVE THE DINDER.	297

Preface.

The work entitled "The Albert N'yanza Great Basin of the Nile," published in 1866, has given an account of the equatorial lake system from which the Egyptian river derives its source. It has been determined by the joint explorations of Speke, Grant, and myself, that the rainfall of the equatorial districts supplies two vast lakes, the Victoria and the Albert, of sufficient volume to support the Nile throughout its entire course of thirty degrees of latitude. Thus the parent stream, fed by never-failing reservoirs, supplied by the ten months' rainfall of the equator, rolls steadily on its way through arid sands and burning deserts until it reaches the Delta of Lower Egypt.

It would at first sight appear that the discovery of the lake sources of the Nile had completely solved the mystery of ages, and that the fertility of Egypt depended upon the rainfall of the equator concentrated in the lakes Victoria and Albert; but the exploration of the Nile tributaries of Abyssinia divides the Nile system into two proportions, and unravels the entire mystery of the river, by assigning to each its due share in ministering to the prosperity of Egypt.

The lake sources of Central Africa support the life of Egypt, by supplying a stream, throughout all seasons, that has sufficient volume to support the exhaustion of evaporation and absorption; but this stream, if unaided, could never overflow its banks, and Egypt, thus deprived of the annual inundation, would simply exist, and cultivation would be confined to the close vicinity of the river.

The inundation, which by its annual deposit of mud has actually created the Delta of Lower Egypt, upon the overflow of which the fertility of Egypt depends, has an origin entirely separate from the lake-sources of Central Africa, and the supply of water is derived exclusively from Abyssinia.

The two grand affluents of Abyssinia are, the Blue Nile and the Atbara, which join the main stream respectively in N. lat. 15 degrees 30 minutes and 17 degrees 37 minutes. These rivers, although streams of extreme grandeur during the period of the Abyssinian rains, from the middle of June until September, are reduced during the dry months to utter insignificance; the Blue Nile becoming so shallow as to be unnavigable, and the Atbara perfectly dry. At that time the water supply of Abyssinia having ceased, Egypt depends solely upon the equatorial lakes and the affluents of the White Nile, until the rainy season shall again have flooded the two great Abyssinian arteries. That flood occurs suddenly about the 20th of June, and the grand rush of water pouring down the Blue Nile and the Atbara into the parent channel, inundates Lower Egypt, and is the cause of its extreme fertility.

Not only is the inundation the effect of the Abyssinian rains, but the deposit of mud that has formed the Delta, and which is annually precipitated by the rising waters, is also due to the Abyssinian streams, more especially to the river Atbara, which, known as the Bahr el Aswat (Black River), carries a larger proportion of soil than any other tributary of the Nile; therefore, to the Atbara, above all other rivers, must the wealth and fertility of Egypt be attributed.

It may thus be stated: The equatorial lakes *feed* Egypt; but the Abyssinian rivers *cause the inundation.*

This being a concise summary of the Nile system, I shall describe twelve months' exploration, during which I examined every individual river that is tributary to the Nile from Abyssinia, including the Atbara, Settite, Royan, Salaam, Angrab, Rahad, Dinder, and the Blue Nile. The interest attached to these portions of Africa differs entirely from that of the White Nile regions, as the whole of Upper Egypt and Abyssinia is capable of development, and is inhabited by races either Mohammedan or Christian; while Central Africa is peopled by a hopeless race of savages, for whom there is no prospect of civilization.

The exploration of the Nile tributaries of Abyssinia occupied the first twelve months of my journey towards the Nile sources. During this time, I had the opportunity of learning Arabic and of studying the character of the people; both necessary acquirements, which led to my ultimate success in reaching the "Albert N'yanza." As the readers of the work of that title are aware, I was accompanied throughout the entire journey by my wife, who, with extraordinary hardihood and devotion, shared every difficulty with which African travel is beset.

Chapter I.

Above the Cataract.

Without troubling the public with a description of that portion of the Nile to the north of the first cataract, or with a detailed account of the Egyptian ruins, that have been visited by a thousand tourists, I will commence by a few extracts from my journal, written at the close of the boat voyage from Cairo : –

"May 8, 1861. – No air. The thermometer 104 degrees Fahr.; a stifling heat. Becalmed, we have been lying the entire day below the ruins of Philae. These are the most imposing monuments of the Nile, owing to their peculiar situation upon a rocky island that commands the passage of the river above the cataract. The banks of the stream are here hemmed in by ranges of hills from 100 to 250 feet high; these are entirely destitute of soil, being composed of enormous masses of red granite, piled block upon block, the rude masonry of Nature that has walled in the river. The hollows between the hills are choked with a yellow sand, which, drifted by the wind, has, in many instances, completely filled the narrow valleys. Upon either side of the Nile are vestiges of ancient forts. The land appears as though it bore the curse of Heaven; misery, barrenness, and the heat of a furnace are its features. The glowing rocks, devoid of a trace of vegetation, reflect the sun with an intensity that must be felt to be understood. The miserable people who dwell in villages upon the river's banks snatch every sandbank from the retiring stream, and immediately plant their scanty garden with melons, gourds, lentils, &c. this being their only resource for cultivation. Not an inch of available soil is lost; but day by day, as the river decreases, fresh rows of vegetables are sown upon the newly-acquired land. At Assouan, the sandbanks are purely sand brought down by the cataracts, therefore soil must be added to enable the people to cultivate. They dig earth from the ruins of the ancient town; this they boat across the river and spread upon the sandbank, by which excessive labour they secure sufficient mould to support their crops.

In the vicinity of Philae the very barrenness of the scenery possesses a charm. The iron-like sterility of the granite rocks, naked except in spots where the wind has sheeted them with sand; the groves of palms springing unexpectedly into view in this desert wilderness, as a sudden bend of the river discovers a village; the ever blue and never clouded sky above, and, the only blessing of this blighted land, the Nile, silently flowing between its stern walls of rocks towards the distant land of Lower Egypt, form a total that produces a scene to be met with nowhere but upon the Nile. In this miserable spot the unfortunate inhabitants are taxed equally with those of the richer districts – about fivepence annually for each date palm.

"May 9. – A good breeze, but tremendous heat. Although the floor and the curtains of the cabin are continually wetted, and the Venetian blinds are closed, the thermometer, at 4 P.M., stood at 105 degrees in the shade; and upon deck, 137 degrees in the sun. This day we passed the ruins of several small temples. The country is generally rocky, with intervals of ten or twelve miles of desert plains.

"May 10. – Fine breeze, the boat sailing well. Passed several small temples. The henna grows in considerable quantities on the left bank of the river. The leaf resembles that of the myrtle; the blossom has a powerful fragrance; it grows like a feather, about eighteen inches long, forming a cluster of small yellow flowers. The day pleasantly cool; thermometer, 95 degrees.

"May 11. – At 5 A.M. we arrived at Korosko; lat. 22 degrees 50 minutes N.; the halting-place for all vessels from Lower Egypt with merchandise for the Soudan."

At this wretched spot the Nile is dreary beyond description, as a vast desert, unenlivened by cultivation, forms its borders, through which the melancholy river rolls towards Lower Egypt in the cloudless glare of a tropical sun. From whence came this extraordinary stream that could flow through these burning sandy deserts, unaided by tributary channels? That was the mysterious question as we stepped upon the shore now, to commence our land journey in search of the distant sources. We climbed the steep sandy bank, and sat down beneath a solitary sycamore.

We had been twenty-six days sailing from Cairo to this point. The boat returned, and left us on the east bank of the Nile, with the great Nubian desert before us.

Korosko is not rich in supplies. A few miserable Arab huts, with the usual fringe of dusty date palms, compose the village; the muddy river is the frontier on the west, the burning desert on the east. Thus hemmed in, Korosko is a narrow strip of a few yards' width on the margin of the Nile, with only one redeeming feature in its wretchedness – the green shade of the old sycamore beneath which we sat.

I had a firman from the Viceroy, a cook, and a dragoman. Thus my impedimenta were not numerous. The firman was an order to all Egyptian officials for assistance; the cook was dirty and incapable; and the interpreter was nearly ignorant of English, although a professed polyglot. With this small beginning, Africa was before me, and thus I commenced the search for the Nile sources. Absurd as this may appear, it was a correct commencement. Ignorant of Arabic, I could not have commanded a large party, who would have been at the mercy of the interpreter or dragoman; thus, the first qualification necessary to success was a knowledge of the language.

After a delay of some days, I obtained sixteen camels from the sheik. I had taken the precaution to provide water-barrels, in addition to the usual goat-skins; and, with a trustworthy guide, we quitted Korosko on the 16th May, 1861, and launched into the desert.

The route from Korosko across the Nubian desert cuts off the chord of an arc made by the great westerly bend of the Nile. This chord is about 230 miles in length. Throughout this barren desert there is no water, except at the half-way station, Moorahd (from moorra, bitter); this, although salt and bitter, is relished by camels. During the hot season in which we unfortunately travelled, the heat was intense, the thermometer ranging from 106 degrees to 114 degrees Fahr. in the shade. The parching blast of the simoom was of such exhausting power, that the water rapidly evaporated from the closed water-skins. It was, therefore, necessary to save the supply by a forced march of seven days, in which period we were to accomplish the distance, and to reach Abou Hammed, on the southern bend of the welcome Nile.

During the cool months, from November until February, the desert journey is not disagreeable; but the vast area of glowing sand exposed to the scorching sun of summer, in addition to the withering breath of the simoom, renders the forced march of 230 miles in seven days, at two and a half miles per hour, the most fatiguing journey that can be endured.

Farewell to the Nile! We turned our backs upon the life-giving river, and our caravan commenced the silent desert march.

A few hours from Korosko the misery of the scene surpassed description. Glowing like a furnace, the vast extent of yellow sand stretched to the horizon. Rows of broken hills, all of volcanic origin, broke the flat plain. Conical tumuli of volcanic slag here and there rose to the height of several hundred feet, and in the far distance resembled the Pyramids of Lower Egypt – doubtless they were the models for that ancient and everlasting architecture; hills of black basalt jutted out from the barren base of sand, and the molten air quivered on the overheated surface of the fearful desert. 114 degrees Fahr. in the shade under the water-skins; 137 degrees in the sun. Noiselessly the spongy tread of the camels crept along the sand – the only sound was the rattle of some loosely secured baggage of their packs. The Arab camel-drivers followed silently at intervals, and hour by hour we struck deeper into the solitude of the Nubian desert.

We entered a dead level plain of orange-coloured sand, surrounded by pyramidical hills: the surface was strewn with objects resembling cannon shot and grape of all sizes from a 32-pounder downwards – the spot looked like the old battle-field of some infernal region; rocks glowing with heat – not a vestige of vegetation – barren, withering desolation. – The slow rocking step of the camels was most irksome, and despite the heat, I dismounted to examine the Satanic bombs and cannon shot. Many of them were as perfectly round as though cast in a mould, others were egg-shaped, and all were hollow. With some difficulty I broke them, and found them to contain a bright red sand: they were, in fact, volcanic bombs that had been formed by the ejection of molten lava to a great height from active volcanoes; these had become globular in falling, and, having cooled before they reached the earth, they retained their forms as hard spherical bodies, precisely resembling cannon shot. The exterior was brown, and appeared to be rich in iron. The smaller specimens were the more perfect spheres, as they cooled quickly, but many of the heavier masses had evidently reached the earth when only half solidified, and had collapsed upon falling. The sandy plain was covered with such vestiges of volcanic action, and the infernal bombs lay as imperishable relics of a hail-storm such as may have destroyed Sodom and Gomorrah.

Passing through this wretched solitude we entered upon a scene of surpassing desolation. Far as the eye could reach were waves like a stormy sea, grey, cold-looking waves in the burning heat; but no drop of water: it appeared as though a sudden curse had turned a raging sea to stone. The simoom blew over this horrible wilderness, and drifted the hot sand into the crevices of the rocks, and the camels drooped their heads before the suffocating wind; but still the caravan noiselessly crept along over the rocky undulations, until the stormy sea was passed: once more we were upon a boundless plain of sand and pebbles.

Here every now and then we discovered withered melons (Cucumis colocynthis); the leaves had long since disappeared, and the shrivelled stalks were brittle as glass. They proved that even the desert had a season of life, however short; but the desert fruits were bitter. So intensely bitter was the dry white interior of these melons, that it exactly resembled quinine in taste; when rubbed between the fingers, it became a fine white powder. The Arabs use this medicinally; a small piece placed in a cup of milk, and allowed to stand for a few hours, renders the draught a strong aperient. The sun – that relentless persecutor of the desert traveller – sank behind the western hills, and the long wished for night arrived; cool, delicious night! the thermometer 78 degrees Fahr. a difference of 36 degrees between the shade of day.

The guide commanded the caravan, – he was the desert pilot, and no one dared question his directions; he ordered a halt for *two hours'* rest. This was the usual stage and halting-place by the side of a perpendicular rock, the base of which was strewn thick with camel's dung; this excellent fuel soon produced a blazing fire, the coffee began to boil, and fowls were roasting for a hasty dinner. A short snatch of sleep upon the sand, and the voice of the guide again disturbed us. The camels had not been unloaded, but had lain down to rest with their packs, and had thus eaten their feed of dhurra (Sorghum vulgare) from a mat. In a few minutes we started, once more the silent and monotonous desert march.

In the cool night I preferred walking to the uneasy motion of the camel; the air was most invigorating after the intense heat of the day and the prostration caused by the simoom. The desert had a charm by night, as the horizon of its nakedness was limited; the rocks assumed fantastic shapes in the bright moonlight, and the profound stillness produced an effect of the supernatural in that wild and mysterious solitude; the Arab belief in the genii and afreet, and all the demon enemies of man, was a natural consequence of a wandering life in this desert wilderness, where nature is hostile to all living beings.

In forty-six hours and forty-five minutes' actual marching from Korosko we reached Moorahd, "the bitter well."

This is a mournful spot, well known to the tired and thirsty camel, the hope of reaching which has urged him fainting on his weary way to drink one draught before he dies: this is the camel's grave. Situated half way between Korosko and Abou Hammed, the well of Moorahd is in an extinct crater, surrounded upon all sides but one by precipitous cliffs about 300 feet high. The bottom is a dead flat, and forms a valley of sand about 250 yards wide. In this bosom of a crater, salt and bitter water is found at a depth of only six feet from the surface. To this our tired camels frantically rushed upon being unloaded.

The valley was a "valley of dry bones." Innumerable skeletons of camels lay in all directions; the ships of the desert thus stranded on their voyage. Withered heaps of parched skin and bone lay here and there, in the distinct forms in which the camels had gasped their last; the dry desert air had converted the hide into a coffin. There were no flies here, thus there were no worms to devour the carcases; but the usual sextons were the crows, although sometimes too few to perform their office. These were perched upon the overhanging cliffs; but no sooner had our overworked camels taken their long draught and lain down exhausted on the sand, than by common consent they descended from their high places, and walked round and round each tired beast.

As many wretched animals simply crawl to this spot to die, the crows, from long experience and constant practice, can form a pretty correct diagnosis upon the case of a sick camel; they had evidently paid a professional visit to my caravan, and were especially attentive in studying the case of one particular camel that was in a very weakly condition and had stretched itself full length upon the sand; nor would they leave it until it was driven forward.

The heat of Moorahd was terrific; there was no shade of any kind, and the narrow valley surrounded by glowing rocks formed a natural oven. The intense dryness of the overheated atmosphere was such, that many of our water-skins that appeared full were nearly empty; the precious supply had evaporated through the porous leather, and the skins were simply distended by the expanded air within. Fortunately I had taken about 108 gallons from Korosko, and I possessed a grand reserve in my two barrels which could not waste; these were invaluable as a resource when the supply in the skins should be exhausted. My Arab camel-men were supposed to be provided with their own private supply; but, as they had calculated upon stealing from my stock, in which they were disappointed, they were on exceedingly short allowance, and were suffering much from thirst. During our forced march of three days and a half it had been impossible to perform the usual toilette, therefore, as water was life, washing had been out of the question. Moorahd had been looked forward to as the spot of six hours' rest, where we could indulge in the luxury of a bath on a limited scale after the heat and fatigue of the journey. Accordingly, about two quarts of water were measured into a large Turkish copper basin; the tent, although the heat was unendurable, was the only dressing-room, and the two quarts of water, with a due proportion of soap, having washed two people, was about to be thrown away, when the Arab guide, who had been waiting his opportunity, snatched the basin from the servant, and in the agony of thirst drank nearly the whole of its contents, handing the residue to a brother Arab, with the hearty ejaculation, "El hambd el Illah!" (Thank God!)

My wife was seriously ill from the fatigue and intense heat, but there can be no halt in the desert; dead or alive, with the caravan you must travel, as the party depends upon the supply of water. A few extracts verbatim from my journal will describe the journey: –

"May 20. – Started at 12.30 P.M. and halted at 6.30. Off again at 7.30 P.M. till 2.45 A.M. About four miles from Moorahd, grey granite takes the place of the volcanic slag and schist that formed the rocks to that point. The desert is now a vast plain, bounded by a range of rugged hills on the south. On the north side of Moorahd, at a distance of above eight miles, slate is met with; this continues for about three miles of the route, but it is of impure quality, with the exception of one vein, of a beautiful blue colour. A few miserable stunted thorny mimosas are here to be seen scattered irregularly, as though lost in this horrible desert."

Many years ago, when the Egyptian troops first conquered Nubia, a regiment was destroyed by thirst in crossing this desert. The men, being upon a limited allowance of water, suffered from extreme thirst, and deceived by the appearance of a mirage that exactly resembled a beautiful lake, they insisted on being taken to its banks by the Arab guide. It was in vain that the guide assured them that the lake was unreal, and he refused to lose the precious time by wandering from his course. Words led to blows, and he was killed by the soldiers, whose lives depended upon his guidance. The whole regiment turned from the track and rushed towards the welcome waters. Thirsty and faint, over the burning sands they hurried; heavier and heavier their footsteps became – hotter and hotter their breath, as deeper they pushed into the desert – farther and farther from the lost track where the pilot lay in his blood; and still the mocking spirits of the desert, the afreets of the mirage, led them on, and the lake glistening in the sunshine tempted them to bathe in its cool waters, close to their eyes, but never at their lips. At length the delusion vanished – the fatal lake had turned to burning sand! Raging thirst and horrible despair! the pathless desert and the murdered guide! lost! lost! all lost! Not a man ever left the desert, but they were subsequently discovered, parched and withered corpses, by the Arabs sent upon the search.

"May 21. – Started at 5.45 A.M. till 8.45; again, at 1.45 P.M. till 7 P.M.; again, at 9.30 P.M. till 4 A.M. Saw two gazelles, the first living creatures, except the crows at Moorahd, that we have seen since we left Korosko; there must be a supply of water in the mountains known only to these animals. Thermometer, 111 degrees Fahr. in the shade; at night, 78 degrees. The water in the leather bottle that I repaired is deliciously cool. N.B. – In sewing leather bottles or skins for holding water, no thread should be used, but a leathern thong, which should be dry; it will then swell when wetted, and the seam will be watertight.

"May 22. – Started at 5.30 A.M. till 9.30; again, at 2.15 P.M. till 7.15 P.M. Rested to dine, and started again at 8.30 P.M. till 4.25 A.M.; reaching Abou Hammed, thank heaven!

"Yesterday evening we passed through a second chain of rugged hills of grey granite, about 600 feet high, and descended through a pass to an extensive plain, in which rose abruptly, like huge pyramids, four granite hills, at great distances apart. So exactly do they resemble artificial pyramids at a distance, that it is difficult to believe they are natural objects. I feel persuaded that the ancient Egyptians took their designs for monuments and buildings from the hills themselves, and raised in the plains of Lower Egypt artificial pyramids in imitation of the granite hills of this form. Their temples were in form like many of the granite ranges, and were thoroughly encased with stone. The extraordinary massiveness of these works suggests that Nature assisted the design; the stone columns are imitations of the date palms, and the buildings are copies of the rocky hills – the two common features of Egyptian scenery.

"Throughout the route from Korosko, the skeletons of camels number about eight per mile, with the exception of the last march on either side of the watering-place Moorahd, on which there are double that number, as the animals have become exhausted as they approach the well. In the steep pass through the hills, where the heat is intense, and the sand deep, the mortality is dreadful; in some places I counted six and eight in a heap; and this difficult portion of the route is a mass of bones, as every weak animal gives in at the trying place.

"So dreadful a desert is this between Korosko and Abou Hammed, that Said Pasha ordered the route to be closed; but it was re-opened upon the application of foreign consuls, as the most direct road to the Soudan. Our Bishareen Arabs are first-rate walkers, as they have performed the entire journey on foot. Their water and provisions were all exhausted yesterday, but fortunately I had guarded the key of my two water-casks; thus I had a supply when every water-skin was empty, and on the last day I divided my sacred stock amongst the men, and the still more thirsty camels. In the hot months, a camel cannot march longer than three days without drinking, unless at the cost of great suffering.

"Having arrived here (Abou Hammed) at 4.25 this morning, 23d May, I had the luxury of a bath. The very sight of the Nile was delightful, after the parched desolation of the last seven days. The small village is utterly destitute of everything, and the sterile desert extends to the very margin of the Nile. The journey having occupied ninety-two hours of actual marching across the desert, gives 230 miles as the distance from Korosko, at the loaded-camel rate of two and a half miles per hour. The average duration of daily march has been upwards of thirteen hours, including a day's halt at Moorahd. My camels have arrived in tolerable condition, as their loads did not exceed 400 lbs. each; the usual load is 500 lbs.

"May 24. – Rested both men and beasts. A caravan of about thirty camels arrived, having lost three during the route.

"May 25. – Started at 5 a.m. The route is along the margin of the Nile, to which the desert extends. A fringe of stunted bushes, and groves of the coarse and inelegant dome palm, mark the banks of the river by a thicket of about half a mile in width. I saw many gazelles, and succeeded in stalking a fine buck, and killing him with a rifle.

"May 26. – Marched ten hours. Saw gazelles, but so wild that it was impossible to shoot. Thermometer 110 degrees Fahr.

"May 27. – Marched four hours and forty-five minutes, when we were obliged to halt, as F. is very ill. In the evening I shot two gazelles, which kept the party in meat.

"May 28. – Marched fifteen hours, to make up for the delay of yesterday. Shot a buck on the route.

"May 29. – The march of yesterday cut off an angle of the river, and we made a straight course through the desert, avoiding a bend of the stream. At 7.30 this morning we met the Nile again; the same character of country as before, the river full of rocks, and forming a succession of rapids the entire distance from Abou Hammed. Navigation at this season is impossible, and is most dangerous even at flood-time. The simoom is fearful, and the heat is so intense that it was impossible to draw the gun-cases out of their leather covers, which it was necessary to cut open. All woodwork is warped; ivory knife-handles are split; paper breaks when crunched in the hand, and the very marrow seems to be dried out of the bones by this horrible simoom. One of our camels fell down to die. Shot two buck gazelles; I saw many, but they are very wild.

"May 30. – The extreme dryness of the air induces an extraordinary amount of electricity in the hair, and in all woollen materials. A Scotch plaid laid upon a blanket for a few hours adheres to it, and upon being roughly withdrawn at night a sheet of flame is produced, accompanied by tolerably loud reports.

"May 31. – After an early march of three hours and twenty minutes, we arrived at the town of Berber, on the Nile, at 9.35 a.m. We have been fifty-seven hours and five minutes actually marching from Abou Hammed, which, at two and a half miles per hour, equals 143 miles. We have thus marched 373 miles from Korosko to Berber in fifteen days; the entire route is the monotonous Nubian desert. Our camels have averaged twenty-five miles per day, with loads of 400 lbs. at a cost of ninety piastres (about 19s.) each, for the whole distance. This rate, with the addition of the guide's expenses, equals about 5s. 6d. per 100 lbs. for carriage throughout 373 miles of burning desert. Although this frightful country appears to be cut off from all communication with the world, the extremely low rate of transport charges affords great facility for commerce." [1]

Berber is a large town, and in appearance is similar to the Nile towns of Lower Egypt, consisting of the usual dusty, unpaved streets, and flat-roofed houses of sun-baked bricks. It is the seat of a Governor, or Mudir, and is generally the quarters for about 1,500 troops. We were very kindly received by Halleem Effendi, the ex-Governor, who at once gave us permission to pitch the tents in his garden, close to the Nile, on the southern outskirt of the town. After fifteen days of desert marching, the sight of a well-cultivated garden was an Eden in our eyes. About eight acres of land, on the margin of the river, were thickly planted with lofty date groves, and shady citron and lemon trees, beneath which we revelled in luxury on our Persian rugs, and enjoyed complete rest after the fatigue of our long journey. Countless birds were chirping and singing in the trees above us; innumerable ring-doves were cooing in the shady palms; and the sudden change from the dead sterility of the desert to the scene of verdure and of life, produced an extraordinary effect upon the spirits. What caused this curious transition? Why should this charming oasis, teeming with vegetation and with life, be found in the yellow, sandy desert? . . . Water had worked this change; the spirit of the Nile, more potent than any genii of the Arabian fables, had transformed the desert into a fruitful garden. Halleem Effendi, the former Governor, had, many years ago, planted this garden, irrigated by numerous water-wheels; and we now enjoyed the fruits, and thanked Heaven for its greatest blessings in that burning land, shade and cool water.

 The tents were soon arranged, the camels were paid for and discharged, and in the cool of the evening we were visited by the Governor and suite.

 The firman having been officially presented by the dragoman upon our arrival in the morning, the Governor had called with much civility to inquire into our projects and to offer assistance. We were shortly seated on carpets outside the tent, and after pipes and coffee, and the usual preliminary compliments, my dragoman explained, that the main object of our

---

[1] Since that date, 31st May, 1861, the epidemic or cattle plague carried off an immense number of camels, and the charges of transport rose in 1864 and 1865 to a rate that completely paralysed the trade of Upper Egypt.

journey was to search for the sources of the Nile, or, as he described it, "the head of the river."

Both the Governor and Halleem Effendi, with many officers who had accompanied them, were Turks; but, in spite of the gravity and solidity for which the Turk is renowned, their faces relaxed into a variety of expressions at this (to them) absurd announcement. "The head of the Nile!" they exclaimed, "impossible!" "Do they know where it is?" inquired the Governor, of the dragoman; and upon an explanation being given, that, as we did not know where it was, we had proposed to discover it, the Turks merely shook their heads, sipped their coffee, and took extra whiffs at their long pipes, until at length the white-haired old Halleem Effendi spoke. He gave good and parental advice, as follows: –

"Don't go upon so absurd an errand; nobody knows anything about the Nile, neither will any one discover its source. We do not even know the source of the Atbara; how should we know the source of the great Nile. A great portion of the Atbara flows through the Pasha of Egypt's dominions; the firman in your possession with his signature, will insure you respect, so long as you remain within his territory; but if you cross his frontier, you will be in the hands of savages. The White Nile is the country of the negroes; wild, ferocious races who have neither knowledge of God nor respect for the Pasha, and you must travel with a powerful armed force; the climate is deadly; how could you penetrate such a region to search for what is useless even should you attain it? But how would it be possible for a lady, young and delicate, to endure what would kill the strongest man? Travel along the Atbara river into the Taka country, there is much to be seen that is unexplored; but give up the mad scheme of the Nile source."

There was some sense in old Halleem Effendi's advice; it was the cool and cautious wisdom of old age, but as I was not so elderly, I took it "cum grano salis." He was a charming old gentleman, the perfect beau ideal of the true old style of Turk, but few specimens of which remain; all that he had said was spoken in sincerity, and I resolved to collect as much information as possible from the grey-headed authorities before I should commence the expedition. I was deeply impressed with one fact, that until I could dispense with an interpreter it would be impossible to succeed, therefore I determined to learn Arabic as speedily as possible.

A week's rest in the garden of Halleem Effendi prepared us for the journey. I resolved to explore the Atbara river and the Abyssinian affluents, prior to commencing the White Nile voyage. The Governor promised me two Turkish soldiers as attendants, and I arranged to send my heavy baggage by boat to Khartoum, and secure the advantage of travelling light; a comfort that no one can appreciate who has not felt the daily delay in loading a long string of camels. Both my wife and I had suffered from a short attack of fever brought on by the prostrating effect of the simoom, which at this season (June) was at its height. The Nile was slowly rising, although it was still low; occasionally it fell about eighteen inches in one night, but again rose; this proved that, although the rains had commenced, they were not constant, as the steady and rapid increase of the river had not taken place. The authorities assured me that the Blue Nile was now rising at Khartoum, which accounted for the increase of the river at Berber.

The garden of Halleem Effendi was attended by a number of fine powerful slaves from the White Nile, whose stout frames and glossy skins were undeniable witnesses of their master's care. A charmingly pretty slave girl paid us daily visits, with presents of fruit from her kind master and numerous mistresses, who, with the usual Turkish compliments as a preliminary message, requested permission to visit the English lady.

In the cool hour of evening a bevy of ladies approached through the dark groves of citron trees, so gaily dressed in silks of the brightest dyes of yellow, blue, and scarlet, that no bouquet of flowers could have been more gaudy. They were attended by numerous slaves, and the head servant politely requested me to withdraw during the interview. Thus turned out of my tent, I was compelled to patience and solitude beneath a neighbouring date palm.

The result of the interview with my wife was most satisfactory; the usual womanish questions had been replied to, and hosts of compliments exchanged. We were then rich in all kinds of European trifles that excited their curiosity, and a few little presents established so great an amount of confidence that they gave the individual history of each member of the family from childhood, that would have filled a column of the Times with births, deaths, and marriages.

Some of these ladies were very young and pretty, and of course exercised a certain influence over their husbands; thus, on the following morning, we were inundated with visitors, as the male members of the family came to thank us for the manner in which their ladies had been received; and fruit, flowers, and the general produce of the garden were presented to us in profusion. However pleasant, there were drawbacks to our garden of Eden; there was dust in our Paradise; not the dust that we see in Europe upon unwatered roads, that simply fills the eyes, but sudden clouds raised by whirlwinds in the desert which fairly choked the ears and nostrils when thus attacked. June is the season when these phenomena are most prevalent. At that time the rains have commenced in the south, and are extending towards the north; the cold and heavy air of the southern rain-clouds sweeps down upon the overheated atmosphere of the desert, and produces sudden violent squalls and whirlwinds when least expected, as at that time the sky is cloudless.

The effect of these desert whirlwinds is most curious, as their force is sufficient to raise dense columns of sand and dust several thousand feet high; these are not the evanescent creations of a changing wind, but they frequently exist for many hours, and travel forward, or more usually in circles, resembling in the distance solid pillars of sand. The Arab superstition invests these appearances with the supernatural, and the mysterious sand-column of the desert wandering in its burning solitude, is an evil spirit, a "Gin" ("genii" plural, of the Arabian Nights). I have frequently seen many such columns at the same time in the boundless desert, all travelling or waltzing in various directions at the wilful choice of each whirlwind: this vagrancy of character is an undoubted proof to the Arab mind of their independent and diabolical origin.

The Abyssinian traveller, Bruce, appears to have entertained a peculiar dread of the dangers of such sand columns, but on this point his fear was exaggerated. Cases may have occurred where caravans have been suffocated by whirlwinds of sand, but these are rare exceptions, and the usual effects of the dust storm are the unroofing of thatched huts, the destruction of a few date palms, and the disagreeable amount of sand that not only half chokes both man and beast, but buries all objects that may be lying on the ground some inches deep in dust.

The wind at this season (June) was changeable, and strong blasts from the south were the harbingers of the approaching rainy season. We had no time to lose, and we accordingly arranged to start. I discharged my dirty cook, and engaged a man who was brought by a coffee-house keeper, by whom he was highly recommended; but, as a precaution against deception, I led him before the Mudir, or Governor, to be registered before our departure. To my astonishment, and to his infinite disgust, he was immediately recognised as an old offender, who had formerly been imprisoned for theft! The Governor, to prove his friendship, and his interest in my welfare, immediately sent the police to capture the coffee-house keeper who had recommended the cook. No sooner was the unlucky surety brought to the Divan than he was condemned to receive 200 lashes for having given a false character. The sentence was literally carried out, in spite of my remonstrance, and the police were ordered to make the case public to prevent a recurrence. The Governor assured me, that as I held a firman from the Viceroy he could not do otherwise, and that I must believe him to be my truest friend. "Save me from my friends," was an adage quickly proved. I could not procure a cook, neither any other attendants, as every one was afraid to guarantee a character, lest he might come in for his share of the 200 lashes!

The Governor came to my rescue, and sent immediately the promised Turkish soldiers, who were to act in the double capacity of escort and servants. They were men of totally opposite characters. Hadji Achmet was a hardy, powerful, dare-devil-looking Turk, while Hadji Velli was the perfection of politeness, and as gentle as a lamb. My new allies procured me three donkeys in addition to the necessary baggage camels, and we started from the pleasant garden of Halleem Effendi on the evening of the 10th of June for the junction of the Atbara river with the Nile.

Chapter II.

*"'Mongst them were several Englishmen of pith,
Sixteen named Thompson, and nineteen named Smith."*
                                                    Don Juan.

MAHOMET, Achmet, and Ali are equivalent to Smith, Brown, and Thompson. Accordingly, of my few attendants, my dragoman was Mahomet, and my principal guide was Achmet; and subsequently I had a number of Alis. Mahomet was a regular Cairo dragoman, a native of Dongola, almost black, but exceedingly tenacious regarding his shade of colour, which he declared to be light brown. He spoke very bad English, was excessively conceited, and irascible to a degree. No pasha was so bumptious or overbearing to his inferiors, but to me and to his mistress while in Cairo he had the gentleness of the dove, and I had engaged him at 5l. per month to accompany me to the White Nile. Men change with circumstances; climate affects the health and temper; the sleek and well-fed dog is amiable, but he would be vicious when thin and hungry; the man in luxury and the man in need are not equally angelic. Now Mahomet was one of those dragomen who are accustomed to the civilized expeditions of the British tourist to the first or second cataract, in a Nile boat replete with conveniences and luxuries, upon which the dragoman is monarch supreme, a whale among the minnows, who rules the vessel, purchases daily a host of unnecessary supplies, upon which he clears his profit, until he returns to Cairo with his pockets filled sufficiently to support him until the following Nile season. The short three months' harvest, from November until February, fills his granary for the year. Under such circumstances the temper should be angelic. But times had changed: the luxurious Mahomet had left the comfortable Nile boat at Korosko, and he had crossed the burning desert upon a jolting camel; he had left the well-known route where the dragoman was supreme, and he found himself among people who treated him in the light of a common servant. "A change came o'er the spirit of his dream;" Mahomet was no longer a great man, and his temper changed with circumstances; in fact, Mahomet became unbearable, and still he was absolutely necessary, as he was the tongue of the expedition until we should accomplish Arabic. To him the very idea of exploration was an absurdity; he had never believed in it from the first, and he now became impressed with the fact that he was positively committed to an undertaking that would end most likely in his death, if not in terrible difficulties; he determined, under the circumstances, to make himself as disagreeable as possible to all parties. With this amiable resolution Mahomet adopted a physical infirmity in the shape of deafness; in reality, no one was more acute in hearing, but as there are no bells where there are no houses, he of course could not answer such a summons, and he was compelled to attend to the call of his own name – "Mahomet! Mahomet!" No reply, although the individual was sitting within a few feet, apparently absorbed in the contemplation of his own boots. "Mahomet!" with an additional emphasis upon the second syllable. Again no response. "Mahomet, you rascal, why don't you answer?" This energetic address would effect a change in his position; the mild and lamb-like dragoman of Cairo would suddenly start from the ground, tear his own hair from his head in handfuls, and shout, "Mahomet! Mahomet! Mahomet! always Mahomet! D – n Mahomet! I wish he were dead, or back in Cairo, this brute Mahomet!" The irascible dragoman would then beat his own head unmercifully with his fists, in a paroxysm of rage.

To comfort him I could only exclaim, "Well done, Mahomet! thrash him; pommel him well; punch his head; you know him best; he deserves it; don't spare him!" This advice, acting upon the natural perversity of his disposition, generally soothed him, and he ceased punching his head. This man was entirely out of his place, if not out of his mind, at certain moments, and having upon one occasion smashed a basin by throwing it in the face of the cook, and upon another occasion narrowly escaped homicide, by throwing an axe at a man's head, which missed by an inch, he became a notorious character in the little expedition.

We left Berber in the evening at sunset; we were mounted upon donkeys, while our Turkish attendants rode upon excellent dromedaries that belonged to their regiment of irregular cavalry. As usual, when ready to start, Mahomet was the last; he had piled a huge mass of bags and various luggage upon his donkey, that almost obscured the animal, and he sat mounted upon this pinnacle dressed in gorgeous clothes, with a brace of handsome pistols in his belt, and his gun slung across his shoulders. Upon my remonstrating with him upon the cruelty of thus overloading the donkey, he flew into a fit of rage, and dismounting immediately, he drew his pistols from his belt and dashed them upon the ground; his gun shared the same fate, and heaving his weapons upon the sand, he sullenly walked behind his donkey, which he drove forward with the caravan.

We pushed forward at the usual rapid amble of the donkeys; and, accompanied by Hadji Achmet upon his dromedary, with the coffee-pot, &c. and a large Persian rug slung behind the saddle, we quickly distanced the slower caravan under the charge of Hadji Velli and the sullen Mahomet.

There was no difficulty in the route, as the sterile desert of sand and pebbles was bounded by a fringe of bush amid mimosa that marked the course of the Nile, to which our way lay parallel. There was no object to attract particular attention, and no sound but that of the bleating goats driven homeward by the Arab boys, and the sharp cry of the desert sand grouse as they arrived in flocks to drink in the welcome river. The flight of these birds is extremely rapid, and is more like that of the pigeon than the grouse; they inhabit the desert, but they travel great distances both night and morning to water, as they invariably drink twice a day. As they approach the river they utter the cry "Chuckow, chuckow," in a loud clear note, and immediately after drinking they return upon their long flight to the desert. There are several varieties of the sand grouse. I have met with three, but they are dry, tough, and worthless as game.

We slept in the desert about five miles from Berber, and on the following day, after a scorching march of about twenty miles, we arrived at the junction of the Atbara river with the Nile. Throughout the route the barren sand stretched to the horizon on the left, while on the right, within a mile of the Nile, the soil was sufficiently rich to support a certain amount of vegetation – chiefly dwarf mimosas and the Asclepias gigantea. The latter I had frequently seen in Ceylon, where it is used medicinally by the native doctors; but here it was ignored, except for the produce of a beautiful silky down which is used for stuffing cushions and pillows. This vegetable silk is contained in a soft pod or bladder about the size of an orange. Both the leaves and the stem of this plant emit a highly poisonous milk, that exudes from the bark when cut or bruised; the least drop of this will cause total blindness, if in contact with the eye. I have seen several instances of acute ophthalmia that have terminated in loss of sight from the accidental rubbing of the eye with the hand when engaged in cutting firewood from the asclepias. The wood is extremely light, and is frequently tied into fagots and used by the Arabs as a support while swimming, in lieu of cork. Although the poisonous qualities of the plant cause it to be shunned by all other animals, it is nevertheless greedily devoured by goats, who eat it unharmed.

It was about two hours after sunset when we arrived at the steep bank of the Atbara river. Pushing through the fringe of young dome palms that formed a thick covert upon the margin, we cautiously descended the bank for about twenty-five feet, as the bright glare of the river's bed deceived me by the resemblance to water. We found a broad surface of white sand, which at that season formed the dry bed of the river. Crossing this arid bottom of about 400 yards in width, we unsaddled on the opposite side, by a bed of water melons planted near a small pool of water. A few of these we chopped in pieces for our tired donkeys, and we shared in the cool and welcome luxury ourselves that was most refreshing after the fatigue of the day's journey. Long before our camels arrived, we had drunk our coffee and were sound asleep upon the sandy bed of the Atbara.

At daybreak on the following morning, while the camels were being loaded, I strolled to a small pool in the sand, tempted by a couple of wild geese; these were sufficiently unsophisticated as to allow me to approach within shot, and I bagged them both, and secured our breakfast; they were the common Egyptian geese, which are not very delicate eating. The donkeys being saddled, we at once started with our attendant, Hadji Achmet, at about five miles per hour, in advance of our slower caravan. The route was upon the river's margin, due east, through a sandy copse of thorny mimosas which fringed the river's course for about a quarter of a mile on either side; beyond this all was desert.

The Atbara had a curious appearance; in no part was it less than 400 yards in width, while in many places this breadth was much exceeded. The banks were from twenty-five to thirty feet deep: these had evidently been over-flowed during floods, bnt at the present time the river was dead; not only partially dry, but so glaring was the sandy bed, that the reflection of the sun was almost unbearable.

Great numbers of the dome palm (Hyphoene Thebaica, Mart.) grew upon the banks; these trees are of great service to the Arab tribes, who at this season of drought forsake the deserts and flock upon the margin of the Atbara. The leaves of the dome supply them with excellent material for mats and ropes, while the fruit is used both for man and beast. The dome palm resembles the palmyra in the form and texture of its fan-shaped leaves, but there is a distinguishing peculiarity in the growth: instead of the straight single stem of the palmyra, the dome palm spreads into branches, each of which invariably represents the letter Y. The fruit grows in dense clusters, numbering several hundred, of the size of a small orange, but of an irregular oval shape; these are of a rich brown colour, and bear a natural polish as though varnished. So hard is the fruit and uninviting to the teeth, that a deal board would be equally practicable for mastication; the Arabs pound them between stones, by which rough process they detach the edible portion in the form of a resinous powder. The rind of the nut which produces this powder is about a quarter of an inch thick; this coating covers a strong shell which contains a nut of vegetable ivory, a little larger than a full-sized walnut. When the resinous powder is detached, it is either eaten raw, or it is boiled into a delicious porridge, with milk; this has a strong flavour of gingerbread.

The vegetable ivory nuts are then soaked in water for about twenty-four hours, after which they are heaped in large piles upon a fire until nearly dry, and thoroughly steamed; this process renders them sufficiently tractable to be reduced by pounding in a heavy mortar. Thus, broken into small pieces they somewhat resemble half-roasted chestnuts, and in this state they form excellent food for cattle. The useful dome palm is the chief support of the desert Arabs when in times of drought and scarcity the supply of corn has failed. At this season (June) there was not a blade of even the withered grass of the desert oases. Our donkeys lived exclusively upon the dhurra (Sorghum Egyptiaca) that we carried with us, and the camels required a daily supply of corn in addition to the dry twigs and bushes that formed their dusty food. The margin of the river was miserable and uninviting; the trees and bushes were entirely leafless from the intense heat, as are the trees in England during winter. The only shade was afforded by the evergreen dome palms; nevertheless, the Arabs occupied the banks at intervals of three or four miles, wherever a pool of water in some deep bend of the dried river's bed offered an attraction; in such places were Arab villages or camps, of the usual mat tents formed of the dome palm leaves.

Many pools were of considerable size and of great depth. In flood-time a tremendous torrent sweeps down the course of the Atbara, and the sudden bends of the river are hollowed out by the force of the stream to a depth of twenty or thirty feet below the level of the bed. Accordingly these holes become reservoirs of water when the river is otherwise exhausted. In such asylums all the usual inhabitants of this large river are crowded together in a comparatively narrow space. Although these pools vary in size, from only a few hundred yards to a mile in length, they are positively full of life; huge fish, crocodiles of immense size, turtles, and occasionally hippopotami, consort together in close and unwished-for proximity.

The animals of the desert – gazelles, hyaenas, and wild asses – are compelled to resort to these crowded drinking-places, occupied by the flocks of the Arabs equally with the timid beasts of the chase. The birds that during the cooler months would wander free throughout the country, are now collected in vast numbers along the margin of the exhausted river; innumerable doves, varying in species, throng the trees and seek the shade of the dome palms; thousands of desert grouse arrive morning and evening to drink and to depart; while birds in multitudes, of lovely plumage, escape from the burning desert, and colonize the poor but welcome bushes that fringe the Atbara river.

The heat was intense. As we travelled along the margin of the Atbara, and felt with the suffering animals the exhaustion of the clinmate, I acknowledged the grandeur of the Nile that could overcome the absorption of such thirsty sands, and the evaporation caused by the burning atmosphere of Nubia. For nearly 1,200 miles from the junction of the Atbara with the parent stream to the Mediterranean, not one streamlet joined the mysterious river, neither one drop of rain ruffled its waters, unless a rare thunder-shower, as a curious phenomenon, startled the Arabs as they travelled along the desert. Nevertheless the Nile overcame its enemies, while the Atbara shrank to a skeleton, bare and exhausted, reduced to a few pools that lay like blotches along the broad surface of glowing sand.

Notwithstanding the overpowering sun, there were certain advantages to the traveller at this season; it was unnecessary to carry a large supply of water, as it could be obtained at intervals of a few miles. There was an indescribable delight in the cool night, when, in the perfect certainty of fine weather, we could rest in the open air with the clear bright starlit sky above us. There were no mosquitoes, neither were there any of the insect plagues of the tropics; the air was too dry for the gnat tribe, and the moment of sunset was the signal for perfect enjoyment, free from the usual drawbacks of African travel. As the river pools were the only drinking-places for birds and game, the gun supplied not only my own party, but I had much to give away to the Arabs in exchange for goat's milk, the meal of the dome nuts, &c. Gazelles were exceedingly numerous, but shy, and so difficult to approach that they required most careful stalking. At this season of intense heat they drank twice a day – at about an hour after sunrise, and half an hour before sunset.

The great comfort of travelling along the bank of the river in a desert country is the perfect freedom, as a continual supply of water enables the explorer to rest at his leisure in any attractive spot where game is plentiful, or where the natural features of the country invite investigation. We accordingly halted, after some days' journey, at a spot named Collodabad, where an angle of the river had left a deep pool of about a mile in length: this was the largest sheet of water that we had seen throughout the course of the Atbara. A number of Arabs had congregated at this spot with their flocks and herds; the total absence of verdure had reduced the animals to extreme leanness, as the goats gathered their scanty sustenance from the seed-pods of the mimosas, which were shaken down to the expectant flocks by the Arab boys, with long hooked poles. These seeds were extremely oily, and resembled linseed, but the rank flavour was disagreeable and acrid.

This spot was seven days' march from the Nile junction, or about 160 miles. The journey had been extremely monotonous, as there had been no change in the scenery; it was the interminable desert, with the solitary streak of vegetation in the belt of mimosas and dome palms, about a mile and a half in width, that marked the course of the river. I had daily shot gazelles, geese, pigeons, desert grouse, &c. but no larger game. I was informed that at this spot, Collodabad, I should be introduced for the first time to the hippopotamus.

Owing to the total absence of nourishing food, the cattle produced a scanty supply of milk; thus the Arabs, who depended chiefly upon their flocks for their subsistence, were in great distress, and men and beasts mutually suffered extreme hardship. The Arabs that occupy the desert north of the Atbara are the Bishareens; it was among a large concourse of these people that we pitched our tents on the banks of the river at Collodabad.

This being the principal watering-place along the deserted bed of the Atbara, the neighbourhood literally swarmed with doves, sand grouse, and other birds, in addition to many geese and pelicans.

Early in the morning I procured an Arab guide to search for the reported hippopotami. My tents were among a grove of dome palms on the margin of the river; thus I had a clear view of the bed for a distance of about half a mile on either side. This portion of the Atbara was about 500 yards in width, the banks were about thirty feet perpendicular depth; and the bend of the river had caused the formation of the deep hollow on the opposite side which now formed the pool, while every other part was dry. This pool occupied about one-third the breadth of the river, bounded by the sand upon one side, and by a perpendicular cliff upon the other, upon which grew a fringe of green bushes similar to willows. These were the only succulent leaves that I had seen since I left Berber.

We descended the steep sandy bank in a spot that the Arabs had broken down to reach the water, and after trudging across about 400 yards of deep sand, we reached the extreme and narrowest end of the pool; here for the first time I saw the peculiar four-toed print of the hippopotamus's foot. A bed of melons had been planted here by the Arabs in the moist sand near the water, but the fruit had been entirely robbed by the hippopotami. A melon is exactly adapted for the mouth of this animal, as he could crunch the largest at one squeeze, and revel in the juice. Not contented with the simple fruits of the garden, a large bull hippopotamus had recently killed the proprietor. The Arab wished to drive it from his plantation, but was immediately attacked by the hippo, who caught him in its mouth and killed him by one crunch. This little incident had rendered the hippo exceedingly daring, and it had upon several occasions charged out of the water, when the people had driven their goats to drink; therefore it would be the more satisfactory to obtain a shot, and to supply the hungry Arabs with meat at the expense of their enemy.

At this early hour, 6 A.M., no one had descended to the pool, thus all the tracks upon the margin were fresh and undisturbed: there were the huge marks of crocodiles that had recently returned to the water, while many of great size were still lying upon the sand in the distance: these slowly crept into the pool as we approached. The Arabs had dug small holes in the sand within a few yards of the water: these were the artificial drinking-places for their goats and sheep, that would have been snapped up by the crocodiles had they ventured to drink in the pool of crowded monsters. I walked for about a mile and a half along the sand without seeing a sign of hippopotami, except their numerous tracks upon the margin. There was no wind, and the surface of the water was unruffled; thus I could see every creature that rose in the pool either to breathe or to bask in the morning sunshine. The number and size of the fish, turtles, and crocodiles were extraordinary; many beautiful gazelles approached from all sides for their morning draught: wild geese, generally in pairs, disturbed the wary crocodiles by their cry of alarm as we drew near, and the desert grouse in flocks of many thousands had gathered together, and were circling in a rapid flight above the water, wishing, but afraid, to descend and drink. Having a shot gun with me, I fired and killed six at one discharge, but one of the wounded birds having fallen into the water at a distance of about 120 yards, it was immediately seized by a white-throated fish-eagle, which perched upon a tree, swooped down upon the bird, utterly disregarding the report of the gun. The Bishareen Arabs have no fire-arms, thus the sound of a gun was unknown to the game of the desert.

I had killed several wild geese for breakfast in the absence of the hippopotami, when I suddenly heard the peculiar loud snorting neigh of these animals in my rear; we had passed them unperceived, as they had been beneath the surface. After a quick walk of about half a mile, during which time the cry of the hippos had been several times repeated, I observed six of these curious animals standing in the water about shoulder-deep. There was no cover, therefore I could only advance upon the sand without a chance of stalking them; this caused them to retreat to deeper water, but upon my arrival within about eighty yards, they raised their heads well up, and snorted an impudent challenge. I had my old Ceylon No. 10 double rifle, and, taking a steady aim at the temple of one that appeared to be the largest, the ball cracked loudly upon the skull. Never had there been such a commotion in the pool as now! At the report of the rifle, five heads sank and disappeared like stones, but the sixth hippo leaped half out of the water, and, falling backwards, commenced a series of violent struggles: now upon his back; then upon one side, with all four legs frantically paddling, and raising a cloud of spray and foam; then waltzing round and round with its huge jaws wide open, raising a swell in the hitherto calm surface of the water. A quick shot with the left-hand barrel produced no effect, as the movements of the animal were too rapid to allow a steady aim at the forehead; I accordingly took my trmisty little Fletcher[2] double rifle No. 24, and, running knee-deep into the water to obtain a close shot, I fired exactly between the eyes, near the crown of the head. At the report of the little Fletcher the hippo disappeared; the tiny waves raised by the commotion broke upon the sand, but the game was gone.

This being my first vis-a-vis with a hippo, I was not certain whether I could claim the victory; he was gone, but where? However, while I was speculating upon the case, I heard a tremendous rush of water, and I saw five hippopotami tearing along in full trot through a portion of the pool that was not deep enough to cover them above the shoulder: this was the affair of about half a minute, as they quickly reached deep water, and disappeared at about a hundred and fifty yards' distance.

The fact of five hippos in retreat after I had counted six in the onset was conclusive that my waltzing friend was either dead or disabled; I accordingly lost no time in following the direction of the herd. Hardly had I arrived at the spot where they had disappeared, when first one and then another head popped up and again sank, until one more hardy than the rest ventured to appear within fifty yards, and to bellow as before. Once more the No. 10 crashed through his head, and again the waltzing and struggling commenced like the paddling of a steamer: this time, however, the stunned hippo in its convulsive efforts came so close to the shore that I killed it directly in shallow water, by a forehead shot with the little Fletcher. I concluded from this result that my first hippo must also be lying dead in deep water.

The Arabs, having heard the shots fired, had begun to gather towards the spot, and, upon my men shouting that a hippo was killed, crowds came running to the place with their knives and ropes, while others returned to their encampment to fetch camels and mat bags to convey the flesh. In half an hour at least three hundred Arabs were on the spot; the hippo had been hauled to shore by ropes, and, by the united efforts of the crowd, the heavy carcase had been rolled to the edge of the water. Here the attack commenced; no pack of hungry hyaenas could have been more savage. I gave them permission to take the flesh, and in an instant a hundred knives were

---

2   This excellent and handy rifle was made by Thomas Fletcher, of Gloucester, and accompanied me like a faithful dog throughout my journey of nearly five years to the Albert N'yanza, and returned with me to England as good as new.

at work: they fought over the spoil like wolves. No sooner was the carcase flayed than the struggle commenced for the meat; the people were a mass of blood, as some stood thigh-deep in the reeking intestines wrestling for the fat, while many hacked at each other's hands for coveted portions that were striven for as a bonne bouche. I left the savage crowd in their ferocious enjoyment of flesh and blood, and I returned to camp for breakfast, my Turk, Hadji Achmet, carrying some hippopotamus steaks.

That morning my wife and I breakfasted upon our first hippo, an animal that was destined to be our general food throughout our journey among the Abyssinian tributaries of the Nile. After breakfast we strolled down to the pool to search for the hippopotamus No. 1. This we at once found, dead, as it had risen to the surface, and was floating like the back of a turtle a few inches above the water. The Arabs had been so intent upon the division of their spoil that they had not observed their new prize; accordingly, upon the signal being given, a general rush took place, and in half an hour a similar scene was enacted to that of hippo No. 2.

The entire Arab camp was in commotion and full of joy at this unlooked-for arrival of flesh. Camels laden with meat and hide toiled along the sandy bed of the river; the women raised their long and shrill cry of delight; and we were looked upon as general benefactors for having brought them a supply of good food in this season of distress. In the afternoon I arranged my tackle, and strolled down to the pool to fish. There was a difficulty in procuring bait; a worm was never heard of in the burning deserts of Nubia, neither had I a net to catch small fish; I was therefore obliged to bait with pieces of hippopotamnus. Fishing in such a pool as that of the Atbara was sufficiently exciting, as it was impossible to speculate upon what creature might accept the invitation; but the Arabs who accompanied me were particular in guarding me against the position I had taken under a willow-bush close to the water, as they explained, that most probably a crocodile would take me instead of the bait; they declared that accidents had frequently happened when people had sat upon the bank either to drink with their hands, or even while watching their goats. I accordingly fished at a few feet distant from the margin, and presently I had a bite; I landed a species of perch about two pounds' weight; this was the "boulti," one of the best Nile fish mentioned by the traveller Bruce. In a short time I had caught a respectable dish of fish, but hitherto no monster had paid me the slightest attention; accordingly I changed my bait, and upon a powerful hook, fitted upon treble-twisted wire, I fastened an enticing strip of a boulti. The bait was about four ounces, and glistened like silver; the water was tolerably clear, but not too bright, and with such an attraction I expected something heavy. My float was a large-sized pike-float for live bait, and this civilized sign had been only a few minutes in the wild waters of the Atbara, when, bob! and away it went! I had a very large reel, with nearly three hundred yards of line that had been specially made for monsters; down went the top of my rod, as though a grindstone was suspended on it, and, as I recovered its position, away went the line, and the reel revolved, not with the sudden dash of a spirited fish, but with the steady determined pull of a trotting horse. What on earth have I got hold of? In a few minutes about a hundred yards of line were out, and as the creature was steadily but slowly travelling down the centre of the channel, I determined to cry "halt!" if possible, as my tackle was extremely strong, and my rod was a single bamboo. Accordingly, I put on a powerful strain, which was replied to by a sullen tug, a shake, and again my rod was pulled suddenly down to the water's edge. At length, after the roughest handling, I began to reel in slack line, as my unknown friend had doubled in upon me; and upon once more putting severe pressure upon him or her, as it might be, I perceived a great swirl in the water, about twenty yards from the rod. The tackle would bear anything, and I strained so heavily upon my adversary, that I soon reduced our distance; but the water was exceedingly deep, the bank precipitous, and he was still invisible. At length, after much tugging and counter-tugging, he began to show; eagerly I gazed into the water to examine my new acquaintance, when I made out something below, in shape between a coach-wheel and a sponging-bath; in a few moments more I brought to the surface an enormous turtle, well hooked. I felt like the old lady who won an elephant in a lottery: that I had him was certain, but what was I to do with my prize? It was at the least a hundred pounds' weight, and the bank was steep and covered with bushes; thus it was impossible to land the monster, that now tugged and dived with the determination of the grindstone that his first pull had suggested. Once I attempted the gaff but the trusty weapon that had landed many a fish in Scotland broke in the hard shell of the turtle, and I was helpless. My Arab now came to my assistance, and at once terminated the struggle. Seizing the line with both hands, utterly regardless of all remonstrance (which, being in English, he did not understand), he quickly hauled our turtle to the surface, and held it, struggling and gnashing its jaws, close to the steep bank. In a few moments the line slackened, and the turtle disappeared. The fight was over! The sharp horny jaws had bitten through treble-twisted brass wire as clean as though cut by shears. My visions of turtle soup had faded.

The heavy fish were not in the humour to take; I therefore shot one with a rifle as it came to the surface to blow, and, the water in this spot being shallow, we brought it to shore; it was a species of carp, between thirty and forty pounds; the scales were rather larger than a crown piece, and so hard that they would have been difficult to pierce with a harpoon. It proved to be useless for the table, being of an oily nature that was only acceptable to the Arabs.

In the evening I went out stalking in the desert, and returned with five fine buck gazelles. These beautiful creatures so exactly resemble the colour of the sandy deserts which they inhabit, that they are most difficult to distinguish, and their extreme shyness renders stalking upon foot very uncertain. I accordingly employed an Arab to lead a camel, under cover of which I could generally manage to approach within a hundred yards. A buck gazelle weighs from sixty to seventy pounds, and is the perfection of muscular development. No person who has seen the gazelles in confinement in a temperate climate can form an idea of the beauty of the animal in its native desert. Born in the scorching sun, nursed on the burning sand of the treeless and shadowless wilderness, the gazelle is among the antelope tribe as the Arab horse is among its brethren, the high-bred and superlative beauty of the race. The skin is as sleek as satin, of a colour difficult to describe, as it varies between the lightest mauve and yellowish brown; the belly is snow-white; the legs, from the knee downwards, are also white, and are as fine as though carved from ivory; the hoof is beautifully shaped, and tapers to a sharp point; the head of the buck is ornamented by gracefully-curved annulated horns, perfectly black, and generally from nine to twelve inches long in the bend; the eye is the well-known perfection – the full, large, soft, and jet-black eye of the gazelle. Although the desert appears incapable of supporting animmial life, there are in the undulating surface numerous shallow sandy ravines, in which are tufts of a herbage so coarse that, as a source of nourishment, it would be valueless to a domestic animal: nevertheless, upon this dry and wiry substance the delicate gazelles subsist; and, although they never fatten, they are exceedingly fleshy and in excellent condition. Entirely free from fat, and nevertheless a mass of muscle and sinew, the gazelle is the fastest of the antelope tribe. Proud of its strength, and confident in its agility, it will generally bound perpendicularly four or five feet from the ground several times before it starts at full speed, as though to test the quality of its sinews before the race. The Arabs course them with greyhounds, and sometimes they are caught by running several dogs at the same time; but this result is from the folly of the gazelle, who at first distances his pursuers like the wind; but, secure in its speed, it halts and faces the dogs, exhausting itself by bounding exultingly in the air; in the meantime the greyhounds are closing up, and diminishing the chance of escape. As a rule, notwithstanding this absurdity of the gazelle, it has the best of the race, and the greyhounds return crestfallen and beaten. Altogether it is the most beautiful specimen of game that exists, far too lovely and harmless to be hunted and killed for the mere love of sport. But when dinner depends upon the rifle, beauty is no protection; accordingly, throughout our desert march we lived upon gazelles, and I am sorry to confess that I became very expert at stalking these wary little animals. The flesh, although tolerably good, has a slight flavour of musk; this is not peculiar to the gazelle, as the odour is common to most of the small varieties of antelopes.

Having a good supply of meat, all hands were busily engaged in cutting it into strips and drying it for future use; the bushes were covered with festoons of flesh of gazelles and hippopotami, and the skins of the former were prepared for making girbas, or water-sacks. The flaying process for this purpose is a delicate operation, as the knife must be so dexterously used that no false cut should injure the hide. The animal is hung up by the hind legs; an incision is then made along the inside of both thighs to the tail, and with some trouble the skin is drawn off the body towards the head, precisely as a stocking might be drawn from the leg; by this operation the skin forms a seamless bag, open at both ends. To form a girba, the skin must be buried in the earth for about twenty hours: it is then washed in water, and the hair is easily detached. Thus rendered clean, it is tanned by soaking for several days in a mixture of the bark of a mimosa and water; from this it is daily withdrawn, and stretched out with pegs upon the ground; it is then well scrubbed with a rough stone, and fresh mimosa bark well bruised, with water, is rubbed in by the friction. About four days are sufficient to tan the thin skin of a gazelle, which is much valued for its toughness and durability; the aperture at the hind quarters is sewn together, and the opening of the neck is closed, when required, by tying. A good water-skin should be porous, to allow the water to exude sufficiently to moisten the exterior: thus the action of the air upon the exposed surface causes evaporation, and imparts to the water within the skin a delicious coolness. The Arabs usually prepare their tanned skins with an empyreumatical oil made from a variety of substances, the best of which is that from the sesame grain; this has a powerful smell, and renders the water so disagreeable that few Europeans could drink it. This oil is black, and much resembles tar in appearance; it has the effect of preserving the leather, and of rendering it perfectly water-tight. In desert travelling each person should have his own private water-skin slung upon his dromedary; for this purpose none are so good as a small-sized gazelle skin that will contain about two gallons.

On the 23d June we were nearly suffocated by a whirlwind that buried everything within the tents several inches in dust; the heat was intense;

as usual the sky was spotless, but the simoom was more overpowering than I had yet experienced. I accordingly took my rifle and went down to the pool, as any movement, even in the burning sun, was preferable to inaction in that sultry heat and dust. The crocodiles had dragged the skeletons of the hippopotami into the water; several huge heads appeared and then vanished from the surface, and the ribs of the carcase that projected, trembled and jerked as the jaws of the crocodiles were at work beneath. I shot one of very large size through the head, but it sank to the bottom; I expected to find it on the following morning floating upon the surface when the gas should have distended the body.

I also shot a large single bull hippopotamus late in the evening, which was alone at the extremity of the pool; he sank at the forehead shot, and, as he never rose again, I concluded that he was dead, and that I should find him on the morrow with the crocodile. Tired with the heat, I trudged homeward over the hot and fatiguing sand of the river's bed.

The cool night arrived, and at about half-past eight I was lying half asleep upon my bed by the margin of the river, when I fancied that I heard a rumbling like distant thunder: I had not heard such a sound for months, but a low uninterrupted roll appeared to increase in volume, although far distant. Hardly had I raised my head to listen more attentively when a confusion of voices arose from the Arabs' camp, with a sound of many feet, and in a few minutes they rushed into my camp, shouting to my men in the darkness, "El Bahr! El Bahr!" (the river! the river!)

We were up in an instant, and my interpreter, Mahomet, in a state of intense confusion, explained that the river was coming down, and that the supposed distant thunder was the roar of approaching water.

Many of the people were asleep on the clean sand on the river's bed; these were quickly awakened by the Arabs, who rushed down the steep bank to save the skulls of my two hippopotami that were exposed to dry. Hardly had they descended, when the sound of the river in the darkness beneath told us that the water had arrived, and the men, dripping with wet, had just sufficient time to drag their heavy burdens up the bank.

All was darkness and confusion; everybody was talking and no one listening; but the great event had occurred the river had arrived "like a thief in the night." On the morning of the 24th June, I stood on the banks of the noble Atbara river, at the break of day. The wonder of the desert! – yesterday there was a barren sheet of glaring sand, with a fringe of withered bush and trees upon its borders, that cut the yellow expanse of desert. For days we had journeyed along the exhausted bed: all Nature, even in Nature's poverty, was most poor: no bush could boast a leaf: no tree could throw a shade: crisp gums crackled upon the stems of the mimosas, the sap dried upon the burst bark, sprung with the withering heat of the simoom. In one night there was a mysterious change – wonders of the mighty Nile! – an army of water was hastening to the wasted river: there was no drop of rain, no thunder-cloud on the horizon to give hope, all had been dry and sultry; dust and desolation yesterday, to-day a magnificent stream, some 500 yards in width and from fifteen to twenty feet in depth, flowed through the dreary desert! Bamboos and reeds, with trash of all kinds, were hurried along the muddy waters. Where were all the crowded inhabitants of the pool? The prison doors were broken, the prisoners were released, and rejoiced in the mighty stream of the Atbara.

The 24th June, 1861, was a memorable day. Although this was actually the beginning of my work, I felt that by the experience of this night I had obtained a clue to one portion of the Nile mystery, and that, as "coming events cast their shadows before them," this sudden creation of a river was but the shadow of the great cause.

The rains were pouring in Abyssinia! these were sources of the Nile!

One of my Turks, Hadji Achmet, was ill; therefore, although I longed to travel, it was necessary to wait. I extract verbatim from my journal, 26th June: – "The river has still risen; the weather is cooler, and the withered trees and bushes are giving signs of bursting into leaf. This season may be termed the spring of this country. The frightful simoom of April, May, and June, burns everything as though parched by fire, and not even a withered leaf hangs to a bough, but the trees wear a wintry appearance in the midst of intense heat. The wild geese have paired, the birds are building their nests, and, although not even a drop of dew has fallen, all Nature seems to be aware of an approaching change, as the south wind blowing cool from the wet quarter is the harbinger of rain. Already some of the mimosas begin to afford a shade, under which the gazelles may be surely found at mid-day; the does are now in fawn, and the young will be dropped when this now withered land shall be green with herbage.

"Busy, packing for a start to-morrow; I send Hadji Velli back to Berber in charge of the two hippos' heads to the care of the good old Halleem Effendi. No time for shooting to-day. I took out all the hippos' teeth, of which he possesses 40, $\frac{10-10}{10-10}$,

six tusks and fourteen molars in each jaw. The bones of the hippopotamus, like those of the elephant, are solid, and without marrow."

Chapter III.

Wild Asses of the Desert.

The journey along the margin of the Atbara was similar to the entire route from Berber, a vast desert, with the narrow band of trees that marked the course of the river; the only change was the magical growth of the leaves, which burst hourly from the swollen buds of the mimosas: this could be accounted for by the sudden arrival of the river, as the water percolated rapidly through the sand and nourished the famishing roots.

The tracks of wild asses had been frequent, but hitherto I had not seen the animals, as their drinking-hour was at night, after which they travelled far into the desert: however, on the morning of the 29th June, shortly after the start at about 6 A.M., we perceived three of these beautiful creatures on our left – an ass, a female, and a foal. They were about half a mile distant when first observed, and upon our approach to within half that distance they halted and faced about; they were evidently on their return to the desert from the river. Those who have seen donkeys in their civilized state have no conception of the beauty of the wild and original animal. Far from the passive and subdued appearance of the English ass, the animal in its native desert is the perfection of activity and courage; there is a high-bred tone in the deportment, a high-actioned step when it trots freely over the rocks and sand, with the speed of a horse when it gallops over the boundless desert. No animal is more difficult of approach; and, although they are frequently captured by the Arabs, those taken are invariably the foals, which are ridden down by fast dromedaries, while the mothers escape. The colour of the wild ass is a reddish cream tinged with the shade most prevalent of the ground that it inhabits; thus it much resembles the sand of the desert. I wished to obtain a specimen, and accordingly I exerted my utmost knowledge of stalking to obtain a shot at the male. After at least an hour and a half I succeeded in obtaining a long shot with a single rifle, which passed through the shoulder, and I secured my first and last donkey. It was with extreme regret that I saw my beautiful prize in the last gasp, and

I resolved never to fire another shot at one of its race. This fine specimen was in excellent condition, although the miserable pasturage of the desert is confined to the wiry herbage already mentioned; of this the stomach was full, chewed into morsels like chopped reeds. The height of this male ass was about 13.3 or 14 hands; the shoulder was far more sloping than that of the domestic ass, the hoofs were remarkable for their size; they were wide, firm, and as broad as those of a horse of 15 hands. I skinned this animal carefully, and the Arabs divided the flesh among them, while Hadji Achmet selected a choice piece for our own dinner. At the close of our march that evening, the morsel of wild ass was cooked in the form of "rissoles:" the flavour resembled beef but it was extremely tough.

On the following day, 30th June, we reached Gozerajup, a large permanent village on the south bank of the river. By dead reckoning we had marched 246 miles from Berber. This spot was therefore about 220 miles from the junction of the Atbara with the Nile. Here we remained for a few days to rest the donkeys and to engage fresh camels. An extract from my journal will give a general idea of this miserable country: –

"July 3. – I went out early to get something for breakfast, and shot a hare and seven pigeons. On my return to camp, an Arab immediately skinned the hare, and pulling out the liver, lungs, and kidneys, he ate them raw and bloody. The Arabs invariably eat the lungs, liver, kidneys, and the thorax of sheep, gazelles, &c. while they are engaged in skinning the beasts, after which they crack the leg bones between stones, and suck out the raw marrow."

A Bishareen Arab wears his hair in hundreds of minute plaits which hang down to his shoulders, surmounted by a circular bushy topknot upon the crown, about the size of a large breakfast-cup, from the base of which the plaits descend. When in full dress, the plaits are carefully combed out with an ivory skewer about eighteen inches in length; after this operation, the head appears like a huge black mop surmounted by a fellow mop of a small size. Through this mass of hair he carries his skewer, which is generally ornamented, and which answers the double purpose of comb and general scratcher.

The men have remarkably fine features, but the women are not generally pretty. The Bishareen is the largest Arab tribe of Nubia. Like all the Arabs of Upper Egypt, they pay taxes to the Viceroy; these are gathered by parties of soldiers, who take the opportunity of visiting them during the drought, at which time they can be certainly found near the river; but at any other season it would be as easy to collect tribute from the gazelles of the desert as from the wandering Bishareens. The appearance of Turkish soldiers is anything but agreeable to the Arabs; therefore my escort of

Turks was generally received with the "cold shoulder" upon our arrival at an Arab camp, and no supplies were forthcoming in the shape of milk, &c. until the long coorbatch (hippopotamus whip) of Hadji Achmet had cracked several times across the shoulders of the village headman. At first this appeared to me extremely brutal, but I was given to understand that I was utterly ignorant of the Arab character, and that he knew best. I found by experience that Hadji Achmet was correct; even where milk was abundant, the Arabs invariably declared that they had not a drop, that the goats were dry, or had strayed away; and some paltry excuses were offered until the temper of the Turk became exhausted, and the coorbatch assisted in the argument. A magician's rod could not have produced a greater miracle than the hippopotamus whip. The goats were no longer dry, and in a few minutes large gourds of milk were brought, and liberally paid for, while I was ridiculed by the Turk, Hadji Achmet, for so foolishly throwing away money to the "Arab dogs."

Our route was to change. We had hitherto followed the course of the Atbara, but we were now to leave that river on our right, while we should travel s.e. about ninety miles to Cassala, the capital of the Taka country, on the confines of Abyssinia, the great depot upon that frontier for Egyptian troops, military stores, &c.

Having procured fresh camels, we started on 5th July. This portion of the desert was rich in agates and numerous specimens of bloodstone. Exactly opposite the village of Gozerajup are curious natural landmarks, – four pyramidical hills of granite that can be seen for many miles' distance in this perfectly level country. One of these hills is about 500 feet high, and is composed entirely of flaked blocks of grey granite piled one upon the other; some of these stand perpendicularly in single masses from 30 to 50 feet high, and from a distance might be taken for giants climbing the hill-side. The pinnacle has a peculiar conical cap, which appears to have been placed there by design, but upon closer inspection it is found to be natural, as no stone of such immense size could have been placed in such a position.

For the first two hours' march from this landmark, the country was covered with scrubby bush abounding in gazelles and guinea-fowl. Here, for the first time, I saw the secretary bird, known to the Arabs as the "Devil's horse." A pair of these magnificent birds were actively employed in their useful avocation of hunting reptiles, which they chased with wonderful speed. Great numbers of wild asses passed us during the march towards evening; they were on their way from the desert to the Atbara river, some miles distant upon the west. Veritable thunder we now heard for the first time in Africa, and a cloud rose with great rapidity from the horizon.

A cloud was a wonder that we had not enjoyed for months, but as this increased both in size and density, accompanied by a gust of cool wind, we were led to expect a still greater wonder – *rain!* Hardly had we halted for the night, when down it came in torrents, accompanied by a heavy thunderstorm. On the following morning, we experienced the disadvantage of rain; the ground was so slippery that the camels could not march, and we were obliged to defer our start until the sun had dried the surface.

We had now arrived at the most interesting point to an explorer. From Cairo to within a few miles south of Gozerajup stretched the unbroken desert through which we had toiled from Korosko, and which had so firmly impressed its dreariness upon the mind that nothing but desert had been expected: we had learned to be content in a world of hot sand, rocks, and pebbles; but we had arrived upon the limit; the curious landmark of Gozerajup was an everlasting beacon that marked the frontier of the Nubian desert; it was a giant warder, that seemed to guard the living south from the dreadful skeleton of nature on the north; the desert had ceased!

It was a curious and happy coincidence that onr arrival upon the limits of the desert should have been celebrated by the first shower of rain: we no longer travelled upon sand and stones, but we stood upon a fertile loam, rendered soapy and adhesive by the recent shower. The country was utterly barren at that season, as the extreme heat of the sun and simoom destroys all vegetation so thoroughly that it becomes as crisp as glass; the dried grass breaks in the wind, and is carried away in dust, leaving the earth so utterly naked and bare that it is rendered a complete desert.

In the rainy season, the whole of this country, from the south to Gozerajup, is covered with excellent pasturage, and, far from resembling a desert, it becomes a mass of bright green herbage. The Arabs and their flocks are driven from the south by the flies and by the heavy rains, and Gozerajup offers a paradise to both men and beasts; thousands of camels with their young, hundreds of thousands of goats, sheep, and cattle, are accompanied by the Arabs and their families, who encamp on the happy pastures during the season of plenty.

We had now passed the hunts occupied by the Bishareens, and we had entered upon the country of the Hadendowa Arabs. These are an exceedingly bad tribe, and, together with their neighbours, the Hallonga Arabs, they fought determinedly against the Egyptians, until finally conquered during the reign of the famous Mehemet Ala Pasha, when the provinces of Nubia submitted unconditionally, and became a portion of Upper Egypt.

Upon arrival at Soojalup we came upon the principal encampment of the Hadendowa during the dry season. Within a few miles of this spot the scene had changed: instead of the bare earth denuded of vegetation, the country was covered with jungle, already nearly green, while the vast plains of grass, enlivened by beautiful herds of antelopes, proved not only the fertility of the soil, but the presence of moisture. Although there was no stream, nor any appearance of a river's bed, Soojalup was well supplied with water throughout the hottest season by numerous wells. This spot is about forty miles distant from Gozerajup, and is the first watering-place upon the route to Cassala. As we approached the wells, we passed several large villages surrounded by fenced gardens of cotton, and tobacco, both of which throve exceedingly. Every village possessed a series of wells, with a simple contrivance for watering their cattle: – Adjoining the mouth of each well was a basin formed of clay, raised sufficiently high above the level of the ground to prevent the animals from treading it while drinking. With a rope and a leathern bag distended by pieces of stick, the water was raised from the wells and emptied into the clay basins; the latter were circular, about nine feet in diameter, and two feet deep. I measured the depth of some of the wells, and found a uniformity of forty feet. We halted at Soojalup for the night: here for the first time I saw the beautiful antelope known by the Arabs as the Ariel (Gazelle Dama). This is a species of gazelle, being similar in form and in shape of the horns, but as large as a fallow deer: the colour also nearly resembles that of the gazelle, with the exception of the rump, which is milk-white.

These animals had no water nearer than the Atbara river, unless they could obtain a stealthy supply from the cattle basins of the Arabs during the night; they were so wild, from being constantly disturbed and hunted by the Arab dogs, that I found it impossible to stalk them upon the evening of our arrival. The jungles literally swarmed with guinea-fowl – I shot nine in a few minutes, and returned to camp with dinner for my whole party. The only species of guinea-fowl that I have seen in Africa is that with the blue comb and wattles. These birds are a blessing to the traveller, as not only are they generally to be met with from the desert frontier throughout the fertile portions of the south, but they are extremely good eating, and far superior to the domestic guinea-fowl of Europe. In this spot, Soojalup, I could have killed any number, had I wished to expend my shot: but this most necessary ammunition required much nursing during a long exploration. I had a good supply, four hundredweight of the most useful sizes, No. 6 for general shooting, and B B. for geese, &c.; also a bag of No. 10, for firing into dense flocks of small birds. On the following morning we left Soojalup; for several miles on our route were Arab camps and wells, with immense herds of goats, sheep, and cattle. Antelopes were very numerous, and it was exceedingly interesting to observe the new varieties as we increased our distance from the north. I shot two from my camel (G. Dorcas); they were about the size of a fine roebuck; – the horns were like those of the gazelle, but the animals were larger and darker in colour, with a distinguishing mark in a jet black stripe longitudinally dividing the white of the belly from the reddish colour of the flank. These antelopes were exceedingly wild, and without the aid of a camel it would have been impossible to approach them. I had exchanged my donkey for Hadji Achmet's dromedary; thus mounted, I could generally succeed in stalking to within ninety or a hundred yards, by allowing the animal to feed upon the various bushes, as though I had mounted it for the purpose of leading it to graze. This deceived the antelopes, and by carefully ascertaining the correct wind, I obtained several shots, some of which failed, owing to the unsteadiness of my steed, which had a strong objection to the rifle.

The entire country from Gozerajup to Cassala is a dead flat, upon which there is not one tree sufficiently large to shade a full-sized tent: there is no real timber in the country, but the vast level extent of soil is a series of open plains and low bush of thorny mimosa: there is no drainage upon this perfect level; thus, during the rainy season, the soakage actually melts the soil, and forms deep holes throughout the country, which then becomes an impracticable slough, bearing grass and jungle. Upon this fertile tract of land, cotton might be cultivated to a large extent, and sent to Berber, via Atbara, from Gozerajup, during the season of flood. At the present time, the growth is restricted to the supply required by the Arabs for the manufacture of their cloths. These are woven by themselves, the weaver sitting in a hole excavated in the ground before his rude loom, shaded by a rough thatch about ten feet square, supported upon poles. There is a uniformity in dress throughout all the Nubian tribes of Arabs, the simple toga of the Romans this is worn in many ways, as occasion may suggest, very similar to the Scotch plaid. The quality of cotton produced is the same as that of Lower Egypt, and the cloths manufactured by the Arabs, although coarse, are remarkably soft. The toga or tope is generally ornamented with a few red stripes at either extremity, and is terminated by a fringe.

As we approached within about twenty-five miles o Cassala, I remarked that the country on our left was in many places flooded; the Arabs, who had hitherto been encamped in this neighbourhood during the dry season, were migrating to other localities in the neighbourhood of Soojalup and Gozerajup, with their vast herds of camels and goats. As rain had not fallen in sufficient quantity to account for the flood, I was informed that it was due to the river Gash, or Mareb, which, flowing from Abyssinia, passed beneath the walls of Cassala, and then divided into innumerable ramifications; it was eventually lost, and disappeared in the porous soil, after having flooded a large extent of country. This cause accounted for the never-failing wells of Soojalup – doubtless a substratum of clay prevented the total escape of the water, which remained at a depth of forty feet from the surface. The large tract of country thus annually flooded by the river Gash is rendered extremely fruitful, and is the resort of both the Hadendowa and the Hallonga Arabs during the dry season, who cultivate large quantities of dhurra, and other grain. Unfortunately, in these climates, fertility of soil is generally combined with unhealthiness, and the commencement of the rainy season is the signal for fevers and other maladies. No sooner had we arrived in the flooded country than my wife was seized with a sudden and severe attack, which necessitated a halt upon the march, as she could no longer sit upon her camel. In the evening, several hundreds of Arabs arrived, and encamped around our fire. It was shortly after sunset, and it was interesting to watch the extreme rapidity with which these swarthy sons of the desert pitched their camp – a hundred fires were quickly blazing; the women prepared the food, children sat in clusters round the blaze, as all were wet from paddling through the puddled ground, from which they were retreating.

No sooner was the bustle of arrangement completed, than a grey old man stepped forward, and, responding to his call, every man of the hundreds present formed in line, three or four deep. At once there was total silence, disturbed only by the crackling of the fires, or by the cry of a child; and with faces turned to the east, in attitudes of profound devotion, the wild but fervent followers of Mahomet repeated their evening prayer.

The flickering red light of the fires illumined the bronze faces of the congregation, and as I stood before the front line of devotees, I took off my cap in respect for their faith, and at the close of their prayer I made my salaam to their venerable Faky (priest); he returned the salutation with the cold dignity of an Arab. In this part the coorbatch of the Turk was unnecessary, and we shortly obtained supplies of milk. I ordered the dragoman Mahomet to inform the Faky that I was a doctor, and that I had the best medicines at the service of the sick, with advice gratis. In a short time I had many applicants, to whom I served out a quantity of Holloway's pills. These are most useful to an explorer, as, possessing unmistakeable purgative properties, they create an undeniable effect upon the patient, which satisfies him of their value. They are also extremely convenient, as they may be carried by the pound in a tin box, and served out in infinitesimal doses from one to ten at a time, according to the age of the patients. I had a large medicine chest, with all necessary drugs, but I was sorely troubled by the Arab women, many of whom were barren, who insisted upon my supplying them with some medicine that would remove this stigma and render them fruitful. It was in vain to deny them; I therefore gave them usually a small dose of ipecacuanha, with the comforting word to an Arab, "Inshallah," "if it please God." At the same time I explained that the medicine was of little value.

On the following morning, during the march, my wife had a renewal of fever. We had already passed a large village named Abre, and the country was a forest of small trees, which, being in leaf, threw a delicious shade. Under a tree, upon a comfortable bed of dry sand, we wer obliged to lay her for several hours, until the paroxysm passed, and she could remount her dromedary. This she did with extreme difficulty, and we hurried toward Cassala, from which town we were only a few miles distant.

For the last fifty or sixty miles we had seen the Cassala mountain – at first a blue speck above the horizon. It now rose in all the beauty of a smooth and bare block of granite, about 3,500 feet above the level of the country with the town of Cassala at the base, and the roaring torrent Gash flowing at our feet. When we reached the end of the day's march, it was between 5 and 6 p.m. The walled town was almost washed by the river, which was at least 500 yards wide. However, our guides assured us that it was fordable, although dangerous on account of the strength of the current. Camels are most stupid and nervous animals in water; that ridden by my wife was fortunately better than the generality. I sent two Arabs with poles, ahead of my camel, and carefully led the way. After considerable difficulty, we forded the river safely; the water was nowhere above four feet deep, and, in most places, it did not exceed three; but the great rapidity of the stream would have rendered it impossible for the me to cross without the assistance of poles. One of our camels lost its footing, and was carried helplessly down the river for some hundred yards, until it stranded upon a bank.

The sun had sunk when we entered Cassala. It is a walled town, surrounded by a ditch and flanking towers, and containing about 8,000 inhabitants, exclusive of troops. The houses and walls were of unburnt brick, smeared with clay and cow-dung. As we rode through the dusty streets, I sent off Mahomet with my firman to the Mudir; and, not finding a suitable place inside the town, I returned outside the walls, where I ordered the tents to be pitched in a convenient spot among some wild fig-trees. Hardly were the tents pitched than Mahomet returned, accompanied by an officer and ten soldiers as a guard, with a polite message from the Mudir or governor, who had, as usual, kissed the potent firman, and raised it to his forehead, with the declaration that he was "my servant, and that all that I required should be immediately attended to." Shortly after, we were called upon by several Greeks, one of whom was the army doctor, Signor

Georgis, who, with great kindness, offered to supply all our wants. My wife was dreadfully weak and exhausted, therefore an undisturbed night's rest was all that was required, with the independence of our own tent.

Cassala is rich in hyaenas, and the night was passed in the discordant howling of these disgusting but useful animals: they are the scavengers of the country, devouring every species of filth, and clearing all carrion from the earth. Without the hyaenas and vultures, the neighbourhood of a Nubian village would be unbearable; it is the idle custom of the people to leave unburied all animals that die. Thus, among the numerous flocks and herds, the casualties would create a pestilence were it not for the birds and beasts of prey.

On the following morning the fever had yielded to quinine, and we were enabled to receive a round of visits – the governor and suite, Elias Bey, the doctor and a friend, and, lastly, Malem Georgis, an elderly Greek merchant, who, with great hospitality, insisted upon our quitting the sultry tent and sharing his own roof. We therefore became his guests in a most comfortable house for some days. Our Turk, Hadji Achmet, returned on his way to Berber; we discharged our camels, and prepared -to start afresh from this point for the Nile tributaries of Abyssinia.

Chapter IV.

Route from Cassala to Souakim.

By dead reckoning, Cassala is ninety-three miles s.s.e. of Gozerajup, or about 340 miles from Berber. We had ridden about 710 miles from Korosko, 630 miles of which had been through scorching deserts during the hottest season. We were, therefore, thankful to exchange the intense heat of the tent for a solid roof, and to rest for a short time in the picturesque country of Taka.

The direct route to Cassala, the capital of Taka, should be from Suez to Souakim, on the Red Sea, and from thence in sixteen days, by camel. Thus, were there a line from Suez to Souakim by steamers, similar to that already established to Jedda, Cassala would be only twenty-two days' journey from Cairo. At present, the arrival of steamers at Souakim is entirely uncertain; therefore the trade of the country is paralysed by the apathy of the Egyptian Government. The Abdul Azziz Company run their steamers regularly from Suez to Jedda; and, although they advertise Souakim as a port of call, there is no dependence to be placed upon the announcement; therefore, all merchants are afraid not only of delay, but of high warehouse charges at Souakim. The latter port is only four days' steaming from Suez, and, being the most central depot for all merchandise both to and from Upper Egypt, it would become a point of great importance were regular means of transport established.

Cotton of excellent quality may be grown to an unlimited amount in the provinces of Upper Egypt, and could be delivered at Souakim at a trifling cost of transport. A large quantity of gum arabic is collected throughout this country, which sells in Cassala at 20 piastres (4s. 2d.) the cantar of 100 lbs. There are three varieties, produced from various mimosas; the finest quality is gathered in the province of Kordofan, but I subsequently met with large quantities of this species in the Base country. Senna grows wild in the deserts, but the low price hardly pays for the cost of collection. There are several varieties; that with extremely narrow and sharp-pointed leaves is preferred. It grows in sandy situations where few plants would exist. The bush seldom exceeds three feet in height, and is generally below that standard; but it is exceedingly thick, and rich in a pale green foliage, which is a strong temptation to the hungry camel. Curiously, this purgative plant is the animal's bonne bouche, and is considered most nourishing as fodder.

The exports of the Soudan are limited to gum arabic, ivory, hides, senna, and bees'-wax; the latter is the produce of Abyssinia. These articles are generally collected by travelling native traders, who sell to the larger merchants resident in Cassala and Khartoum, the two principal towns of the Soudan. The bazaar in Cassala was poor, as the principal articles were those of low price, adapted to the wants of the Arabs, who flock to the capital as a small London, to make their purchases of cloths, perfumery for the women, copper cooking pots, &c.

The fortifications of the town, although useless against cannon, are considered by the Arabs as impregnable. The walls are of solid mud and sun-baked bricks, carefully loopholed for musketry, while a deep fosse, by which it is surrounded, is a safeguard against a sudden surprise.

These engineering precautions were rendered necessary by the ferocity of the Arabs, who fought the Egyptians with great determination for some years before they were finally subdued. Although the weapons of all the Arab tribes are the simple sword and lance, they defended their country against the regular troops of Egypt until they were completely defeated by a scarcity of water, against which there could be no resistance. The Egyptians turned the course of the river Gash, and entirely shut off the supply from one portion of the country, while they inundated another. This was effected by an immense dam, formed of the stems of the dome palms, as a double row of piles, while the interior was rendered water-tight by a lining of matting filled up with sand.

Cassala was built about twenty years before I visited the country, after Taka had been conquered and annexed to Egypt. The general annexation of the Soudan and the submission of the numerous Arab tribes to the Viceroy have been the first steps necessary to the improvement of the country. Although the Egyptians are hard masters, and do not trouble themselves about the future well-being of the conquered races, it must be remembered that, prior to the annexation, all the tribes were at war among themselves. There was neither government nor law; thus the whole country was closed to Europeans. At present, there is no more danger in travelling in Upper Egypt than in crossing Hyde Park after dark, provided the traveller be just and courteous. At the time of my visit to Cassala in 1861, the Arab tribes were separately governed by their own chiefs or sheiks, who were responsible to the Egyptian authorities for the taxes due from their people: since that period, the entire tribes of all denominations have been placed under the authority of that grand old Arab patriarch Achmet Abou Sinn, to be hereafter mentioned. The Sheik Moosa, of the Hadendowa tribe, was in prison during our stay in that country, for some breach of discipline in his dealings with the Egyptian Government. The iron hand of despotism has produced a marvellous change among the Arabs, who are rendered utterly powerless by the system of government adopted by the Egyptians; unfortunately, this harsh system has the effect of paralysing all industry.

The principal object of Turks and Egyptians in annexation, is to increase their power of taxation by gaining an additional number of subjects. Thus, although many advantages have accrued to the Arab provinces of Nubia through Egyptian rule, there exists an amount of mistrust between the governed and the governing. Not only are the camels, cattle, and sheep subjected to a tax, but every attempt at cultivation is thwarted by the authorities, who impose a fine or tax upon the superficial area of the cultivated land. Thus, no one will cultivate more than is absolutely necessary, as he dreads the difficulties that the broad acres of waving crops would entail upon his family. The bona fide tax is a bagatelle to the amounts squeezed from him by the extortionate soldiery, who are the agents employed by the sheik; these must have their share of the plunder, in excess of the amount to be delivered to their employer; he, also, must have his plunder before he parts with the bags of dollars to the governor of the province. Thus the unfortunate cultivator is ground down; should he refuse to pay the necessary "baksheesh" or present to the tax-collectors, some false charge is trumped up against him, and he is thrown into prison. As a green field is an attraction to a flight of locusts in their desolating voyage, so is a luxuriant farm in the Soudan a point for the tax-collectors of Upper Egypt. I have frequently ridden several days' journey through a succession of empty villages, deserted by the inhabitants upon the report of the soldiers' approach; the women and children, goats and cattle, camels and asses, have all been removed into the wilderness for refuge, while their crops of corn have been left standing for the plunderers, who would be too idle to reap and thrash the grain.

Notwithstanding the misrule that fetters the steps of improvement, Nature has bestowed such great capabilities of production in the fertile soil of this country, that the yield of a small surface is more than sufficient for the requirements of the population, and actual poverty is unknown. The average price of dhurra is fifteen piastres per "rachel," or about 3s. 2d. for 500 lbs. upon the spot where it is grown. The dhurra (Sorghum andropogon) is the grain most commonly used throughout the Soudan; there are great varieties of this plant, of which the most common are the white and the red. The land is not only favoured by Nature by its fertility, but the intense heat of the summer is the labourer's great assistant. As before described, all vegetation entirely disappears in the glaring Sun, or becomes so dry that it is swept off by fire; thus the soil is perfectly clean and fit for immediate cultivation upon the arrival of the rains. The tool generally used is similar to the Dutch hoe. With this simple implement the surface is scratched to the depth of about two inches, and the seeds of the dhurra are dibbled in about three feet apart, in rows from four to five feet in width. Two seeds are dropped into each hole. A few days after the first shower they rise above the ground, and when about six inches high, the whole population turn out of their villages at break of day to weed the dhurra fields. Sown in July, it is harvested in February and March. Eight months are thus required for the cultivation of this cereal in the intense heat of Nubia. For the first three months the growth is extremely rapid, and the stem attains a height of six or seven feet. When at perfection on the rich soil of the Taka country, the plant averages a height of ten feet, the circumference of the stem being about four inches. The crown is a feather very similar to that of the sugar cane; the blossom falls, and the feather becomes a head of dhurra, weighing about two pounds. Each grain is about the size of hemp-seed. I took the trouble of counting the corns contained in an average-sized head, the result being 4,848. The process of harvesting and thrashing are remarkably simple, as the heads are simply detached from the straw and beaten out in piles. The dried straw is a substitute for sticks in forming the walls of the village huts; these are plastered with clay and cow-dung, which form the Arab's lath and plaster.

The millers' work is exclusively the province of the women. There are no circular hand-mills, as among Oriental nations; but the corn is ground upon a simple flat stone, of either gneiss or granite, about two feet in length by fourteen inches in width. The face of this is roughened by beating with a sharp-pointed piece of harder stone, such as quartz, or hornblende, and the grain is reduced to flour by great labour and repeated grinding or rubbing with a stone rolling-pin. The flour is mixed with water and allowed to ferment; it is then made into thin pancakes upon an earthenware flat portable hearth. This species of leavened bread is known to the Arabs as the kisra. It is not very palatable, but it is extremely well suited to Arab cookery, as it can be rolled up like a pancake and dipped in the general dish of meat and gravy very conveniently, in the absence of spoons and forks. No man will condescend to grind the corn, and even the Arab women have such an objection to this labour, that one of the conditions of matrimony enforced upon the husband, if possible, provides the wife with a slave woman to prepare the flour.

Hitherto we had a large stock of biscuits, but as our dragoman Mahomet had, in a curious fit of amiability, dispensed them among the camel-drivers, we were now reduced to the Arab kisras. Although not as palatable as wheaten bread, the flour of dhurra is exceedingly nourishing, containing, according to Professor Johnston's analysis, eleven and a half per cent. of gluten, or one and a half per cent. more than English wheaten flour. Thus men and beasts thrive, especially horses, which acquire an excellent condition.

The neighbourhood of Cassala is well adapted for the presence of a large town and military station, as the fertile soil produces the necessary supplies, while the river Gash affords excellent water. In the rainy season this should be filtered, as it brings down many impurities from the torrents of Abyssinia, but in the heat of summer the river is entirely dry, and clear and wholesome water is procured from wells in the sandy bed. The south and south-east of Cassala is wild and mountainous, affording excellent localities for hill stations during the unhealthy rainy season; but such sanitary arrangements for the preservation of troops are about as much heeded by the Egyptian Government as by our own, and regiments are left in unwholesome climates to take their chance, although the means of safety are at hand.

The Taka country being the extreme frontier of Egypt, constant raids are made by the Egyptians upon their neighbours – the hostile Base, through which country the river Gash or Mareb descends. I was anxious to procure all the information possible concerning the Base, as it would be necessary to traverse the greater portion in exploring the Settite river, which is the principal tributary of the Atbara, and which is in fact the main and parent stream, although bearing a different name. I heard but one opinion of the Base – it was a wild and independent country, inhabited by a ferocious race, whose hand was against every man, and who in return were the enemies of all by whom they were surrounded – Egyptians, Abyssinians, Arabs, and Mek Nimmur; nevertheless, secure in their mountainous stronghold, they defied all adversaries. The Base is a portion of Abyssinia, but the origin of the tribe that occupies this ineradicable hornet's nest is unknown. Whether they are the remnant of the original Ethiopians, who possessed the country prior to the conquests of the Abyssinians, or whether they are descended from the woolly-haired tribes of the south banks of the Blue Nile, is equally a mystery; all we know is that they are of the same type as the inhabitants of Fazogle, of the upper portion of the Blue River; they are exceedingly black, with woolly hair, resembling in that respect the negro, but without the flat nose or prognathous jaw. No quarter is given on either side, should the Base meet the Arabs, with whom war is to the knife. In spite of the overwhelming superiority of their adversaries, the Base cannot be positively subdued; armed with the lance as their only weapon, but depending upon extreme agility and the natural difficulties of their mountain passes, the attack of the Base is always by stealth; their spies are ever prowling about unseen like the leopard, and their onset is invariably a surprise; success or defeat are alike followed by a rapid retreat to their mountains.

As there is nothing to be obtained by the plunder of the Base but women and children as slaves, the country is generally avoided, unless visited for the express purpose of a slave razzia. Cultivation being extremely limited, the greater portion of the country is perfectly wild, and is never visited even by the Base themselves unless for the purpose of hunting. Several beautiful rivers descend from the mountain ranges, which ultimately flow into the Atbara; these, unlike the latter river, are never dry: thus, with a constant supply of water, in a country of forest and herbage, the Base abounds in elephants, rhinoceroses, hippopotami, giraffes, buffaloes, lions, leopards, and great numbers of the antelope tribe.

Cassala, thus situated on the confines of the Taka country, is an important military point in the event of war between Egypt and Abyssinia, as the Base would be invaluable as allies to the Egyptians; their country commands the very heart of Abyssinia, and their knowledge of the roads would be an incalculable advantage to an invading force. On the 14th July I had concluded my arrangements for the start; there had been some difficulty in procuring camels, but the all-powerful firman was a never-failing talisman, and, as the Arabs had declined to let their animals for hire, the Governor despatched a number of soldiers and seized the required number, including their owners. I engaged two wild young Arabs of eighteen and twenty years of age, named Bacheet and Wat Gamma: the latter being interpreted signifies "Son of the Moon." This in no way suggests lunacy, but the young Arab had happened to enter this world on the day of the new moon, which was considered to be a particularly fortunate and brilliant omen at his birth. Whether the climax of his good fortune had arrived at the moment he entered my service I know not, but, if so, there was a cloud over his happiness in his subjection to Mahomet the dragoman, who rejoiced in the opportunity of bullying the two inferiors. Wat Gamma was a quiet, steady, well-conducted lad, who bore oppression mildly; but the younger, Bacheet, was a fiery, wild young Arab, who, although an excellent boy in his peculiar way, was almost incapable of being tamed and domesticated. I at once perceived that Mahomet would have a determined rebel to control, which I confess I did not regret. Wages were not high in this part of the world, – the lads were engaged at one and a half dollar per month and their keep. Mahomet, who was a great man, suffered from the same complaint to which great men are (in those countries) particularly subject: wherever he went, he was attacked with claimants of relationship; he was overwhelmed with professions of friendship from people who claimed to be connexions of some of his family; in fact, if all the ramifications of his race were correctly represented by the claimants of relationship, Mahomet's family tree would have shaded the Nubian desert.

We all have our foibles: the strongest fort has its feeble point, as the chain snaps at its weakest link; – family pride was Mahomet's weak link. This was his tender point; and Mahomet, the great and the imperious, yielded to the gentle scratching of his ear if a stranger claimed connexion with his ancient lineage. Of course he had no family, with the exception of his wife and two children, whom he had left in Cairo. The lady whom he had honoured by an admission to the domestic circle of the Mahomets was suffering from a broken arm when we started from Egypt, as she had cooked the dinner badly, and the "gaddah," or large wooden bowl, had been thrown at her by the naturally indignant husband, precisely as he had thrown the axe at one man and the basin at another, while in our service: these were little contretemps that could hardly disturb the dignity of so great a man. Mahomet met several relations at Cassala: one borrowed money of him; another stole his pipe; the third, who declared that nothing should separate them now that "by the blessing of God" they had met, determined to accompany him through all the difficulties of our expedition, provided that Mahomet would only permit him to serve for love, without wages. I gave Mahomet some little advice upon this point, reminding him that, although the clothes of the party were only worth a few piastres, the spoons and forks were silver, therefore I should hold him responsible for the honesty of his friend. This reflection upon the family gave great offence, and he assured me that Achmet, our quondam acquaintance, was so near a relation that he was – I assisted him in the genealogical distinction: "Mother's brother's cousin's sister's mother's son? Eh, Mahomet?" "Yes, sar, that's it!" "Very well, Mahomet; mind he don't steal the spoons, and thrash him if he doesn't do his work!" "Yes, sar," replied Mahomet; "he all same like one brother, he one good man will do his business quietly; if not, master lick him." The new relation not understanding English, was perfectly satisfied with the success of his introduction, and from that moment he became one of the party. One more addition, and our arrangements were completed: – the Governor of Cassala was determined that we should not start without a representative of the Government, in the shape of a soldier guide; he accordingly gave us a black man, a corporal in one of the Nubian regiments, who was so renowned as a sportsman that he went by the name of "El Baggar" (the cow), on account of his having killed several of the oryx antelope, known as "El Baggar et Wahash" (the cow of the desert).

The rains had fairly commenced, as a heavy thunder-shower generally fell at about 2 P.M. On the 15th, the entire day was passed in transporting our baggage across the river Gash to the point from which we had started upon our arrival at Cassala: this we accomplished with much difficulty, with the assistance of about a hundred men supplied by the Governor, from whom we had received much attention and politeness. We camped for the night upon the margin of the river, and marched on the following morning at daybreak due west towards the Atbara.

The country was a great improvement upon that we had hitherto passed; the trees were larger, and vast plains of young grass, interspersed with green bush, stretched to the horizon. The soil was an exceedingly rich loam, most tenacious when wetted: far as the eye could reach to the north and west of Cassala was the dead level plain, while to the south and east arose a broken chain of mountains.

We had not proceeded many miles, when the numerous tracks of antelopes upon the soil, moistened by the shower of yesterday, proved that we had arrived in a sporting country; shortly after, we saw a herd of about fifty ariels (Gazelle Dama). To stalk these wary antelopes I was obliged to separate from my party, who continued on their direct route. Riding upon my camel, I tried every conceivable dodge without success. I could not approach them nearer than about 300 yards. They did not gallop off at once, but made a rush for a few hundred paces, and then faced about to gaze at the approaching camel. After having exhausted my patience to no purpose, I tried another plan: instead of advancing against the wind as before, I made a great circuit and gave them the wind. No sooner was I in good cover behind a mimosa bush than I dismounted from my camel, and, leading it until within view of the shy herd, I tied it to a tree, keeping behind the animal so as to be well concealed. I succeeded in retreating through the bushes unobserved, leaving the camel as a gazing point to attract their attention. Running at my best speed to the same point from which I had commenced my circuit, and keeping under cover of the scattered bushes, I thus obtained the correct wind, and stalked up from bush to bush behind the herd, who were curiously watching the tied camel, that was quietly gazing on a mimosa. In this way I had succeeded in getting within 150 yards of the beautiful herd, when a sudden fright seized them, and they rushed off in an opposite direction to the camel, so as to pass about 120 yards on my left; as they came by in full speed, I singled out a superb animal, and tried the first barrel of the little Fletcher rifle. I heard the crack of the ball, and almost immediately afterwards the herd passed on, leaving one lagging behind at a slow canter; this was my wounded ariel, who shortly halted, and laid down in an open glade. Having no dog, I took the greatest precaution in stalking, as a wounded antelope is almost certain to escape if once disturbed when it has lain down. There was a small withered stem of a tree not thicker than a man's thigh; this grew within thirty yards of the antelope; my only chance of approach was to take a line direct for this slight object of cover. The wind was favourable, and I crept along the ground. I had succeeded in arriving within a few yards of the tree when up jumped the antelope, and bounded off as though unhurt; but there was no chance for it at this distance, and I rolled it over with a shot through the spine.

Having done the needful with my beautiful prize, and extracted the interior, I returned for my camel that had well assisted in the stalk. Hardly had I led the animal to the body of the ariel, when I heard a rushing sound like a strong wind, and down came a vulture with its wings collapsed, falling from an immense height direct to its prey, in its eagerness to be the first in the race. By the time that I had fastened the ariel across the back of the camel, many vultures were sitting upon the ground at a few yards' distance, while others were arriving every minute: before I had shot the ariel, not a vulture had been in sight; the instant that I retreated from the spot a flock of ravenous beaks were tearing at the offal.

In the constant doubling necessary during the stalk I had quite lost my way. The level plain to the horizon, covered with scattered mimosas, offered no object as a guide. I was exceedingly thirsty, as the heat was intense, and I had been taking rapid exercise; unfortunately my water-skin was slung upon my wife's camel. However unpleasant the situation, my pocket compass would give me the direction, as we had been steering due west; therefore, as I had turned to my left when I left my party, a course N.W. should bring me across their tracks, if they had continued on their route. The position of the Cassala mountain agreed with this course; therefore, remounting my dromedary, with the ariel slung behind the saddle, I hastened to rejoin our caravan. After about half an hour I heard a shot fired not far in advance, and I shortly joined the party, who had fired a gun to give me the direction. A long and deep pull at the water-skin was the first salutation.

We halted that night near a small pond formed by the recent heavy rain. Fortunately the sky was clear; there was abundance of fuel, and pots were shortly boiling an excellent stew of ariel venison and burnt onions. The latter delicious bulbs are the blessing of Upper Egypt: I have lived for days upon nothing but raw onions and sun-dried rusks. Nothing is so good a substitute for meat as an onion; but if raw, it should be cut into thin slices, and allowed to soak for half an hour in water, which should be poured off: the onion thus loses its pungency, and becomes mild and agreeable; with the accompaniment of a little oil and vinegar it forms an excellent salad.

The following day's march led us through the same dead level of grassy plains and mimosas, enlivened with numerous herds of ariels and large black-striped gazelles (Dorcas), one of which I succeeded in shooting for my people. After nine hours' journey we arrived at the, valley of the Atbara, in all sixteen hours' actual marching from Cassala.

There was an extraordinary change in the appearance of the river between Gozerajup and this spot. There was no longer the vast sandy desert with the river flowing through its sterile course on a level with the surface of the country, but after traversing an apparently perfect flat of forty-five miles of rich alluvial soil, we had suddenly arrived upon the edge of a deep valley, between five and six miles wide, at the bottom of which, about 200 feet below the general level of the country, flowed the river Atbara. On the opposite side of the valley, the same vast table lands continued to the western horizon.

We commenced the descent towards the river; the valley was a succession of gullies and ravines, of landslips and watercourses; the entire hollow, of miles in width, had evidently been the work of the river. How many ages had the rains and the stream been at work to scoop out from the flat table land this deep and broad valley? Here was the giant labourer that had shovelled the rich loam upon the delta of Lower Egypt! Upon these vast flats of fertile soil there can be no drainage except through soakage. The deep valley is therefore the receptacle not only for the water that oozes from its sides, but subterranean channels, bursting as land-springs from all parts of the walls of the valley, wash down the more soluble portions of earth, and continually waste away the soil. Landslips occur daily during the rainy season; streams of rich mud pour down the valley's slopes, and as the river flows beneath in a swollen torrent, the friable banks topple down into the stream and dissolve. The Atbara becomes the thickness of pea-soup, as its muddy waters steadily perform the duty they have fulfilled from age to age. Thus was the great river at work upon our arrival on its bank at the bottom of the valley. The Arab name, "Bahr el Aswat" (black river) was well bestowed; it was the black mother of Egypt, still carrying to her offspring the nourishment that had first formed the Delta.

At this point of interest, the journey had commenced; the deserts were passed, all was fertility and life: wherever the sources of the Nile might be, the Atbara was the parent of Egypt! This was my first impression, to be proved hereafter.

Chapter V.

The Storm.

A violent thunderstorm, with a deluge of rain, broke upon our camp upon the banks of the Atbara, fortunately just after the tents were pitched. We thus had an example of the extraordinary effects of the heavy rain in tearing away the soil of the valley. Trifling watercourses were swollen to torrents; banks of earth became loosened and fell in, and the rush of mud and water upon all sides swept forward into the river with a rapidity which threatened the destruction of the country, could such a tempest endure for a few days. In a couple of hours all was over. The river was narrower than in its passage through the desert, but was proportionately deeper. The name of the village on the opposite bank was Goorashee, with which a means of communication had been established by a ferry-boat belonging to our friend and late host, Malem Georgis, the Greek merchant of Cassala. He had much trouble in obtaining permission from the authorities to introduce this novelty, which was looked upon as an innovation, as such a convenience had never before existed. The enterprising proprietor had likewise established a cotton farm at Goorashee, which appeared to succeed admirably, and was an undeniable example of what could be produced in this fertile country were the spirit of improvement awakened. Notwithstanding the advantage of the ferry-boat, many of the Arabs preferred to swim their camels across the river to paying a trifle to the ferryman. A camel either cannot or will not swim unless it is supported by inflated skins: thus the passage of the broad river Atbara (at this spot about 300 yards wide) is an affair of great difficulty. Two water-skins are inflated, and attached to the camel by a band passed like a girth beneath the belly. Thus arranged, a man sits upon its back, while one or two swim by the side as guides. The current of the Atbara runs at a rapid rate; thus the camel is generally carried at least half a mile down the river before it can gain the opposite bank. A few days before our arrival, a man had been snatched from the back of his camel while crossing, and was carried off by a crocodile. Another man had been taken during the last week while swimming the river upon a log. It was supposed that these accidents were due to the same crocodile, who was accustomed to bask upon a mud bank at the foot of the cotton plantation. On the day following our arrival at the Atbara, we found that our camel-drivers had absconded during the night with their camels; these were the men who had been forced to serve by the Governor of Cassala. There was no possibility of proceeding for some days, therefore I sent El Baggar across the river to endeavour to engage camels, while I devoted myself to a search for the crocodile. I shortly discovered that it was unfair in the extreme to charge one particular animal with the death of the two Arabs, as several large crocodiles were lying upon the mud in various places. A smaller one was lying asleep high and dry upon the bank; the wind was blowing strong, so that, by carefully approaching, I secured a good shot within thirty yards, and killed it on the spot by a bullet through the head, placed about an inch above the eyes.

After some time, the large crocodiles, who had taken to the water at the report of the gun, again appeared, and crawled slowly out of the muddy river to their basking-places upon the bank. A crocodile usually sleeps with its mouth wide open; I therefore waited until the immense jaws of the nearest were well expanded, showing a grand row of glittering teeth, when I crept carefully towards it through the garden of thickly-planted cotton. Bacheet and Wat Gamma followed in great eagerness. In a short time I arrived within about forty yards of the beast, as it lay upon a flat mud bank formed by one of the numerous torrents that had carried down the soil during the storm of yesterday. The cover ceased, and it was impossible to approach nearer without alarming the crocodile; it was a fine specimen, apparently nineteen or twenty feet in length, and I took a steady shot with the little Fletcher rifle at the temple, exactly in front of the point of union of the head with the spine. The jaws clashed together, and a convulsive start followed by a twitching of the tail led me to suppose that sudden death had succeeded the shot; but, knowing the peculiar tenacity of life possessed by the crocodile, I fired another shot at the shoulder, as the huge body lay so close to the river's edge that the slightest struggle would cause it to disappear. To my surprise, this shot, far from producing a quietus, gave rise to a series of extraordinary convulsive struggles. One moment it rolled upon its back, lashed out right and left with its tail, and ended by toppling over into the river.

This was too much for the excitable Bacheet, who, followed by his friend, Wat Gamma, with more courage than discretion, rushed into the river, and endeavoured to catch the crocodile by the tail. Before I had time to call them back, these two Arab water-dogs were up to their necks in the river, screaming out directions to each other while they were feeling for the body of the monster with their feet. At length I succeeded in calling them to shore, and we almost immediately saw the body of the crocodile appear belly upwards, about fifty yards down the stream; the forepaws were above the water, but, after rolling round several times, it once more disappeared, rapidly carried away by the muddy torrent. This was quite enough for the Arabs, who had been watching the event from the opposite bank of the river, and the report quickly spread that two crocodiles were killed, one of which they declared to be the public enemy that had taken the men at the ferry, but upon what evidence I cannot understand. Although my Arabs looked forward to a dinner of crocodile flesh, I was obliged to search for something of rather milder flavour for ourselves. I waited for about an hour while the first crocodile was being divided, when I took a shot gun and succeeded in killing three geese and a species of antelope no larger than a hare, known by the Arabs as the Dik-dik (Nanotragus Hemprichianus). This little creature inhabits thick bush. Since my return to England, I have seen a good specimen in the Zoological Gardens of the Regent's Park.

Upon my arrival at the tents, I found the camp redolent of musk from the flesh of the crocodile, and the people were quarrelling for the musk glands, which they had extracted, and which are much prized by the Arab women, who wear them strung like beads upon a necklace.

A crocodile possesses four of such glands; they vary in size according to the age of the reptile, but they are generally about as large as a hazelnut, when dried. Two glands are situated in the groin, and two in the throat, a little in advance of the fore-legs. I have noticed two species of crocodiles throughout all the rivers of Abyssinia, and in the White Nile. One of these is of a dark brown colour, and much shorter and thicker in proportion than the other, which grows to an immense length, an is generally of a pale greenish yellow. Throughout the Atbara, crocodiles are extremely mischievous and bold; this can be accounted for by the constant presence of Arabs and their flocks, which the crocodiles have ceased to fear, as they exact a heavy tribute in their frequent passages of the river. The Arabs assert that the dark-coloured, thick-bodied species is more to be dreaded than the other.

The common belief that the scales of the crocodile will stop a bullet is very erroneous. If a rifle is loaded with the moderate charge of two and a half drachms it will throw an ounce ball through the scales of the hardest portion of the back; but were the scales struck obliquely, the bullet might possibly glance from the surface, as in like manner it would ricochet from the surface of water. The crocodile is so difficult to kill outright, that people are apt to imagine that the scales have resisted their bullets. The only shots that will produce instant death are those that strike the brain or the spine through the neck. A shot through the shoulder is fatal; but as the body immediately sinks, and does not reappear upon the surface until the gases have distended the carcase, the game is generally carried away by the stream before it has had time to float. The body of a crocodile requires from twelve to eighteen hours before it will rise to the surface, while that of the hippopotamus will never remain longer than two hours beneath the water, and will generally rise in an hour and a half after death. This difference in time depends upon the depth and temperature; in deep holes of the river of from thirty to fifty feet, the water is much cooler near the bottom, thus the gas is not generated in the body so quickly as in shallow and warmer water. The crocodile is not a grass-feeder, therefore the stomach is comparatively small, and the contents do not generate the amount of gas that so quickly distends the huge stomach of the hippopotamus; thus the body of the former requires a longer period before it will rise to the surface.

In the evening we crossed with our baggage and people to the opposite side of the river, and pitched our tents at the village of Goorashee. A small watercourse had brought down a large quantity of black sand. Thinking it probable that gold might exist in the same locality, I washed some earth in a copper basin, and quickly discovered a few specks of the precious metal. Gold is found in small quantities in the sand of the Atbara; at Fazogle, on the Blue Nile, there are mines of this metal worked by the Egyptian Govermnent. From my subsequent experience I have no doubt that valuable minerals exist in large quantities throughout the lofty chain of Abyssinian mountains from which these rivers derive their sources.

The camels arrived, and once more we were ready to start. Our factotum, El Baggar, had collected a number of both baggage-camels and riding dromedaries or "hygeens;" the latter he had brought for approval, as we had suffered much from the extreme roughness of our late camels. There is the same difference between a good hygeen or dromedary and a baggage-camel as between the thoroughbred and the cart-horse; and it appears absurd in the eyes of the Arabs that a man of any position should ride a baggage-camel. Apart from all ideas of etiquette, the motion of the latter animal is quite sufficient warning. Of all species of fatigue, the back-breaking monotonous swing of a heavy camel is the worst; and, should the rider lose patience, and administer a sharp cut with the coorbatch that induces the creature to break into a trot, the torture of the rack is a pleasant tickling compared to the sensation of having your spine driven by a sledge-hammer from below, half a foot deeper into the skull. The human frame may be inured to almost anything; thus the Arabs, who have always been accustomed to this kind of exercise, hardly feel the motion, and the portion of the body most subject to pain in riding a rough camel upon two bare pieces of wood for a saddle, becomes naturally adapted for such rough service, as monkeys become hardened from constantly sitting upon rough substances. The children commence almost as soon as they are born, as they must accompany their mothers in their annual migrations; and no sooner can the young Arab sit astride and hold on, than he is placed behind his father's saddle, to which he clings, while he bumps upon the bare back of the jolting camel. Nature quickly arranges a horny protection to the nerves, by the thickening of the skin; thus, an Arab's opinion of the action of a riding hygeen should never be accepted without a personal trial. What appears delightful to him may be torture to you, as a strong breeze and a rough sea may be charming to a sailor, but worse than death to a landsman.

I was determined not to accept the camels now offered as hygeens until I had seen them tried; I accordingly ordered our black soldier El Baggar to saddle the most easy-actioned animal for my wife, but I wished to see him put it through a variety of paces before she should accept it. The delighted El Baggar, who from long practice was as hard as the heel of a boot, disdained a saddle; the animal knelt, was mounted, and off he started at full trot, performing a circle of about fifty yards' diameter as though in a circus. I never saw such an exhibition! "Warranted quiet to ride, of easy action, and fit for a lady!" This had been the character received with the rampant brute, who now, with head and tail erect, went tearing round the circle, screaming and roaring like a wild beast, throwing his fore-legs forward, and stepping at least three feet high in his trot. Where was El Baggar? A disjointed-looking black figure was sometimes on the back of this easy-going camel, sometimes a foot high in the air; arms, head, legs, hands appeared like a confused mass of dislocations; the woolly hair of this unearthly individual, that had been carefully trained in long stiff narrow curls, precisely similar to the tobacco known as "negro-head," alternately started upright en masse, as though under the influence of electricity, and then fell as suddenly upon his shoulders: had the dark individual been a "black dose," he or it could not have been more thoroughly shaken. This object, so thoroughly disguised by rapidity of movement, was El Baggar; happy, delighted El Baggar! As he came rapidly round towards us flourishing his coorbatch, I called to him, "Is that a nice hygeen for the Sit (lady), El Baggar? is it *very* easy?" He was almost incapable of a reply. "V-e-r-y e-e-a-a-s-y," replied the trustworthy authority, "j-j-j-just the thin-n-n-g for the S-i-i-i-t-t-t." "All right, that will do," I answered, and the jockey pulled up his steed. "Are the other camels better or worse than that?" I asked. "Much worse," replied El Baggar; "the others are rather rough, but this is an easy-goer, and will suit the lady well."

It was impossible to hire a good hygeen; an Arab prizes his riding animal too much, and invariably refuses to let it to a stranger, but generally imposes upon him by substituting some lightly-built camel, that he thinks will pass muster. I accordingly chose for my wife a steady-going animal from among the baggage-camels, trusting to be able to obtain a hygeen from the great sheik Abou Sinn, who was encamped upon the road we were about to take along the valley of the Atbara; we arranged to leave Goorashee on the following day.

Upon arriving at the highest point of the valley, we found ourselves on the vast table land that stretches from the Atbara to the Nile. At this season the entire surface had a faint tint of green, as the young shoots of grass had replied to the late showers of rain; so perfect a level was this great tract of fertile country, that within a mile of the valley of the Atbara there was neither furrow nor watercourse, but the escape of the rainfall was by simple soakage. As usual, the land was dotted with mimosas, all of which were now bursting into leaf. The thorns of the different varieties of these trees are an extraordinary freak of Nature, as she appears to have exhausted all her art in producing an apparently useless arrangement of defence. The mimosas that are most common in the Soudan provinces are mere bushes, seldom exceeding six feet in height; these spread out towards the top like mushrooms, but the branches commence within two feet of the ground; they are armed with thorns in the shape of fish-hooks, which they resemble in sharpness and strength. A thick jungle composed of such bushes is perfectly impenetrable to any animals but elephants, rhinoceroses, and buffaloes; and should the clothes of a man become entangled in such thorns, either they must give way, or he must remain a prisoner. The mimosa that is known among the Arabs as the Kittar is one of the worst species, and is probably similar to that which caught Absalom by the hair; this differs from the well-known "Wait-a-bit" of South Africa, as no milder nickname could be applied than "Dead-stop." Were the clothes of strong material, it would be perfectly impossible to break through a kittar-bush.

A magnificent specimen of a kittar, with a wide-spreading head in the young glory of green leaf, tempted my hungry camel during our march; it was determined to procure a mouthful, and I was equally determined that it should keep to the straight path, and avoid the attraction of the green food. After some strong remonstrance upon my part, the perverse beast shook its ugly head, gave a roar, and started off in full trot straight at the thorny bush. I had not the slightest control over the animal, and in a few seconds it charged the bush with the mad intention of rushing either through or beneath it. To my disgust I perceived that the wide-spreading branches were only just sufficiently high to permit the back of the camel to pass underneath. There was no time for further consideration; we charged the bush; I held my head doubled up between my arms, and the next moment I was on my back, half stunned by the fall. The camel-saddle lay upon the ground; my rifle, that had been slung behind, my coffee-pot, the water-skin burst, and a host of other impedimenta, lay around me in all directions; worst of all, my beautiful gold repeater lay at some distance from me, rendered entirely useless. I was as nearly naked as I could be; a few rags held together, but my shirt was gone, with the exception of some shreds that adhered to my arms. I was, of course, streaming with blood, and looked much more as though I had been clawed by a leopard than as having simply charged a bush. The camel had fallen down with the shock after I had been swept off by the thorny branches. To this day I have the marks of the scratching.

Unless a riding-camel is perfectly trained, it is the most tiresome animal to ride after the first green leaves appear; every bush tempts it from the path, and it is a perpetual fight between the rider and his beast throughout the journey.

We shortly halted for the night, as I had noticed unmistakeable signs of an approaching storm. We quickly pitched the tents, grubbed up the root and stem of a decayed mimosa, and lighted a fire, by the side of which our people sat in a circle. Hardly had the pile begun to blaze, when a cry from Mahomet's new relative, Achmet, informed us that he had been bitten by a scorpion. Mahomet appeared to think this highly entertaining, until suddenly he screamed out likewise, and springing from the ground, he began to stamp and wring his hands in great agony: he had himself been bitten, and we found that a whole nest of scorpions were in the rotten wood lately thrown upon the fire; in their flight from the heat they stung all whom they met. There was no time to prepare food; the thunder already roared above us, and in a few minutes the sky, lately so clear, was as black as ink. I had already prepared for the storm, and the baggage was piled within the tent; the ropes of the tents had been left slack to allow for the contraction, and we were ready for the rain. It was fortunate that we were in order; a rain descended, with an accompaniment of thunder and lightning, of a volume unknown to the inhabitants of cooler climates; for several hours there was almost an uninterrupted roar of the most deafening peals, with lightning so vivid that our tent was completely lighted up in the darkness of the night, and its misery displayed. Not only was the rain pouring through the roof so that we were wet through as we crouched upon our angareps (stretchers), but the legs of our bedstead stood in more than six inches of water. Being as wet as I could be, I resolved to enjoy the scene outside the tent; it was curious in the extreme. Flash after flash of sharp forked lightning played upon the surface of a boundless lake; there was not a foot of land visible, but the numerous dark bushes projecting from the surface of the water destroyed the illusion of depth that the scene would otherwise have suggested. The rain ceased, but the entire country was flooded several inches deep; and when the more distant lightning flashed as the storm rolled away, I saw the camels lying like statues built into the lake. On the following morning the whole of this great mass of water had been absorbed by the soil, which had become so adhesive and slippery that it was impossible for the camels to move; we therefore waited for some hours, until the intense heat of the sun had dried the surface sufficiently to allow the animals to proceed.

Upon striking the tent, we found beneath the valance between the crown and the walls a regiment of scorpions; the flood had doubtless destroyed great numbers within their holes, but these, having been disturbed by the deluge, had found an asylum by crawling up the tent walls: with great difficulty we lighted a fire, and committed them all to the flames. Mahomet made a great fuss about his hand, which was certainly much swollen, but not worse than that of Achmet, who did not complain, although during the night he had been again bitten on the leg by one of these venomous insects, that had crawled from the water upon his clothes. During our journey that morning parallel with the valley of the Atbara, I had an excellent opportunity of watching the effect of the storm. We rode along the abrupt margin of the table land, where it broke suddenly into the deep valley; from the sides of this the water was oozing in all directions, creating little avalanches of earth, which fell as they lost their solidity from too much moisture. This wonderfully rich soil was rolling gradually towards Lower Egypt. From the heights above the river we had a beautiful view of the stream, which at this distance, reflecting the bright sunlight, did not appear like the thick liquid mud that we knew it to be. The valley was of the same general character that we had remarked at Goorashee, but more abrupt – a mass of landslips, deep ravines, shaded by mimosas, while the immediate neighbour hood of the Atbara was clothed with the brightest green foliage. In this part, the valley was about three miles in width, and two hundred feet deep.

The commencement of the rainy season was a warning to all the Arabs of this country, who were preparing for their annual migration to the sandy and firm desert on the west bank of the river, at Gozerajup; that region, so barren and desolate during the hot season, would shortly be covered with a delicate grass about eighteen inches high. At that favoured spot the rains fell with less violence, and it formed a nucleus for the general gathering of the people with their flocks.

We were travelling south at the very season when the natives were migrating north. I saw plainly that it would be impossible for us to continue our journey during the wet season, as the camels had the greatest difficulty in carrying their loads even now, at the commencement: their feet sank deep into the soil; this formed adhesive clods upon their spongy toes, that almost disabled them. The farther we travelled south, the more violent would the rains become, and a long tropical experience warned me that the rainy season was the signal for fevers. All the camels of the Arabs were being driven from the country; we had already met many herds travelling northward, but this day's march was through crowds of these animals, principally females with their young, many thousands of which were on the road. Some of the young foals were so small that they could not endure the march; these were slung in nets upon the backs of camels, while the mother followed behind. We revelled in milk, as we had not been able to procure it since we left Cassala. Some persons dislike the milk of the camel; I think it is excellent to drink pure, but it does not answer in general use for mixing with coffee, with which it immediately curdles; it is extremely rich, and is considered by the Arabs to be more nourishing than that of the cow. To persons of delicate health I should invariably recommend boiled milk in preference to plain; and should the digestion be so extremely weak that liquid milk disagrees with the stomach, they should allow it to become thick, similar to curds and whey: this should be then beaten together, with the admixture of a little salt and cayenne pepper; it then assumes the thickness of cream, and is very palatable. The Arabs generally prepare it in this manner; it is not only considered to be more wholesome, but in its thickened state it is easier to carry upon a journey. With an apology to European medical men, I would suggest that they should try the Arab system whenever they prescribe a milk diet for a delicate patient. The first operation of curdling, which is a severe trial to a weak stomach, is performed in hot climates by the atmosphere, as in temperate climates by the admixture of rennet, &c.; thus the most difficult work of the stomach is effected by a foreign agency, and it is spared the first act of its performance. I have witnessed almost marvellous results from a milk diet given as now advised.

Milk, if drunk warm from the animal in hot climates will affect many persons in the same manner as a powerful dose of senna and salts. Our party appeared to be proof against such an accident, as they drank enough to have stocked a moderate-sized dairy. This was most good-naturedly supplied gratis by the Arabs.

It was the season of rejoicing; everybody appeared in good humour; the distended udders of thousands of camels were an assurance of plenty. The burning sun that for nine months had scorched the earth was veiled by passing clouds; the cattle that had panted for water, and whose food was withered straw, were filled with juicy fodder: the camels that had subsisted upon the dried and leafless twigs and branches, now feasted upon the succulent tops of the mimosas. Throngs of women and children mounted upon camels, protected by the peculiar gaudy saddle hood, ornamented with cowrie-shells, accompanied the march; thousands of sheep and goats, driven by Arab boys, were straggling in all directions; baggage-camels, heavily laden with the quaint household goods, blocked up the way; the fine bronzed figures of Arabs, with sword and shield, and white topes, or plaids, guided their milk-white dromedaries through the confused throng with the usual placid dignity of their race, simply passing by with the usual greeting, "Salaam aleikum," "Peace be with you."

It was the Exodus; all were hurrying towards the promised land – "the land flowing with milk and honey," where men and beasts would be secure, not only from the fevers of the south, but from that deadly enemy to camels and cattle, the fly; this terrible insect drove all before it.

If all were right in migrating to the north, it was a logical conclusion that we were wrong in going to the south during the rainy season; however, we now heard from the Arabs that we were within a couple of hours' march from the camp of the great Sheik Achmet Abou Sinn, to whom I had a letter of introduction. At the expiration of about that time we halted, and pitched the tents among some shady mimosas, while I sent Mahomet to Abou Sinn with the letter, and my firman.

I was busily engaged in making sundry necessary arrangements in the tent, when Mahomet returned, and announced the arrival of the great sheik in person. He was attended by several of his principal people, and as he approached through the bright green mimosas, mounted upon a beautiful snow-white hygeen, I was exceedingly struck with his venerable and dignified appearance. Upon near arrival I went forward to meet him, and to assist him from his camel; but his animal knelt immediately at his command, and he dismounted with the ease and agility of a man of twenty.

He was the most magnificent specimen of an Arab that I have ever seen. Although upwards of eighty years of age, he was as erect as a lance, and did not appear more than between fifty and sixty; he was of Herculean stature, about six feet three inches high, with immensely broad shoulders and chest; a remarkably arched nose; eyes like an eagle, beneath large, shaggy, but perfectly white eyebrows; a snow-white beard of great thickness descended below the middle of his breast. He wore a large white turban, and a white cashmere abbai, or long robe, from the throat to the ankles. As a desert patriarch he was superb, the very perfection of all that the imagination could paint, if we would personify Abraham at the head of his people. This grand old Arab with the greatest politeness insisted upon our immediately accompanying him to his camp, as he could not allow us to remain in his country as strangers. He would hear of no excuses, but he at once gave orders to Mahomet to have the baggage repacked and the tents removed, while we were requested to mount two superb white hygeens, with saddle-cloths of blue Persian sheep-skins, that he had immediately accoutred when he heard from Mahomet of our miserable camels. The tent was struck, and we joined our venerable host with a line of wild and splendidly-mounted attendants, who followed us towards the sheik's encampment.

Chapter VI.

Sheik Achmet Abou Sinn.

Among the retinue of the aged sheik, whom we now accompanied, were ten of his sons, some of whom appeared to be quite as old as their father. We had ridden about two miles, when we were suddenly met by a crowd of mounted men, armed with the usual swords and shields; many were on horses, others upon hygeens, and all drew up in lines parallel with our approach. These were Abou Sinn's people, who had assembled to give us the honorary welcome as guests of their chief; this etiquette of the Arabs consists in galloping singly at full speed across the line of advance, the rider flourishing the sword over his head, and at the same moment reining up his horse upon its haunches so as to bring it to a sudden halt. This having been performed by about a hundred riders upon both horses and hygeens, they fell into line behind our party, and, thus escorted, we shortly arrived at the Arab encampment. In all countries the warmth of a public welcome appears to be exhibited by noise – the whole neighbourhood had congregated to meet us; crowds of women raised the wild shrill cry that is sounded alike for joy or sorrow; drums were beat; men dashed about with drawn swords and engaged in mimic fight, and in the midst of din and confusion we halted and dismounted. With peculiar grace of manner the old sheik assisted my wife to dismount, and led her to an open shed arranged with angareps (stretchers) covered with Persian carpets and cushions, so as to form a divan. Sherbet, pipes, and coffee were shortly handed to us, and Mahomet, as dragoman, translated the customary interchange of compliments; the sheik assured us that our unexpected arrival among them was "like the blessing of a new moon," the depth of which expression no one can understand who has not experienced life in the desert, where the first faint crescent is greeted with such enthusiasm. After a long conversation we were led to an excellent mat tent that had been vacated by one of his sons, and shortly afterwards an admirable dinner of several dishes was sent to us, while with extreme good taste we were left undisturbed by visitors until the following morning. Our men had been regaled with a fat sheep, presented by the sheik, and all slept contentedly.

At sunrise we were visited by Abou Sinn. It appeared that, after our conversation of the preceding evening, he had inquired of Mahomet concerning my future plans and intentions; he now came specially to implore us not to proceed south at this season of the year, as it would be perfectly impossible to travel; he described the country as a mass of mud, rendered so deep by the rains that no animal could move; that the fly called the "seroot" had appeared, and that no domestic animal except a goat could survive its attack; he declared that to continue our route would be mere insanity: and he concluded by giving us a most hospitable invitation to join his people on their road to the healthy country at Gozerajup, and to become his guests for three or four months, until travelling would be feasible in the south, at which time he promised to assist me in my explorations by an escort of his own people, who were celebrated elephant hunters, and knew the entire country before us. This was an alluring programme; but after thanking him for his kindness, I explained how much I disliked to retrace my steps, which I should do by returning to Gozerajup; and that as I had heard of a German who was living at the village of Sofi, on the Atbara, I should prefer to pass the season of the rains at that place, where I could gather information, and be ready on the spot to start for the neighbouring Base country when the change of season should permit. After some hesitation he consented to this plan, and promised not only to mount us on our journey, but to send with us an escort commanded by one of his grandsons. Sofi was about seventy-eight miles distant.

Abou Sinn had arranged to move northwards on the following day; we therefore agreed to pass one day in his camp, and to leave for Sofi the next morning. The ground upon which the Arab encampment was situated was a tolerably flat surface, like a shelf, upon the slope of the Atbara valley, about thirty or forty feet below the rich table lands; the surface of this was perfectly firm, as by the constant rains it had been entirely denuded of the loam that had formed the upper stratum. This formed a charming place for the encampment of a large party, as the ground was perfectly clean, a mixture of quartz pebbles upon a hard white sandstone. Numerous mimosas afforded a shade, beneath which the Arabs sat in groups, and at the bottom of the valley flowed the Atbara.

This tribe, which was peculiarly that of Abou Sinn, and from which he had sprung, was the Shookeriyah, one of the most powerful among the numerous tribes of Upper Egypt.

From Korosko to this point we had already passed the Bedouins, Bishareens, Hadendowas, Hallongas, until we had entered the Shookeriyahs.

On the west of our present position were the Jalyns, and to the south near Sofi were the Dabainas. Many of the tribes claim a right to the title of Bedouins, as descended from that race. The customs of all the Arabs are nearly similar, and the distinction in appearance is confined to a peculiarity in dressing the hair; this is a matter of great importance among both men and women. It would be tedious to describe the minutiae of the various coiffures, but the great desire with all tribes, except the Jalyn, is to have a vast quantity of hair arranged in their own peculiar fashion, and not only smeared, but covered with as much fat as can be made to adhere. Thus, should a man wish to get himself up as a great dandy, he would put at least half a pound of butter or other fat upon his head; this would be worked up with his coarse locks by a friend, until it somewhat resembled a cauliflower. He would then arrange his tope or plaid of thick cotton cloth, and throw one end over his left shoulder, while slung from the same shoulder his circular shield would hang upon his back; suspended by a strap over the right shoulder would hang his long two-edged broadsword.

Fat is the great desideratum of an Arab; his head, as I have described, should be a mass of grease; he rubs his body with oil or other ointment; his clothes, i.e. his one garment or tope, is covered with grease, and internally he swallows as much as he can procure.

The great Sheik Abou Sinn, who is upwards of eighty, as upright as a dart, a perfect Hercules, and whose children and grandchildren are like the sand of the sea-shore, has always consumed daily throughout his life two rottolis (pounds) of melted butter. A short time before I left the country he married a new young wife about fourteen years of age. This may be a hint to octogenarians.

The fat most esteemed for dressing the hair is that of the sheep. This undergoes a curious preparation, which renders it similar in appearance to cold cream; upon the raw fat being taken from the animal it is chewed in the mouth by an Arab for about two hours, being frequently taken out for examination during that time, until it has assumed the desired consistency. To prepare sufficient to enable a man to appear in full dress, several persons must be employed in masticating fat at the same time. This species of pomade, when properly made, is perfectly white, and exceedingly light and frothy. It may be imagined that when exposed to a burning sun, the beauty of the head-dress quickly disappears, but the oil then runs down the neck and back, which is considered quite correct, especially when the tope becomes thoroughly greased; the man is then perfectly anointed. We had seen an amusing exanmple of this when on the march from Berber to Gozerajup. The Turk, Hadji Achmet, had pressed into our service, as a guide for a few miles, a dandy who had just been arranged as a cauliflower, with at least half a pound of white fat upon his head. As we were travelling upwards of four miles an hour in an intense heat, during which he was obliged to run, the fat ran quicker than he did, and at the end of a couple of hours both the dandy and his pomade were exhausted; the poor fellow had to return to his friends with the total loss of personal appearance and half a pound of butter.

Not only are the Arabs particular in their pomade, but great attention is bestowed upon perfumery, especially by the women. Various perfumes are brought from Cairo by the travelling native merchants; among which those most in demand are oil of roses, oil of sandalwood, an essence from the blossom of a species of mimosa, essence of musk, and the oil of cloves. The women have a peculiar method of scenting their bodies and clothes by an operation that is considered to be one of the necessaries of life, and which is repeated at regular intervals. In the floor of the tent, or hut, as it may chance to be, a small hole is excavated sufficiently large to contain a common-sized champagne bottle: a fire of charcoal, or of simply glowing enmbers, is made within the hole, into which the woman about to be scented throws a handful of various drugs; she then takes off the cloth or tope which forms her dress, and crouches naked over the fumes, while she arranges her robe to fall as a mantle from her neck to the ground like a tent. When this arrangement is concluded she is perfectly happy, as none of the precious fumes can escape, all being retained beneath the robe, precisely as if she wore a crinoline with an incense-burner beneath it, which would be a far more simple way of performing the operation. She now begins to perspire freely in the hot-air bath, and the pores of the skin being thus opened and moist, the volatile oil from the smoke of the burning perfumes is immediately absorbed.

By the time that the fire has expired, the scenting process is completed, and both her person and robe are redolent of incense, with which they are so thoroughly impregnated that I have frequently smelt a party of women strongly at full a hundred yards' distance, when the wind has been blowing from their direction. Of course this kind of perfumery is only adapted for those who live in tents and in the open air, but it is considered by the ladies to have a peculiar attraction for the other sex, as valerian is said to ensnare the genus felis. As the men are said to be allured by this particular combination of sweet smells, and to fall victims to the delicacy of their nasal organs, it will be necessary to give the receipt for the fatal mixture, to be made up in proportions according to taste : – Ginger, cloves, cinnamon, frankincense, sandal-wood, myrrh, a species of sea-weed that is brought from the Red Sea, and lastly, what I mistook for shells, but which I subsequently discovered to be the horny disc that closes the aperture when a shell-fish withdraws itself within its shell; these are also brought from the Red Sea, in which they abound throughout the shores of Nubia and Abyssinia. In addition to the charm of sweet perfumes, the women who can afford the luxury, suspend from their necks a few pieces of the dried glands of the musk cat, which is a native of the country; such an addition completes the toilet, when the coiffure has been carefully arranged.

Hair-dressing in all parts of the world, both civilized and savage, is a branch of science; savage negro tribes are distinguished by the various arrangements of their woolly heads. Arabs are marked by similar peculiarities, that have never changed for thousands of years, and may be yet seen depicted upon the walls of Egyptian temples in the precise forms as worn at present, while in modern times the perfection of art has been in the wig of a Lord Chancellor. Although this latter example of the result of science is not the actual hair of the wearer, it adds an imposing glow of wisdom to the general appearance, and may have originated as a necessity where a deficiency of sagacity had existed, and where the absence of years required the fictitious crown of grey old age. A barrister in his wig, and the same amount of learning without the wig, is a very different affair; he is an imperfect shadow of himself. Nevertheless, among civilized nations, the men do not generally bestow much anxiety upon the fashion of their hair; the labour in this branch of art is generally performed by the women, who in all countries and climes, and in every stage of civilization, bestow the greatest pains upon the perfection of the coiffure, the various arrangements of which might, I should imagine, be estimated by the million. In some countries they are not even contented with the natural colour of the hair, either if black or blonde, but they use a pigment that turns it red. I only noticed this among the Somauli tribe; and that of the Nuehr, some of the wildest savages of the White Nile, until I returned to England, where I found the custom was becoming general among the civilized, and that ladies were adopting the lovely tint of the British fox. The Arab women do not indulge in fashions; strictly conservative in their manners and customs, they never imitate, but they simply vie with each other in the superlativeness of their own style; thus the dressing of the hair is a most elaborate affair, which occupies a considerable portion of their time. It is quite impossible for an Arab woman to arrange her own hair; she therefore employs an assistant, who, if clever in the art, will generally occupy about three days before it is satisfactorily concluded. First, the hair must be combed with a long skewer-like pin; then, when well divided, it becomes possible to use an exceedingly coarse wooden comb. When the hair is reduced to reasonable order by the latter process, a vigorous hunt takes place, which occupies about an hour, according to the amount of game preserved; the sport concluded, the hair is rubbed with a mixture of oil of roses, myrrh, and sandal-wood dust mixed with a powder of cloves and cassia. When well greased and rendered somewhat stiff by the solids thus introduced, it is plaited into at least two hundred fine plaits; each of these plaits is then smeared with a mixture of sandal-wood dust and either gum water or paste of dhurra flour. On the last day of the operation, each tiny plait is carefully opened by the long hair-pin or skewer, and the head is ravissante. Scented and frizzled in this manner, with a well-greased tope or robe, the Arab lady's toilet is complete, her head is then a little larger than the largest sized English mop, and her perfume is something between the aroma of a perfumer's shop and the monkey-house at the Zoological Gardens. This is considered "very killing," and I have been quite of that opinion when a crowd of women have visited my wife in our tent, with the thermometer at 95 degrees, and they have kindly consented to allow me to remain as one of the party. It is hardly necessary to add, that the operation of hair-dressing is not often performed, but that the effect is permanent for about a week, during which time the game become so excessively lively, that the creatures require stirring up with the long hair-pin or skewer whenever too unruly; this appears to be constantly necessary from the vigorous employment of the ruling sceptre during conversation. A levee of Arab women in the tent was therefore a disagreeable invasion, as we dreaded the fugitives; fortunately, they appeared to cling to the followers of Mahomet in preference to Christians.

The plague of lice brought upon the Egyptians by Moses has certainly adhered to the country ever since, if "lice" is the proper translation of the Hebrew word in the Old Testament: it is my own opinion that the insects thus inflicted upon the population were not lice, but ticks. Exod. viii. 16, "The dust became lice throughout all Egypt;" again, Exod. viii. 17, "Smote dust . . . it became lice in man and beast." Now the louse that infects the human body and hair has no connexion whatever with "dust," and if subject to a few hours' exposure to the dry heat of the burning sand, it would shrivel and die; but the tick is an inhabitant of the dust, a dry horny insect without any apparent moisture in its composition; it lives in hot sand and dust, where it cannot possibly obtain nourishment, until some wretched animal should lie down upon the spot, and become covered with these horrible vermin. I have frequently seen desert places so infested with ticks, that the ground was perfectly alive with them, and it would have been impossible to have rested on the earth; in such spots, the passage in Exodus has frequently occurred to me as bearing reference to these vermin, which are the greatest enemies to man and beast. It is well known that, from the size of a grain of sand in their natural state, they will distend to the size of a hazel-nut after having preyed for some days upon the blood of an animal. The Arabs are invariably infested with lice, not only in their hair, but upon their bodies and clothes; even the small charms or spells worn upon the arm in neatly-sewn leathern packets are full of these vermin. Such spells are generally verses copied from the Koran by the Faky, or priest, who receives some small gratuity in exchange; the men wear several of such talismans upon the arm above the elbow, but the women wear a large bunch of charms, as a sort of chatelaine, suspended beneath their clothes round the waist. Although the tope or robe, loosely but gracefully arranged around the body, appears to be the whole of the costume, the women wear beneath this garment a thin blue cotton cloth tightly bound round the loins, which descends to a little above the knee; beneath this, next to the skin, is the last garment, the rahat – the latter is the only clothing of young girls, and may be either perfectly simple or adorned with beads and cowrie shells according to the fancy of the wearer; it is perfectly effective as a dress, and admirably adapted to the climate.

The rahat is a fringe of fine dark brown or reddish twine, fastened to a belt, and worn round the waist. On either side are two long tassels, that are generally ornamented with beads or cowries, and dangle nearly to the ankles, while the rahat itself should descend to a little above the knee, rather shorter than a Highland kilt. Nothing can be prettier or more simple than this dress, which, although short, is of such thickly hanging fringe, that it perfectly answers the purpose for which it is intended. Many of the Arab girls are remarkably good-looking, with fine figures until they become mothers. They generally marry at the age of thirteen or fourteen, but frequently at twelve, or even earlier. Until married, the rahat is their sole garment. Throughout the Arab tribes of Upper Egypt, chastity is a necessity, as an operation is performed at the early age of from three to five years that thoroughly protects all females, and which renders them physically proof against incontinency.

There is but little love-making among the Arabs. The affair of matrimony usually commences by a present to the father of the girl, which, if accepted, is followed by a similar advance to the girl herself, and the arrangement is completed. All the friends of both parties are called together for the wedding; pistols and guns are fired off, if possessed. There is much feasting, and the unfortunate bridegroom undergoes the ordeal of whipping by the relations of his bride, in order to test his courage. Sometimes this punishment is exceedingly severe, being inflicted with the coorbatch or whip of hippopotamus hide, which is cracked vigorously about his ribs and back. If the happy husband wishes to be considered a man worth having, he must receive the chastisement with an expression of enjoyment; in which case the crowds of women again raise their thrilling cry in admiration. After the rejoicings of the day are over, the bride is led in the evening to the residence of her husband, while a beating of drums and strumming of guitars (rhababas) are kept up for some hours during the night, with the usual discordant idea of singing.

There is no divorce court among the Arabs. They are not sufficiently advanced in civilization to accept a pecuniary fine as the price of a wife's dishonour; but a stroke of the husband's sword, or a stab with the knife, is generally the ready remedy for infidelity. Although strictly Mahometans, the women are never veiled; neither do they adopt the excessive reserve assumed by the Turks and Egyptians. The Arab women are generally idle; and one of the conditions of accepting a suitor is, that a female slave is to be provided for the special use of the wife. No Arab woman will engage herself as a domestic servant; thus, so long as their present customs shall remain unchanged, slaves are creatures of necessity. Although the law of Mahomet limits the number of wives for each man to four at one time, the Arab women do not appear to restrict their husbands to this allowance, and the slaves of the establishment occupy the position of concubines.

The customs of the Arabs in almost every detail have remained unchanged. Thus, in dress, in their nomadic habits, food, the anointing with oil (Eccles. ix. 8, "Let thy garments be always white, and let thy head lack no ointment"), they retain the habits and formalities of the distant past, and the present is but the exact picture of those periods which are historically recorded in the Old Testament. The perfumery of the women already described, bears a resemblance to that prepared by Moses for the altar, which was forbidden to be used by the people. "Take thou also unto thee principal spices, of pure myrrh five hundred shekels, and of sweet cinnamon half so much, even two hundred and fifty shekels, and of sweet calamus two hundred and fifty shekels, and of cassia five hundred shekels, after the shekel of the sanctuary, and of oil olive an hin: and thou shalt make it an oil of holy ointment, an ointment compound after the art of the apothecary: it shall be an holy anointing oil." – Exod. xxx. 23-25.

The manner of anointing by the ancients is exhibited by the Arabs at the present day, who, as I have already described, make use of so large a quantity of grease at one application that, when melted, it runs down over their persons and clothes. In Ps. cxxxiii. 2, "It is like the precious ointment upon the head, that ran down upon the beard, even Aaron's beard, that went down to the skirts of his garments."

In all hot climates, oil or other fat is necessary to the skin as a protection from the sun, where the body is either naked or very thinly clad. I have frequently seen both Arabs and the negro tribes of Africa suffer great discomfort when for some days the supply of grease has been exhausted; the skin has become coarse, rough, almost scaly, and peculiarly unsightly, until the much-loved fat has been obtained, and the general appearance of smoothness has been at once restored by an active smearing. The expression in Ps. civ. 15, "And oil to make his face to shine," describes the effect that was then considered beautifying, as it is at the present time.

The Arabs generally adhere strictly to their ancient customs, independently of the comparatively recent laws established by Mahomet. Thus, concubinage is not considered a breach of morality; neither is it regarded by the legitimate wives with jealousy. They attach great importance to the laws of Moses, and to the customs of their forefathers; neither can they understand the reason for a change of habit in any respect where necessity has not suggested the reform. The Arabs are creatures of necessity; their nomadic life is compulsory, as the existence of their flocks and herds depends upon the pasturage. Thus, with the change of seasons they must change their localities, according to the presence of fodder for their cattle. Driven to and fro by the accidents of climate, the Arab has been compelled to become a wanderer; and precisely as the wild beasts of the country are driven from place to place either by the arrival of the fly, the lack of pasturage, or by the want of water, even so must the flocks of the Arab obey the law of necessity, in a country where the burning sun and total absence of rain for nine months of the year convert the green pastures into a sandy desert. The Arabs and their herds must follow the example of the wild beasts, and live as wild and wandering a life. In the absence of a fixed home, without a city, or even a village that is permanent, there can be no change of custom. There is no stimulus to competition in the style of architecture that is to endure only for a few months; no municipal laws suggest deficiencies that originate improvements. The Arab cannot halt in one spot longer than the pasturage will support his flocks; therefore his necessity is food for his beasts. The object of his life being fodder, he must wander in search of the ever-changing supply. His wants must be few, as the constant changes of encampment necessitate the transport of all his household goods; thus he reduces to a minimum the domestic furniture and utensils. No desires for strange and fresh objects excite his mind to improvement, or alter his original habits; he must limit his impedimenta, not increase them. Thus with a few necessary articles he is contented. Mats for his tent, ropes manufactured with the hair of his goats and camels, pots for carrying fat; water-jars and earthenware pots or gourd-shells for containing milk; leather water-skins for the desert, and sheep-skin bags for his clothes, – these are the requirements of the Arabs. Their patterns have never changed, but the water-jar of to-day is of the same form that was carried to the well by the women of thousands of years ago. The conversation of the Arabs is in the exact style of the Old Testament. The name of God is coupled with every trifling incident in life, and they believe in the continual action of Divine special interference. Should a famine afflict the country, it is expressed in the stern language of the Bible – "The Lord has sent a grievous famine upon the land;" or, "The Lord called for a famine, and it came upon the land." Should their cattle fall sick, it is considered to be an affliction by Divine command; or should the flocks prosper and multiply particularly during one season, the prosperity is attributed to special interference. Nothing can happen in the usual routine of daily life without a direct connexion with the hand of God, according to the Arab's belief.

This striking similarity to the descriptions of the Old Testament is exceedingly interesting to a traveller when residing among these curious and original people. With the Bible in one hand, and these unchanged tribes before the eyes, there is a thrilling illustration of the sacred record; the past becomes the present; the veil of three thousand years is raised, and the living picture is a witness to the exactness of the historical description. At the same time, there is a light thrown upon many obscure passages in the Old Testament by the experience of the present customs and figures of speech of the Arabs which are precisely those that were practised at the periods described. I do not attempt to enter upon a theological treatise, therefore it is unnecessary to allude specially to these particular points. The sudden and desolating arrival of a flight of locusts, the plague, or any other unforeseen calamity, is attributed to the anger of God, and is believed to be an infliction of punishment upon the people thus visited, precisely as the plagues of Egypt were specially inflicted upon Pharaoh and the Egyptians.

Should the present history of the country be written by an Arab scribe, the style of the description would be purely that of the Old Testament; and the various calamities or the good fortunes that have in the course of nature befallen both the tribes and individuals, would be recounted either as special visitations of Divine wrath, or blessings for good deeds performed. If in a dream a particular course of action is suggested, the Arab believes that God has spoken and directed him. The Arab scribe or historian would describe the event as the "voice of the Lord" ("kallam el Allah"), having spoken unto the person; or, that God appeared to him in a dream and "said," &c. Thus much allowance would be necessary on the part of a European reader for the figurative ideas and expressions of the people. As the Arabs are unchanged, the theological opinions which they now hold are the same as those which prevailed in remote ages, with the simple addition of their belief in Mahomet as the Prophet.

There is a fascination in the unchangeable features of the Nile regions. There are the vast Pyramids that have defied time; the river upon which Moses was cradled in infancy; the same sandy deserts through which he led his people; and the watering-places where their flocks were led to drink. The wild and wandering tribes of Arabs who thousands of years ago dug out the wells in the wilderness, are represented by their descendants unchanged, who now draw water from the deep wells of their forefathers with the skins that have never altered their fashion. The Arabs, gathering with their goats and sheep around the wells to-day, recall the recollection of that distant time when "Jacob went on his journey, and came into the land of the people of the east. And he looked, and behold a well in the field; and, lo, there were three flocks of sheep lying by it, for out of that well they watered the flocks; and a great stone was upon the well's mouth. And thither were all the flocks gathered; and they rolled the stone from the well's mouth, and watered the sheep, and put the stone again upon the well's mouth in his place." The picture of that scene would be an illustration of Arab daily life in the Nubian deserts, where the present is the mirror of the past.

Chapter VII.

The Departure.

On the morning of the 25th July, 1861, Abou Sinn arrived at our tent with a number of his followers, in their whitest apparel, accompanied by one of his grandsons, Sheik Ali, who was to command our escort and to accompany us to the frontier of the Dabaina tribe, at which spot we were to be handed over to the care of the sheik of those Arabs, Atalan Wat Said, who would conduct us to Sofi. There were two superb hygeens duly equipped for my wife and myself: they were snow-white, without speck or blemish, and as clean and silk-like as good grooming could accomplish. One of these beautiful creatures I subsequently measured, – seven feet three and a half inches to the top of the hump; this was much above the average. The baggage-camels were left to the charge of the servants, and we were requested to mount immediately, as the Sheik Abou Sinn was determined to accompany us for some distance as a mark of courtesy, although he was himself to march with his people on that day in the opposite direction towards Gozerajup. Escorted by our grand old host, with a great number of mounted attendants, we left the hospitable camp, and followed the margin of the Atbara valley towards the south, until, at the distance of about two miles, Abou Sinn took leave, and returned with his people.

We now enjoyed the contrast between the light active step of first-class hygeens, and the heavy swinging action of the camels we had hitherto ridden. Travelling was for the first time a pleasure; there was a delightful movement in the elasticity of the hygeens, who ambled at about five miles and a half an hour, as their natural pace; this they can continue for nine or ten hours without fatigue. Having no care for the luggage, and the coffee-pot being slung upon the saddle of an attendant, who also carried our carpet, we were perfectly independent, as we were prepared with the usual luxuries upon halting, – the carpet to recline upon beneath a shady tree, and a cup of good Turkish coffee. Thus we could afford to travel at a rapid rate, and await the arrival of the baggage-camels at the end of the day's journey. In this manner the march should be arranged in these wild countries, where there is no resting-place upon the path beyond the first inviting shade that suggests a halt. The day's journey should be about twenty-four miles. A loaded camel seldom exceeds two miles and a half per hour; at this rate nearly ten hours would be consumed upon the road daily, during which time the traveller would be exposed to the intense heat of the sun, and to the fatigue inseparable from a long and slow march. A servant mounted upon a good hygeen should accompany him with the coffee apparatus and a cold roast fowl and biscuits; the ever necessary carpet should form the cover to his saddle, to be ready when required; he then rides far in advance of the caravan. This simple arrangement insures comfort, and lessens the ennui of the journey; the baggage-camels are left in charge of responsible servants, to be brought forward at their usual pace, until they shall arrive at the place selected for the halt by the traveller. The usual hour of starting is about 5.30 A.M. The entire day's journey can be accomplished in something under five hours upon hygeens, instead of the ten hours dreary pace of the caravan; thus, the final halt would be made at about 10.30 A.M. at which time the traveller would be ready for breakfast. The carpet would be spread under a shady tree; upon a branch of this his water-skin should be suspended, and the day's work over, he can write up his journal and enjoy his pipe while coffee is being prepared. After breakfast he can take his gun or rifle and explore the neighbourhood, until the baggage-camels shall arrive in the evening, by which time, if he is a sportsman, he will have procured something for the dinner of the entire party. The servants will have collected firewood, and all will be ready for the arrival of the caravan, without the confusion and bustle of a general scramble, inseparable from the work to be suddenly performed, when camels must be unloaded, fuel collected, fires lighted, the meals prepared, beds made, &c. &c. all at the same moment, with the chance of little to eat. Nothing keeps the camel-drivers and attendants in such good humour as a successful rifle. While they are on their long and slow march, they speculate upon the good luck that may attend the master's gun, and upon arrival at the general bivouac in the evening they are always on the alert to skin and divide the antelopes, pluck the guinea-fowls, &c. &c. We now travelled in this delightful manner; there were great numbers of guinea-fowl throughout the country, which was the same everlasting flat and rich table land, extending for several hundred miles to the south, and dotted with green mimosas; while upon our left was the broken valley of the Atbara.

The only drawback to the journey was the rain. At about 2 P.M. daily we were subjected to a violent storm, which generally lasted until the evening; and although our guides invariably hurried forward on the march to the neighbourhood of some deserted huts, whose occupants had migrated north, our baggage and servants upon the road were exposed to the storm, and arrived late in the evening, wet and miserable. There could be no doubt that the season for travelling was past. Every day's journey south had proved by the increased vegetation that we were invading the rainy zone, and that, although the northern deserts possessed their horrors of sandy desolation, they at the same time afforded that great advantage to the traveller, a dry climate.

In a few rapid marches we arrived at Tomat, the commencement of the Dabainas and the principal head-quarters of the sheik of that tribe, Atalan Wat Said. This was a lovely spot, where the country appeared like green velvet, as the delicate young grass was about two inches above the ground. The Arab camp was situated upon a series of knolls about a hundred and fifty feet above the Atbara, upon the hard ground denuded by the rains, as this formed a portion of the valley. At this spot, the valley on the west bank of the river was about two miles broad, and exhibited the usual features of innumerable knolls, ravines, and landslips, in succession, like broken terraces from the high level table land, sloping down irregularly to the water's edge. On the opposite side of the river was the most important feature of the country; the land on the east bank was considerably higher than upon the west, and a long tongue formed a bluff cliff that divided the Atbara valley from the sister valley of the Settite, which, corresponding exactly in character and apparent dimensions, joined that of the Atbara from the s.e., forming an angle like the letter V, in a sudden bend of the river. Through the valley of the eastern bank flowed the grand river Settite, which here formed a junction with the Atbara.

Looking down upon the beautifully wooded banks of the two rivers at this interesting point, we rode leisurely across a ravine, and ascended a steep incline of bright green grass, upon the summit of which was a fine level space of several acres that formed the Arab head-quarters. This surface was nearly covered with the usual mat tents, and in a few moments our camels knelt before that of the sheik, at which we dismounted. A crowd of inquisitive Arabs surrounded us upon seeing so large a party of hygeens, and the firman having been delivered by our guide, Sheik Ali, we were almost immediately visited by Sheik Atalan Wat Said. He was a man in the prime of life, of an intelligent countenance, and he received us with much politeness, immediately ordering a fat sheep to be brought and slaughtered for our acceptance.

The usual welcome upon the arrival of a traveller, who is well received in an Arab camp, is the sacrifice of a fat sheep, that should be slaughtered at the door of his hut or tent, so that the blood flows to the threshold. This custom has evidently some connexion with the ancient rites of sacrifice.

Should an important expedition be undertaken, a calf is slaughtered at the entrance of the camp, and every individual steps over the body as the party starts upon the enterprise.

Upon learning my plans, he begged us to remain through the rainy season at Tomat, as it was the head-quarters of a party of Egyptian irregular troops, who would assist me in every way. This was no great temptation, as they were the people whom I most wished to avoid; I therefore explained that I was bound to Sofi by the advice of Abou Sinn, from whence I could easily return if I thought proper, but I wished to proceed on the following morning. He promised to act as our guide, and that hygeens should be waiting at the tent-door at sunrise. After our interview, I strolled down to the river's side and shot some guinea-fowl.

The Settite is the river par excellence, as it is the principal stream of Abyssinia, in which country it bears the name of "Tacazzy." Above the junction, the Atbara does not exceed two hundred yards in width. Both rivers have scooped out deep and broad valleys throughout their course; this fact confirmed my first impression of the supply of soil having been brought down by the Atbara to the Nile. The country on the opposite or eastern bank of the Atbara is contested ground; in reality it forms the western frontier of Abyssinia, of which the Atbara river is the boundary, but since the annexation of the Nubian provinces to Egypt there has been no safety for life or property upon the line of frontier; thus a large tract of country actually forming a portion of Abyssinia is uninhabited.

Upon my return to the camp, I was informed by the Sheik Wat Said that a detachment of troops was stationed at Tomat expressly to protect the Egyptian frontier from the raids of Mek Nimmur, who was in the habit of crossing the Atbara and pillaging the Arab villages during the dry season, when the river was fordable. This Mek Nimmur was a son of the celebrated Mek Nimmur, the chief of Shendy, a district upon the west bank of the Nile between Berber and Khartoum. When the Egyptian forces, under the command of Ismael Pasha, the son of the Viceroy Mehemet Ali Pasha, arrived at Shendy, at the time of the conquest of Nubia, he called the great Sheik Mek (from Melek, signifying king) Nimmur before him, and demanded the following supplies for his army, as tribute for the Pasha: – 1,000 young girls as slaves; 1,000 oxen; and of camels, goats, sheep, each 1,000; also camel-loads of corn and straw each 1,000, with a variety of other demands expressed by the same figure. It is said that Mek Nimmur replied to these demands with much courtesy, "Your arithmetic exhibits a charming simplicity, as the only figure appears to be 1,000." In a short time the supplies began to arrive, strings of camels, laden with corn, assembled at Shendy in the Egyptian camp; cattle, goats, sheep, came in from all sides; fodder for the Egyptian cavalry, to the amount of 1,000 camel-loads, was brought to head-quarters, and piled in a huge wall that encircled the tent of the General Ismael Pasha. In the dead of night, while he slept, the crackling of fire was heard, and flames burst out upon all sides of the dry and combustible fodder; the Arabs had fired the straw in all directions, and a roar of flame in a fatal ring surrounded the Pasha's tent, which caught the fire. There was no escape! In the confusion, the Arabs fell upon the troops, and massacred a considerable number. After this success, Mek Nimmur succeeded in retiring with his people and herds to Sofi, on the Atbara, to which place we were bound; this was about twelve miles from Tomat. The body of Ismael Pasha was found beneath those of some of his women, all of whom that were within the inclosure having perished.

After this calamity the Egyptians recovered Shendy, and in revenge they collected a number of the inhabitants of all ages and both sexes. These were penned together like cattle in a zareeba or kraal, and were surrounded with dhurra-straw, which was fired in a similar manner to that which destroyed the Pasha. Thus were these unfortunate creatures destroyed en masse, while the remaining portion of the population fled to the new settlement of their chief at Sofi.

Within the last few years preceding my arrival, the Egyptians had attacked and utterly destroyed the old town of Sofi. Mek Nimmur had retired across the Atbara, and had taken refuge in Abyssinia, where he had been welcomed by the king of that country as the enemy of the Turks, and had been presented with a considerable territory at the western base of the high mountain range. When I arrived on the Atbara in 1861, the original Mek Nimnmur was dead, and his son, who also was called Mek Nimmur, reigned in his stead. "Nimmur" signifies in Arabic "leopard:" thus "Mek Nimmur" is the "Leopard King."

This man was constantly at war with the Egyptians, and such Arabs who were friendly to Egypt. His principal head-quarters were about seventy miles from Tomat, at a village named Mai Gubba, from which country he made successful razzias upon the Egyptian territory, which compelled a vigilant look-out during the dry season. During the rains there was no danger, as the river was immensely deep, and impassable from the total absence of boats.

The uninhabited country exactly opposite Tomat was said to abound with large game, such as elephants, giraffes, &c. as there were no enemies to disturb them.

At break of day, 29th July, the grandson of Abou Sinn, Sheik Ali, who had been our guide, paid us his parting visit, and returned with his people, while at the same time Atalan Wat Said arrived with a large retinue of his own Arabs and Egyptian soldiers to escort us to Sofi. Two splendid hygeens were already saddled for us, one of which was specially intended for my wife; this was the most thorough-bred looking animal I have ever seen; both were milk-white, but there was a delicacy in the latter that was unequalled. This was rather small, and although the ribs were so well covered that the animal appeared rather fleshy, it was in the hardiest condition, and was shaped in the depth of brisket and width of loins like a greyhound; the legs were remarkably fine, and as clean as ivory. The Sheik Atalan was charmed at our admiration of his much-prized hygeen, and to prove its speed and easy action we were no sooner mounted than he led the way at about ten miles an hour, down the steep slopes, across the rough watercourses, and up the hill-sides, assuring my wife that she might sip a cup of coffee on the back of the animal she rode, without spilling a drop: although an exaggeration, this is the usual figure of speech by which an Arab describes the easy action of a first-rate hygeen. It was a beautiful sight to watch the extraordinary ease with which the hygeen glided along over the numerous inequalities of the ground without the slightest discomfort to the rider; the numerous escort became a long and irregular line of stragglers, until at length they were lost in the distance, with the exception of three or four, who, well mounted, were proud of keeping their position. Emerging from the uneven valley of the Atbara, we arrived upon the high and level table land above; here the speed increased, and in the exhilaration of the pace in the cool morning air, with all nature glowing in the fresh green of a Nubian spring, we only regretted the shortness of the journey to Sofi, which we reached before the heat of the day had commenced. We were met by the sheik of the village, and by a German who had been a resident of Sofi for some years; he was delighted to see Europeans, especially those who were conversant with his own language, and he very politely insisted that we should dismount at his house. Accordingly our camels knelt at the door of a little circular stone building about twelve feet in diameter, with a roof thatched according to Arab fashion. This dwelling was the model of an Arab hut, but the walls were of masonry instead of mud and sticks, and two small windows formed an innovation upon the Arab style, which had much astonished the natives, who are contented with the light afforded by the doorway.

We were shortly sitting in the only stone building in the country, among a crowd of Arabs, who, according to their annoying custom, had thronged to the hut upon our arrival, and not only had filled the room, but were sitting in a mob at the doorway, while masses of mop-like heads were peering over the shoulders of the front rank, excluding both light and air; even the windows were blocked with highly frizzled heads, while all were talking at the same time.

Coffee having been handed to the principal people while our tents were being pitched outside the village, we at length silenced the crowd; our new acquaintance explained in Arabic the object of our arrival, and our intention of passing the rainy season at Sofi, and of exploring the various rivers of Abyssinia at the earliest opportunity. Atalan Wat Said promised every assistance when the time should arrive; he described the country as abounding with large game of all kinds, and he agreed to furnish me with guides and hunters at the commencement of the hunting season; in the meantime he ordered the sheik of the village, Hassan bel Kader, to pay us every attention.

After the departure of Atalan and his people, and the usual yelling of the women, we had time to examine Sofi, and accompanied by the German, Florian, we strolled through the village. At this position the slope of the valley towards the river was exceedingly gradual upon the west bank, until within a hundred and fifty yards of the Atbara, when the ground rapidly fell, and terminated in an abrupt cliff of white sandstone.

The miserable little village of modern Sofi comprised about thirty straw huts, but the situation was worthy of a more important settlement. A plateau of hard sandy soil of about twenty acres was bordered upon either side by two deep ravines that formed a natural protection, while below the steep cliff, within two hundred paces in front of the village, flowed the river Atbara; for mounted men there was only one approach, that which we had taken from the main land. There could not have been a more inviting spot adopted for a resting-place during the rains. Although the soil was thoroughly denuded of loam, and nothing remained but the original substratum of sandstone and pebbles, the grass was at this season about three inches high throughout the entire valley of the Atbara, the trees were in full leaf, and the vivid green, contrasting with the snow-white sandstone rocks, produced the effect of an ornamental park. My tents were pitched upon a level piece of ground, outside the village, about a hundred paces from the river, where the grass had been so closely nibbled by the goats that it formed a natural lawn, and was perfection for a camp; drains were dug around the tent walls, and everything was arranged for a permanency. I agreed with the sheik for the erection of a comfortabie hut for ourselves, a kitchen adjoining, and a hut for the servants, as the heavy storms were too severe for a life under canvas; in the meantime we sat in our tent, and had a quiet chat with Florian, the German.

He was a sallow, sickly-looking man, who with a large bony frame had been reduced from constant hard work and frequent sickness to little but skin and sinew; he was a mason, who had left Germany with the Austrian Mission to Khartoum, but finding the work too laborious in such a climate, he and a friend, who was a carpenter, had declared for independence, and they had left the Mission.

They were both enterprising fellows, and sportsmen; therefore they had purchased rifles and ammunition, and had commenced life as hunters; at the same time they employed their leisure hours in earning money by the work of their hands in various ways. Florian, being a stonemason, had of course built his hut of stone; he was a fair blacksmith and carpenter, and was well provided with tools; but his principal occupation was whipmaking, from the hides of hippopotami. As coorbatches were required throughout the country there was an extensive demand for his camel-whips, which were far superior to those of native manufacture; these he sold to the Arabs at about two shillings each. He had lately met with a serious accident by the bursting of one of the wretched guns that formed his sporting battery; this had blown away his thumb from the wrist joint, and had so shattered his hand that it would most likely have suffered amputation had he enjoyed the advantage of European surgical assistance; but with the simple aid of his young black lad, Richarn, who cut off the dangling thumb and flesh with his knife, he had preserved his hand, minus one portion.

Florian had had considerable experience in some parts of the country that I was about to visit, and he gave me much valuable information that was of great assistance in directing my first operations. The close of the rainy season would be about the middle of September, but travelling would be impossible until November, as the fly would not quit the country until the grass should become dry; therefore the Arabs would not return with their camels until that period.

It appeared that this peculiar fly, which tortured all domestic animals, invaded the country shortly after the commencement of the rains, when the grass was about two feet high; a few had already been seen, but Sofi was a favoured spot that was generally exempt from this plague, which clung more particularly to the flat and rich table lands, where the quality of grass was totally different to that produced upon the pebbly and denuded soil of the sandstone slopes of the valley. The grass of the slopes was exceedingly fine, and would not exceed a height of about two feet, while that of the table lands would exceed nine feet, and become impassable, until sufficiently dry to be cleared by fire. In November, the entire country would become a vast prairie of dried straw, the burning of which would then render travelling and hunting possible.

Florian had hunted for some distance along the Settite river with his companions, and had killed fifty-three hippopotami during the last season. I therefore agreed that he should accompany me until I should have sufficiently explored that river, after which I proposed to examine the rivers Salaam and Angrab, of which great tributaries of the Atbara nothing definite was known, except that they joined that river about fifty miles south of Sofi.

Florian described the country as very healthy during the dry season, but extremely dangerous during the rains, especially in the month of October, when, on the cessation of rain, the sun evaporated the moisture from the sodden ground and rank vegetation. I accordingly determined to arrange our winter quarters as comfortably as possible at Sofi for three months, during which holiday I should have ample time for gaining information and completing my arrangements for the future. Violent storms were now of daily occurrence; they had first commenced at about 2 P.M., but they had gradually altered the hour of their arrival to between 3 and 4. This night, 29th July, we were visited at about 11 P.M. with the most tremendous tempest that we had yet experienced, which lasted until the morning. Fortunately the tent was well secured with four powerful storm-ropes fastened from the top of the pole, and pinned about twenty-five yards from the base to iron bars driven deep into the hard ground; but the night was passed in the discomforts of a deluge that, driven by the hurricane, swept through the tent, which threatened every minute to desert us in shreds. On the following morning the storm had passed away, and the small tent had done likewise, having been blown down and carried many yards from the spot where it had been pitched. Mahomet, who was the occupant, had found himself suddenly enveloped in wet canvas, from which he had emerged like a frog in the storm. There was no time to be lost in completing my permanent camp; I therefore sent for the sheik of the village, and proceeded to purchase a house. I accompanied him through the narrow lanes of Sofi, and was quickly shown a remarkably neat house, which I succeeded in purchasing from the owner for the sum of ten piastres (two shillings). This did not seem an extravagant outlay for a neat dwelling with a sound roof; neither were there any legal expenses in the form of conveyance, as in that happy and practical land the simple form of conveyance is the transportation of the house (the roof) upon the shoulders of about thirty men, and thus it is conveyed to any spot that the purchaser may consider desirable. Accordingly, our mansion was at once seized by a crowd of Arabs, and carried off in triumph, while the sticks that formed the wall were quickly arranged upon the site I had chosen for our camp. In the short space of about three hours I found myself the proprietor of an eligible freehold residence, situated upon an eminence in park-like grounds, commanding extensive and romantic views of the beautifully-wooded valley of the Atbara, within a minute's walk of the neighbouring village of Sofi, perfect immunity from all poor-rates, tithes, taxes, and other public burthens, not more than 2,000 miles from a church, with the advantage of a post-town at the easy distance of seventy leagues. The manor comprised the right of shooting throughout the parishes of Ahyssinia and Soudan, plentifully stocked with elephants, lions, rhinoceroses, giraffes, buffaloes, hippopotami, leopards, and a great variety of antelopes; while the right of fishing extended throughout the Atbara and neighbouring rivers, that were well stocked with fish ranging from five to a hundred and fifty pounds; also with turtles and crocodiles.

The mansion comprised entrance-hall, dining-room, drawing-roomn, lady's boudoir, library, breakfast-room, bed-room and dressing-room (with the great advantage of their combination in one circular room fourteen feet in diameter). The architecture was of an ancient style, from the original design of a pill-box surmounted by a candle extinguisher.

Thus might my estate have been described by an English estate agent and auctioneer, with a better foundation of fact than many newspaper advertisements.

I purchased two additional huts, one of which was erected at the back (if a circle has a back) of our mansion, as the kitchen, while the other at a greater distance formed the "servants' hall." We all worked hard for several days in beautifying our house and grounds. In the lovely short grass that resembled green velvet, we cut walks to the edge of a declivity, and surrounded the house with a path of snow-white sand, resembling coarsely pounded sugar; this we obtained from some decomposed sandstone rock which crumbled upon the slightest pressure. We collected curiously-shaped blocks of rock, and masses of fossil wood that were imbedded in the sandstone; these we formed into borders for our walks, and opposite to our front door (there was no back door) we arranged a half-circle or "carriage-drive," of white sand, to the extreme edge of the declivity, which we bordered with large rocks; one of which I believe may remain to this day, as I carried it to the spot to form a seat, and my vanity was touched by the fact that it required two Arabs to raise it from the ground. I made a rustic table of split bamboos, and two garden seats opposite the entrance of the house, and we collected a number of wild plants and bulbs which we planted in little beds; we also sowed the seeds of different gourds that were to climb up on our roof.

In the course of a week we had formed as pretty a camp as Robinson Crusoe himself could have coveted; but he, poor unfortunate, had only his man Friday to assist him, while in our arrangements there were many charms and indescribable little comforts that could only be effected by a lady's hand. Not only were our walks covered with snow-white sand and the borders ornamented with beautiful agates that we had collected in the neighbourhood, but the interior of our house was the perfection of neatness: the floor was covered with white sand beaten firmly together to the depth of about six inches; the surface was swept and replaced with fresh material daily; the travelling bedsteads, with their bright green mosquito curtains, stood by either side, affording a clear space in the centre of the circle, while exactly opposite the door stood the gun-rack, with as goodly an array of weapons as the heart of a sportsman could desire: –

- My little Fletcher double rifle, No. 24.
- One double rifle, No. 10, by Tatham.
- Two double rifles, No. 10, by Reilly.
- One double rifle, No. 10, by Beattie (one of my old Ceylon tools).
- One double gun, No. 10, by Beattie.
- One double gun, No. 10, by Purdey, belonging to Mr. Oswell, of South African celebrity.
- One single rifle, No. 8, by Manton.
- One single rifle, No. 14, by Beattie.
- One single rifle that carried a half-pouud explosive shell, by Holland of Bond Street; this was nicknamed by the Arabs "Jenna el Mootfah" (child of a cannon), and for the sake of brevity I called it the "Baby."

My revolver and a brace of double-barrelled pistols hung upon the wall, which, although the exterior of the house was straw, we had lined with the bright coloured canvas of the tent. Suspended by loops were little ornamental baskets worked by the Arabs, that contained a host of useful articles, such as needles, thread, &c. &c., and the remaining surface was hung with hunting knives, fishing lines, and a variety of instruments belonging to the chase. A travelling table, with maps and a few books, stood against the wall, and one more article completed our furniture, – an exceedingly neat toilet table, the base of which was a flat-topped portmanteau, concealed by a cunning device of chintz and muslin; this, covered with the usual arrangement of brushes, mirror, scent-bottles, &c. threw an air of civilization over the establishment, which was increased by the presence of an immense sponging-bath, that, being flat and circular, could be fitted underneath a bed. In the draught of air next the door stood our filter in a wooden frame, beneath which was a porous jar that received and cooled the clear water as it fell.

Our camp was a perfect model; we had a view of about five miles in extent along the valley of the Atbara, and it was my daily amusement to scan with my telescope the uninhabited country upon the opposite side of the river, and watch the wild animals as they grazed in perfect security. I regret that at that time I did not smoke; in the cool of the evening we used to sit by the bamboo table outside the door of our house, and drink our coffee in perfect contentment amidst the beautiful scene of a tropical sunset and the deep shadows in the valley; but a pipe! – the long "chibbook" of the Turk would have made our home a Paradise! Nevertheless we were thoroughly happy at Sofi; – there was a delightful calm, and a sense of rest; a total estrangement from the cares of the world, and an enchanting contrast in the soft green verdure of the landscape before us to the many hundred weary miles of burning desert through which we had toiled from Lower Egypt. In those barren tracts, the eye had become so accustomed to sterility and yellow sand, that it had appeared impossible to change the scene, and Africa afforded no prospect beyond the blank hitherto shown upon the chart of the interior; we were now in a land of rich pastures, and apparently in another world, after the toil of a hard life; – it was the haven of a pilgrim, rest!

While we were enjoying a few months' repose, the elements were hard at work. Every day, without exception, and generally for several hours of the night, the lightning flashed and thunder roared with little intermission, while the rain poured in such torrents that the entire country became perfectly impassable, with the exception of the hard ground of the Atbara valley. The rich loam of the table land had risen like leavened dough, and was knee-deep in adhesive mud; the grass upon this surface grew with such rapidity that in a few weeks it reached a height of nine or ten feet. The mud rushed in torrents down the countless watercourses, which were now in their greatest activity in hurrying away the fertile soil of Egypt; and the glorious Atbara was at its maximum.

Chapter VIII.

The Plagues of Egypt.

Time glided away smoothly at our camp amidst the storms of the rainy season. The Arabs had nothing to do, and suffered much from the absence of their herds, as there was a great scarcity of milk. The only animals that had not been sent to the north were a few goats; these were so teased by the flies that they produced but a small supply. Fever had appeared at the same time with the flies, and every one was suffering more or less, especially Florian, who was seriously ill. I was in full practice as physician, and we congratulated ourselves upon the healthiness of our little isolated camp, when suddenly my wife was prostrated by a severe attack of gastric fever, which for nine days rendered her recovery almost hopeless. At length the fever gave way to careful attendance, and my Arab patients and Florian were also in a fair way towards recovery. The plagues of Egypt were upon us; the common house-flies were in billions, in addition to the cattle-tormentor. Our donkeys would not graze, but stood day and night in the dense smoke of fires, made of sticks and green grass, for protection.

The plague of boils broke out, and every one was attacked more or less severely. Then came a plague of which Moses must have been ignorant, or he would surely have inflicted it upon Pharaoh. This was a species of itch, which affected all ages and both sexes equally; it attacked all parts of the body, but principally the extremities. The irritation was beyond description; small vesicles rose above the skin, containing a watery fluid, which, upon bursting, appeared to spread the disease. The Arabs had no control over this malady, which they called "coorash," and the whole country was scratching. The popular belief attributed the disease to the water of the Atbara at this particular season: although a horrible plague, I do not believe it to have any connexion with the well-known itch or "scabies" of Europe.

I adopted a remedy that I had found a specific for mange in dogs, and this treatment became equally successful in cases of coorash. Gunpowder, with the addition of one-fourth of sulphur, made into a soft paste with water, and then formed into an ointment with fat: this should be rubbed over the whole body. The effect upon a black man is that of a well-cleaned boot – upon a white man it is still more striking; but it quickly cures the malady. I went into half mourning by this process, and I should have adopted deep mourning had it been necessary; I was only attacked from the feet to a little above the knees. Florian was in a dreadful state, and the vigorous and peculiar action of his arms at once explained the origin of the term "Scotch fiddle," the musical instrument commonly attributed to the north of Great Britain.

The Arabs are wretchedly ignorant of the healing art, and they suffer accordingly. At least fifty per cent. of the population in Sofi had a permanent enlargement of the spleen, which could be felt with a slight pressure of the hand, frequently as large as an orange; this was called "Jenna el Wirde" (child of the fever), and was the result of constant attacks of fever in successive rainy seasons.

Faith is the drug that is supposed to cure the Arab; whatever his complaint may be, he applies to his Faky or priest. This minister is not troubled with a confusion of book-learning, neither are the shelves of his library bending beneath weighty treatises upon the various maladies of human nature; but he possesses the key to all learning, the talisman that will apply to all cases, in that one holy book the Koran. This is his complete pharmacopoeia: his medicine chest, combining purgatives, blisters, sudorifics, styptics, narcotics, emetics, and all that the most profound M.D. could prescribe. With this "multum in parvo" stock-in-trade the Faky receives his patients. No. 1 arrives, a barren woman who requests some medicine that will promote the blessing of childbirth. No. 2, a man who was strong in his youth, but from excessive dissipation has become useless. No. 3, a man deformed from his birth, who wishes to become straight as other men. No. 4, a blind child. No. 5, a dying old woman, carried on a litter; and sundry other impossible cases, with others of a more simple character.

The Faky produces his book, the holy Koran, and with a pen formed of a reed he proceeds to write a prescription; not to be made up by an apothecary, as such dangerous people do not exist, but the prescription itself is to be *swallowed!* Upon a smooth board, like a slate, he rubs sufficient lime to produce a perfectly white surface; upon this he writes in large characters, with thick glutinous ink, a verse or verses from the Koran that he considers applicable to the case; this completed, he washes off the holy quotation, and converts it into a potation by the addition of a little water; this is swallowed in perfect faith by the patient, who in return pays a fee according to the demand of the Faky. Of course it cannot be supposed that this effects a cure, or that it is in any way superior to the prescriptions of a thorough-bred English doctor; the only advantage possessed by the system is complete innocence, in which it may perhaps claim superiority. If no good result is attained by the first holy dose, the patient returns with undiminished confidence, and the prescription is repeated as "the draught as before," well known to the physic-drinkers of England, and in like manner attended with the bill. The fakeers make a considerable amount by this simple practice, and they add to their small earnings by the sale of verses of the Koran as talismans.

As few people can read or write, there is an air of mystery in the art of writing which much enhances the value of a scrap of paper upon which is written a verse from the Koran. A few piastres are willingly expended in the purchase of such talismans, which are carefully and very neatly sewn into small envelopes of leather, and are worn by all people, being handed down from father to son.

The Arabs are especially fond of relics; thus, upon the return from a pilgrimage to Mecca, the "hadji," or pilgrim, is certain to have purchased from some religious Faky of the sacred shrine either a few square inches of cloth, or some such trifle, that belonged to the prophet Mahomet. This is exhibited to his friends and strangers as a wonderful spell against some particular malady, and it is handed about and received with extreme reverence by the assembled crowd. I once formed one of a circle when a pilgrim returned to his native village: we sat in a considerable number upon the ground, while he drew from his bosom a leather envelope, suspended from his neck, from which he produced a piece of extremely greasy woollen cloth, about three inches square, the original colour of which it would have been impossible to guess. This was a piece of Mahomet's garment, but what portion he could not say. The pilgrim had paid largely for this blessed relic, and it was passed round our circle from hand to hand, after having first been kissed by the proprietor, who raised it to the crown of his head, which he touched with the cloth, and then wiped both his eyes. Each person who received it went through a similar performance, and as ophthalmia and other diseases of the eyes were extremely prevalent, several of the party had eyes that had not the brightness of the gazelle's; nevertheless, these were supposed to become brighter after having been wiped by the holy cloth. How many eyes this same piece of cloth had wiped it would be impossible to say, but such facts are sufficient to prove the danger of holy relics, that are inoculators of all manner of contagious diseases.

I believe in holy shrines as the pest spots of the world. We generally have experienced in Western Europe that all violent epidemics arrive from the East. The great breadth of the Atlantic boundary would naturally protect us from the West, but infectious disorders, such as plague, cholera, small-pox, &c. may be generally tracked throughout their gradations from their original nests; those nests are in the East, where the heat of the climate acting upon the filth of semi-savage communities engenders pestilence.

The holy places of both Christians and Mahometans are the receptacles for the masses of people of all nations and classes who have arrived from all points of the compass; the greater number of such people are of poor estate; many, who have toiled on foot from immense distances, suffering from hunger and fatigue, and bringing with them not only the diseases of their own remote countries, but arriving in that weak state that courts the attack of any epidemic. Thus crowded together, with a scarcity of provisions, a want of water, and no possibility of cleanliness, with clothes that have been unwashed for weeks or months, in a camp of dirty pilgrims, without any attempt at drainage, an accumulation of filth takes place that generates either cholera or typhus; the latter, in its most malignant form, appears as the dreaded "plague." Should such an epidemic attack the mass of pilgrims debilitated by the want of nourishing food, and exhausted by their fatiguing march, it runs riot like a fire among combustibles, and the loss of life is terrific. The survivors radiate from this common centre, upon their return to their respective homes, to which they carry the seeds of the pestilence to germinate upon new soils in different countries. Doubtless the clothes of the dead furnish materials for innumerable holy relics as vestiges of the wardrobe of the Prophet; these are disseminated by the pilgrims throughout all countries, pregnant with disease; and, being brought into personal contact with hosts of true believers, Pandora's box could not be more fatal.

Not only are relics upon a pocket scale conveyed by pilgrims, and reverenced by the Arabs, but the body of any Faky, who in lifetime was considered extra holy, is brought from a great distance to be interred in some particular spot. In countries where a tree is a rarity, a plank for a coffin is unknown; thus the reverend Faky, who may have died of typhus, is wrapped in cloths and packed in a mat. In this form he is transported, perhaps, some hundred miles, slung upon a camel, with the thermometer above 130 degrees Fahr. in the sun, and he is conveyed to the village that is so fortunate as to be honoured with his remains. It may be readily imagined that with a favourable wind, the inhabitants are warned of his approach some time before his arrival. Happily, long before we arrived at Sofi, the village had been blessed by the death of a celebrated Faky, a holy man who would have been described as a second Isaiah were the annals of the country duly chronicled. This great "man of God," as he was termed, had departed this life at a village on the borders of the Nile, about eight days' hard camel-journey from Sofi; but from some assumed right, mingled no doubt with jobbery, the inhabitants of Sofi had laid claim to his body, and he had arrived upon a camel horizontally, and had been buried about fifty yards from our present camp. His grave was beneath a clump of mimosas that shaded the spot, and formed the most prominent object in the foreground of our landscape. Thither every Friday the women of the village congregated, with offerings of a few handfuls of dhurra in small gourd-shells, which they laid upon the grave, while they *ate the holy earth* in small pinches, which they scraped like rabbits, from a hole they had burrowed towards the venerated corpse; this hole was about two feet deep from continual scratching, and must have been very near the Faky.

Although bamboos did not grow in Sofi, great numbers were brought down by the river during the rains; these were eagerly collected by the Arabs, and the grave of the Faky was ornamented with selected specimens, upon which were hung small pieces of rag-like banners. The people could not explain why they were thus ornamented, but I imagine the custom had originated from the necessity of scaring the wild animals that might have exhumed the body.

Although the grave of this revered Faky was considered a sacred spot, the women had a curious custom that we should not consider an honour to the sanctity of the place: they met in parties beneath the shade of the mimosas that covered the grave, for the express purpose of freeing each other's heads from vermin; the creatures thus caught, instead of being killed, were turned loose upon the Faky.

Although the Arabs in places remote from the immediate action of the Egyptian authorities are generally lawless, they are extremely obedient to their own sheiks, and especially to the fakeers: thus it is important to secure such heads of the people as friends. My success as a physician had gained me many friends, as I studiously avoided the acceptance of any present in return for my services, which I wished them to receive as simple acts of kindness; thus I had placed the Sheik Hassan bel Kader under an obligation, by curing him of a fever; and as he chanced to combine in his own person the titles of both sheik and faky, I had acquired a great ascendency in the village, as my medicines had proved more efficacious than the talismans. "Physician, cure thyself," applied to the Faky, who found three grains of my tartar emetic more powerful than a whole chapter of the Koran.

We frequently had medical discussions, and the contents of my large medicine-chest were examined with wonder by a curious crowd; the simple effect of mixing a seidlitz powder was a source of astonishment; but a few drops of sulphuric acid upon a piece of strong cotton cloth which it destroyed immediately, was a miracle that invested the medicine-chest with a specific character for all diseases. The Arab style of doctoring is rather rough. If a horse or other animal has inflammation, they hobble the legs and throw it upon the ground, after which operation a number of men kick it in the belly until it is relieved – (by death). Should a man be attacked with fever, his friends prescribe a system of diet, in addition to the Koran of the Faky: he is made to drink, as hot as he can swallow it, about a quart of melted sheep's fat or butter. Young dogs, as a cure for distemper, are thrown from the roof of a house to the ground – a height of about ten feet. One night we were sitting at dinner, when we suddenly heard a great noise, and the air was illumined by the blaze of a hut on fire. In the midst of the tumult I heard the unmistakeable cries of dogs, and thinking that they were unable to escape from the fire, I ran towards the spot. As I approached, first one and then another dog ran screaming from the flames, until a regular pack of about twenty scorched animals appeared in quick succession, all half mad with fright and fire. I was informed that hydrophobia was very prevalent in the country, and that the certain preventive from that frightful malady was to make all the dogs of the village pass through the fire. Accordingly an old hut had been filled with straw and fired; after which, each dog was brought by its owner and thrown into the flames. Upon another occasion I heard a great yelling and commotion, and I found Mahomet's "mother's brother's cousin's sister's mother's son," Achmet, struggling on the ground, and nearly overpowered by a number of Arabs, who were determined to operate upon a large boil in his groin, which they had condemned to be squeezed, although it was not in a state that admitted of such treatment. The patient was biting and kicking liberally on all sides in self-defence, and his obstinate surgeons could hardly be persuaded to desist.

Syphilis is common throughout the country, and there are several varieties of food that are supposed to effect a cure. A sheep is killed, and the entire flesh is cooked with the fat, being cut into small pieces and baked in a pot; several pounds of butter or other grease are then boiled, and in that state are poured into the jars containing the baked meat; the patient is then shut up by himself in a hut with this large quantity of fat food, with which he is to gorge himself until the whole is consumed. Another supposed cure for the same disease is a pig dressed in a similar manner, which meat, although forbidden by the Koran, may be taken medicinally. The flesh of the crocodile is eaten greedily, being supposed to promote desire. There are few animals that the Arabs of the Nubian provinces will refuse; the wild boar is invariably eaten by the Arab hunters, although in direct opposition to the rules of the Koran. I once asked them what their Faky would say if he were aware of such a transgression. "Oh!" they replied, "we have already asked his permission, as we are sometimes severely pressed for food in the jungles; he says, 'If you have the *koran* in your hand and *no pig*, you are forbidden to eat pork; but if you have the *pig* in your hand and *no koran*, you had better eat what God has given you.'"

This is a charming example of simplicity in theological discussion that might perhaps be followed with advantage in graver questions; we might cease to strain at the gnats and swallow our pigs.

I had an audience of a party of hunters whom I had long wished to meet. Before my arrival at Sofi I had heard of a particular tribe of Arabs that inhabited the country south of Cassala, between that town and the Base country; these were the Hamrans, who were described as the most extraordinary Nimrods, who hunted and kiled all wild animals, from the antelope to the elephant, with no other weapon than the sword; the lion and the rhinoceros fell alike before the invincible sabres of these mighty hunters, to whom as an old elephant-hunter I wished to make my salaam, and humbly confess my inferiority.

From the manner in which their exploits had been hitherto explained to me, I could not understand how it could be possible to kill an elephant with the sword, unless the animal should be mobbed by a crowd of men and hacked to death, but I was assured that the most savage elephant had no chance upon good riding ground, against four aggageers (as the hunters with the sword are designated). I had determined to engage a party of these hunters to accompany me throughout my exploration of the Abyssinian rivers at the proper season, when I should have an excellent opportunity of combining sport with an examination of the country. My intentions had become known, and the visit of the hunters was the consequence.

The Hamran Arabs are distinguished from the other tribes by an extra length of hair, worn parted down the centre, and arranged in long curls; otherwise there is no perceptible difference in their appearance from other Arabs. They are armed, as are all others, with swords and shields; the latter are circular, and are generally formed of rhinoceros hide. There are two forms of shields used by the various tribes of Arabs: one is a narrow oval, about four feet in length, of either bull's or buffalo's hide, stiffened by a strong stick which passes down the centre; the other is circular, about two feet in diameter, with a projection in the centre as a protection for the hand. When laid flat upon the ground, the shield somewhat resembles an immensely broad-brimmed hat, with a low crown terminating in a point. In the inside of the crown is a strong bar of leather as a grip for the hand, while the outside is generally guarded by a strip of the scaly hide of a crocodile.

The skins most prized for shields are those of the giraffe and the rhinoceros; those of the buffalo and elephant are likewise in general use, but they are considered inferior to the former, while the hide of the hippopotamus is too thick and heavy.

The hide of the giraffe is wonderfully tough, and combines the great advantage of extreme lightness with strength. The Arabs never ornament their shields; they are made for rough and actual service, and the gashes upon many are proofs of the necessity of such a protection for the owner.

Although there are two patterns of shields among the Arabs, there is no difference in the form of their swords, which simply vary in size according to the strength of the wearer. The blade is long and straight, two-edged, with a simple cross handle, having no other guard for the hand than the plain bar, which at right angles with the hilt forms the cross. I believe this form was adopted after the Crusades, when the long, straight, cross-handled blades of the Christian knights left an impression behind them that established the fashion. All these blades are manufactured at Sollingen, and are exported to Egypt for the trade of the interior. Of course they differ in quality and price, but they are of excellent temper. The Arabs are extremely proud of a good sword, and a blade of great value is carefully handed down through many generations. The sheiks and principal people wear silver-hilted swords. The scabbards are usually formed of two thin strips of elastic but soft wood, covered with leather. No Arab would accept a metal scabbard, as it would destroy the keen edge of his weapon. The greatest care is taken in sharpening the swords. While on the march, the Arab carries his weapon slung on the pommel of his saddle, from which it passes beneath his thigh. There are two projecting pieces of leather, about twelve inches apart, upon the scabbard, between which the thigh of the horseman fits, and thus prevents the sword from slipping from its place. Carried in this position at full speed, there is an absence of that absurd dangling and jumping of the sword that is exhibited in our British cavalry, and the weapon seems to form a portion of the rider. The first action of an Arab when he dismounts at a halt upon the march, and sits beneath a tree, is to draw his sword; and after trying both edges with his thumb, he carefully strops the blade to and fro upon his shield until a satisfactory proof of the edge is made by shaving the hair off his arm, after which it is returned to the sheath. I have measured these swords; that of a fair average size is three feet in the length of blade, and one inch and seven-eighths in breadth; the hilt, from the top of the guard to the extremity, five and a half inches. Thus the sword complete would be about three feet five or six inches. Such a weapon possesses immense power, as the edge is nearly as sharp as a razor. But the Arabs have not the slightest knowledge of swordsmanship; they never parry with the blade, but trust entirely to the shield, and content themselves with slashing either at their adversary or at the animal that he rides; one good cut delivered by a powerful arm would sever a man at the waist like a carrot. The Arabs are not very powerful men; they are extremely light and active, and generally average about five feet eight inches in height. But their swords are far too heavy for their strength; and although they can deliver a severe cut, they cannot recover the sword sufficiently quick to parry, therefore they are contented with the shield as their only guard. If opposed to a good swordsman they would be perfectly at his mercy, as a feint at the head causes them to raise the shield; this prevents them from seeing the point, that would immediately pass through the body.

Notwithstanding their deficiency in the art of the sword, they are wonderful fellows to cut and slash; and when the sharp edge of the heavy weapon touches an enemy, the effect is terrible.

The elephant-hunters, or aggageers, exhibited their swords, which differed in no respect from those usually worn; but they were bound with cord very closely from the guard for about nine inches along the blade, to enable them to be grasped by the right hand, while the hilt was held by the left; the weapon was thus converted into a two-handed sword. The scabbards were strengthened by an extra covering, formed of the skin of the elephant's ear.

In a long conversation with these men, I found a corroboration of all that I had previously heard of their exploits, and they described the various methods of killing the elephant with the sword. Those hunters who could not afford to purchase horses hunted on foot, in parties not exceeding two persons. Their method was to follow the tracks of an elephant, so as to arrive at their game between the hours of 10 A.M. and noon, at which time the animal is either asleep, or extremely listless, and easy to approach. Should they discover the animal asleep, one of the hunters would creep stealthily towards the head, and with one blow sever the trunk while stretched upon the ground; in which case the elephant would start upon his feet, while the hunters escaped in the confusion of the moment. The trunk severed would cause an haemorrhage sufficient to insure the death of the elephant within about an hour. On time other hand, should the animal be awake upon their arrival, it would be impossible to approach the trunk; in such a case, they would creep up from behind, and give a tremendous cut at the back sinew of the hind leg, about a foot above the heel. Such a blow would disable the elephant at once, and would render comparatively easy a second cut to the remaining leg; the arteries being divided, the animal would quickly bleed to death. These were the methods adopted by poor hunters, until, by the sale of ivory, they could purchase horses for the higher branch of the art. Provided with horses, the party of hunters should not exceed four. They start before daybreak, and ride slowly throughout the country in search of elephants, generally keeping along the course of a river until they come upon the tracks where a herd or a single elephant may have drunk during the night. When once upon the tracks, they follow fast towards the retreating game. The elephants may be twenty miles distant; but it matters little to the aggageers. At length they discover them, and the hunt begins. The first step is to single out the bull with the largest tusks; this is the commencement of the fight. After a short hunt, the elephant turns upon his pursuers, who scatter and fly from his headlong charge until he gives up the pursuit; he at length turns to bay when again pressed by the hunters. It is the duty of one man in particular to ride up close to the head of the elephant, and thus to absorb its attention upon himself. This insures a desperate charge. The greatest coolness and dexterity are then required by the hunter, who now, the *hunted*, must so adapt the speed of his horse to the pace of the elephant, that the enraged beast gains in the race until it almost reaches the tail of the horse. In this manner the race continues. In the meantime, two hunters gallop up behind the elephant, unseen by the animal, whose attention is completely directed to the horse almost within his grasp. With extreme agility, when close to the heels of the elephant, one of the hunters, while at full speed, springs to the ground with his drawn sword, as his companion seizes the bridle, and with one dexterous two-handed blow he severs the back sinew. He immediately jumps out of the way and remounts his horse; but if the blow is successful, the elephant becomes disabled by the first pressure of its foot upon the ground; the enormous weight of the animal dislocates the joint, and it is rendered helpless. The hunter who has hitherto led the elephant immediately turns, and riding to within a few feet of the trunk, he induces the animal to attempt another charge. This, clumsily made, affords an easy opportunity for the aggageers behind to slash the sinew of the remaining leg, and the immense brute is reduced to a standstill; it dies of loss of blood in a short time, *thus positively killed by one man with two strokes of the sword!*

This extraordinary hunting is attended with superlative danger, and the hunters frequently fall victims to their intrepidity. I felt inclined to take off my cap and make a low bow to the gallant and swarthy fellows who sat before me, when I knew the toughness of their hearts and the activity of their limbs. One of them was disabled for life by a cut from his own sword, that had severed the knee-cap and bitten deep into the joint, leaving a scar that appeared as though the leg had been nearly off; he had missed his blow at the elephant, owing to the high and tough dried grass that had partially stopped the sword, and in springing upon one side, to avoid the animal that had turned upon him, he fell over his own sharp blade, which cut through the bone, and he lay helpless; he was saved by one of his comrades, who immediately rushed in from behind, and with a desperate cut severed the back sinew of the elephant. As I listened to these fine fellows, who in a modest and unassuming manner recounted their adventures as matters of course, I felt exceedingly small. My whole life had been passed in wild sports from early manhood, and I had imagined that I understood as much as most people of this subject; but here were men who, without the aid of the best rifles and deadly projectiles, went straight at their game, and faced the lion in his den with shield and sabre. There is a freemasonry among hunters, and my heart was drawn towards these aggageers. We fraternised upon the spot, and I looked forward with intense pleasure to the day when we might become allies in action.

I have been rewarded by this alliance in being now able to speak of the deeds of others that far excel my own, and of bearing testimony to the wonderful courage and dexterity of these Nimrods, instead of continually relating anecdotes of dangers in the first person, which cannot be more disagreeable to the reader than to the narrator.

Without inflicting a description of five months passed in Sofi, it will be necessary to make a few extracts from my journal, to convey an idea of the manner in which the time was occupied.

"August 7, 1861. – There is plenty of game on the other side of the river, but nothing upon this; there are no means of crossing, as the stream is exceedingly strong, and about two hundred yards in width. We felled a tree for a canoe, but there is nothing worthy of the name of timber, and the wood is extremely heavy.

"There are several varieties of wild spinach, and a plant that makes a good salad, known by the Arabs as 'Regly;' also wild onions as large as a man's fist, but uneatable.

"Angust 8. – I counted seventy-six giraffes on the opposite side of the river. This magnificent sight is most tantalizing. The sheik made his appearance to-day with a present of butter and honey, and some small money in exchange for dollars that I had given him. The Austrian dollar of Maria Theresa is the only large coin current in this country; the effigy of the empress, with a very low dress and a profusion of bust, is, I believe, the charm that suits the Arab taste. So particular are these people, that they reject the coin after careful examination, unless they can distinctly count seven dots that form the star upon the coronet. No clean money will pass current in this country; all coins must be dirty and gummy, otherwise they are rejected: this may be accounted for, as the Arabs have no method of detecting false money; thus they are afraid to accept any new coin.

"Auqust 16. – Great failure! We launched the canoe, but although it was carefully hollowed out, the wood was so heavy that it would only carry one person, and even then it threatened to become a bathing-machine; thus nine days' hard work are lost. Florian is in despair, but 'Nil desperandum!' I shall set to work instanter, and make a raft. Counted twenty-eight giraffes on the opposite side of the river.

"August 17. – I set to work at daybreak to make a raft of bamboo and inflated skins. There is a wood called ambatch (Anemone mirabilis) that is brought down by the river from the upper country; this is lighter than cork, and I have obtained four large pieces for my raft. Mahomet has been very saucy to-day; he has been offensively impertinent for a long time, so this morning I punched his head.

"August 18. – Launched the raft; it carries four persons safely; but the current is too strong, and it is therefore unmanageable. In the afternoon I shot a large crocodile on the other side of the river (about two hundred yards) with the little Fletcher rifle, and after struggling for some time upon the steep bank it rolled into the water.

"The large tamarind trees on the opposite bank are generally full of the dog-faced baboons (Cynocephalus) in the evening, at their drinking-hour. I watched a large crocodile creep slyly out of the water, and lie in waiting among the rocks at the usual drinking-place before they arrived, but the baboons were too wide awake to be taken in so easily. A young fellow was the first to discover the enemy; he had accompanied several wise and experienced old hands, to the extremity of the bough that at a considerable height overhung the river; from this post they had a bird's-eye view, and reconnoitred before one of the numerous party descended to drink. The sharp eyes of the young one at once detected the crocodile, who matched in colour so well with the rocks, that most probably a man would not have noticed it until too late. At once the young one commenced shaking the bough and screaming with all his might to attract the attention of the crocodile, and to induce it to move. In this he was immediately joined by the whole party, who yelled in chorus, while the large old males bellowed defiance, and descended to the lowest branches within eight or ten feet of the crocodile. It was of no use – the pretender never stirred, and I watched it until dark; it remained still inn the same place, waiting for some unfortunate baboon whose thirst might provoke his fate; but not one was sufficiently foolish, although the perpendicular banks prevented them from drinking except at that particular spot.

"The birds in this country moult twice during the year, and those of the most brilliant colours exchange their gaudy hues for a sober grey or brown. Several varieties sing beautifully; the swallow also sings, although in Europe I have never heard it attempt more than its well-known twitter.

"One of the mimosas yields an excellent fibre for rope-making, in which my people are busily engaged; the bark is as tough as leather, and forms an admirable material for the manufacture of sacks. This business is carried to a considerable extent by the Arabs, as there is a large demand for sacks of sufficient size to contain two hundred and fifty or three hundred pounds of gum arabic (half a camel load). Thus one sack slung upon each side can be packed easily to the animal.

"August 19. – A dead elephant floated down the river to-day: this is the second that has passed within the last few days; they have been most probably drowned in attempting to cross some powerful torrent tributary to the Atbara. As usual, upon the fact becoming known, the entire village rushed out, and, despite the crocodiles, a crowd of men plunged into the river about a quarter of a mile below Sofi, and swimming out they intercepted the swollen carcase, which was quickly covered with people; they were carried several miles down the river before they could tow the body to shore, by ropes fastened to the swimmers. Afterwards, there was a general quarrel over the division of the spoil: the skin, in sections, and the tusks, were brought home in triumph.

"The country being now bright green, the antelopes are distinctly visible on the opposite side. Three tetel (Antelopus Bubalis) graze regularly together in the same place daily. This antelope is a variety of the hartebeest of South Africa; it is a reddish-chestnut colour, and is about the size of an Alderney cow.

"One of the mimosas (Acacia Arabica) produces a fruit in appearance resembling a tamarind: this is a powerful astringent and a valuable medicine in cases of fever and diarrhoea; it is generally used by the Arabs for preparing hides; when dry and broken it is rich in a hard gum, which appears to be almost pure tannin.

"August 20. – Close, hot, and damp weather; violent rain about sixteen hours out of the twenty-four. When the hot season sets in, the country will almost boil. This morning I counted 154 giraffes in one herd on the other side of the river; there were many more, but they passed each other so rapidly that I could not reckon the entire troop.

"August 21. – I counted 103 giraffes. There is literally no game upon this side (west) of the Atbara, as the country for twelve hours' journey from Sofi is thronged with Arabs during the dry season.

"All my people are more or less ill; I am not very well myself; but I have staved off an attack of fever by preventive measures.

"August 25. – Such a magnificent sunset I have never seen! From all quarters were gathering storms of the blackest description, each cloud emitting lightning without intermission, and as the sun touched the horizon upon the only clear point, it illumined like a fire the pitch-black clouds, producing the most extraordinary effect of vivid colouring, combined with lightning, and a rainbow.

"Rain in torrents throughout the night. It is now impossible to walk on the flat table land, as the soil is so saturated that it clings to the feet like birdlime, in masses that will pull the shoes off unless they fit tight. All this immense tract of rich land would grow any amount of cotton, or wheat, as in this country the rain falls with great regularity – this might be sent to Berber by boats during the season of flood.

"August 27. – My antelope skins are just completed and are thoroughly tanned. Each skin required a double handful of the 'garra,' or fruit of the Acacia Arabica. The process is simple: the skin being thoroughly wetted, the garra is pounded into a paste; this is rubbed into the hide with a rough piece of sandstone, until it becomes perfectly clean, and free from impurities; it is then wrapped up with a quantity of the paste, and is deposited in a trough and kept in the shade for twenty-four hours. It should undergo a similar rubbing daily, and be kept in the trough to soak in the garra for four or five days. After this process it should be well rubbed with fat, if required to keep soft and pliable when wetted. If soaked in milk after tanning, the leather will become waterproof. The large tanned ox-hides used by the Arabs as coverlets are perfectly waterproof, and are simply prepared with milk. These are made in Abyssinia, and can be purchased at from ten piastres to a dollar each. The Arabs thoroughly appreciate the value of leather, as they are entirely dependent upon such material for coverlets, watersacks, travelling bags, &c. &c. The sac de voyage is a simple skin of either goat or sheep drawn off the animal as a stocking is drawn from the leg; this is very neatly ornamented, and arranged with loops which close the mouth, secured by a padlock. Very large sacks, capable of containing three hundred pounds of corn, are made in the same manner by drawing off entire the skins of the larger antelopes – that of the tetel is considered the most valuable for this purpose. The hide of the wild ass is the finest of all leather, and is so close in the grain that before tanning, when dry and hardened in the sun, it resembles horn in transparency. I have made excellent mocassins with this skin, which are admirable if kept wetted.

"August 28. – Sofi being upon the frontier, the laws are merely nominal; accordingly there is an interesting mixture in the society. Should any man commit a crime in Abyssinia, he takes refuge over the border; thus criminals of the blackest character are at large. One fellow who has paid us daily visits killed his brother with a knife a few months since. I have excluded this gentleman from the select circle of our acquaintance.

"The Arab women are very clever in basket-work and matting – they carry their milk in baskets that are so closely fitted as to be completely water-tight; these are made of the leaves of the dome palm, shred into fine strips. In addition to the coarse matting required for their tents, they manufacture very fine sleeping mats, curiously arranged in various coloured patterns; these are to cover the angareps, or native bedsteads, which are simple frameworks upon legs, covered with a network of raw hide worked in a soft state, after which it hardens to the tightness of a drum when thoroughly dry. No bed is more comfortable for a warm climate than a native angarep with a simple mat covering; it is beautifully elastic, and is always cool, as free ventilation is permitted from below. I have employed the Arab women to make me a hunting-cap of the basket-work of dome palm, to my old pattern.

"August 28. – I have been busily employed in putting new soles to my shoes, having cut up the leather cover of a gun-case for material. No person can walk barefooted in this country, as the grass is armed with thorns. A peculiar species, that resembles a vetch, bears a circular pod as large as a horse-bean; the exterior of the pod is armed with long and sharp spikes like the head of an ancient mace; these pods when ripe are exceedingly hard, and falling to the ground in great numbers, the spikes will pierce the sole of any shoe unless of a stout substance.

"August 29. – Florian is very ill with fever. The mosquitoes are so troublesome that the Arabs cannot sleep in their huts, but are forced to arrange platforms about six feet high, upon which the whole family rest until they are awakened by a sudden thunderstorm, and are compelled to rush into their huts; – this has been the case nightly for some time past.

"I find that the whole village has been trying on my new hunting-cap, that an Arab woman has just completed; this was brought to me to-day, thick with butter and dirt from their greasy pates. This is a trifle: yesterday Florian was ill and required some tea; his servant tried the degree of heat by plunging his dirty black finger to the bottom.

"Shortly after our wild Arab lad, Bacheet, was engaged, we drilled him as table servant. The flies were very troublesome, and continually committed suicide by drowning themselves in the tea. One morning during breakfast there were many cases of felo de se, or 'temporary insanity,' and my wife's tea-cup was full of victims; Bacheet, wishing to be attentive, picked out the bodies with his finger and thumb! – 'Now, my good fellow, Bacheet,' I exclaimed, 'you really must not put your dirty fingers in the tea: you should take them out with the tea-spoon. Look here,' and I performed the operation, and safely landed several flies that were still kicking. 'But mind, Bacheet,' I continued, 'that you wipe the tea-spoon first, to be sure that it is clean!' On the following morning at breakfast we covered up the cups with saucers to prevent accidents; but to our astonishment Bacheet, who was in waiting, suddenly took a tea-spoon from the table, wiped it carefully with a corner of the table-cloth, and stooping down beneath the bed, most carefully saved from drowning, with the tea-spoon, several flies that were in the last extremity within a vessel by no means adapted for a spoon. Perfectly satisfied with the result, he carefully rewiped the tea-spoon upon the table-cloth, and replaced it in its proper position. 'Oh Bacheet! Bacheet! you ignoramus, you extraordinary and impossible animal!' However, there was no help for it – the boy thought he was doing the right thing exactly.

"September 1. – The animals are worried almost to death by the countless flies, especially by that species that drives the camels from the country. This peculiar fly is about the size of a wasp, with an orange-coloured body, with black and white rings; the proboscis is terrific; it is double, and appears to be disproportioned, being two-thirds the length of the entire insect. When this fly attacks an animal, or man, it pierces the skin instantaneously, like the prick of a red-hot needle driven deep into the flesh, at the same time the insect exerts every muscle of its body by buzzing with its wings as it buries the instrument to its greatest depth. The blood starts from the wound immediately, and continues to flow for a considerable time; this is an attraction to other flies in great numbers, many of which would lay their eggs upon the wound.

"I much prefer the intense heat of summer to the damp of the rainy season, which breeds all kinds of vermin. During the hot season the nights are cool and delightful, there is not one drop of dew, and we live entirely in the open air beneath the shade of a tree in the day, and under a roof of glittering stars at night. The guns never rust, although lying upon the ground, and we are as independent as the antelopes of the desert, any bush affording a home within its limit of shadow. During the rainy season hunting and travelling would be equally impossible; the rifles would constantly miss fire. The mud is in most places knee-deep, and a malignant fever would shortly settle the hunter. The rains cease early in September, after which we are to expect a complete vapour-bath until the end of October, by which time the fiery sun will have evaporated the moisture from the sodden earth; that interval will be the most unhealthy season.

"As this fertile country can depend upon three months' periodical rain, from the middle of June until September there is no reason for unproductiveness; it would produce a large revenue if in industrious hands.

"September 2. – For many days past we have seen large herds of giraffes and many antelopes on the opposite side of the river, about two miles distant, on the borders of the Atbara, into which valley the giraffes apparently dared not descend but remained on the table land, although the antelopes appearmed to prefer the harder soil of the valley slopes. This day a herd of twenty-eight giraffes tantalized me by descending a short distance below the level flats, and I was tempted at all hazards across the river. Accordingly preparations were immediately made for a start. The sheik of the village and several of the Arabs were hippopotami hunters by profession; these fellows could swim like otters, and, despite the crocodiles, they seemed as much at home in the water as on land. We prepared an impromptu raft. My angarep (bedstead) was quickly inverted; six water-skins were inflated, and lashed, three on either side. A shallow packing-case, lined with tin, containing my gun, was fastened in the centre of the angarep, and two tow-lines were attached to the front part of the raft, by which swimmers were to draw it across the river. Two men were to hang on behind, and, if possible, keep it straight in the rapid current.

"The Arabs were full of mettle, as their minds were fixed upon giraffe venison. A number of people, including my wife, climbed upon the mosquito platforms, to obtain a good view of the projected hunt, and we quickly carried our raft to the edge of the river. There was not much delay in the launch. I stepped carefully into my coffin-shaped case, and squatted down, with a rifle on either side, and my ammunition at the bottom of the tin-lined water-proof case; thus, in case of an upset, I was ready for a swim. Off we went! The current, running at nearly five miles an hour, carried us away at a great pace, and the whirlpools caused us much trouble, as we several times waltzed round when we should have preferred a straight course, but the towing swimmers being well mounted upon logs of light ambatch-wood, swam across in fine style, and after some difficulty we arrived at the opposite bank, and scrambled through thick bushes, upon our hands and knees, to the summit.

"For about two miles' breadth on this side of the river the valley is rough broken ground, full of gullies and ravines sixty or seventy feet deep, beds of torrents, bare sandstone rocks, bushy crags, fine grassy knolls, and long strips of mimosa covert, forming a most perfect locality for shooting.

"I had observed by the telescope that the giraffes were standing as usual upon an elevated position, from whence they could keep a good look-out. I knew it would be useless to ascend the slope direct, as their long necks give these animals an advantage similar to that of the man at the mast-head; therefore, although we had the wind in our favour, we should have been observed. I therefore determined to make a great circuit of about five miles, and thus to approach them from above, with the advantage of the broken ground for stalking. It was the perfection of uneven country: by clambering broken cliff, wading shoulder-deep through muddy gullies, sliding down the steep ravines, and winding through narrow bottoms of high grass and mimosas for about two hours, during which we disturbed many superb nellut (Ant. strepsiceros) and tetel (Ant. Bubalis), we at length arrived at the point of the high table land upon the verge of which I had first noticed the giraffes with the telescope. Almost immediately I distinguished the tall neck of one of these splendid animals about half a mile distant upon my left, a little below the table land; it was feeding on the bushes, and I quickly discovered several others near the leader of the herd. I was not far enough advanced in the circuit that I had intended to bring me exactly above them, therefore I turned sharp to my right, intending to make a short half circle, and to arrive on the leeward side of the herd, as I was now to windward: this I fortunately completed, but I had marked a thick bush as my point of cover, and upon arrival I found that the herd had fed down wind, and that I was within two hundred yards of the great bull sentinel that, having moved from his former position, was now standing directly before me. I lay down quietly behind the bush with my two followers, and anxiously watched the great leader, momentarily expecting that it would get my wind. It was shortly joined by two others, and I perceived the heads of several giraffes lower down the incline, that were now feeding on their way to the higher ground. The seroot fly was teasing them, and I remarked that several birds were fluttering about their heads, sometimes perching upon their noses and catching the fly that attacked their nostrils, while the giraffes appeared relieved by their attentions: these were a peculiar species of bird that attacks the domestic animals, and not only relieves them of vermin, but eats into the flesh, and establishes dangerous sores. A puff of wind now gently fanned the back of my neck; it was cool and delightful, but no sooner did I feel the refreshing breeze than I knew it would convey our scent direct to the giraffes. A few seconds afterwards, the three grand obelisks threw their heads still higher in the air, and fixing their great black eyes upon the spot from which the danger came, they remained as motionless as though carved from stone. From their great height they could see over the bush behind which we were lying at some paces distant, and although I do not think they could distinguish us to be men, they could see enough to convince them of hidden enemies.

"The attitude of fixed attention and surprise of the three giraffes was sufficient warning for the rest of the herd, who immediately filed up from the lower ground, and joined their comrades. All now halted, and gazed steadfastly in our direction, forming a superb tableau; their beautiful mottled skins glancing like the summer coat of a thoroughbred horse, the orange-coloured statues standing out in high relief from a background of dark-green mimosas.

"This beautiful picture soon changed; I knew that my chance of a close shot was hopeless, as they would presently make a rush, and be off; thus I determined to get the first start. I had previously studied the ground, and I concluded that they would push forward at right angles with my position, as they had thus ascended the hill, and that, on reaching the higher ground, they would turn to the right, in order to reach an immense tract of high grass, as level as a billiard-table, from which no danger could approach them unobserved.

"I accordingly with a gentle movement of my hand directed my people to follow me, and I made a sudden rush forward at full speed. Off went the herd; shambling along at a tremendous pace, whisking their long tails above their hind quarters, and taking exactly the direction I had anticipated, they offered me a shoulder shot at a little within two hundred yards' distance. Unfortunately, I fell into a deep hole concealed by the high grass, and by the time that I resumed the hunt they had increased their distance, but I observed the leader turned sharp to the right, through some low mimosa bush, to make direct for the open table land. I made a short cut oblquely at my best speed, and only halted when I saw that I should lose ground by altering my position. Stopping short, I was exactiy opposite the herd as they filed by me at right angles in full speed, within about a hundred and eighty yards. I had my old Ceylon No. 10 double rifle, and I took a steady shot at a large dark-coloured bull: the satisfactory sound of the ball upon his hide was followed almost immediately by his blundering forward for about twenty yards, and falling heavily in the low bush. I heard the crack of the ball of my left-hand barrel upon another fine beast, but no effects followed. Bacheet quickly gave me the single 2-ounce Manton rifle, and I singled out a fine dark-coloured bull, who fell on his knees to the shot, but recovering, hobbled off disabled, apart from the herd, with a foreleg broken just below the shoulder. Reloading immediately, I ran up to the spot, where I found my first giraffe lying dead, with the ball clean through both shoulders: the second was standing about one hundred paces distant; upon my approach he attempted to move, but immediately fell, and was despatched by my eager Arabs. I followed the herd for about a mile to no purpose, through deep clammy ground and high grass, and I returned to our game.

"These were my first giraffes, and I admired them as they lay before me with a hunter's pride and satisfaction, but mingled with a feeling of pity for such beautiful and utterly helpless creatures. The giraffe, although from sixteen to twenty feet in height, is perfectly defenceless, and can only trust to the swiftness of its pace, and the extraordinary power of vision, for its means of protection. The eye of this animal is the most beautiful exaggeration of that of the gazelle, while the colour of the reddish-orange hide, mottled with darker spots, changes the tints of the skin with the differing rays of light, according to the muscular movement of the body. No one who has merely seen the giraffe in a cold climate can form the least idea of its beauty in its native land. By the time that we had skinned one of the aninmals, it was nearly six o'clock, and it was necessary to hurry forward to reach the river before night; we therefore arranged some thorny boughs over the bodies, to which we intended to return on the following morning.

"When about half-way to the river, as we were passing through grass about four feet high, three tetel bounded from a ravine, and, passing directly before us, gave me a splendid shot at about sixty yards. The Ceylon No. 10 struck the foremost through the shoulder, and it fell dead after running a few yards. This was also my first tetel (Antelopus Bubalis); it was in splendid condition, the red coat was like satin, and the animal would weigh about five hundred pounds live weight.

"I had made very successful shots, having bagged three out of four large game; this perfectly delighted the Arabs, and was very satisfactory to myself, as I was quite aware that my men would be only too willing to accompany me upon future excursions.

"It was quite dark before we reached the river; we had been much delayed by repeated falls into deep holes, and over hidden stones; thus I was well satisfied to find myself once more at home after having crossed the river, in pitchy darkness, in a similar manner as before. Every person in the village had had a good view of the stalk; therefore, as two giraffes had been seen to fall, the Arabs were waiting on the bank in expectation of meat.

"September 3. – This morning I crossed the river with about twenty men, some swimming with inflated skins, and others supported by logs of ambatch. A number of swimmers were holding on to a pole to which four inflated girbas were attached; this is an excellent plan for assisting soldiers to cross a river, as they can land together in parties, instead of singly, with their guns dry, should the opposite bank be occupied by an enemy. I sat in my gun-case, with the two rifles that I used yesterday, in addition to the little Fletcher; heaps of clothes and sandals belonging to the swimmers formed my cargo; while, in case of accident, I had taken off my belt and shoes, and tied my ammunition within an inflated skin. Neptune in his car drawn by dolphins was not more completely at home than I in my gun-case, towed by my fish-like hippopotami hunters. After pirouetting in several strong whirlpools, during which time a crowd of women on the Sofi side of the river were screaming to Allah and the Prophet to protect us from crocodiles, we at length arrived.

"We took a direct course towards the animals I had shot on the previous evening, meeting with no game except a large troop of dog-faced baboons (Cynocephali), until we reached the body of the tetel (Antelopus Bubalis), which lay undisturbed; leaving people to flay it carefully, so that the skin should serve as a water or corn sack, we continued our path towards the dead giraffes.

"I had not proceeded far, before I saw, at about a mile distant, a motionless figure, as though carved from red granite; this I felt sure was a giraffe acting as sentry for another party that was not yet in view; I therefore sent my men on towards the dead giraffes, while, accompanied by Florian's black servant Richarn,[3] who was a good sportsman, and a couple of additional men, I endeavoured to stalk the giraffe. It was impossible to obtain a favourable wind, without exposing ourselves upon flat ground, where we should have been immediately perceived; I therefore arranged that my men should make a long circuit and drive the giraffe, while I would endeavour to intercept it. This plan failed; but shortly after the attempt, I observed a herd of about a hundred of these splendid creatures, browsing on the mimosas about half a mile distant. For upwards of three hours I employed every artifice to obtain a shot, but to no purpose, as upon my approach to within a quarter of a mile, they invariably chose open ground, leaving a sentry posted behind the herd, while two or three kept a look-out well in advance. No animal is so difficult to approach as the giraffe; however, by great patience and caution, I succeeded in reaching a long and deep ravine, by which I hoped to arrive within a close shot, as many of the herd were standing upon the level table-ground, from which this natural trench suddenly descended. I believe I should have arrived within fifty yards of the herd by this admirable approach, had it not been for the unlucky chance that brought me vis-a-vis with two tetel, that by galloping off attracted the attention of the giraffes. To add to my misfortune, after a long and tedious crawl on hands and knees up the narrow amid steep extremity of the gully, just as I raised my head above the edge of the table land, expecting to see the giraffes within fifty paces, I found three gazelles feeding within ten yards of me, while three magnificent giraffes were standing about a hundred and fifty yards distant.

"Off bounded the gazelles the instant that we were perceived; they of course gave the alarm immediately, and away went the giraffes; but I took a quick shot at the great leader as he turned to the right, and he staggered a few paces and fell headlong into the bush. Hurrah for the Ceylon No. 10! – however, neither the second barrel, nor a shot with the Manton 2-ounce, produced any effect. It was a glorious sight to see the herd of upwards of a hundred of these superb animals close up at the alarm of the shots, and

---

3   This faithful black, a native of the White Nile regions, subsequently became my servant, and, for four years accompanied us honestly and courageously through all our difficulties to the Albert N'yanza.

pelt away in a dense body through the dark green mimosa bush that hardly reached to their shoulders; but pursuit was useless. My giraffe was not quite dead, and, the throat having been cut by the Arabs and Richarn, we attempted to flay our game; this was simply impossible. The seroot fly was in swarms about the carcase, thousands were buzzing about our ears and biting like bull-dogs: the blood was streaming from our necks, and, as I wore no sleeves, my naked arms suffered terribly. I never saw such an extraordinary sight; although we had killed our giraffe, we could not take possession; it was no wonder that camels and all domestic animals were killed by this horrible plague, the only wonder was the possibility of wild animals resisting the attack. The long tails of the giraffes are admirable fly-whippers, but they would be of little service against such a determined and blood-thirsty enemy as the seroot. They were now like a swarm of bees, and we immediately made war upon the scourge, by lighting several fires within a few feet to windward of the giraffe; when the sticks blazed briskly, we piled green grass upon the tops, and quickly produced a smoke that vanquished the enemy.

"It was now about 3 P.M. and intensely hot; I had been in constant exercise since 6 A.M., therefore I determined upon luncheon under the shade of a welcome mimosa upon which I had already hung my water-skin to cool. We cut sonne long thin strips of flesh from the giraffe, and lighted a fire of dry babanoose wood expressly for cooking. This species of wood is exceedingly inflammable, and burns like a torch; it is intensely hard, and in colour and grain it is similar to lignum vitae. The festoons of giraffe flesh were hung upon forked sticks, driven into the ground to leeward of the fire, while others were simply thrown upon the embers by my men, who, while the food was roasting, employed themselves in skinning the animal, and in eating the flesh raw. The meat was quickly roasted, and was the best I have ever tasted, fully corroborating the praises I had frequently heard of giraffe meat from the Arab hunters. It would be natural to suppose that the long legs of this animal would furnish the perfection of marrow bones, but these are a disappointment, as the bones of the giraffe are solid, like those of the elephant and hippopotamus; the long tendons of the legs are exceedingly prized by the Arabs in lieu of thread for sewing leather, also for guitar strings.

"After luncheon, I took my little Fletcher rifle, and strolled down to the spot from whence I had fired the shot, as I wished to measure the distance, but no sooner had I arrived at the place than I observed at about a quarter of a mile below me, in the valley, a fine tetel; it was standing on the summit of one of the numerous knolls, evidently driven fronm the high grass by the flies. I stalked it very carefully until I arrived within about a hundred yards, and just as I reached the stem of a tree that I had resolved upon as my covering-point, the tetel got my wind, and immediately bounded off, receiving the bullet in the right hip at the same moment. After a few bounds it fell, and I ran forward to secure it, but it suddenly sprang to its feet, and went off at a surprising rate upon three legs. I believed I missed it, as I fired a quick shot just as it disappeared in the thick bushes. Whistling for my people, I was now joined by Bacheet and Richarn, my other men remaining with the giraffe. For about four miles we followed on the track through the broken valley of the Atbara, during which we several times disturbed the tetel, but could not obtain a good shot, on account of the high grass and thick bushes. Several times I tried a snap shot, as for a moment I caught sight of its red hide galloping through the bush, but as it ran down wind I had no chance of getting close to my game. At length, after following rapidly down a grassy ravine, I presently heard it pelting through the bushes; the ravine made a bend to the right, therefore, by taking a short cut, I arrived just in time to catch sight of the tetel as it passed over an open space below me; this time the little Fletcher bagged him. On examination I found that I had struck it four times. I had fired five shots, but as three of those had been fired almost at random, when the animal was in full speed through the bushes, one had missed, and the others were badly placed.

"Fortunately this long hunt had been in the direction of Sofi, to which we were near; still more fortunately, after we had marked the spot, we shortly met my first party of Arabs returning towards the village, heavily laden with giraffe's flesh, and the hide of one that I had killed yesterday. It appeared that during the night, lions and hyaenas had completely devoured one of the giraffes, not even leaving a vestige of skin or bone, but the immediate neighbourhood of the spot where it lay had been trampled into mud by the savage crowd who had left their footprints as witnesses to the robbery; the hide and bones had evidently been dragged away piecemeal.

"On arrival at the river we were all busy in preparing for the passage with so large a quantity of meat. The water-skins for the raft were quickly inflated, and I learnt from the Arabs an excellent contrivance for carrying a quantity of flesh across a river, without its becoming sodden. The skin of the tetel was nearly as capacious as that of an Alderney cow; this had been drawn off in the usual manner, so as to form a sack. The Arabs immediately proceeded to tie up the neck like the mouth of a bag, and to secure the apertures at the knees in like manner; when this operation was concluded, the skin became an immense sack, the mouth being at the aperture left at the hind-quarters. The No. 10 bullet had gone completely through the shoulders of the tetel, thus the two holes in the hide required stopping; this was dexterously performed by inserting a stone into either hole, of a size so much larger than the aperture, that it was impossible to squeeze them through. These stones were inserted from the inside of the sack; they were then grasped by the hand from the outside, and pulled forward, while a tight ligature was made behind each stone, which effectually stopped the holes. The skin of the tetel was thus converted into a waterproof bag, into which was packed a quantity of flesh sufficient to fill two-thirds of its capacity; the edges of the mouth were then carefully drawn together, and secured by tying. Thus carefully packed, one of the foreleg ligatures was untied, and the whole skin was inflated by blowing through the tube formed by the skin of the limb; the inflation completed, this was suddenly twisted round and tied. The skin thus filled looked like an exaggerated water-skin; the power of flotation was so great, that about a dozen men hung on to the legs of the tetel, and to each other's shoulders, when we launched it in the river. This plan is well worthy of the attention of military men; troops, when on service, are seldom without bullocks; in the absence of boats or rafts, not only can the men be thus safely conveyed across the river, but the ammunition can be packed within the skins, wrapped up in straw, and will be kept perfectly dry.

"The Arabs were much afraid of crocodiles this night, as it was perfectly dark when we had completed our preparations, and they feared that the snmell of so large a quantity of raw flesh, more especially the hide of the giraffe, which must be towed, would attract these beasts to the party; accordingly I fired several shots to alarm them, and the men plunged into the river, amidst the usual yelling of the women on the opposite side. Fires had been lighted to direct us, and all passed safely across.

"The sport upon the Abyssinian side of the river had been most satisfactory, and I resolved upon the first opportunity to change my quarters, and to form an encampment upon that bank of the Atbara until the proper season should arrive for travelling. I had killed three giraffes and two tetel in only two excursions. Florian, who was ill, had not been able to accompany me; although he had been shooting in this neighbourhood for two years he had never killed a giraffe. This want of success was owing to the inferiority of his weapons, that were not adapted to correct shooting at a range exceeding a hundred yards.

"On the following morning about fifty Arabs crossed the river with the intention of bringing the flesh of the giraffe, but they returned crestfallen in the evening, as again the lions and hyaenas had been before them, and nothing was left. I therefore resolved not to shoot again until I should be settled in my new camp on the other side of the river, as it was a wasteful expenditure of these beautiful animals unless the flesh could be preserved.

"The rainy season was drawing to a close, and I longed to quit the dulness of Sofi.

"September 12. – The river has fallen nearly eighteen feet, as the amount of rain has much decreased during the last week. Immense crocodiles are now to be seen daily, basking upon the muddy banks. One monster in particular, who is well known to the Arabs as having devoured a woman a few months ago, invariably sleeps upon a small island up the river.

"This evening I counted seven elephants on the east side of the river on the table lands.

"To-day the Arabs kept one of their holy feasts; accordingly, a sheep was slaughtered as a sacrifice, with an accompaniment of music and singing, i.e. howling to several guitars.

"The Arab system of an offering is peculiar. Should a friend be dangerously ill, or rain be demanded, or should any calamity befall them, they slaughter an ox if they possess it, or a sheep or goat in the absence of a larger animal, but the owner of the beast *sells* the meat in small portions to the assembled party, and the whole affair of sacrifice resolves itself into a feast; thus having filled thenmselves with good meat, they feel satisfied that they have made a religious sacrifice, and they expect the beneficial results. The guitar music and singing that attend the occasion are simply abominable. Music, although beloved like dancing by both the savage and civilized, varies in character according to the civilization of the race; that which is agreeable to the uneducated ear is discord to the refined nerves of the educated. The uutuned ear of the savage can no more enjoy the tones of civilized music than his palate would relish the elaborate dishes of a French chef de cuisine. As the stomach of the Arab prefers the raw meat and reeking liver taken hot from the animal, so does his ear prefer his equally coarse and discordant music to all other. The guitar most common is made of either the shell of a large gourd, or that of a turtle; over this is stretched an untanned skin, that of a large fish being preferred; through this two sticks are fixed about two feet three inches in length; the ends of these are fastened to a cross piece upon which are secured the strings; these are stretched over a bridge similar to those of a violin, and are either tightened or relaxed by rings of waxed rag fastened upon the cross piece – these rings are turned by the hand, and retain their position in spite of the strain upon the strings. Nothing delights an Arab more than to sit idly in his hut and strum this wretched instrument from morning until night."

I was thoroughly tired of Sofi, and I determined to move my party across the river to camp on the uninhabited side; the rains had almost ceased, therefore we should be able to live in the tent at night, and to form a shady nook beneath some mimosas by day; accordingly we busily prepared for a move.

Chapter IX.

Form a Raft With the Sponging Bath.

On the 15th September the entire male population of Sofi turned out to assist us in crossing the river, as I had promised them a certain sum should the move be effected without the loss or destruction of baggage. I had arranged a very superior raft to that I had formerly used, as I now had eight inflated skins attached to the bedstead, upon which I lashed our large circular sponging bath, which, being three feet eight inches in diameter, and of the best description, would be perfectly safe for my wife, and dry and commodious for the luggage. In a very short time the whole of our effects were carried to the water's edge, and the passage of the river commenced. The rifles were the first to cross with Bacheet, while the water-tight iron box that contained the gunpowder was towed like a pinnace behind the raft. Four hippopotami hunters were harnessed as tug steamers, while a change of swimmers waited to relieve them every alternate voyage. The raft answered admirably, and would easily support about three hundred pounds. The power of flotation of the sponging bath alone I had proved would support a hundred and ninety pounds, thus the only danger in crossing was the chance of a crocodile making a dash either at the inflated skins in mistake for the body of a man, or at the swimmers themselves. All the usual necessaries were safely transported, with the tents and personal baggage, before I crossed myself, with a number of Arabs. We quickly cleared the grass from the hard pebbly soil of a beautiful plateau on the summit of a craggy sandstone cliff, about eighty feet above the river; here we pitched the tents, close to some mimosas of dense foliage, and all being in order, I went down to the river to receive the next arrival. My wife now came across the ferry, and so perfectly had this means of transport succeeded, that by the evening, the whole of our stores and baggage had been delivered without the slightest damage, with the exception of a very heavy load of corn, that had caused the sponging bath to ship a sea during a strong squall of wind. The only person who had shown the least nervousness in trusting his precious body to my ferry-boat was Mahomet the dragoman, who, having been simply accustomed to the grand vessels of the Nile, was not prepared to risk himself in a voyage across the Atbara in a sponging bath. He put off the desperate attempt until the last moment, when every other person of my party had crossed; I believe he hoped that a wreck would take place before his turn should arrive, and thus spare him the painful necessity, but when at length the awful moment arrived, he was assisted carefully imito the bath by his servant Achmet and a number of Arabs, all of whom were delighted at his imbecility. Perched nervously in the centre of the bath, and holding on tight by either side, he was towed across with his travelling bag of clothes, while Achmet remained in charge of his best clothes and sundry other personal effects, that were to form the last cargo across the ferry. It appeared that Achmet, the dearly beloved and affectionate relative of Mahomet, who had engaged to serve him for simple love instead of money, was suddenly tempted by Satan, and seeing that Mahomet and the entire party were divided from him and the property in his charge, by a river two hundred yards wide, about forty feet deep, with a powerful current, he made up his mind to bolt with the valuables; therefore while Mahomet, in a nervous state in the ferry-bath, was being towed towards the east, Achmet turned in another direction and fled towards the west. Mahomet having been much frightened by the nautical effort he had been forced to make, was in an exceedingly bad temper upon the arrival on the opposite bank, and having at length succeeded in climbing up the steep ascent, in shoes that were about four sizes too large for him, he arrived on the lofty plateau of our camp, and doubtless would like ourselves have been charmed with the view of the noble river rushing between the cliffs of white sandstone, had he only seen Achmet his fond relative with his effects on the opposite bank. Mahomet strained his eyes, but the blank was no optical delusion; neither Achmet nor his effects were there. The Arabs, who hated the unfortunate Mahomet for his general overbearing conduct, now comforted him with the suggestion that Achmet had run away, and that his only chance was to re-cross the river and give chase. Mahomet would not have ventured upon another voyage to the other side and back again, for the world, and as to giving chase in boots (highlows) four sizes too big, and without strings, that would have been as absurd as to employ a donkey to catch a horse. Mahomet could do nothing but rush frantically to the very edge of the cliff, and scream and gesticulate to a crowd of Arab women who had passed the day beneath the shady trees by the Faky's grave, watching our passage of the Atbara. Beating his own head and tearing his hair were always the safety valves of Mahomet's rage, but as hair is not of that mushroom growth that reappears in a night, he had patches upon his cranium as bald as a pumpkin shell, from the constant plucking, attendant upon losses of temper; he now not only tore a few extra locks from his head, but he shouted out a tirade of abuse towards the far-distant Achmet, calling him a "son of a dog," cursing his father, and paying a few compliments to the memory of his mother, which if only half were founded upon fact were sad blots upon the morality of the family to which Mahomet himself belonged, through his close relationship to Achmet, whom he had declared to be his mother's brother's cousin's sister's mother's son.

A heavy shower of rain fell shortly after our camp was completed, when fortunately the baggage was under cover; this proved to be the last rain of the season, and from that moment the burning sun ruled the sodden country, and rapidly dried up not only the soil but all vegetation. The grass within a few days of the cessation of the rain assumed a tinge of yellow, and by the end of October there was not a green spot to relieve the eye from the golden blaze of the landscape, except the patches of grass and reeds that sprang from the mud banks of the retiring river. The climate was exceedingly unhealthy, but we were fortunately exceptions to the general rule, and although the inhabitants of Sofi were all sufferers, our camp had no invalids, with the exception of Mahomet, who had upon one occasion so gorged himself with half-putrid fish, that he nearly died in consequence. It would be impossible to commence our explorations in the Base until the grass should be sufficiently dry to burn; there were two varieties: that upon the slopes and hollows of the stony soil of the Atbara valley had been a pest ever since it had ripened; as the head formed three barbed darts, these detached themselves from the plant with such facility, that the slightest touch was sufficient to dislodge them; they immediately pierced the clothes, from which they could not be withdrawn, as the barbed heads broke off and remained. It was simply impossible to walk in this grass as it became ripe, without special protection; I accordingly tanned some gazelle skins, with which my wife constructed stocking gaiters, to be drawn over the foot and tied above and below the knee; thus fortified I could defy the grass, and indulge in shooting and exploring the neighbourhood until the season should arrive for firing the country. The high grass upon the table lands, although yellow, would not be sufficiently inflammable until the end of November.

The numerous watercourses that drained the table lands during the rainy season were now dry. No sooner had the grass turned yellow, than the pest of the country, the seroot fly, disappeared; thus the presence of this insect may be dated from about 10th July to 10th October. As the fly vanished, the giraffes also left the neighbourhood. By a few days' exploration, I found that the point of land from the junction of the Settite river with the Atbara, formed a narrow peninsula which was no wider than eight miles across from our encampment: thus the herds of game retreating from the south before the attacks of the seroot, found themselves driven into a cut-de-sac upon the strip of land between the broad and deep rivers the Settite and Atbara, which in the rainy season they dared not cross. All this country being uninhabited, there were several varieties of game at all seasons, but the three rainy months insure a good supply of elephants and giraffes; these retreat about thirty miles farther south, when permitted by the cessation of the flies to return to their favourite haunts.

My camp was in a very commanding position, as it was protected in front by the Atbara, and on the left by a perpendicular ravine about eighty feet deep, at the bottom of which flowed the rivulet called by the Arabs the "Till;" this joined the river immediately below our plateau. On our right was a steep and rugged incline covered with rocks of the whitest sandstone, through which ran veins of rich iron ore from four to five feet in width. I found a considerable quantity of fossil wood in the sandstone, and I had previously discovered on the Sofi side of the river, the fossil stem of a tree about twelve feet long; the grain appeared to be exceedingly close, but I could not determine the class to which the tree had belonged.

As the Atbara had fallen to the level of the small tributary, the Till, that stream was nearly exhausted, and the fish that inhabited its deep and shady waters during the rainy season were now fast retiring to the parent river. At the mouth of the stream were a number of rocks, that, as the water of the Atbara retreated, daily increased in size; these were evidently blocks that had been detached from the cliffs that walled in the Till. As we were now entirely dependent upon the rod and the rifle for the support of our party, I determined to try for a fish, as I felt quite certain that some big fellows in the main river would be waiting to receive the small fry that were hurrying away from the exhausted waters of the Till.

I had a good supply of tackle, and I chose a beautifully straight and tapering bamboo that had been brought down by the river floods. I cut off the large brass ring from a game-bag, which I lashed to the end of my rod; and having well secured my largest winch, that carried upwards of 200 yards of the strongest line, I arranged to fish with a live bait upon a set of treble hooks. In one of the rocks at the water's edge was a circular hole about three feet in diameter and five or six feet deep; this appeared like an artificial well, but it was simply the effect of natural boring by the joint exertions of the strong current conmbined with hard sand and gravel. This had perhaps years ago settled in some slight hollow in the rock, and had gradually worked out a deep well by perpetual revolutions. I emptied this natural bait box of its contents of sand and rounded pebbles, and having thoroughly cleaned and supplied it with fresh water, I caught a large number of excellent baits by emptying a hole in the Till; these I consigned to my aquarium. The baits were of various kinds: some were small "boulti" (a species of perch), but the greater number were young fish of the Silurus species; these were excellent, as they were exceedingly tough in the skin, and so hardy in constitution, that they rather enjoyed the fun of fishing. I chose a little fellow about four inches in length to begin with, and I delicately inserted the hook under the back fin. Gently dropping my alluring and lively little friend in a deep channel between the rocks and the mouth of the Till, I watched my large float with great interest, as, carried by the stream, it swept past the corner of a large rock into the open river; that corner was the very place where, if I had been a big fish, I should have concealed myself for a sudden rush upon an unwary youngster. The large green float sailed leisurely along, simply indicating, by its uneasy movement, that the bait was playing; and now it passed the point of the rock and hurried round the corner in the sharper current towards the open river. Off it went! – Down dipped the tip of the rod, with a rush so sudden that the line caught somewhere, I don't know where, and broke!

"Well, that was a monster!" I exclaimed, as I recovered my inglorious line; fortunately the float was not lost, as the hooks had been carried away at the fastening to the main line; a few yards of this I cut off, as it had partially lost its strength from frequent immersion.

I replaced the lost hooks by a still larger set, with the stoutest gimp and swivels, and once more I tried my fortune with a bait exactly resembling the first. In a short time I had a brisk run, and quickly landed a fish of about twelve pounds: this was a species known by the Arabs as the "bayard;" it has a blackish green back, the brightest silver sides and belly, with very peculiar back fins, that nearest to the tail being a simple piece of flesh free from rays. This fish has four long barbules in the upper jaw, and two in the lower: the air-bladder, when dried, forms a superior quality of isinglass, and the flesh of this fish is excellent. I have frequently seen the bayard sixty or seventy pounds' weight, therefore I was not proud of my catch, and I recommenced fishing. Nothing large could be tempted, and I only succeeded in landing two others of the same kind, one of about nine pounds, the smaller about six. I resolved upon my next trial to use a much larger bait, and I returned to camp with my fish for dinner.

The life at our new camp was charmingly independent; we were upon Abyssinian territory; but, as the country was uninhabited, we considered it as our own. I had previously arranged with the sheik of Sofi that, whenever the rifle should be successful and I could spare meat, I would hoist the English flag upon my flagstaff; thus I could at any time summon a crowd of hungry visitors, who were ever ready to swim the river and defy the crocodiles in the hope of obtaining flesh. We were exceedingly comfortable, having a large stock of supplies; in addition to our servants we had acquired a treasure in a nice old slave woman, whom we had hired from the sheik at a dollar per month to grind the corn. Masara (Sarah) was a dear old creature, the most willing and obliging specimen of a good slave; and she was one of those bright exceptions of the negro race that would have driven Exeter Hall frantic with enthusiasm. Poor old Masara! she had now fallen into the hands of a kind mistress, and as we were improving in Arabic, my wife used to converse with her upon the past and present; future had never been suggested to her simple mind. Masara had a weighty care; her daily bread was provided; money she had none, neither did she require it; husband she could not have had, as a slave has none, but is the common property of all who purchase her: but poor Masara had a daughter, a charming pretty girl of about seventeen, the offspring of one of the old woman's Arab masters. Sometimes this girl came to see her mother, and we arranged the bath on the inflated skins, and had her towed across for a few days. This was Masara's greatest happiness, but her constant apprehension; the nightmare of her life was the possibility that her daughter should be sold and parted from her. The girl was her only and all absorbing thought, the sole object of her affection: she was the moon in her mother's long night of slavery; without her, all was dark and hopeless. The hearts of slaves are crushed and hardened by the constant pressure of the yoke; nevertheless some have still those holy feelings of affection that nature has implanted in the human mind: it is the tearing asunder of those tender chains that renders slavery the horrible curse that it really is; human beings are reduced to the position of animals, without the blessings enjoyed by the brute creation – short memories and obtuse feelings.

Masara, Mahomet, Wat Gamma, and Bacheet, formed the establishment of Ehetilla, which was the Arab name of our locality. Bacheet was an inveterate sportsman and was my constant and sole attendant when shooting; his great desire was to accompany me in elephant-hunting, when he promised to carry one of my spare rifles as a trusty gun-bearer, and he vowed that no animal should ever frighten him.

A few extracts from my journal written at that time will convey a tolerable idea of the place and our employments.

"September 23. – Started for the Settite river. In about four hours' good marching N.N.E. through a country of grass and mimosa bush that forms the high land between that river and the Atbara, I reached the Settite about a mile from the junction. The river is about 250 yards wide, and flows through a broken valley of innumerable hillocks and deep ravines of about five miles in width, precisely similar in character to that of the Atbara; the soil having been denuded by the rains, and carried away by the floods of the river towards the Nile. The heat was intense; there was no air stirring; a cloudless sky and a sun like a burning-glass. We saw several nellut (Taurotragus strepsiceros), but these superb antelopes were too wild to allow a close approach. The evening drew near, and we had nothing to eat, when fortunately I espied a fine black-striped gazelle (Gazella Dorcas), and with the greatest caution I stalked it to within about a hundred paces, and made a successful shot with the Fletcher rifle, and secured our dinner. Thus provided, we selected a steep sugar-loaf-shaped hill, upon the peak of which we intended to pass the night. We therefore cleared away the grass, spread boughs upon the ground, lighted fires, and prepared for a bivouac. Having a gridiron, and pepper and salt, I made a grand dinner of liver and kidneys, while my men ate a great portion of the gazelle raw, and cooked the remainder in their usual careless manner by simply laying it upon the fire for a few seconds until warmed half through. There is nothing like a good gridiron for rough cooking; a frying-pan is good if you have fat, but without it, the pan is utterly useless. With a gridiron and a couple of iron skewers a man is independent: – the liver cut in strips and grilled with pepper and salt is excellent, but kabobs are sublime, if simply arranged upon the skewer in alternate pieces of liver and kidney cut as small as walnuts, and rubbed with chopped garlic, onions, cayenne, black pepper, and salt. The skewers thus arranged should be laid either upon the glowing embers, or across the gridiron.

"Not a man closed his eyes that night – not that the dinner disagreed with them – but the mosquitoes! Lying on the ground, the smoke of the fires did not protect us; we were beneath it, as were the mosquitoes likewise; in fact the fires added to our misery, as they brought new plagues in thousands of flying bugs; with beetles of all sizes and kinds: these, becoming stupified in the smoke, tumbled clumsily upon me, entangling themselves in my long beard and whiskers, crawling over my body, down my neck, and up my sleeping-drawers, until I was swarming with them; the bugs upon being handled squashed like lumps of butter, and emitted a perfume that was unbearable. The night seemed endless; it was passed in alternately walking to and fro, flapping right and left with a towel, covering my head with a pillow-case, and gasping for air through the button-hole, in an atmosphere insufferably sultry.

"At length morning dawned, thank Heaven! I made a cup of strong coffee, ate a morsel of dhurra bread, and started along the high ground parallel with the course of the Settite river up stream.

"After walking for upwards of four hours over ground covered with tracks of giraffes, elephants, and antelopes about a fortnight old, I saw four tetel (Antelopus Bubalis), but I was unfortunate in my shot at a long range in high grass. We had been marching south-east, and as I intended to return to camp, we now turned sharp to the west. The country was beautiful, composed of alternate glades, copses, and low mimosa forest. At length I espied the towering head of a giraffe about half a mile distant; he was in the mimosa forest, and was already speculating upon our party, which he had quickly observed. Leaving my men in this spot to fix his attention, I succeeded in making a good stalk to within one hundred and twenty yards of him. He was exactly facing me, and I waited for him to turn and expose the flank, but he suddenly turned so quickly that I lost the opportunity, and he received the bullet in his back as he started at full speed; for the moment he reeled crippled among the mimosas, but, recovering, he made off. I could not fire the left-hand barrel on account of the numerous trees and bushes. I called my men, and followed for a few hundred yards upon his track, but as this was directly in an opposite direction to that of my camp I was forced to give up the hunt.[4]

"About an hour later I hit a tetel with both barrels of the little Fletcher, at full gallop; but although we followed the blood-track for sonme distance, we did not recover it. At this season the grass is in most places from seven to ten feet high, and being trodden by numerous old tracks of animals, it is difficult to find a wounded beast without the assistance of a dog. The luck was against me to-day; I could only shoot well enough to hit everything, but to bag nothing, owing to a sleepless night. I killed a guinea-fowl to secure dinner upon my return, and we at length reached the welcome Atbara within two miles of my head-quarters. My men made a rush to the river, and threw themselves into the water, as all were more or less exhausted by the intense heat of the long day's work after a restless night. I took a good drink through my gazelle shank-bone, which I wear suspended from my neck for that purpose, and I went on alone, leaving my bathing party to refresh themselves. I reached the tent a little after 4 P.M. after more than ten hours' continual walking in the burning sun. I felt almost red hot, but my bath and clean linen being ready, thanks to the careful preparation of my wife, I was quickly refreshed, and sat down with a lion's appetite to good curry and rice, and a cup of black coffee.

---

4   We found the remains of the Giraffe a few days later.

"September 25. – Having nothing to eat, I took my fishing-rod and strolled down to the river, and chose from my aquarium a fish of about half a pound for a live bait; I dropped this in the river about twenty yards beyond the mouth of the Till, and allowed it to swim naturally down the stream so as to pass across the Till junction, and descend the deep channel between the rocks. For about ten minutes I had no run; I had twice tried the same water without success, nothing would admire my charming bait; when, just as it had reached the favourite turning-point at the extremity of a rock, away dashed the line, with the tremendous rush that follows the attack of a heavy fish. Trusting to the soundness of my tackle, I struck hard and fixed my new acquaintance thoroughly, but off he dashed down the stream for about fifty yards at one rush, making for a narrow channel between two rocks, through which the stream ran like a mill-race. Should he pass this channel, I knew he would cut the line across the rock; therefore, giving him the butt, I held him by main force, and by the great swirl in the water I saw that I was bringing him to the surface; but just as I expected to see him, my float having already appeared, away he darted in another direction, taking sixty or seventy yards of line without a check. I at once observed that he must pass a shallow sandbank favourable for landing a heavy fish; I therefore checked him as he reached this spot, and I followed him down the bank, reeling up line as I ran parallel with his course. Now came the tug of war! I knew my hooks were good and the line sound, therefore I was determined not to let him escape beyond the favourable ground; and I put a strain upon him, that after much struggling brought to the surface a great shovel-head, followed by a pair of broad silvery sides, as I led him gradualhy into shallow water. Bacheet now cleverly secured him by the gills, and dragged him in triumph to the shore. This was a splendid bayard, at least forty pounds' weight.

"I laid my prize upon some green reeds, and covered it carefully with the same cool material. I then replaced my bait by a lively fish, and once more tried the river. In a very short time I had another run, and landed a small fish of about nine pounds of the same species. Not wishing to catch fish of that size, I put on a large bait, and threw it about forty yards into the river, well up the stream, and allowed the float to sweep the water in a half circle, thus taking the chance of different distances from the shore. For about half an hour nothing moved; I was just preparing to alter my position, when out rushed my line, and striking hard, I believed I fixed the old gentleman himself, for I had no control over him whatever; holding him was out of the question; the line flew through my hands, cutting them till the blood flowed, and I was obliged to let the fish take his own way: this he did for about eighty yards, when he suddenly stopped. This unexpected halt was a great calamity, for the reel overran itself, having no check-wheel, and the slack bends of the line caught the handle just as he again rushed forward, and with a jerk that nearly pulled the rod from my hands he was gone! I found one of my large hooks broken short off; the confounded reel! The fish was a monster!

"After this bad luck I had no run until the evening, when putting on a large bait, and fishing at the tail of a rock between the stream and still water, I once more had a grand rush, and hooked a big one. There were no rocks down stream, all was fair play and clear water, and away he went at racing pace straight for the middle of the river. To check the pace, I grasped the line with the stuff of my loose trousers, and pressed it between my fingers so as to act as a break, and compel him to labour for every yard; but he pulled like a horse, and nearly cut through the thick cotton cloth, making straight running for at least a hundred yards without a halt. I now put so severe a strain upon him, that my strong bamboo bent nearly double, and the fish presently so far yielded to the pressure, that I could enforce his running in half circles instead of straight away. I kept gaining line, until I at length led him into a shallow bay, and after a great fight, Bacheet embraced him by falling upon him, and clutching the monster with hands and knees; he then tugged to the shore a magnificent fish of upwards of sixty pounds. For about twenty minutes he had fought against such a strain as I had never before used upon a fish, but I had now adopted hooks of such a large size and thickness that it was hardly possible for them to break, unless snapped by a crocodile. My reel was so loosened from the rod, that had the struggle lasted a few minutes longer I must have been vanquished. This fish measured three feet eight inches to the root of the tail, and two feet three inches in girth of shoulders; the head measured one foot ten inches in circumference – it was the same species as those I had already caught.

"This closed the sport for the day. We called all hands to carry the fish to camp, and hoisted the flag, which was quickly followed by the arrival of a number of men from Sofi, to receive all that we could spare. The largest fish we cut into thin strips, – these we salted and dried; the head made delicious soup, with a teaspoonful of curry-powder.

"September 26. – The weather is now intensely hot, and the short spear grass is drying so rapidly that in some stony places it can be fired. The birds appear to build their nests at various seasons. Many that built three months ago are again at work; among others is a species of black Mina, that takes entire possession of a tree, which it completely covers with nests coarsely constructed of sticks. A few days ago I found several trees converted into colonies of many hundred dwellings.

"I never allow either the monkeys or baboons to be disturbed: thus they have no fear of our party, but with perfect confidence they approach within thirty or forty yards of the tents, sitting upon the rocks and trees, and curiously watching all that takes place in the camp. I have only seen one species of monkey in this neighbourhood – a handsome dark grey animal with white whiskers. The baboons are also of one species, the great dog-faced ape (Cynocephalus); these grow to a very large size, and old Masara fully expects to be carried off and become the wife of an old baboon, if they are allowed to become so bold.

"This afternoon I took a stroll with the rifle, but saw nothing except a young crocodile about six feet long; this was on the dry summit of a hill, far from water. I shot it and took the skin. I can only conclude that the small stream in which he had wandered from the river-bed had become dry, and the creature had lost its way in searching for other water.

"September 27. – I started from the tent at 6 A.M. and made a circuit of about eighteen miles, seeing nothing but tetel and gazelles, but I had no luck. Hot and disgusted, I returned home, and took the rod, hoping for better luck in the river. I hooked, but lost, a small fish, and I began to think that the fates were against me by land and water, when I suddenly had a tremendous run, and about a hundred and fifty yards rushed off the reel without the possibility of stopping the fish. The river was very low; thus I followed along the bank, holding hard, and after about half an hour of difference of opinion, the fish began to show itself, and I coaxed it into the shallows; here it was cleverly managed by Bacheet, who lugged it out by the tail. It was an ugly monster, of about fifty pounds, a species of silurus, known by the Arabs as the 'coor;' it differed from the silurus of Europe by haviimg a dorsal fin, like a fringe, that extended along the back to the tail. This fish had lungs resembling delicate branches of red coral, and, if kept moist, it would exist upon the land for many hours like an eel. It smelt strongly of musk, but it was gladly accepted by the Sheik of Sofi, who immediately answered to the flag.

"While shooting this morning I came suddenly upon a small species of leopard that had just killed a snake about five feet in length; the head was neatly bitten off and lay upon the ground near the body; the animal was commencing a meal off the snake when it was disturbed, and I lost sight of it immediately in the high grass.

"September 28. – The heat is most oppressive: even the nights are hot, until about 2 A.M., at which hour a cool breeze springs up. The wind now blows from the south until about 1 P.M., when it changes suddenly to the north, and then varies between these two points during the rest of the day; this leads me to hope that the north wind will shortly set in. September, as in England, is the autumn of this land; the wild fruits are ripe, some of which are not unpleasant, but they are generally too sweet, – they lack the acidity that would be agreeable in this burning climate. There is an orange-coloured berry that has a pleasant flavour, but it is extremely oily; this has a peculiarly disagreeable effect upon the system, if eaten in any quantity. Several varieties of excellent wild vegetables grow in great abundance throughout this country: beans, three kinds of spinach; the juicy, brittle plant cultivated in Lower Egypt, and known as the 'regle;' and lastly, that main-stay of Arab cookery, 'waker,' well known in Ceylon and India under the names of 'Barmian' and 'Bandikai.' This grows to the height of thirteen or fourteen feet in the rich soil of the table lands: the Arabs gather the pods and cut them into thin slices; these are dried in the sun, and then packed in large sacks for market. The harvest of waker is most important, as no Arab dish would be perfect without the admixture of this agreeable vegetable. The dried waker is ground into powder between two stones; this, if boiled with a little gravy, produces a gelatinous and highly-flavoured soup.

"September 29. – We have just heard that Atalan Wat Said, by whom we were so well received, is dead! The Arabs have a disagreeable custom of paying honours to a guest by keeping the anniversary of the death of any relatives whose decease should be known to them; thus, when Atalan Wat Said paid a visit to Sheik Achmet Abou Sinn, the latter celebrated with much pomp the anniversary of his (Atalan's) late father's death. The unfortunate guest, who happened to arrive in Abou Sinn's camp upon the exact day upon which his father had died in the precedimig year, was met by a mourning crowd, with the beating of drums, the howling of women, and the loud weeping and sorrowful condoling of the men. This scene affected Atalan Wat Said to such a degree, that, being rather unwell, he immediately sickened with fever, and died in three days. In this country any grief of mind will insure an attack of fever, when all are more or less predisposed during the unhealthy season, from the commencement of July until the end of October.

"This afternoon I took the rod, and having caught a beautiful silver-sided fish of about a pound weight, I placed it upon a large single hook fastened under the back fin. In about an hour I had a run, but upon striking, I pulled the bait out of the fish's mouth, as the point of the hook had not touched the jaw. I had wound up slowly for about thirty yards, hoping that the big fellow would follow his lost prize, as I knew him to be a large fish by his attack upon a bait of a pound weight. I found my bait was killed, but having readjusted the hook, I again cast it in the same direction, and slowly played it towards me. I had him! He took it immediately, and I determined to allow him to swallow it before I should strike. Without a halt, about a hundred yards of line were taken at the first rush towards the middle of the river; he then stopped, and I waited for about a minute, and then fixed him with a jerk that bent my bamboo like a fly-rod. To this he replied by a splendid challenge; in one jump he flew about six feet above the water, and showed himself to be one of the most beautiful fish I had ever seen; not one of those nondescript antediluvian brutes that you expect to catch in these extraordinary rivers, but in colour he appeared like a clean run salmon. He gave tremendous play, several times leaping out of the water, and shaking his head furiously to free himself from the hook; then darting away with eighty or a hundred yards of fresh line, until he at last was forced to yield to the strong and elastic bamboo, and his deep body stranded upon the fatal shallows.

"Bacheet was a charming lad to land a fish: he was always quiet and thoughtful, and never got in the way of the line; this time he closely approached him from behind, slipped both his hands along his side, and hooked his fingers into the broad gills; thus he dragged him, splashing through the shallows, to the sandbank. What a beauty! What was he? The colour was that of a salmon, and the scales were not larger in proportion: he was about fifty pounds' weight. The back fin resembled that of a perch, with seven rays; the second, dorsal fin towards the tail had fourteen rays; the head was well shaped, and small in proportion; the eyes were bright red, and shone like rubies; and the teeth were very small. I cut away my line, as the hook was deeply swallowed; and after having washed this beautiful fish, I assisted Bacheet to carry it to the camp, where it was laid upon a clean mat at the tent-door for admiration. This species of fish is considered by the Arabs to be the best in the river; it is therefore called 'El Baggar' (the cow). It is a species of perch, and we found it excellent – quite equal to a fine trout. I made an exact sketch of it on the spot, after which the greater portion was cut up and salted; it was then smoked for about four hours. The latter process is necessary to prevent the flies from blowing it, before it becomes sufficiently dry to resist their attacks.

"For several days I passed my time in fishing, with the varying success that must attend all fishermen. Upon the extreme verge of the river's bank were dense bushes of the nabbuk, about fifteen feet high, but so thickly massed with green foliage that I cut out a tunnel with my hunting-knife, and completed a capacious arbour, thoroughly protected from the sun. In this it was far more agreeable to pass the day than at the camp; accordingly we arranged the ground with mats and carpets, and my wife converted the thorny bower into an African drawing-room, where she could sit with her work and enjoy the view of the river at her feet, and moreover watch the fishing."

Chapter X.

A Few Notes at Ehetilla.

I will not follow the dates of the journal consecutively, but merely pounce from time to time upon such passages as will complete the description of our life at Ehetilla.

"October 4. – I went out fishing in the usual place, where the Till joins the Atbara; the little stream has disappeared, and the bed is now perfectly dry, but there are many large rocks and sandbanks in the river, which are excellent places for heavy fish. I had only three runs, but I landed them all. The first was a beautiful baggar about forty pounds, from which time a long interval elapsed before I had another. I placed a bait of about a pound upon my treble hook, and this being a fine lively fellow, was likely to entice a monster. I was kept waiting for a considerable time, but at last he came with the usual tremendous rush. I gave him about fifty yards of line before I fixed him, and the struggle then commenced, as usual with the baggar, by his springing out of the water, and showing his superb form and size. This was a magnificent fish, and his strength was so great, that in his violent rushes he would take sixty or seventy yards of line without my permission. I could not check him, as the line burnt and cut my fingers to such a degree that I was forced to let it go, and my only way of working him was to project the butt of the rod in the usual manner; this was a very feeble break upon the rush of such a fish. At last, after about half an hour of alternate bullying and coaxing, I got him into the shallows, and Bacheet attempted to manage him; this time he required the assistance of Wat Gamma, who quickly ran down from the camp, and after much struggling, an enormous baggar of between seventy and eighty pounds was hauled to the shore by the two delighted Arabs.

"I never enjoyed the landing of a fish more than on the present occasion, and I immediately had the flag hoisted for a signal, and sent the largest that I had just caught as a present to Florian and his people. The two fish as they lay upon the green reeds, glittering in silvery scales, were a sight to gladden the eyes of a fisherman, as their joint weight was above one hundred and twenty pounds. I caught another fish in the evening something over twenty pounds, an ugly and useful creature, the coor, that I despised, although it is a determined enemy while in play.

"October 10. – Set fire to the low spear grass of the valley. The river is now very low, exposing in many places large beds of shingle, and rocks hitherto concealed. The water level is now about thirty feet below the dried sedges and trash left by the high floods upon the overhanging boughs. The bed of the Atbara, and that of the Settite, are composed of rounded pebbles of all sizes, and masses of iron ore. Large oysters (Etheria), resembling the pearl oysters of Ceylon, are very numerous, and, from their internal appearance, with large protuberances of pearl matter, I should imagine they would most probably yield pearls.

"The wild animals have now deserted this immediate neighbourhood; the only creatures that are to be seen in numbers are the apes and monkeys: these throng the sides of the river, eating the tamarinds from the few large trees, and collecting gum from the mimosas. These hungry animals gather the tamarinds before they ripen, and I fear they will not leave a handful for us; nothing is more agreeable in this hot climate than the acidity of tamarind water. I remarked a few days ago, when walking along the dry sandy bed of the Till about five miles from the river, that the monkeys had been digging wells in the sand for water.

"Many changes are now taking place in the arrival and departure of various birds according to their migrations; immense numbers of buzzards and hawks have arrived, and keep my fowls in perpetual alarm. Ducks fly in large flocks up stream invariably, every day; storks of different kinds are arriving. Among the new comers is a beautiful little bird, in size and shape like a canary, but of a deep bluish black, with an ivory white bill and yellow lips. The beasts of prey are hungry, as the game has become scarce: – there is no safety for tame animals, and our goats will not feed, as they are constantly on the look-out for danger, starting at the least sound in the bushes, and running to the tents for security: thus their supply of milk is much reduced.

"The Sheik of Sofi, Hassan bel Kader, swam across the river with a present of fowls; these he had tied upon his head to prevent them from drowning. This man is a celebrated hippopotamus hunter, and I look forward to accompanying him upon a harpooning expedition, when the river is lower. His father was killed by a bull hippo that he had harpooned; the infuriated animal caught the unfortunate hunter in his jaws, and with one nip disembowelled him before his son's eyes. Accidents are constantly occurring in this dangerous sport, as the hunters are so continually in the water that they are exposed, like baits, to the attacks of crocodiles. During the last season one of the sheik's party was killed; several men were swimming the river, supported by inflated skins, when one was suddenly seized by a crocodile. Retaining his hold upon the support, his comrades had time to clutch him by the hair, and beneath the arms; thus the crocodile could not drag the buoyant skins beneath the surface. Once he was dragged from their grasp, but holding to his inflated skin, he regained the surface, and was again supported by his friends, who clung to him, while he implored them to hold him tight, as the crocodile still held him by the leg. In this way the hunters assisted him; at the same time they struck downwards with their spears at the determined brute, until they at last drove it from its hold. Upon gaining the shore, they found that the flesh of the leg from the knee downwards had been stripped from the bone, and the poor fellow shortly died.

"October 11. – The Arabs have murdered one of the Egyptian soldiers, about five miles from Sofi. All my people are more or less ill, but we, thank Heaven, are in excellent health; in fact, I have never been better than in this country, although I am constantly in hard exercise in the burning sun.

"October 15. – A fine breeze, therefore I set fire to the grass in all directions, which spread into a blaze over many miles of country. The fire immediately attracts great numbers of fly-catchers and buzzards; these hover in the smoke to catch the locusts and other insects that escape from the heat. Buzzards are so exceedingly bold, that it is one person's special duty to protect the strips of flesh when an animal is being cut up, at which time many scores collect, and swoop down upon their prey clutching a piece of meat with their claws, if left unguarded for a moment. Upon one occasion, the cook had just cleaned a fish of about a pound and a half weight, which he laid upon the ground while he stooped to blow the fire; in an instant a large buzzard darted upon it, and carried it off.

"Africa may have some charms, but it certainly is rather a trying country; in the rainy weather we have the impenetrable high grass, the flies, and the mud; when those entertainments are over, and the grass has ripened, every variety of herb and bush is more or less armed with lances, swords, daggers, bayonets, knives, spikes, needles, pins, fish-hooks, hay-forks, harpoons, and every abomination in the shape of points which render a leather suit indispensable to a sportsman, even in this hot climate. My knickerbockers are made of the coarse but strong Arab cotton cloth, that I have dyed brown with the fruit of the Acacia Arabica; but after a walk of a few minutes, I am one mass of horrible points from the spear grass, for about a foot from the upper part of my gaiters; the barbed points having penetrated, break off, and my trousers are as comfortable as a hedgehog's skin turned inside out, with the 'woolly side in.'

"I long for the time when the entire country will be dry enough to burn, when fire will make a clean sweep of these nuisances.

"October 17. – The sheik and several Arabs went to the Settite to sow tobacco; they simply cast the seed upon the sandy loam left by the receding river, without even scratching the soil; it is thus left to take its chance. I accompanied him to the Settite, and came upon the tracks of a herd of about fifty elephants that had crossed the river a few days previous. As we were walking through the high grass we came upon a fine boa-constrictor (python), and not wishing to fire, as I thought I might disturb elephants in the neighbourhood, I made a cut at it with my heavy hunting-knife, nearly severing about four feet from the tail, but it escaped in the high grass.

"October 18. – A lion paid us a visit last night, roaring close to the tent at intervals, frightening Mahomet out of his wits.

"The seroot fly has entirely disappeared, and immense dragon flies are now arrived, and are greedily attacking all other flying insects.

"October 19. – Troops of baboons are now exceedingly numerous, as the country being entirely dried up, they are forced to the river for water, and the shady banks covered with berry-bearing shrubs induce them to remain. It is very amusing to watch these great male baboons stalking majestically along, followed by a large herd of all ages, the mothers carrying their little ones upon their backs, the latter with a regular jockey-seat riding most comfortably, while at other times they relieve the monotony of the position by sprawling at full length and holding on by their mother's back hair. Suddenly a sharp-eyed young ape discovers a bush well covered with berries, and his greedy munching being quickly observed, a general rush of youngsters takes place, and much squabbling for the best places ensues among the boys; this ends in great uproar when down comes a great male, who cuffs one, pulls another by the hair, bites another on the hind quarters just as he thinks he has escaped, drags back a would-be deserter by his tail and shakes him thoroughly, and thus he shortly restores order, preventing all further disputes by sitting under the bush and quietly enjoying the berries by himself. These baboons have a great variety of expressions that may perhaps represent their vocabulary: a few of these I begin to understand, such as their notes of alarm, and the cry to attract attention; thus, when I am sitting alone beneath the shade of a tree to watch their habits, they are at first not quite certain what kind of a creature I may be, and they give a peculiar cry to induce me to move and show myself more distinctly.

"October 20. – A lion was roaring throughout the night not far from the tent on his way towards the river to drink; at every roar he was answered by the deep angry cry of the baboons, who challenged him immediately from their secure positions on the high rocks and trees. I found the tracks of his large feet upon the bank of the river, but there is no possibility of finding these animals in the daytime, as they retire to the high grass upon the table lands.

"The banks of the Atbara are now swarming with small birds that throng the bushes (a species of willow), growing by the water's edge; the weight of a large flock bends down the slender boughs until they touch the water: this is their opportunity for drinking, as their beaks for an instant kiss the stream. These unfortunate little birds get no rest, the large fish and the crocodiles grab at them when they attempt to drink, while the falcons and hawks pursue them at all times and in every direction. Nothing is fat, as nothing can obtain rest, the innumerable birds and beasts of prey give no peace to the weaker kinds; the fattest alderman of the city of London would become a skeleton, if hunted for two hours daily by a hyaena.

"October 23. – This evening I took a walk, accompanied by my wife, and Bacheet with a spare gun, to try for a shot at guinea-fowl. We were strolling along the margin of the river, when we heard a great shrieking of women on the opposite side, in the spot from which the people of Sofi fetch their water. About a dozen women had been filling their water-skins, when suddenly they were attacked by a large crocodile, who attempted to seize a woman, but she, springing back, avoided it, and the animal swallowed her girba (water-skin), that, being full of water and of a brown exterior, resembled the body of a woman. The women rushed out of the river, when the crocodile made a second dash at them, and seized another water-skin that a woman had dropped in her flight. They believe this to be the same monster that took a woman a few months ago. Few creatures are so sly and wary as the crocodile. I watch them continually as they attack the dense flocks of small birds that throng the bushes at the water's edge. These birds are perfectly aware of the danger, and they fly from the attack, if possible. The crocodile then quietly and innocently lies upon the surface, as though it had appeared quite by an accident; it thus attracts the attention of the birds, and it slowly sails away to a considerable distance, exposed to their view. The birds, thus beguiled by the deceiver, believe that the danger is removed, and they again flock to the bush, and once more dip their thirsty beaks into the stream. Thus absorbed in slaking their thirst, they do not observe that their enemy is no longer on the surface. A sudden splash, followed by a huge pair of jaws beneath the bush that engulfs some dozens of victims, is the signal unexpectedly given of the crocodile's return, who has thus slyly dived, and hastened under cover of water to his victims. I have seen the crocodiles repeat this manoeuvre constantly; they deceive by a feigned retreat, and then attack from below.

"In like manner the crocodile perceives, while it is floating on the surface in mid-stream, or from the opposite side of the river, a woman filling her girba, or an animal drinking, &c. &c. Sinking immediately, it swims perhaps a hundred yards nearer, and again appearing for an instant upon the surface, it assures itself of the position of its prey by a stealthy look; once more it sinks, and reaches the exact spot above which the person or animal may be. Seeing distinctly through the water, it generally makes its fatal rush from beneath – sometimes seizing with its jaws, and at other times striking the object into the water with its tail, after which it is seized and carried off.

"The crocodile does not attempt to swallow a large prey at once, but generally carries it away and keeps it for a considerable time in its jaws in some deep hole beneath a rock, or the root of a tree, where it eats it at leisure. The tongue of the crocodile is so unlike that of any other creature that it can hardly be called by the same name; no portion throughout the entire length is detached from the flesh of the lower jaw – it is more like a thickened membrane from the gullet to about half way along the length of jaw.

"October 4. – Having burnt off a large surface of high grass, I discovered a quantity of gourds and wild cucumbers – the latter are bright crimson, covered with long fleshy prickles, with black horny tips; these are eaten by the baboons, but not by the Arabs. The gourds are only serviceable for cups and ladles manufactured from their shells.

"I find a good pair of Highland shooting shoes of great value; the soles were exceedingly thick, and they have resisted, until now, the intensely hard and coarse-grained sandstone which grinds through all leather. My soles are at length worn out, and I have repaired them with the tanned hide of giraffe. Much of the sandstone is white and soft and friable; but this appears to have been decomposed by time and exposure, as the generality is hard and would make excellent grindstones.

"October 25. – Three elephant-hunters arrived to-day with horses for sale. I purchased three – a bay and two greys. They are all of Abyssinian breed, and are handsome animals, although none exceed fourteen hands and a half. The prices were high for this part of the world where dollars are scarce; but to me, they appeared to be absurdly cheap. The bay horse was a regular strong-built cob; for him I paid nineteen dollars – about 4*l*. including a native saddle and bridle; for the greys, I paid fifteen and thirteen dollars, saddles and bridles also included. The bay I named Tetel (hartebeest), the greys Aggahr[5] and Gazelle. Tetel was a trained hunter, as was Aggahr likewise. Gazelle was quite inexperienced, but remarkably handsome. None of these horses had ever been shod, but their hoofs were beautifully shaped, and as hard as ivory. The saddles had no stuffing on the seats, but were simple wooden frames, with high backs and pommels, the various pieces being sewn together with raw hide, and the front and back covered with crocodile skin. The stirrups were simple iron rings, sufficiently large to admit the great toe of the rider, according to Arab fashion in these parts. The bits were dreadfully severe; but perhaps not unnecessarily, as the sword allows only one bridle-hand to a pulling horse. Each horse was furnished with a leathern nose-bag, and a long leathern thong as a picket strap. All these horses and saddlery I had purchased for forty-seven dollars, or 9l. 10s. Fortunately, both my wife and I were well provided with the best English saddles, bridles, &c. or the 'big toe' stirrup would have been an awkward necessity.

"October 26. – We left our camp this morning for a few days' reconnaissance of the country, accompanied by Florian, prior to commencing our regular expedition. Nine miles s.e. of Ehetilla we passed through a village called Wat el Negur, after which we continued along a great tract of table land, on the eastern side of the Atbara valley, bounded by a mimosa forest about four miles on the east. Very large quantities of dhurra (Sorghum vulgare) are grown upon this fertile soil; it is now higher than a man's head when mounted upon a camel. Far as the eye can reach, the great table lands extend on either side the broad valley of the Atbara. The cotton that was planted many years ago by the inhabitants who have vanished, still flourishes, although choked with grass six or seven feet high. At 4 P.M. we reached a large village, Sherif el Ibrahim, twenty-eight miles s.e. from Sofi by the route upon the east bank of the Atbara, which cuts off a bend in the river. A species of dhurra, as sweet as the sugar-cane, grows here in abundance, being regularly sown and cultivated; it is called ankoleep. This is generally chewed in the mouth as a cane; but it is also peeled by the women, and, when dried, it is boiled with milk to give it sweetness. A grain called dochan, a species of millet, is likewise cultivated to a considerable extent; when ripe, it somewhat resembles the head of the bulrush. The whole of this country would grow cotton and sugar to perfection.

"October 28. – Having slept at the village, we went to the river, and Florian shot a hippopotamus. The natives, having skinned it, rushed at the carcase with knives and axes, and fought over it like a pack of wolves; neither did they leave the spot until they had severed each bone, and walked off with every morsel, of this immense beast.

---

5 Aggahr is the designation of a hunter with the sword.

"October 31. – Having passed a couple of days at Sherif el Ibrahim, we started for the Settite. When about half way, we arrived at a curious plateau of granite rock, with a pool of water in the centre. Formerly a large village occupied this position, named Gerrarat; but it was destroyed in a raid by the Egyptians, as being one of Mek Nimmur's strongholds. The rock is a flat surface of about five acres, covered with large detached fragments of granite; near this are several pools of water, which form the source of the rivulet, the Till, that bounds our camp at Ehetilla. A large homera-tree (Adansonia digitata) grows among the blocks of granite by the pool; in the shade of its enormous boughs we breakfasted, and again started at 4 P.M. reaching the Settite river at 7.30, at a spot named Geera. In the dark we had some difficulty in finding our way down the rugged slopes of the valley to the river. We had not taken beds, as these incumbrances were unnecessary when in light marching order. We therefore made separate bivouacs, Florian and his people about a hundred yards distant, while a rug laid upon the ground was sufficient for my wife. I made myself comfortable in a similar manner. Lions were roaring all night.

"On the following morning we took a long stroll along the wild and rugged valley of the Settite, that was precisely similar to that of the Atbara. The river, although low, was a noble stream, and the water was at this season beautifully clear as it ran over a bed of clean pebbles. The pass between the cliffs of Geera was exceedingly lovely. At that point the river did not exceed 200 yards in width, and it flowed through abrupt cliffs of beautiful rose-coloured limestone; so fine and pure was the surface of the stone, that in places it resembled artificially-smoothed marble; in other places, the cliffs, equally abrupt, were of milk-white limestone of similar quality. This was the first spot in which I had found limestone since I had left Lower Egypt. The name 'Geera,' in Arabic, signifies lime. Formerly this was an important village belonging to Mek Nimmur, but it had been destroyed by the Egyptians, and the renowned Mek Nimmur was obliged to fall back to the strongholds of the mountains.

"I started off a man to recall Mahomet and my entire camp fronm Ehetilla to Wat el Negur, as that village was only seven hours' march from Geera; the three points, Sherif el Ibrahim, Geera, and Wat el Negur formed almost an equilateral triangle. We reached the latter village on the following day, and found that Mahomet and a string of camels from Sofi had already arrived. The country was now thickly populated on the west bank of the Atbara, as the Arabs and their flocks had returned after the disappearance of the seroot fly. Mahomet had had an accident, having fallen from his camel and broken no bones, but he had smashed the stock of my single-barrel rifle; this was in two pieces; I mended it, and it become stronger than ever. The wood had broken short off in the neck of the stock, I therefore bored a hole about three inches deep up the centre of either piece, so that it was hollowed like a marrow-bone; in one of them I inserted a piece of an iron ramrod, red-hot, I then drew the other piece over the iron in a similar manner, and gently tapped the shoulder-plate until I had driven the broken joint firmly together. I then took off from a couple of old boxes two strong brass hasps; these I let neatly into the wood on each side of the broken stock, and secured them by screws, filing off all projections, so that they fitted exactly. I finished the work by stretching a piece of well-soaked crocodile's skin over the joint, which, when drawn tight, I sewed strongly together. When this dried it became as hard as horn, and very much stronger; the extreme contraction held the work together like a vice, and my rifle was perfectly restored. A traveller in wild countries should always preserve sundry treasures that will become invaluable, such as strips of crocodile skin, the hide of the iguana, &c. which should be kept in the tool-box for cases of need. The tool-box should not exceed two feet six inches in length, and one foot in depth, but it should contain the very best implements that can be made, with an extra supply of gimlets, awls, centre-bits, and borers of every description, also tools for boring iron; at least two dozen files of different sorts should be included."

Wat el Negur was governed by a most excellent and polite sheik of the Jalyn tribe. Sheik Achmet Wat el Negur was his name and title; being of the same race as Mek Nimmur, he dared to occupy the east bank of the Atbara. Sheik Achmet was a wise man; he was a friend of the Egyptian authorities, to whom he paid tribute as though it were his greatest pleasure; he also paid tribute to Mek Nimmur, with whom he was upon the best of terms; therefore, in the constant fights that took place upon the borders, the cattle and people of Sheik Achmet were respected by the contending parties, while those of all others were sufferers. This was exactly the spot for my head-quarters, as, like Sheik Achmet, I wished to be on good terms with everybody, and through him I should be able to obtain an introduction to Mek Nimmur, whom I particularly wished to visit, as I had heard that there never was such a brigand. Accordingly, I pitched the tents and formed a camp upon the bank of the river, about two hundred yards below the village of Wat el Negur, and in a short time Sheik Achmet and I became the greatest friends.

There is nothing more delightful when travelling in a strange country, a thousand miles away from the track of the wildest tourist, than to come upon the footprint of a countryman; not the actual mark of his sole upon the sand, which the dust quickly obscures, but to find imprinted deeply upon the minds and recollections of the people, the good character of a former traveller, that insures you a favourable introduction. Many years before I visited Wat el Negur, Mr. Mansfield Parkyns, who has certainly written the best book on Abyssinia that I have ever read, passed through this country, having visited Mek Nimmur, the father of the present Mek. He was, I believe, the only European that had ever been in Mek Nimmur's territory, neither had his footsteps been followed until my arrival. Mr. Parkyns had left behind him what the Arabs call a "sweet name;" and as I happened to have his book, "Life in Abyssinia," with me, I showed it to the sheik as his production, and explained the illustrations, &c.; at the same time I told him that Mr. Parkyns had described his visit to Mek Nimmur, of whom he had spoken very highly, and that I wished to have an opportunity of telling the great chief in person how much his good reception had been appreciated. The good Sheik Achmet immediately promised to present me to Mek Nimmur, and wished particularly to know whether I intended to write a book like Mr. Parkyns upon my return. Should I do so, he requested me to mention HIS name. I promised at once to do this trifling favour; thus I have the greatest pleasure in certifying that Sheik Achmet Wat el Negur is one of the best and most agreeable fellows that I have ever met in Africa; he does not keep an hotel, or I would strongly recommend it to all travellers, but his welcome is given gratis, with the warmest hospitality.

The country for several miles upon the table land above Wat el Negur was highly cultivated, and several thousand acres were planted with dhurra, that was at this season in full grain, and nearly ripe. Much sesame was grown for the manufacture of oil; cotton was also cultivated, and the neighbourhood was a fair example of the wonderful capabilities of the entire country that was allowed to lie in idleness. There was little rest for the inhabitants at this time, as the nights were spent in watching their extensive plantations, and endeavouring to scare away the elephants. These animals, with extreme cunning, invaded the dhurra crops at different positions every night, and retreated before morning to great distances in the thick thorny jungles of the Settite.

Our arrival was welcomed with general enthusiasm, as the Arabs were unprovided with fire-arms, and the celebrated aggageers or swordhunters were useless, as the elephants only appeared at night, and were far too cunning to give them a chance. There was a particular range of almost impenetrable thorny covert in the neighbourhood of Geera, well known as the asylum for these animals, to which they retreated, after having satiated themselves by a few hours' feeding upon the crops of corn. I promised to assist in protecting the plantations, although the Arabs assured me that, in spite of our rifles, the elephants would return every night.

Wishing to judge personally of the damage, I rode up to the dhurra-fields, and for a few hours I examined the crops, through which I could ride with ease, as the plants were arranged like hops.

Many acres were absolutely destroyed, as the elephants had not only carefully stripped off the heavy heads of corn, but had trampled down and wilfully broken much more than they had consumed. The Arabs knew nothing about guns, or their effect upon elephants, and I felt quite sure that a few nights with the heavy rifles would very soon scare them from the fields.

I return to my journal.

"November 7. – In the middle of last night I was disturbed by the Arabs, who begged me to get up and shoot the elephants that were already in the plantations. This I refused to do, as I will not fire a shot until they call in their watchers, and leave the fields quiet. A few nights ago there was a perfect uproar from a score of watchers, that prevented the elephants from coming at the very time that the people had induced me to pass the whole night in the fields. I have arranged that the sheik shall call in all these watchers, and that they shall accompany me to-morrow night. I will then post myself in the centre of the plantations, dividing the men into many parties at all points, to return quietly to me and report the position that the elephants may have taken.

"This morning I purchased a kid for two piastres (five pence). The sheik is exceedingly civil, and insists upon sending me daily supplies of milk and vegetables.

"This afternoon, accompanied by my wife, I accepted an invitation to shoot a savage old bull hippopotamus that had been sufficiently impertinent to chase several of the natives. He lived in a deep and broad portion of the river, about two miles distant. We accordingly rode to the spot, and found the old hippo at home. The river was about 250 yards wide at this place, in an acute bend that had formed a deep pool. In the centre of this was a mud bank, just below the surface; upon this shallow bed the hippo was reposing. Upon perceiving us he was exceedingly saucy, snorting at my party, and behaving himself in a most absurd manner, by shaking his head and leaping half-way out of the water. This plunging demonstration was intended to frighten us. I had previously given Bacheet a pistol, and had ordered him to follow on the opposite bank from the ford at Wat el Negur. I now hallooed to him to fire several shots at the hippo, in order to drive him, if possible, towards me, as I lay in ambush behind a rock in the bed of the river. Bacheet descended the almost perpendicular bank to the water's edge, and after having chaffed the hippo considerably, he fired a shot with the pistol, which was far more dangerous to us on the opposite side than to the animal. The hippo, who was a wicked solitary old bull, accustomed to have his own way, returned the insult by charging towards Bacheet with a tremendous snorting, that sent him scrambling up the steep bank in a panic, amidst a roar of laughter from the people on my side concealed in the bushes. In this peal of merriment I thought I could distinguish a voice closely resembling that of my wife. However, Bacheet, who had always longed to be brought face to face with some foe worthy of his steel, had bolted, and he now stood safe in his elevated position on the top of the bank, thirty feet above the river, and fired the second barrel in bold defiance at the hippopotamus.

"As the hippo had gained confidence, I showed myself above the rock, and called to him, according to Arab custom, 'Hasinth! Hasinth!'[6] He, thinking no doubt that he might as well hunt me away, gave a loud snort, sank, and quickly reappeared about a hundred yards from me; but nearer than this he positively refused to approach. I therefore called to Bacheet to shout from the other side to attract his attention, and as he turned his head, I took a steady shot behind the ear with the little Fletcher rifle. This happened to be one of those fortunate shots that consoles you for many misses, and the saucy old hippo turned upon his back and rolled about in tremendous struggles, lashing the still and deep pool into waves, until he at length disappeared. We knew that he was settled; thus my people started off towards the village, and in a marvellousiy short time a frantic crowd of Arabs arrived with camels, ropes, axes, knives, and everything necessary for an onslaught upon the hippo, who, up to this time, had not appeared upon the surface. In about an hour and a half from the time he received the bullet, we discovered his carcase floating about two hundred yards lower down the river. Several heads of large crocodiles appeared and vanished suddenly within a few feet of the floating carcase, therefore the Arabs considered it prudent to wait until the stream should strand the body upon the pebbly shallows about half a mile below the pool. Upon arrival at that point, there was a general rush, and the excited crowd secured the hippo by many ropes, and hauled it to the shore. It was a very fine bull, as the skin without the head measured twelve feet three inches. I had two haunches kept for the sheik, and a large quantity of fat, which is highly and deservedly prized by the Arabs, as it is the most delicate of any animal. Those portions secured, with a reserve of meat for ourselves, the usual disgusting scene of violence commenced, the crowd falling upon the carcase like maddened hyaenas.

"In the evening I resolved to watch the dhurra fields for elephants. At about 9 P.M. I arrived in the plantations, with three men carrying spare

---

6   Hasinth is the Arabic for hippopotamus.

guns, among whom was Bacheet, who had at length an opportunity for which he had long yearned. I entrusted to him the 'Baby,' which he promised to put into my hands the very moment that I should fire my second barrel. I carried my own Ceylon No. 10, made by Beattie. We had not been half an hour in the dhurra fields before we met a couple of Arab watchers, who informed us that a herd of elephants was already in the plantation; we accordingly followed our guides. In about a quarter of an hour we distinctly heard the cracking of the dhurra stems, as the elephants browsed, and trampled them beneath their feet.

"Taking the proper position of the wind, I led our party cautiously in the direction of the sound, and in about five minutes I came in view of the slate-coloured and dusky forms of the herd. The moon was bright, and I counted nine elephants; they had trampled a space of about fifty yards square into a barren level, and they were now slowly moving forward, feeding as they went. One elephant, unfortunately, was separated from the herd, and was about forty yards in the rear; this fellow I was afraid would render our approach difficult. Cautioning my men, especially Bacheet, to keep close to me with the spare rifles, I crept along the alleys formed by the tall rows of dhurra, and after carefully stalking against the wind, I felt sure that it would be necessary to kill the single elephant before I should be able to attack the herd. Accordingly, I crept nearer and nearer, well concealed in the favourable crop of high and sheltering stems, until I was within fifteen yards of the hindmost animal. As I had never shot one of the African species, I was determined to follow the Ceylon plan, and get as near as possible; therefore I continued to creep from row to row of dhurra, until I at length stood at the very tail of the elephant in the next row. I could easily have touched it with my rifle, but just at this moment, it either obtained my wind, or it heard the rustle of the men. It quickly turned its head half round towards me; in the same instant I took the temple shot, and, by the flash of the rifle, I saw that it fell. Jumping forward past the huge body, I fired the left-hand barrel at an elephant that had advanced from the herd; it fell immediately! Now came the moment for a grand rush, as they stumbled in confusion over the last fallen elephant, and jammed together in a dense mass with their immense ears outspread, forming a picture of intense astonishment! Where were my spare guns? Here was a grand opportunity to run in and floor them right and left!

"Not a man was in sight, everybody had bolted! and I stood in advance of the dead elephant calling for my guns in vain. At length one of my fellows came up, but it was too late, the fallen elephant in the herd had risen from the ground, and they had all hustled off at a great pace, and were gone; I had only bagged one elephant. Where was the valiant

Bacheet? the would-be Nimrod, who for the last three months had been fretting in inactivity, and longing for the moment of action, when he had promised to be my trusty gun-bearer! He was the last man to appear, and he only ventured from his hiding-place in the high dhurra when assured of the elephants' retreat. I was obliged to admonish the whole party by a little physical treatment, and the gallant Bacheet returned with us to the village, crestfallen and completely subdued. On the following day not a vestige remained of the elephant, except the offal: the Arabs had not only cut off the flesh, but they had hacked the skull and the bones in pieces, and carried them off to boil down for soup."

Chapter XI.

The Ford.

Two months had elapsed since the last drop of rain had closed the wet season. It was 15th November, and the river had fallen to so low an ebb that the stream was reduced to a breadth of about eighty yards of bright and clear water, rushing in places with great rapidity through the centre of its broad and stony bed, while in sudden bends of the channel it widened into still, and exceedingly deep pools. We were encamped exactly upon the verge of a perpendicular cliff, from which there was a rugged path to the dry channel some thirty feet below, which shelved rapidly towards the centre occupied by the stream. In this spot were powerful rapids, above which to our left was a ford, at this time about waist-deep, upon a bed of rock that divided the lower rapids from a broad and silent pool above: across this ford the women of the village daily passed to collect their faggots of wood from the bushes on the opposite side. I had shot a crocodile, and a marabou stork, and I was carefully plucking the plume of beautiful feathers from the tail of the bird, surrounded by a number of Arabs, when I observed a throng of women, each laden with a bundle of wood, crossing the ford in single file from the opposite bank. Among them were two young girls of about fifteen, and I remarked that these, instead of marching in a line with the women, were wading hand-in-hand in dangerous proximity to the head of the rapids. A few seconds later, I noticed that they were inclining their bodies up stream, and were evidently struggling with the current. Hardly had I pointed out the danger to the men around me, when the girls clung to each other, and striving against their fate they tottered down the stream towards the rapids, which rushed with such violence that the waves were about two feet high. With praiseworthy speed the Arabs started to their feet, and dashed down the deep descent towards the river, but before they had reached half way, the girls uttered a shriek, lost their footing, and in another instant they threw their arms wildly above their heads, and were hurried away in the foam of the rapids. One disappeared immediately; the other was visible, as her long black hair floated on the surface; she also sank. Presently, about twenty yards below the spot, a pair of naked arms protruded high above the surface, with ivory bracelets upon the wrists, and twice the hands clapped together as though imploring help; again she disappeared. The water was by this time full of men, who had rushed to the rescue; but they had foolishly jumped in at the spot where they had first seen the girls, who were of course by this time carried far away by the torrent. Once more, farther down the river, the hands and bracelets appeared; again they wildly clapped together, and in the clear water we could plainly see the dark hair beneath. Still, she sank again; but almost immediately she rose head and shoulders above the surface, and thrice she again clapped her hands for aid.

This was her last effort; she disappeared. By the time several men had wisely run along the bank below the tail of the rapids, and having formed a line across a very narrow portion of the stream, one of them suddenly clutched an object beneath the water and in another moment he held the body of the girl in his arms. Of course she was dead? or a fit subject for the Royal Humane Society? – So I supposed; when to our intense astonishment, she no sooner was brought to the shore than she gave herself a shake, threw back her long hair, wrung out and arranged her dripping rahat, and walked leisurely back to the ford, which she crossed with the assistance of the Arab who had saved her.

What she was composed of I cannot say; whether she was the offspring of a cross between mermaid and hippopotamus, or hatched from the egg of a crocodile, I know not, but a more wonderfully amphibious being I have rarely seen.

During this painful scene, in which one girl had been entirely lost, the mother of her who was saved had rushed to meet her child as she landed from the ford; but instead of clasping her to her heart, as we had expected, she gave her a maternal welcome by beating her most unmercifully with her fists, bestowing such lusty blows upon her back that we could distinctly hear them at a distance of fifty yards; this punishment, we were given to understand, served her perfectly right, for having been foolish enough to venture near the rapids. The melancholy death-howl was now raised by all the women in the village, while the men explored the river in search of the missing body. On the following morning the sheik appeared at my tent, with a number of Arabs who had been unsuccessful, and he begged me, if possible, to suggest some means for the discovery of the girl, as her remains should be properly interred.

I proposed that they should procure a log of heavy wood, as near as possible the size of the girl, and that this should be thrown into the rapids, in the exact spot where she had disappeared; this, being nearly the same weight, would be equally acted upon by the stream, and would form a guide which they should follow until it should lead them to some deep eddy, or whirlpool formed by a backwater; should the pilot log remain in such a spot, they would most probably find the body in the same place. The men immediately procured a log, and set off with the sheik himself to carry out the experiment. In the afternoon, we heard a terrible howling and crying, and a crowd of men and women returned to the village, some of whom paid us a visit; they had found the body. The log had guided them about two miles distant, and had remained stationary in a backwater near where I had shot the bull hippopotamus; in this still pool, close to the bank, they almost immediately discovered the girl floating slightly beneath the surface. No crocodile had injured the body, but the fish had destroyed a portion of the face; it was already so far advanced in decomposition, that it was necessary to bury it upon the margin of the river, at the spot where it was discovered. The people came to thank me for having originated the idea, and the very agreeable sheik spent the evening with us with a number of his people; this was his greatest delight, and we had become thoroughly accustomed to his daily visits. At such times we sat upon an angarep, while he sat upon a mat stretched upon the ground, with a number of his men, who formed a half-circle around him; he then invariably requested that we would tell him stories about England. Of these he never tired, and with the assistance of Mahomet we established a regular entertainment; the great amusement of the Arabs being the mistakes that they readily perceived were made by Mahomet as interpreter. We knew sufficient Arabic to check and to explain his errors.

The death of the girl gave rise to a conversation upon drowning: this turned upon the subject of the girl herself and ended in a discussion upon the value of women; the question originating in a lament on the part of the sheik that a nice young girl had been drowned instead of a useless old woman. The sheik laid down the law with great force, "that a woman was of no use when she ceased to be young, unless she was a good strong person who could grind corn, and carry water from the river;" in this assertion he was seconded, and supported unanimously by the crowd of Arabs present.

Now it was always a common practice among the Arab women, when they called upon my wife, to request her to show her hands; they would then feel the soft palms and exclaim in astonishment, "Ah! she has never ground corn!" that being the duty of a wife unless she is rich enough to possess slaves. Sheik Achmet requested me to give him some account of our domestic arrangements in England; I did this as briefly as possible, explaining how ladies received our devoted attentions, extolling their beauty and virtue, and in fact giving him an idea that England was paradise, and that the ladies were angels. I described the variety of colours; that instead of all being dark, some were exceedingly fair; that others had red hair; that we had many bright black eyes, and some irresistible dark blue; and at the close of my descriptions I believe the sheik and his party felt disposed to emigrate immediately to the chilly shores of Great Britain; they asked, "How far off is your country?" "Well," said the sheik, with a sigh, "that must be a very charming country; how could you possibly come away from all your beautiful wives? True, you have brought one with you: she is, of course, the youngest and most lovely; perhaps those you have left at home are the *old ones!*" I was obliged to explain, that we are contented with one wife, and that even were people disposed to marry two, or more, they would be punished with imprisonment. This announcement was received with a general expression of indignation; the sheik and his party, who a few minutes ago were disposed to emigrate, and settle upon our shores, would now at the most have ventured upon a return ticket. After some murmurs of disapprobation, there was a decided expression of disbelief in my last statement. "Why," said the sheik, "the fact is simply *impossible!* How *can* a man be contented with one wife? It is ridiculous, absurd! What is he to do when she becomes old? When she is young, if very lovely, perhaps, he might be satisfied with her, but even the young must some day grow old, and the beauty must fade. The man does not fade like the woman; therefore, as he remains the same for many years, but she changes in a few years, Nature has arranged that the man shall have young wives to replace the old; does not the Prophet allow it? Had not our forefathers many wives? and shall we have but one? Look at yourself. Your wife is young, and" (here the sheik indulged in compliments), "but in ten years she will not be the same as now; will you not then let her have a nice house all to herself, when she grows old, while you take a fresh young wife?"

I was obliged to explain to the sheik that, first, our ladies never looked old; secondly, they improved with age; and thirdly, that we were supposed to love our wives with greater ardour as they advanced in years. This was received with an ominous shake of the head, coupled with the exclamation, "Mashallah!" repeated by the whole party. This was the moment for a few remarks on polygamy: I continued, "You men are selfish; you expect from the woman that which you will not give in return, 'constancy and love;' if your wife demanded a multiplicity of husbands, would it not be impossible to love her? how can she love you if you insist upon other wives?" "Ah!" he replied, "our women are different to yours, they would not love anybody; look at your wife, she has travelled with you far away from her own country, and her heart is stronger than a man's; she is afraid of nothing, because you are with her; but our women prefer to be far away from their husbands, and are only happy when they have nothing whatever to do. You don't understand our women, they are ignorant creatures, and when their youth is past are good for nothing but to work. You have explained your customs; your women are adored by the men, and you are satisfied with one wife, either young or old; now I will explain our customs. I have four wives; as one has become old, I have replaced her with a young one; here they all are" (he now marked four strokes upon the sand with his stick). "This one carries water; that grinds the corn; this makes the bread; the last does not do much, as she is the youngest, and my favourite; and if they neglect their work, they get a taste of this!" (shaking a long and, tolerably thick stick). "Now, that's the difference between our establishments; yours is well adapted for your country, and ours is the best plan for our own."

I would not contradict the sheik; the English greatcoat was not the garment for the scorching Soudan, and English ideas were equally unsuited to the climate and requirements of the people. The girls were utterly ignorant, and the Arabs had never heard of a woman who could read and write; they were generally pretty when young, but they rapidly grew old after childbirth. Numbers of young girls and women were accustomed to bathe perfectly naked in the river just before our tent; I employed them to catch small fish for baits and for hours they would amuse themselves in this way, screaming with excitement and fun, and chasing the small fry with their long clothes in lieu of nets; their figures were generally well shaped, but both men and women fell off in the development of the legs. Very few had well-shaped calves, but remarkably thin and cleanly formed ankles, with very delicately shaped feet. The men were constantly bathing in the clear waters of the Atbara, and were perfectly naked, although close to the women; we soon became accustomed to this daily scene, as we do at Brighton and other English bathing-towns.

Our life at Wat el Negur was anything but disagreeable; we had acquired great fame in several ways: the game that I shot I divided among the people; they also took an interest in the fishing, as they generally had a large share of all that I caught; my wife was very kind to all the children, and to the women, who came from great distances to see her; and my character as a physician having been spread far and wide, we became very celebrated people. Of course I was besieged daily by the maimed, the halt, and the blind, and the poor people, with much gratitude, would insist upon bringing fowls and milk in return for our attention to their wants. These I would never accept, but on many occasions, upon my refusal, the women would untie the legs of a bundle of chickens, and allow them to escape in our camp, rather than be compelled to return with their offering. Even the fakeers (priests) were our great friends, although we were Christians, and in my broken Arabic, with the assistance of Mahomet, I used to touch upon theological subjects. At first they expressed surprise that such clever people as the English should worship idols made of wood, or other substances, by the hands of man. I explained to them their error, as we were Protestants in England, who had protested against the practice of bowing down before the figure of Christ or any other form; that we simply worshipped God through Christ, believing Him to be both Saviour and Mediator. I recalled to their recollection that Mahomet and they themselves believed in Christ, as the greatest of all the prophets, therefore in reality there was not so very wide a gulf between their creed and our own; both acknowledging the same God; both believing in Christ, although differing in the degree of that belief. I allowed that Mahomet was a most wonderful man, and that, if a cause is to be valued by its effect, he was as much entitled to the name of prophet as Moses, the first law-giver. Our arguments never became overheated, as these simple yet steadfast Arabs, who held the faith of their forefathers untarnished and uncorrupted by schisms, spoke more with reverence to the great spirit of religion, than with the acrimony of debate. "My brothers," I would reply, "we are all God's creatures, believing in the one great Spirit who created us and all things, who made this atom of dust that we call our world, a tiny star amongst the hosts of heaven; and we, differing in colours and in races, are striving through our short but weary pilgrimage to the same high point; to the same mountain-top, where we trust to meet when the journey shall be accomplished. That mountain is steep, the country is desert; is there but one path, or are there many? Your path and mine are different, but with God's help they will lead us to the top. Shall we quarrel over the well upon the thirsty way? or shall we drink together, and be thankful for the cool waters, and strive to reach the end? Drink from my water-skin when upon the desert we thirst together, scorched by the same sun, exhausted by the same simoom, cooled by the same night, until we sleep at the journey's end, and together thank God, Christian and Mahometan, that we have reached our home."

The good fakeers rejoiced in such simple explanations, and they came to the conclusion that we were "all the same with a little difference," thus we were the best of friends with all the people. If not exactly a cure of their Mahometan souls, they acknowledged that I held the key to their bowels, which were entirely dependent upon my will, when the crowd of applicants daily thronged my medicine chest, and I dispensed jalap, calomel, opium, and tartar emetic. Upon one occasion a woman brought me a child of about fifteen months old, with a broken thigh; she had fallen asleep upon her camel, and had allowed the child to fall from her arms. I set the thigh, and secured it with gum bandages, as the mimosas afforded the requisite material. About twenty yards of old linen in bandages three inches broad, soaked in thick gum-water, will form the best of splints when it becomes dry and hard, which in that climate it will do in about an hour. There was one complaint that I was obliged to leave entirely in the hands of the Arabs, this was called "frendeet;" it was almost the certain effect of drinking the water that in the rainy season is accumulated in pools upon the surface of the rich table lands, especially between the Atbara and Katariff; the latter is a market-town about sixty miles from Wat el Negur, on the west bank of the river. Frendeet commences with a swelling of one of the limbs, generally accompanied with intense pain; this is caused by a worm of several feet in length, but no thicker than pack-thread. The Arab cure is to plaster the limb with cow-dung, which is their common application for almost all complaints. They then proceed to make what they term "doors," through which the worm will be able to escape; but, should it not be able to find one exit, they make a great number by the pleasant and simple operation of pricking the skin in many places with a red-hot lance. In about a week after these means of escape are provided, one of the wounds will inflame, and assume the character of a small boil, from which the head of the worm will issue. This is then seized, and fastened either to a small reed or piece of wood, which is daily and most gently wound round, until, in the course of about a week, the entire worm will be extracted, unless broken during the operation, in which case severe inflammation will ensue.

It was the 22d November, and the time was approaching when the grass throughout the entire country would be sufficiently dry to be fired; we accordingly prepared for our expedition, and it was necessary to go to Katariff to engage men, and to procure a slave in the place of old Masara, whose owner would not trust her in the wild countries we were about to visit. We therefore mounted our horses, and in two days we reached Katariff, rather less than sixty miles distant. The journey was exceedingly uninteresting, as the route lay across the monotonous flats of rich table land, without a single object to attract the attention, except the long line of villages which at intervals of about six miles lined the way. During the dry weather (the present season) there was not a drop of water in this country, except in wells far apart. Thus the cattle within twenty miles of the Atbara were driven every alternate day that great distance to the river, as the wells would not supply the large herds of the Arabs; although the animals could support life by drinking every alternate day, the cows were dry upon the day of fasting; this proved a certain amount of suffering.

Upon arrival at Katariff we were hospitably received by a Greek merchant, Michel Georgis, a nephew of the good old man from whom we had received much attention while at Cassala. The town was a miserable place, composed simply of the usual straw huts of the Arabs; the market, or "Soog," was bi-weekly. Katariff was also known by the name of "Soog Abou Sinn."

I extract an entry from my journal. – "The bazaar held here is most original. Long rows of thatched open sheds, about six feet high, form a street; in these sheds the dealers squat with their various wares exposed on the ground before them. In one, are Manchester goods, the calicoes are printed in England, with the name of the Greek merchant to whom they are consigned; in another, is a curious collection of small wares, as though samples of larger quantities, but in reality they are the dealer's whole stock of sundries, which he deals out to numerous purchasers in minute lots, for paras and half piastres, ginger, cloves, chills, cardamoms, pepper, turmeric, orris root, saffron, sandal-wood, musk, a species of moss that smells like patchouli, antimony for colouring the eyes and lips, henna, glass beads, cowrie shells, steels for striking fire, &c. &c. Other stalls contain sword-blades, files, razors, and other hardware, all of German manufacture, and of the most rubbishing kind. Mingled with these, in the same stall, are looking-glasses, three inches square, framed in coloured paper; slippers, sandals, &c. Other sheds contain camel ropes and bells, saddlery of all descriptions that are in general use, shoes, &c.; but the most numerous stalls are those devoted to red pepper, beads, and perfumery."

Beyond the main street of straw booths are vendors of miscellaneous goods, squatting under temporary fan-shaped straw screens, which are rented at the rate of five paras per day (about a farthing); beneath these may be seen vendors of butter and other grease, contained in a large jar by their side, while upon a stone before them are arranged balls of fat which are sold at five paras a lump. Each morsel is about the size of a cricket-ball: this is supposed to be the smallest quantity required for one dressing of the hair. Other screens are occupied by dealers in ropes, mats, leathern bags, girbas or water-skins, gum sacks, beans, waker, salt, sugar, coffee, &c. &c. Itinerant snmiths are at work, making knife-blades, repairing spears, &c. with small boys working the bellows, formed of simple leathern bags that open and close by the pressure of two sticks. The object that draws a crowd around him is a professional story-teller, wonderfully witty, no doubt, as, being mounted upon a camel from which he addresses his audience, he provokes roars of merriment; his small eyes, overhanging brow, large mouth, with thin and tightly compressed lips and deeply dimpled cheeks, combined with an unlimited amount of brass, completed a picture of professional shrewdness.

Camels, cattle, and donkeys are also exposed for sale. The average price for a baggage camel is twelve dollars; a hygeen, from thirty to sixty dollars; a fat ox, from six to ten dollars (the dollar at four shillings).

Katariff is on the direct merchants' route from Cassala to Khartoum. The charge for transport is accordingly low; a camel loaded with six cantars (600 lbs.) from this spot to Cassala, can be hired for one dollar, and from thence to Souakim, on the Red Sea, for five dollars; thus all produce is delivered from Katariff to the shipping port, at a charge of four shillings per hundred pounds. Cotton might be grown to any extent on this magnificent soil, and would pay the planter a large profit, were regular steam communication established at a reasonable rate between Souakimn and Suez.

There is a fine grey limestone in the neighbourhood of Katariff. The collection of people is exceedingly interesting upon a market day, as Arabs of all tribes, Tokrooris, and some few Abyssinians, concentrate from distant points. Many of the Arab women would be exceedingly pretty were their beauty not destroyed by their custom of gashing the cheeks in three wounds upon either side; this is inflicted during infancy. Scars are considered ornamental, and some of the women are much disfigured by such marks upon their arms and backs; even the men, without exception, are scarified upon their cheeks. The inhabitants of Kordofan and Darfur, who are generally prized as slaves, are invariably marked, not only with simple scars, but by cicatrices raised high above the natural surface by means of salt rubbed into the wounds; these unsightly deformities are considered to be great personal attractions. The Arab women are full of absurd superstitions; should a woman be in an interesting condition, she will creep under the body of a strong camel, believing that the act of passing between the fore and hind legs will endue her child with the strength of the animal. Young infants are scored with a razor longitudinally down the back and abdomen, to improve their constitutions.

I engaged six strong Tokrooris – natives of Darfur – who agreed to accompany me for five months. These people are a tribe of Mahometan negroes, of whom I shall speak more hereafter; they are generally very powerful and courageous, and I preferred a few men of this race to a party entirely composed of Arabs. Our great difficulty was to procure a slave woman to grind the corn and to make the bread for the people. No proprietor would let his slave on hire to go upon such a journey, and it was impossible to start without one; the only resource was to purchase the freedom of some woman, and to engage her as a servant for the trip. Even this was difficult, as slaves were scarce and in great demand: however, at last I heard of a man who had a Galla slave who was clever at making bread, as it had been her duty to make cakes for sale in the bazaar upon market days. After some delays I succeeded in obtaining an interview with both the master and slave at the same time; the former was an Arab, hard at dealing, but, as I did not wish to drive a bargain, I agreed to the price, thirty-five dollars, 7l. The name of the woman was Barrake; she was about twenty-two years of age, brown in complexion, fat, and strong; rather tall, and altogether she was a fine powerful-looking woman, but decidedly not pretty; her hair was elaborately dressed in hundreds of long narrow curls, so thickly smeared with castor oil that the grease had covered her naked shoulders; in addition to this, as she had been recently under the hands of the hairdresser, there was an amount of fat and other nastiness upon her head that gave her the appearance of being nearly grey.

I now counted out thirty-five dollars, which I placed in two piles upon the table, and through the medium of Mahomet I explained to her that she was no longer a slave, as that sum had purchased her freedom; at the same time, as it was a large amount that I had paid, I expected she would remain with us as a servant until our journey should be over, at which time she should receive a certain sum in money, as wages at the usual rate. Mahomet did not agree with this style of address to a slave, therefore he slightly altered it in the translation, which I at once detected. The woman looked frightened and uneasy at the conclusion; I immediately asked Mahomet what he had told her. "Same like master tell to me!" replied the indignant Mahomet. "Then have the kindness to repeat to me in English what you said to her;" I replied. "I tell that slave woman same like master's word; I tell her master one very good master, she Barrake one very bad woman; all that good dollars master pay, too much money for such a bad woman. Now she's master's slave; she belong to master like a dog; if she not make plenty of good bread, work hard all day, early morning, late in night, master take a big stick, break her head."

This was the substance of a translation of my address tinged with Mahomet's colouring, as being more adapted for the ears of a slave!I My wife was present, and being much annoyed, we both assured the woman that Mahomet was wrong, and I insisted upon his explaining to her literally that "no Englishman could hold a slave; that the money I had paid rendered her entirely free; that she would not even be compelled to remain with us, but she could do as she thought proper; that both her mistress and I should be exceedingly kind to her, and we would subsequently find her a good situation in Cairo; in the meantime she would receive good clothes and wages."

This, Mahomet, much against his will, was obliged to translate literally. The effect was magical; the woman, who had looked frightened and unhappy, suddenly beamed with smiles, and without any warning she ran towards me, and in an instant I found myself embraced in her loving arms; she pressed me to her bosom, and smothered me with castor oily kisses, while her greasy ringlets hung upon my face and neck. How long this entertainment would have lasted I cannot tell, but I was obliged to cry "Caffa! Caffa!" (enough! enough!) as it looked improper, and the perfumery was too rich; fortunately my wife was present, but she did not appear to enjoy it more than I did; my snow-white blouse was soiled and greasy, and for the rest of the day I was a disagreeable compound of smells, castor oil, tallow, musk, sandal-wood, burnt shells, and Barrake.

Mahomet and Barrake herself, I believe, were the only people who really enjoyed this little event. "Ha!" Mahomet exclaimed, "this is your own fault! You insisted upon speaking kindly, and telling her that she is not a slave, now she thinks that she is one of your *wives!*" This was the real fact; the unfortunate Barrake had deceived herself; never having been free, she could not understand the use of freedom unless she was to be a wife. She had understood my little address as a proposal, and of course she was disappointed; but, as an action for breach of promise cannot be pressed in the Soudan, poor Barrake, although free, had not the happy rights of a free-born Englishwoman, who can heal her broken heart with a pecuniary plaster, and console herself with damages for the loss of a lover.

We were ready to start, having our party of servants complete, six Tokrooris – Moosa, Abdoolahi, Abderachman, Hassan, Adow, and Hadji Ali, with Mahomet, Wat Gamma, Bacheet, Mahomet secundus (a groom), and Barrake; total eleven men and the cook.

When half way to Wat el Negur, we found the whole country in alarm, Mek Nimmur having suddenly made a foray. He had crossed the Atbara, and plundered the district, and driven off large numbers of cattle and camels, after having killed a considerable number of people. No doubt the reports were somewhat exaggerated, but the inhabitants of the district were flying from their villages, with their herds, and were flocking to Katariff. We arrived at Wat el Negur on the 3d of December, and we now felt the advantage of our friendship with the good Sheik Achmet, who, being a friend of Mek Nimmur, had saved our effects during our absence; these would otherwise have been plundered, as the robbers had paid him a visit; – he had removed our tents and baggage to his own house for protection. Not only had he thus protected our effects, but he had taken the opportunity of delivering the polite message to Mek Nimmur that I had entrusted to his charge – expressing a wish to pay him a visit as a countryman and friend of Mr. Mansfield Parkyns, who had formerly been so well received by his father.

In a few days the whole country was up. Troops of the Dabaina Arabs, under the command of Mahmoud Wat Said (who had now assumed the chieftainship of the tribe after the death of his brother Atalan), gathered on the frontier, while about 2,000 Egyptian regulars marched against Gellabat, and attacked the Abyssinians and Tokrooris, who had united. Several hundreds of the Tokrooris were killed, and the Abyssinians retreated to the mountains. Large bodies of Egyptian irregulars threatened Mek Nimmur's country, but the wily Mek was too much for them. The Jalyn Arabs were his friends; and, although they paid tribute to the Egyptian Government from their frontier villages, they acted as spies, and kept Mek Nimmur au courant of the enemy's movements. The Hamran Arabs, those mighty hunters with the sword, were thorough Ishmaelites, and although nominally subject to Egypt, they were well known as secret friends to Mek Nimmur; and it was believed that they conveyed information of the localities where the Dabaina and Shookeryha Arabs had collected their herds. Upon these Mek Nimmur had a knack of pouncing unexpectedly, when he was supposed to be a hundred miles in an opposite direction.

The dry weather had introduced a season of anarchy along the whole frontier. The Atbara was fordable in many places, and it no longer formed the impassable barrier that necessitated peace. Mek Nimmur (the Leopard King) showed the cunning and ability of his namesake by pouncing upon his prey without a moment's warning, and retreating with equal dexterity. This frontier warfare, skilfully conducted by Mek Nimmur, was most advantageous to Theodorus, the King of Abyssinia, as the defence of the boundary was maintained against Egypt by a constant guerilla warfare. Upon several occasions, expeditions on a large scale had been organized against Mek Nimmur by the Governor-General of the Soudan; but they had invariably failed, as he retreated to the inaccessible mountains, where he had beaten them with loss, and they had simply wreaked their vengeance by burning the deserted villages of straw huts in the low lands, that a few dollars would quickly rebuild. Mek Nimmur was a most unpleasant neighbour to the Egyptian Government, and accordingly he was a great friend of the King Theodorus; he was, in fact, a shield that protected the heart of Abyssinia.

As I have already described, the Base were always at war with everybody; and as Mek Nimmur and the Abyssinians were constantly fighting with the Egyptians, the passage of the Atbara to the east bank was the commencement of a territory where the sword and lance represented the only law. The Hamran Arabs dared not venture with their flocks farther east than Geera, on the Settite, about twenty-five miles from Wat el Negur. From the point of junction of the Settite with the Atbara opposite

Tomat to Geera, they were now encamped with their herds upon the borders of the river for the dry season. I sent a messenger to their sheik, Owat, accompanied by Mahomet, with the firman of the Viceroy, and I requested him to supply me with elephant-hunters (aggageers) and guides to accompany me into the Base and Mek Nimmur's country.

My intention was to thoroughly examine all the great rivers of Abyssinia that were tributaries to the Nile. These were the Settite, Royan, Angrab, Salaam, Rahad, Dinder, and the Blue Nile. If possible, I should traverse the Galla country, and crossing the Blue Nile, I should endeavour to reach the White Nile. But this latter idea I subsequently found impracticable, as it would have interfered with the proper season for my projected journey up the White Nile in search of the sources.

During the absence of Mahomet, I received a very polite message from Mek Nimmur, accompanied by a present of twenty pounds of coffee, with an invitation to pay him a visit. His country lay between the Settite river and the Bahr Salaam; thus without his invitation I might have found it difficult to traverse his territory; – so far, all went well. I returned my salaams, and sent word that we intended to hunt through the Base country, after which we should have the honour of passing a few days with him on our road to the river Salaam, at which place we intended to hunt elephants and rhinoceros. Mahomet returned, accompanied by a large party of Hamran Arabs, including several hunters, one of whom was Sheik Abou Do Roussoul, the nephew of Sheik Owat; as his name in full was too long, he generally went by the abbreviation "Abou Do." He was a splendid fellow, a little above six feet one, with a light active figure, but exceedingly well developed muscles: his face was strikingly handsome; his eyes were like those of a giraffe, but the sudden glance of an eagle lighted them up with a flash during the excitement of conversation, which showed little of the giraffe's gentle character. Abou Do was the only tall man of the party, the others were of middle height, with the exception of a little fellow named Jali, who was not above five feet four inches, but wonderfully muscular, and in expression a regular daredevil. There were two parties of hunters, one under Abou Do, and the other consisting of four brothers Sherrif. The latter were the most celebrated aggageers among the renowned tribe of the Hamran; their father and grandfather had been mighty Nimrods, and the broadswords wielded by their strong arms had descended to the men who now upheld the prestige of the ancient blades. The eldest was Taher Sherrif; his second brother, Roder Sherrif, was a very small, active-looking man, with a withered left arm. An elephant had at one time killed his horse, and on the same occasion had driven its sharp tusk through the arm of the rider, completely splitting the limb, and splintering the bone from the elbow-joint to the wrist to such an extent, that by degrees the fragments had sloughed away, and the arm had become shrivelled and withered. It now resembled a mass of dried leather, twisted into a deformity, without the slightest shape of an arm; this was about fourteen inches in length from the shoulder; the stiff and crippled hand, with contracted fingers, resembled the claw of a vulture.

In spite of his maimed condition, Roder Sherrif was the most celebrated leader in the elephant hunt. His was the dangerous post to ride close to the head of the infuriated animal and provoke the charge, and then to lead the elephant in pursuit, while the aggageers attacked it from behind; it was in the performance of this duty that he had met with the accident, as his horse had fallen over some hidden obstacle, and was immediately caught. Being an exceedingly light weight he had continued to occupy this important position in the hunt, and the rigid fingers of the left hand served as a hook, upon which he could hang the reins.

My battery of rifles was now laid upon a mat for examination; they were in beautiful condition, and they excited the admiration of the entire party. The perfection of workmanship did not appear to interest them so much as the size of the bores; they thrust their fingers down each muzzle, until they at last came to the "Baby," when, finding that two fingers could be easily introduced, they at once fell in love with that rifle in particular. My men explained that it was a "Jenna el Mootfah" (child of a cannon). "Sahe, Jenna el Mootfah kabeer," they replied (it is true, it is the child of a very big cannon). Their delight was made perfect by the exhibition of the half-pound explosive shell, the effects of which were duly explained. I told them that I was an old elephant hunter, but that I did not hunt for the sake of the ivory, as I wished to explore the country to discover the cause of the Nile inundations, therefore I wished to examine carefully the various Abyssinian rivers; but as I had heard they were wonderful sportsmen, I should like them to join my party, and we could both hunt and explore together. They replied that they knew every nook and corner of the entire country as far as Mek Nimmur's and the Base, but that in the latter country we must be prepared to fight, as they made a practice of showing no quarter to the Base, because they received none from them; thus we should require a strong party. I pointed to my rifles, which I explained were odds against the Base, who were without fire-arms; and we arranged to start together on the 17th of December.

In the interval I was busily engaged in making bullets for the journey, with an admixture of one pound of quicksilver to twelve of lead. This hardens the bullet at the same time that it increases the weight, but great caution must be observed in the manufacture, as the mercury, being heavier than the lead, will sink to the bottom, unless stirred with a red-hot iron when mixed. The admixture must take place in small quantities, otherwise the quicksilver will evaporate if exposed to a great heat. Thus the molten lead should be kept upon the fire in a large reservoir, while a portion of quicksilver should be added regularly to every ladleful taken for immediate use. This should be well stirred before it is poured into the mould. Bullets formed of this mixture of metals are far superior to any others.

My preparations for the journey were soon completed. We had passed a most agreeable time at Wat el Negur. Although I had not had much shooting, I gained much experience in the country, having made several extensive journeys in the neighbourhood, and our constant conversations with the sheik had somewhat improved my Arabic. I had discovered several plants hitherto unknown to me, – among others, a peculiar bulb, from which I had prepared excellent arrowroot. This produced several tubers resembling sweet potatoes, but exceedingly long and thin; it was known by the Arabs as "baboon." I pierced with a nail a sheet of tin from the lining of a packing case, and I quickly improvised a grater, upon which I reduced the bulb to pulp. This I washed in water, and when strained through cotton cloth, it was allowed to settle for several hours. The clear water was then poured off; and the thick sediment, when dried in the sun, became arrowroot of the best quality. The Arabs had no idea of this preparation, but simply roasted the roots on the embers.

On the 17th of August, 1861, accompanied by the German Florian, we started from Wat el Negur, and said good-bye to our very kind friend, Sheik Achmet, who insisted upon presenting us with a strong but exceedingly light angarep (bedstead), suitable for camel travelling, and an excellent water-skin, that we should be constantly reminded of him, night and day.

Florian was in a weak condition, as he had suffered much from fever throughout the rainy season. He started under disadvantageous circumstances, as he had purchased a horse that was a bad bargain. The Arabs, who are sharp practitioners, had dealt hardly with him, as they had sold him a wretched brute that could make no other use of its legs than to kick. Of course they had imposed upon poor Florian a long history of how this horse in a giraffe hunt had been the first at the death, &c. &c., and he, the deceived, had promised to shoot a hippopotamus to give them in barter. This he had already done, and he had exchanged a river horse, worth twenty dollars, for a terrestrial horse, worth twenty piastres.

Florian had never mounted a horse in his lifetime as his shooting had always been on foot. This he now explained to us, although the confession was quite unnecessary, as his first attempt at mounting was made upon the wrong side.

Throughout his journey to Geera on the Settite, there was a constant difference of opinion between him and his new purchase, until we suddenly heard a heavy fall. Upon looking back, I perceived Florian like a spread eagle on his stomach upon the ground, lying before the horse, who was quietly looking at his new master. On another occasion, I heard a torrent of abuse expressed in German, and upon turning round I found him clinging to the neck of his animal, having lost both stirrups, while his rifle had fallen to the ground. He was now cursing his beast, whom he accused of wilful murder, for having replied by a kick to a slight tap he had administered with a stick. I could not help suggesting that he would find it awkward should he be obliged to escape from an elephant upon that animal in rough and difficult ground where good riding would be essential; and he declared that nothing should tempt him either to hunt or to escape from any beast on horseback, as he would rather trust to his legs.

Upon arriving at Geera, we bivouacked upon the sandy bed of the river, which had much changed in appearance since our last visit. Although much superior to the Atbara, the stream was confined to a deep channel about 120 yards wide, in the centre of the now dry bed of rounded pebbles and sand. Exactly opposite were extensive encampments of the Hamran Arabs, who were congregated in thousands between this point and the Atbara junction. Their limit for pasturage was about six miles up stream from Geera, beyond which point they dare not trust their flocks on account of their enemies, the Base.

We were immediately visited, upon our arrival, by a number of Arabs, including the Sheik Abou Do, from whom I purchased two good milk goats to accompany us upon our journey. I had already procured one at Wat el Negur in exchange for a few strips of hippopotamus hide for making whips.

Lions were roaring all night close to our sleeping place; there were many of these animals in this neighbourhood, as they were attracted by the flocks of the Arabs.

On the following morning, at daybreak, several Arabs arrived with a report that elephants had been drinking in the river within half an hour's march of our sleeping place. I immediately started with my men, accompanied by Florian, and we shortly arrived upon the tracks of the herd. I had three Hamran Arabs as trackers, one of whom, Taher Noor, had engaged to accompany us throughout the expedition.

For about eight miles we followed the spoor through high-dried grass and thorny bush, until we at length arrived at dense jungle of kittar, – the most formidable of the hooked thorn mimosas. Here the tracks appeared to wander; some elephants having travelled straight ahead, while others had strayed to the right and left. While engaged in determining the path of the herd, we observed four giraffes at about half a mile distant, but they had already perceived us, and were in full flight. For about two hours we travelled upon the circuitous tracks of the elephants to no purpose, when we suddenly were startled by the shrill trumpet of one of these animals in the thick thorns, a few hundred yards to our left. The ground was so intensely hard and dry that it was impossible to distinguish the new tracks from the old, which crossed and recrossed in all directions. I therefore decided to walk carefully along the outskirts of the jungle, trusting to find their place of entrance by the fresh broken boughs. In about an hour we had thus examined two or three miles, without discovering a clue to their recent path, when we turned round a clump of bushes, and suddenly came in view of two grand elephants, standing at the edge of the dense thorns; having our wind, they vanished instantly into the the jungle. We could not follow them, as their course was down wind; we therefore made a circuit to leeward for about a mile, and, finding that the elephants had not crossed in that direction, we felt sure that we must come upon them with the wind in our favour should they still be within the thorny jungle; this was certain, as it was their favourite retreat.

With the greatest labour I led the way, creeping frequently upon my hands and knees to avoid the hooks of the kittar bush, and occasionally listening for a sound. At length, after upwards of an hour passed in this slow and fatiguing advance, I distinctly heard the flap of an elephant's ear, shortly followed by the deep guttural sigh of one of those animals, within a few paces, but so dense was the screen of jungle that I could see nothing. We waited for some minutes, but not the slightest sound could be heard; the elephants were aware of danger, and they were, like ourselves, listening attentively for the first intimation of an enemy. This was a highly exciting moment; should they charge, there would not be a possibility of escape, as the hooked thorns rendered any sudden movement almost impracticable. In another moment, there was a tremendous crash; and, with a sound like a whirlwind, the herd dashed through the crackling jungle. I rushed forward, as I was uncertain whether they were in advance or retreat; leaving a small sample of my nose upon a kittar thorn, and tearing my way, with naked arms, through what, in cold blood, would have appeared impossible, I caught sight of two elephants leading across my path, with the herd following in a dense mass behind them. Firing a shot at the leading elephant, simply in the endeavour to check the herd, I repeated with the left-hand barrel at the head of his companion; this staggered him, and threw the main body into confusion: they immediately closed up in a dense mass, and bore everything before them, but the herd exhibited merely an impenetrable array of hind quarters wedged together so firmly that it was impossible to obtain a head or shoulder shot. I was within fifteen paces of them, and so compactly were they packed, that with all their immense strength they could not at once force so extensive a front through the tough and powerful branches of the dense kittar. For about half a minute they were absolutely checked, and they bored forward with all their might in their determination to open a road through the matted thorns: the elastic boughs, bent from their position, sprang back with dangerous force, and would have fractured the skull of any one who came within their sweep. A very large elephant was on the left flank, and for an instant this turned obliquely to the left; I quickly seized the opportunity and fired the "Baby," with an explosive shell, aimed far back in the flank, trusting that it would penetrate beneath the opposite shoulder. The recoil of the "Baby," loaded with ten drachms of the strongest powder and a half-pound shell, spun me round like a top – it was difficult to say which was staggered the most severely, the elephant or myself; however, we both recovered, and I seized one of my double rifles, a Reilly No. 10, that was quickly pushed into my hand by my Tokroori, Hadji Ali. This was done just in time, as an elephant from the baffled herd turned sharp round, and, with its immense ears cocked, it charged down upon us with a scream of rage. "One of us she must have if I miss!"

This was the first downright charge of an African elephant that I had seen, and instinctively I followed my old Ceylon plan of waiting for a close shot. She lowered her head when within about six yards, and I fired low for the centre of the forehead, exactly in the swelling above the root of the trunk. She collapsed to the shot, and fell dead, with a heavy shock, upon the ground. At the same moment, the thorny barrier gave way before the pressure of the herd, and the elephants disappeared in the thick jungle, through which it was impossible to follow them.

I had suffered terribly from the hooked thorns, and the men likewise. This had been a capital trial for my Tokrooris, who had behaved remarkably well, and had I gained much confidence by my successful forehead shot at the elephant when in full charge; but I must confess that this is the only instance in which I have succeeded in killing an African elephant by the front shot, although I have steadily tried the experiment upon subsequent occasions.

Florian had not had an opportunity of firing a shot, as I had been in his way, and he could not pass on one side owing to the thorns.

We had very little time to examine the elephant, as we were far from home, and the sun was already low. I felt convinced that the other elephant could not be far off, after having received the "Baby's" half-pound shell carefully directed, and I resolved to return on the following morning with many people and camels to divide the flesh. It was dark by the time we arrived at the tents, and the news immediately spread through the Arab camp that two elephants had been killed.

On the following morning we started, and, upon arrival at the dead elephant, we followed the tracks of that wounded by the "Baby." The blood upon the bushes guided us in a few minutes to the spot where the elephant lay dead, at about 300 yards' distance. The whole day passed in flaying the two animals, and cutting off the flesh, which was packed in large gum sacks, with which the camels were loaded. I was curious to examine the effect of the half-pound shell: it had entered the flank on the right side, breaking the rib upon which it had exploded; it had then passed through the stomach and the lower portion of the lungs, both of which were terribly shattered, and breaking one of the fore-ribs on the left side, it had lodged beneath the skin of the shoulder. This was irresistible work, and the elephant had evidently dropped in a few minutes after having received the shell.

The conical bullet of quicksilver and lead, propelled by seven drachms of powder, had entered the exact centre of the forehead of the elephant No. 1, and, having passed completely through the brain and the back part of the skull, we found it sticking fast in the spine, *between the shoulders.* These No. 10 Reillys[7] were wonderfully powerful rifles, and exceedingly handy; they weighed fourteen pounds, and were admirably adapted for dangerous game. I measured both the elephants accurately with a tape: that killed by the "Baby" was nine feet six inches from the forefoot to the shoulder, the other was eight feet three inches. It is a common mistake that twice the circumference of the foot is the height of an elephant; there is no such rule that can be depended upon, as their feet vary in size without any relative proportion to the height of the animal.

A most interesting fact had occurred: when I found the larger elephant, killed by the "Baby," I noticed an old wound unhealed and full of matter in the front of the left shoulder; the bowels were shot through, and were green in various places. Florian suggested that it must be an elephant that I had wounded at Wat el Negur; we tracked the course of the bullet most carefully, until we at length discovered my unmistakeable bullet of quicksilver and lead, almost uninjured, in the fleshy part of the thigh, imbedded in an unhealed wound. Thus, by a curious chance, upon my first interview with African elephants by daylight, I had killed the identical

---

7   They are now in England at Mr. Reilly's, No. 215, Oxford Street, having accompanied me throughout my expedition, and they have never been out of order.

elephant that I had wounded at Wat el Negur forty-three days ago in the dhurra plantation, twenty-eight miles distant! Both these elephants were females. It was the custom of these active creatures to invade the dhurra fields from this great distance, and to return to these almost impenetrable thorny jungles, where they were safe from the attack of the aggageers, but not from the rifles.

On our return to camp, the rejoicings were great; the women yelled as usual, and I delighted the Hamrans by dividing the meat, and presenting them with the hides for shields. I gave Abou Do, and all the hunters, and my camel drivers, large quantities of fat; and I found that I was accredited as a brother hunter by the knights of the sword, who acknowledged that their weapons were useless in the thick jungles of Tooleet, the name of the place where we had killed the elephants.

Chapter XII.

Old Neptune Joins the Party.

We started from Geera, on the 23d of December, with our party complete. The Hamran sword-hunters were Abou Do, Jali, and Suleiman. My chief tracker was Taher Noor, who, although a good hunter, was not a professional aggahr, and I was accompanied by the father of Abou Do, who was a renowned "howarti," or harpooner of hippopotami. This magnificent old man might have been Neptune himself; he stood about six feet two, and his grizzled locks hung upon his shoulders in thick and massive curls, while his deep bronze features could not have been excelled in beauty of outline. A more classical figure I have never beheld than the old Abou Do with his harpoon, as he first breasted the torrent, and then landed dripping from the waves to join our party from the Arab camp on the opposite side of the river. In addition to my Tokrooris, I had engaged nine camels, each with a separate driver, of the Hamrans, who were to accompany us throughout the expedition. These people were glad to engage themselves, with their camels included, at one and a half dollars (six shillings) per month, for man and beast as one. We had not sufficient baggage to load five camels, but four carried a large supply of corn for our horses and people.

Hardly were we mounted and fairly started, than the monkey-like agility of our aggageers was displayed in a variety of antics, that were far more suited to performance in a circus than to a party of steady and experienced hunters, who wished to reserve the strength of their horses for a trying journey.

Abou Do was mounted on a beautiful Abyssinian horse, a grey; Suleiman rode a rough and inferior-looking beast; while little Jali, who was the pet of the party, rode a grey mare, not exceeding fourteen hands in height, which matched her rider exactly in fire, spirit, and speed. Never was there a more perfect picture of a wild Arab horseman than Jali on his mare. Hardly was he in the saddle, than away flew the mare over the loose shingles that formed the dry bed of the river, scattering the rounded pebbles in the air from her flinty hoofs, while her rider in the vigour of delight threw himself almost under her belly while at full speed, and picked up stones from the ground, which he flung, and again caught as they descended. Never were there more complete Centaurs than these Hamran Arabs; the horse and man appeared to be one animal, and that of the most elastic nature, that could twist and turn with the suppleness of a snake; the fact of their being separate beings was proved by the rider springing to the earth with his drawn sword while the horse was in full gallop over rough and difficult ground, and clutching the mane, he again vaulted into the saddle with the agility of a monkey, without once checking the speed. The fact of being on horseback had suddenly altered the character of these Arabs; from a sedate and proud bearing, they had become the wildest examples of the most savage disciples of Nimrod; excited by enthusiasm, they shook their naked blades aloft till the steel trembled in their grasp, and away they dashed over rocks, through thorny bush, across ravines, up and down steep inclinations, engaging in a mimic hunt, and going through the various acts supposed to occur in the attack of a furious elephant. I must acknowledge that, in spite of my admiration for their wonderful dexterity, I began to doubt their prudence. I had three excellent horses for my wife and myself; the Hamran hunters had only one for each; and, if the commencement were an example of their usual style of horsemanship, I felt sure that a dozen horses would not be sufficient for the work before us. However, it was not the moment to offer advice, as they were simply mad with excitement and delight.

The women raised their loud and shrill yell at parting, and our party of about twenty-five persons, with nine camels, six horses, and two donkeys, exclusive of the German Florian, with his kicking giraffe-hunter, and attendants, ascended the broken slope that formed the broad valley of the Settite river.

There was very little game in the neighbourhood, as it was completely overrun by the Arabs and their flocks; and we were to march about fifty miles E.S.E. before we should arrive in the happy hunting-grounds of the Base country, where we were led to expect great results. Previous to leaving Wat el Negur I had thoroughly drilled my Tokrooris in their duties as gun-bearers, which had established a discipline well exemplified in the recent affair with the elephants. I had entrusted to them my favourite rifles, and had instructed them in their use; each man paid particular regard to the rifle that he carried, and, as several were of the same pattern, they had marked them with small pieces of rag tied round the trigger guards. This esprit de corps was most beneficial to the preservation of the arms, which were kept in admirable order. Mahomet, the dragoman, rode my spare horse, and carried my short double-barrelled rifle, slung across his back, in the place of his pistols and gun, which he had wilfully thrown upon the desert when leaving Berber. As the horse was restive, and he had placed the hammers upon the caps, his shirt caught in the lock, and one barrel suddenly exploded, which, with an elephant-charge of six drachms of powder, was rather startling, within a few inches of his ear, and narrowly escaped the back of his skull. Florian possessed a single-barrelled rifle, which he declared had accompanied him through many years of sports: this weapon had become so fond of shooting, that it was constantly going off on its own account, to the great danger of the bystanders, and no sooner were we well off on our journey, than off went this abominable instrument in a spontaneous feu de joie, in the very midst of us! Its master was accordingly *off* likewise, as his horse gave the accustomed kick, that was invariably the deed of separation. However, we cantered on ahead of the dangerous party, and joined the aggageers, until we at length reached the table land above the Settite valley. Hardly were we arrived, than we noticed in the distance a flock of sheep and goats attended by some Arab boys. Suddenly, as Don Quixote charged the sheep, lance in hand, the aggageers started off in full gallop, and as the frightened flock scattered in all directions, in a few moments they were overtaken by the hunters, each of whom snatched a kid, or a goat, from the ground while at full speed, and placed it upon the neck of his horse, without either halting or dismounting. This was a very independent proceeding; but, as the flock belonged to their own tribe, they laughed at the question of property that I had immediately raised, and assured me that this was the Arab custom of insuring their breakfast, as we should kill no game during that day. In this they were mistaken, as I killed sufficient guinea-fowl to render the party independent of other food.

In a day's march through a beautiful country, sometimes upon the high table land to cut off a bend in the river, at other times upon the margin of the stream in the romantic valley, broken into countless hills and ravines covered with mimosas, we arrived at Ombrega (mother of the thorn), about twenty-four miles from Geera. In that country, although uninhabited from fear of the Base, every locality upon the borders of the river has a name. Ombrega is a beautiful situation, where white sandstone cliffs of about two hundred feet perpendicular height, wall in the river, which, even at this dry season, was a noble stream impassable except at certain places, where it was fordable. Having descended the valley we bivouacked in the shade of thick nabbuk trees (Rhamnus lotus), whose evergreen foliage forms a pleasing exception to the general barrenness of the mimosas during the season of drought. We soon arranged a resting-place, and cleared away the grass that produced the thorn which had given rise to the name of Ombrega, and in a short time we were comfortably settled for the night. We were within fifty yards of the river – the horses were luxuriating in the green grass that grew upon its banks, and the camels were hobbled, to prevent them from wandering from the protection of the camp fires, as we were now in the wilderness, where the Base by day, and the lion and leopard by night, were hostile to man and beast. The goats, upon which we depended for our supply of milk, were objects of especial care: these were picketed to pegs driven in the ground close to the fires, and men were ordered to sleep on either side. We had three greyhounds belonging to the Arabs, and it was arranged that, in addition to these guards, a watch should be kept by night.

The dense shade of the nabbuk had been chosen by the Arabs as a screen to the camp-fires, that might otherwise attract the Base, who might be prowling about the country; but, as a rule, however pleasant may be the shade during the day, the thick jungle, and even the overhanging boughs of a tree, should be avoided at night. Snakes and noxious insects generally come forth after dark – many of these inhabit the boughs of trees, and may drop upon the bed of the unwary sleeper; beasts of prey invariably inhabit the thick jungles, in which they may creep unperceived to within springing distance of an object in the camp.

We were fast asleep a little after midnight, when we were awakened by the loud barking of the dogs, and by a confusion in the camp. Jumping up on the instant, I heard the dogs, far away in the dark jungles, barking in different directions. One of the goats was gone! A leopard had sprung into the camp, and had torn a goat from its fastening, although tied to a peg, between two men, close to a large fire. The dogs had given chase; but, as usual in such cases, they were so alarmed as to be almost useless. We quickly collected firebrands, and searched the jungles, and shortly we arrived where a dog was barking violently. Near this spot we heard the moaning of some animal among the bushes, and upon a search with firebrands we discovered the goat, helpless upon the ground, with its throat lacerated by the leopard. A sudden cry from the dog at a few yards' distance, and the barking ceased.

The goat was carried to the camp, when it shortly died. We succeeded in recalling two of the dogs; but the third, that was the best, was missing, having been struck by the leopard. We searched for the body in vain, and concluded that it had been carried off.

On the following day, we discovered fresh tracks of elephants at sunrise. No time was lost in starting, and upon crossing the river, we found that a large herd had been drinking, and had retreated by a peculiar ravine. This cleft through the sandstone rocks, which rose like walls for about a hundred feet upon either side, formed an alley about twenty yards broad, the bottom consisting of snow-white sand that, in the rainy season, formed the bed of a torrent from the upper country. This herd must have comprised about fifty elephants, that must have been in the same locality for several days, as the ground was trampled in all directions, and the mimosas upon the higher land were uprooted in great numnbers: but after following upon the tracks for several hours with great difficulty, owing to the intricacy of their windings upon the dry and hard ground, we met with a sign fatal to success, – the footprints of two men. In a short time we met the men themselves, two elephant-hunters who had followed the herd on foot, with the sword as their only weapon: they had found the elephants, which had obtained their wind and had retreated.

The Sheik Abou Do was furious at the audacity of these two Hamrans, who had dared to disturb our hunting-grounds, and he immediately ordered them to return to Geera.

In addition to the tracks of the herd, we had seen that of a large single bull elephant; this we now carefully followed, and, after many windings, we felt convinced that he was still within the broken ground that formed the Settite valley. After some hours' most difficult tracking, Taher Noor, who was leading the way, suddenly sank gently upon all fours. This movement was immediately, but quietly imitated by the whole party, and I quickly distinguished a large grey mass about sixty yards distant among the bushes, which, being quite leafless, screened the form of the bull elephant, as seen through a veil of treble gauze. I felt quite sure that we should fail in a close approach with so large a party. I therefore proposed that I should lead the way with the Ceylon No. 10, and creep quite close to the elephant, while one of th aggageers should attempt to sabre the back sinew. Jali whispered, that the sword was useless in the high and thick grass in which he was standing, surrounded by thorns; accordingly I told Florian to follow me, and I crept forward. With difficulty, upon hands and knees, I avoided the hooked thorns that would otherwise have fastened upon my clothes, and, with the wind favourable, I at length succeeded in passing through the intervening jungle, and arrived at a small plot of grass that was sufficiently high to reach the shoulder of the elephant. This open space was about fifteen yards in diameter, and was surrounded upon all sides by thick jungle. He was a splendid bull, and stood temptingly for a forehead shot, according to Ceylon practice, as he was exactly facing me at about ten yards' distance. Having been fortunate with the front shot at Geera, I determined to try the effect; I aimed low, and crack went the old Ceylon No. 10 rifle, with seven drachms of powder, and a ball of quicksilver and lead. For an instant the smoke in the high grass obscured the effect, but almost immediately after, I heard a tremendous rush, and, instead of falling, as I had expected, I saw the elephant crash headlong through the thorny jungle. No one was behind me, as Florian had misunderstood the arrangement that he was to endeavour to obtain a quick shot should I fail. I began to believe in what I had frequently heard asserted, that the forehead shot so fatal to the Indian elephant had no effect upon the African species, except by mere chance. I had taken so steady an aim at the convexity at the root of the trunk, that every advantage had been given to the bullet; but the rifle that in Ceylon had been almost certain at an elephant, had completely failed. It was quite impossible to follow the animal through the jungle of hooked thorns. On our way toward the camp we saw tracks of rhinoceroses, giraffes, buffaloes, and a variety of antelopes, but none of the animals themselves.

On the following morning we started, several times fording the river to avoid the bends: our course was due east. After the first three hours' ride through a beautiful country bordering the Settite valley, which we several times descended, we came in clear view of the magnificent range of mountains, that from Geera could hardly be discerned; this was the great range of Abyssinia, some points of which exceed 10,000 feet. The country that we now traversed was so totally uninhabited that it was devoid of all footprints of human beings; even the sand by the river's side, that like the snow confessed every print, was free from all traces of man. The Base were evidently absent from our neighbourhood.

We had several times disturbed antelopes during the early portion of the march, and we had just ascended from the rugged slopes of the valley, when we observed a troop of about a hundred baboons, who were gathering gum arabic from the mimosas; upon seeing us, they immediately waddled off. "Would the lady like to have a girrit (baboon)?" exclaimed the ever-excited Jali: being answered in the affirmative, away dashed the three hunters in full gallop after the astonished apes, who, finding themselves pursued, went off at their best speed. The ground was rough, being full of broken hollows, covered scantily with mimosas, and the stupid baboons, instead of turning to the right into the rugged and steep valley of the Settite, where they would have been secure from the aggageers, kept a straight course before the horses. It was a curious hunt; some of the very young baboons were riding on their mothers' backs: these were now going at their best pace, holding on to their maternal steeds, and looking absurdly human; but, in a few minutes, as we closely followed the Arabs, we were all in the midst of the herd, and with great dexterity two of the aggageers, while at full speed, stooped like falcons from their saddles, and seized each a half-grown ape by the back of the neck and hoisted them upon the necks of the horses. Instead of biting, as I had expected, the astonished captives sat astride of the horses, and clung tenaciously with both arms to the necks of their steeds, screaming with fear. The hunt was over, and we halted to secure the prisoners. Dismounting, to my surprise the Arabs immediately stripped from a mimosa several thongs of bark, and having tied the baboons by the neck, they gave them a merciless whipping with their powerful coorbatches of hippopotamus hide. It was in vain that I remonstrated against this harsh treatment; they persisted in the punishment, otherwise they declared that the baboons would bite, but if well whipped they would become "miskeen" (humble). At length my wife insisted upon mercy, and the unfortunate captives wore an expression of countenance like prisoners about to be led to execution, and they looked imploringly at our faces, in which they evidently discovered some sympathy with their fate. They were quickly placed on horseback before their captors, and once more we continued our journey, highly amused with the little entr'acte.

We had hardly ridden half a mile, when I perceived a fine bull tetel (Antelopus Bubalis) standing near a bush a few hundred yards distant. Motioning to the party to halt, I dismounted, and with the little Fletcher rifle I endeavoured to obtain a shot. When within about a hundred and seventy yards, he observed our party, and I was obliged to take the shot, although I could have approached unseen to a closer distance, had his attention not been attracted by the noise of the horses. He threw his head up preparatory to starting off, and he was just upon the move as I touched the trigger. He fell like a stone to the shot, but almost immediately he regained his feet, and bounded off, receiving a bullet from the second barrel without a flinch; in full speed he rushed away across the party of aggageers about three hundred yards distant. Out dashed Abou Do from the ranks on his active grey horse, and away he flew after the wounded tetel; his long hair floating in the wind, his naked sword in hand, and his heels digging into the flanks of his horse, as though armed with spurs in the last finish of a race. It was a beautiful course; Abou Do hunted like a cunning greyhound; the tetel turned, and taking advantage of the double, he cut off the angle; succeeding by the manoeuvre, he again followed at tremendous speed over the numerous inequalities of the ground, gaining in the race until he was within twenty yards of the tetel, when we lost sight of both game and hunter in the thick bushes. By this time I had regained my horse, that was brought to meet me, and I followed to the spot, towards which my wife, and the aggageers encumbered with the unwilling apes, were already hastening. Upon arrival I found, in high yellow grass beneath a large tree, the tetel dead, and Abou Do wiping his bloody sword, surrounded by the foremost of the party. He had hamstrung the animal so delicately, that the keen edge of the blade was not injured against the bone. My two bullets had passed through the tetel; the first was too high, having entered above the shoulder – this had dropped the animal for a moment; the second was through the flank. The Arabs now tied the baboons to trees, and employed themselves in carefully skinning the tetel so as to form a sack from the hide; they had about half finished the operation, when we were disturbed by a peculiar sound at a considerable distance in the jungle, which, being repeated, we knew to be the cry of buffaloes. In an instant the tetel was neglected, the aggageers mounted their horses, and leaving my wife with a few men to take charge of the game, accompanied by Florian we went in search of the buffaloes. This part of the country was covered with grass about nine feet high, that was reduced to such extreme dryness that the stems broke into several pieces like glass as we brushed through it. The jungle was open, composed of thorny mimosas at such wide intervals, that a horse could be ridden at considerable speed if accustomed to the country. Altogether it was the perfection of ground for shooting, and the chances were in favour of the rifle.

We had proceeded carefully about half a mile when I heard a rustling in the grass, and I shortly perceived a bull buffalo standing alone beneath a tree, close to the sandy bed of a dried stream, about a hundred yards distant between us and the animal; the grass had been entirely destroyed by the trampling of a large herd. I took aim at the shoulder with one of my No. 10 Reilly rifles, and the buffalo rushed forward at the shot, and fell about a hundred paces beyond in the bush. At the report of the shot, the herd that we had not observed, which had been lying upon the sandy bed of the stream, rushed past us with a sound like thunder, in a cloud of dust raised by several hundreds of large animals in full gallop. I could hardly see them distinctly, and I waited for a good chance, when presently a mighty bull separated from the rest, and gave me a fair shoulder shot. I fired a little too forward, and missed the shoulder; but I made a still better shot by mistake, as the Reilly bullet broke the spine through the neck, and dropped him dead. Florian, poor fellow, had not the necessary tools for the work, and one of his light guns produced no effect. Now came the time for the aggageers. Away dashed Jali on his fiery mare, closely followed by Abou Do and Suleiman, who in a few instants were obscured in the cloud of dust raised by the retreating buffaloes. As soon as I could mount my horse that had been led behind me, I followed at full speed, and spurring hard, I shortly came in sight of the three aggageers, not only in the dust, but actually among the rear buffaloes of the herd. Suddenly, Jali almost disappeared from the saddle as he leaned forward with a jerk, and seized a fine young buffalo by the tail. In a moment Abou Do and Suleiman sprang from their horses, and I arrived just in time to assist them in securing a fine little bull of about twelve hands high, whose horns were six or seven inches long. A pretty fight we had with the young Hercules. The Arabs stuck to him like bull-dogs, in spite of his tremendous struggles, and Florian, with other men, shortly arriving, we secured him by lashing his legs together with our belts until impromptu ropes could be made with mimosa bark. I now returned to the spot where we had left my wife and the tetel. I found her standing about fifty yards from the spot with a double rifle cocked, awaiting an expected charge from one of the buffaloes that, separated from the herd, had happened to rush in her direction. Mahomet had been in an awful fright, and was now standing secure behind his mistress. I rode through the grass with the hope of getting a shot, but the animal had disappeared. We returned to the dead tetel and to our captive baboons; but times had changed since we had left them. One had taken advantage of our absence, and, having bitten through his tether, he had escaped; the other had used force instead of cunning, and, in attempting to tear away from confinement, had strangled himself with the slip-knot of the rope.

The aggageers now came up with the young buffalo. This was a great prize, as zoological specimens were much sought after at Cassala by an agent from Italy, who had given contracts for a supply. My hunters, to whom I willingly gave my share in the animal, left one of their party with several of my people to obtain the assistance of the camel-drivers, who were not far distant in the rear; these were to bring the flesh of the animals, and to drive the young bull on the march.

We now pushed on ahead, and at 5 p.m. we arrived at the spot on the margin of the Settite river at which we were to encamp for some time.

In this position, the valley of the Settite had changed its character: instead of the rugged and broken slopes on either side of the river, ascending gradually to the high table lands, the east bank of the river was low, and extended, in a perfect flat for about eight miles, to the foot of an abrupt range of hills; the base had many ages ago formed the margin of the stream, which had washed this enormous mass of soil towards the Atbara river, to be carried by the Nile for a deposit in Lower Egypt. During the rainy season, the river overflowed its banks, and attained a width in many places of six and seven hundred yards. The soil was rich, and, having imbibed much moisture from a periodical overflow, it gave birth to thick jungles of nabbuk (Rhamnus lotus), together with luxuriant grass, which being beautifully green while all other leaves and herbage were parched and withered, afforded pasturage and shade that attracted a number of wild animals. For many miles on either side the river was fringed with dense groves of the green nabbuk, but upon the east bank, an island had been formed of about three hundred acres; this was a perfect oasis of verdure, covered with large nabbuk trees, about thirty feet high, and forming a mixture of the densest coverts, with small open glades of rich but low herbage. To reach this island, upon which we were to encamp, it was necessary to cross the arm of the river, that was now dry, with the exception of deep pools, in one of which we perceived a large bull buffalo drinking, just as we descended the hill. As this would be close to the larder, I stalked to within ninety yards, and fired a Reilly No. 10 into his back, as his head inclined to the water. For the moment he fell upon his knees, but recovering immediately, he rushed up the steep bank of the island, receiving my left-hand barrel between the shoulders, and he disappeared in the dense covert of green nabbuk on the margin. As we were to camp within a few yards of the spot, he was close to home; therefore, having crossed the river, we carefully followed the blood tracks through the jungle; but, after having pushed our way for about twenty paces through the dense covert, I came to the wise conclusion that it was not the place for following a wounded buffalo, and that we should find him dead on the next morning. A few yards upon our right hand was a beautiful open glade, commanding a view of the river, and surrounded by the largest nabbuk trees, that afforded a delightful shade in the midst of the thick covert. This was a spot that in former years had been used by the aggageers as a camp, and we accordingly dismounted, and turned the horses to graze upon the welcome grass. Each horse was secured to a peg by a long leathern thong, as the lions in this neighbourhood were extremely dangerous, having the advantage of thick and opaque jungle.

We employed ourselves until the camels should arrive, in cutting thorn branches, and constructing a zareeba, or fenced camp, to protect our animals during the night from the attack of wild beasts. I also hollowed out a thick green bush to form an arbour, as a retreat during the heat of the day, and in a short space of time we were prepared for the reception of the camels and effects. The river had cast up immense stores of dry wood; this we had collected, and, by the time the camels arrived with the remainder of our party after dark, huge fires were blazing high in air, the light of which had guided them direct to our camp. They were heavily laden with meat, which is the Arab's great source of happiness, therefore in a few minutes the whole party was busily employed in cutting the flesh into long thin strips to dry; these were hung in festoons over the surrounding trees, while the fires were heaped with tit-bits of all descriptions. I had chosen a remarkably snug position for ourselves; the two angareps (stretchers) were neatly arranged in the middle of a small open space free from overhanging boughs; near these blazed a large fire, upon which were roasting a row of marrow-bones of buffalo and tetel, while the table was spread with a clean cloth, and arranged for dinner.

The woman Barrake, who had discovered with regret that she was not a wife but a servant, had got over the disappointment, and was now making dhurra cakes upon the doka: this is a round earthenware tray about eighteen inches in diameter, which, supported upon three stones or lumps of earth, over a fire of glowing embers, forms a hearth. Slices of liver, well peppered with cayenne and salt, were grilling on the gridiron, and we were preparing to dine, when a terrific roar within a hundred and fifty yards informed us that a lion was also thinking of dinner. A confusion of tremendous roars proceeding from several lions followed the first round, and my aggageers quietly remarked, "There is no danger for the horses to-night, the lions have found your wounded buffalo!"

Such a magnificent chorus of bass voices I had never heard; the jungle cracked, as with repeated roars they dragged the carcase of the buffalo through the thorns to the spot where they intended to devour it. That which was music to our ears was discord to that of Mahomet, who with terror in hs face came to us and exclaimed: "Master, what's that? What for master and the missus come to this bad country? That's one bad kind will eat the missus in the night! Perhaps he come and eat Mahomet!" This after-thought was too much for him, and Bacheet immediately comforted him by telling the most horrible tales of death and destruction that had been wrought by lions, until the nerves of Mahomet were completely unhinged.

This was a signal for story-telling, when suddenly the aggageers changed the conversation by a few tales of the Base natives, which so thoroughly eclipsed the dangers of wild beasts, that in a short time the entire party would almost have welcomed a lion, provided would he only have agreed to protect them from the Base. In this very spot where we were then camped, a party of Arab hunters had, two years previous, been surprised at night and killed by the Base, who still boasted of the swords that they possessed as spoils from that occasion. The Base knew this spot as the favourite resting-place of the Hamran hunting-parties, and they might be not far distant now, as we were in the heart of their country. This intelligence was a regular damper to the spirits of some of the party. Mahomet quietly retired and sat down by Barrake, the ex-slave woman, having expressed a resolution to keep awake every hour that he should be compelled to remain in that horrible country. The lions roared louder and louder, but no one appeared to notice such small thunder; all thoughts were fixed upon the Base, so thoroughly had the aggageers succeeded in frightening not only Mahomet, but also our Tokrooris.

Chapter XIII.

The Lions Find the Buffalo.

Early on the following morning the lions were still roaring, apparently within a hundred yards of the camp. I accordingly took a Reilly No. 10 double rifle and accompanied by my wife, who was anxious to see these glorious animals, and who carried my little Fletcher No. 24, I skirted the outside of the jungle on the high bank, on the narrow arm of the river. We were not long in finding traces of the lions. A broad track in the sandy bed of the dried stream showed where the buffalo had been dragged across to the thick and impervious green bushes, exactly beneath us on the margin of the river. A hind quarter of the buffalo, much gnawed, lay within seven or eight paces of us, among the bushes that had been trampled down, and the dung of numerous lions lay upon the open ground near the place of their concealment. We had two Tokrooris with us, carrying spare rifles, and I felt sure that the lions were within the bushes of dense nabbuk, which concealed them as perfectly as though behind a closed curtain. We approached within three or four yards of this effective screen, when suddenly we heard the cracking of bones, as the lions feasted in their den close to us; they would not show themselves, nor was there any possibility of obtaining a shot; therefore, after ascending the high bank, and waiting for some time in the hope that one might emerge to drag away the exposed portion of the buffalo, we returned to camp.

The aggageers had already returned from a reconnaissance of the country, as they had started before daybreak in search of elephants; they reported the fresh tracks of a herd, and they begged me to lose no time in accompanying them, as the elephants might retreat to a great distance. There was no need for this advice; in a few minutes my horse Tetel was saddled, and my six Tokrooris and Bacheet, with spare rifles, were in attendance. Bacheet, who had so ingloriously failed in his first essay at Wat el Negur, had been so laughed at by the girls of the village for his want of pluck, that he had declared himself ready to face the devil rather than the ridicule of the fair sex; and, to do him justice, he subsequently became a first-rate lad in moments of danger.

The aggageers were quickly mounted. It was a sight most grateful to a sportsman to witness the start of these superb hunters, who with the sabres slung from the saddle-bow, as though upon an everyday occasion, now left the camp with these simple weapons, to meet the mightiest animal of the creation in hand-to-hand conflict. The horses' hoofs clattered as we descended the shingly beach, and forded the river shoulder-deep, through the rapid current, while those on foot clung to the manes of the horses, and to the stirrup-leathers, to steady themselves over the loose stones beneath.

Shortly after our arrival upon the opposite side, we came upon numerous antelopes of the nellut (A. Strepsiceros) and tetel (A. Bubalis). I would not fire at these tempting animals, as we were seeking nobler game.

Tracking was very difficult; as there was a total absence of rain, it was next to impossible to distinguish the tracks of two days' date from those most recent upon the hard and parched soil; the only positive clue was the fresh dung of the elephants, and this being deposited at long intervals rendered the search extremely tedious. The greater part of the day passed in useless toil, and, after fording the river backwards and forwards several times, we at length arrived at a large area of sand in the bend of the stream, that was evidently overflowed when the river was full; this surface of many acres was backed by a forest of large trees. Upon arrival at this spot, the aggageers, who appeared to know every inch of the country, declared that, unless the elephants had gone far away, they must be close at hand, within the forest. We were speculating upon the direction of the wind, when we were surprised by the sudden trumpet of an elephant, that proceeded from the forest already declared to be the covert of the herd. In a few minutes later, a fine bull elephant marched majestically from the jungle upon the large area of sand, and proudly stalked direct towards the river.

At that time we were stationed under cover of a high bank of sand that had been left by the retiring river in sweeping round an angle; we immediately dismounted, and remained well concealed. The question of attack was quickly settled; the elephant was quietly stalking towards the water which was about three hundred paces distant from the jungle: this intervening space was heavy dry sand, that had been thrown up by the stream in the sudden bend of the river, which, turning from this point at a right angle, swept beneath a perpendicular cliff of conglomerate rock formed of rounded pebbles cemented together.

I proposed that we should endeavour to stalk the elephant, by creeping along the edge of the river, under cover of a sand bank about three feet high, and that, should the rifles fail, the aggageers should come on at full gallop, and cut off his retreat from the jungle; we should then have a chance for the swords.

Accordingly, I led the way, followed by Hadji Ali, my head Tokroori, with a rifle, while I carried the "Baby." Florian accompanied us. Having the wind fair, we advanced quickly for about half the distance, at which time we were within a hundred and fifty yards of the elephant, who had just arrived at the water, and had commenced drinking. We now crept cautiously towards him; the sand bank had decreased to a height of about two feet, and afforded very little shelter. Not a tree nor bush grew upon the surface of the barren sand, which was so deep that we sank nearly to the ankles at every footstep. Still we crept forward, as the elephant alternately drank, and then spouted the water in a shower over his colossal form; but just as we had arrived within about fifty yards, he happened to turn his head in our direction, and immediately perceived us. He cocked his enormous ears, gave a short trumpet, and for an instant he wavered in his determination whether to attack or fly; but as I rushed towards him with a shout, he turned towards the jungle, and I immediately fired a steady shot at the shoulder with the "Baby." As usual, the fearful recoil of the rifle, with a half-pound shell and twelve drachms of powder, nearly threw me backwards; but I saw the mark upon the elephant's shoulder, in an excellent line, although rather high. The only effect of the shot was to send him off at great speed towards the jungle; but at the same moment the three aggageers came galloping across the sand like greyhounds in a course, and, judiciously keeping parallel with the jungle, they cut off his retreat, and, turning towards the elephant, they confronted him, sword in hand. At once the furious beast charged straight at the enemy; but now came the very gallant, but foolish, part of the hunt. Instead of leading the elephant by the flight of one man and horse, according to their usual method, all the aggageers at the same moment sprang from their saddles, and upon foot in the heavy sand they attacked the elephant with their swords.

In the way of sport, I never saw anything so magnificent, or so absurdly dangerous. No gladiatorial exhibition in the Roman arena could have surpassed this fight. The elephant was mad with rage, and nevertheless he seemed to know that the object of the hunters was to get behind him. This he avoided with great dexterity, turning as it were upon a pivot with extreme quickness, and charging headlong, first at one, and then at another of his assailants, while he blew clouds of sand in the air with his trunk, and screamed with fury. Nimble as monkeys, nevertheless the aggageers could not get behind him. In the folly of excitement they had forsaken their horses, which had escaped from the spot. The depth of the loose sand was in favour of the elephant, and was so much against the men that they avoided his charges with extreme difficulty. It was only by the determined pluck of all three that they alternately saved each other, as two invariably dashed in at the flanks when the elephant charged the third, upon which the wary animal immediately relinquished the chase, and turned round upon his pursuers. During this time, I had been labouring through the heavy sand, and shortly after I arrived at the fight, the elephant charged directly through the aggageers, receiving a shoulder shot from one of my Reilly No. 10 rifles, and at the same time a slash from the sword of Abou Do, who, with great dexterity and speed, had closed in behind him, just in time to reach the leg. Unfortunately, he could not deliver the cut in the right place, as the elephant, with increased speed, completely distanced the aggageers; he charged across the deep sand, and reached the jungle. We were shortly upon his tracks, and after running about a quarter of a mile, he fell dead in a dry watercourse. His tusks were, like the generality of Abyssinian elephants, exceedingly short, but of good thickness.

Some of our men, who had followed the runaway horses, shortly returned, and reported that, during our fight with the bull, they had heard other elephants trumpeting in the dense nabbuk jungle near the river. A portion of thick forest of about two hundred acres, upon this side of the river, was a tempting covert for elephants, and the aggageers, who were perfectly familiar with the habits of the animals, positively declared that the herd must be within this jungle. Accordingly, we proposed to skirt the margin of the river, which, as it made a bend at right angles, commanded two sides of a square. Upon reaching the jungle by the river side, we again heard the trumpet of an elephant and about a quarter of a mile distant we observed a herd of twelve of these animals shoulder-deep in the river, which they were in the act of crossing to the opposite side, to secure themselves in an almost impenetrable jungle of thorny nabbuk. The aggageers advised that we should return to the ford that we had already crossed, and, by repassing the river, we should most probably meet the elephants, as they would not leave the thick jungle until the night. Having implicit confidence in their knowledge of the country, I followed their directions, and we shortly recrossed the ford, and arrived upon a dry portion of the river's bed, banked by a dense thicket of nabbuk.

Jali now took the management of affairs. We all dismounted, and sent the horses to a considerable distance, lest they should by some noise disturb the elephants. We shortly heard a cracking in the jungle on our right, and Jali assured us, that, as he had expected, the elephants were slowly advancing along the jungle on the bank of the river, and they would pass exactly before us. We waited patiently in the bed of the river, and the cracking in the jungle sounded closer as the herd evidently approached.

The strip of thick thorny covert that fringed the margin was in no place wider than half a mile – beyond that, the country was open and park-like, but at this season it was covered with parched grass from eight to ten feet high; the elephants would, therefore, most probably remain in the jungle until driven out.

In about a quarter of an hour, we heard by the noise in the jungle, about a hundred yards from the river, that the elephants were directly opposite to us. I accordingly instructed Jali to creep quietly by himself into the bush and to bring me information of their position: to this he at once agreed.

In three or four minutes he returned; he declared it impossible to use the sword, as the jungle was so dense that it would check the blow, but that I could use the rifle, as the elephants were close to us – he had seen three standing together, between us and the main body of the herd. I told Jali to lead me direct to the spot, and, followed by Fiorian and the aggageers, with my gun-bearers, I kept within a foot of my dependable little guide, who crept gently into the jungle; this was intensely thick, and quite impenetrable, except in such places where elephants and other heavy animals had trodden numerous alleys. Along one of these narrow passages we stealthily advanced, until Jali stepped quietly on one side, and pointed with his finger; I immediately observed two elephants looming through the thick bushes about eight paces from me. One offered a temple shot, which I quickly took with a Reilly No. 10, and floored it on the spot. The smoke hung so thickly, that I could not see sufficiently distinctly to fire my second barrel before the remaining elephant had turned; but Florian, with a three-ounce steel-tipped bullet, by a curious shot at the hind quarters, injured the hip joint to such an extent that we could more than equal the elephant in speed. In a few moments we found ourselves in a small open glade in the middle of the jungle, close to the stern of the elephant we were following. I had taken a fresh rifle, with both barrels loaded, and hardly had I made the exchange, when the elephant turned suddenly, and charged. Determined to try fairly the forehead shot, I kept my ground, and fired a Reilly No. 10, quicksilver and lead bullet, exactly in the centre, when certainly within four yards. The only effect was to make her stagger backwards, when, in another moment, with her immense ears thrown forward, she again rushed on. This was touch-and-go; but I fired my remaining barrel a little lower than the first shot. Checked in her rush, she backed towards the dense jungle, throwing her trunk about and trumpeting with rage. Snatching the Ceylon No. 10 from one of my trusty Tokrooris (Hassan), I ran straight at her, took a most deliberate aim at the forehead, and once more fired. The only effect was a decisive charge; but before I fired my last barrel, Jali rushed in, and, with one blow of his sharp sword, severed the back sinew. She was utterly helpless in the same instant. Bravo, Jali! I had fired three beautifully correct shots with No. 10 bullets, and seven drachms of powder in each charge; these were so nearly together that they occupied a space in her forehead of about three inches, and all had failed to kill! There could no longer be any doubt that the forehead shot at an African elephant could not be relied upon, although so fatal to the Indian species: this increased the danger tenfold, as in Ceylon I had generally made certain of an elephant by steadily waiting until it was close upon me.

I now reloaded my rifles, and the aggageers quitted the jungle to remount their horses, as they expected the herd had broken cover on the other side of the jungle; in which case they intended to give chase, and if possible, to turn them back into the covert, and drive them towards the guns. We accordingly took our stand in the small open glade, and I lent Florian one of my double rifles, as he was only provided with one single-barrelled elephant gun. I did not wish to destroy the prestige of the rifles, by hinting to the aggageers that it would be rather awkward for us to receive the charge of the infuriated herd, as the foreheads were invulnerable; but inwardly I rather hoped that they would not come so direct upon our position as the aggageers wished.

About a quarter of an hour passed in suspense, when we suddenly heard a chorus of wild cries of excitement on the other side of the jungle, raised iy the aggageers, who had headed the herd, and were driving them back towards us. In a few minutes a tremendous crashing in the jungle, accompanied by the occasional shrill scream of a savage elephant, and the continued shouts of the mounted aggageers, assured us that they were bearing down exactly upon our direction; they were apparently followed even through the dense jungle by the wild and reckless Arabs. I called my men close together, and told them to stand fast, and hand me the guns quickly; and we eagerly awaited the onset that rushed towards us like a storm. On they came, tearing everything before them. For a moment the jungle quivered and crashed; a second later, and, headed by an immense elephant, the herd thundered down upon us. The great leader came direct at me, and was received with right and left in the forehead from a Reilly No. 10 as fast as I could pull the triggers. The shock made it reel backwards for an instant, and fortunately turned it and the herd likewise. My second rifle was beautifully handed, and I made a quick right and left at the temples of two fine elephants, dropping them both stone-dead. At this moment the "Baby" was pushed into my hand by Hadji Ali just in time to take the shoulder of the last of the herd, who had already charged headlong after his comrades, and was disappearing in the jungle. Bang! went the "Baby;" round I spun like a weathercock, with the blood pouring from my nose, as the recoil had driven the sharp top of the hammer deep into the bridge. My "Baby" not only screamed, but kicked viciously. However, I knew that the elephant must be bagged, as the half-pound shell had been aimed directly behind the shoulder.

In a few minutes the aggageers arrived; they were bleeding from countless scratches, as, although naked, with the exception of short drawers, they had forced their way on horseback through the thorny path cleft by the herd in rushing through the jungle. Abou Do had blood upon his sword. They had found the elephants commencing a retreat to the interior of the country, and they had arrived just in time to turn them. Following them at full speed, Abou Do had succeeded in overtaking and slashing the sinew of an elephant just as it was entering the jungle. Thus the aggageers had secured one, in addition to Fiorian's elephant that had been slashed by Jali. We now hunted for the "Baby's" elephant, which was almost immediately discovered lying dead within a hundred and fifty yards of the place where it had received the shot. The shell had entered close to the shoulder, and it was extraordinary that an animal should have been able to travel so great a distance with a wound through the lungs by a shell that had exploded within the body.

We had done pretty well. I had been fortunate in bagging four from this herd, in addition to the single bull in the morning; total, five. Florian had killed one, and the aggageers one; total, seven elephants. One had escaped that I had wounded in the shoulder, and two that had been wounded by Florian.

The aggageers were delighted, and they determined to search for the wounded elephants on the following day, as the evening was advancing, and we were about five miles from camp. Having my measuring-tape in a game-bag that was always carried by Abdoolahi, I measured accurately one of the elephants that had fallen with the legs stretched out, so that the height to the shoulder could be exactly taken: – From foot to shoulder in a direct line, nine feet one inch; circumference of foot, four feet eight inches. The elephant lying by her side was still larger, but the legs being doubled up, I could not measure her: these were females.

We now left the jungle, and found our horses waiting for us in the bed of the river by the water side, and we rode towards our camp well satisfied with the day's work. Upon entering an open plain of low withered grass we perceived a boar, who upon our approach showed no signs of fear, but insolently erected his tail and scrutinised our party. Florian dismounted and fired a shot, which passed through his flank, and sent the boar flying off at full speed. Abou Do and I gave chase on horseback, and after a run of a few hundred yards we overtook the boar, which turned resolutely to bay.

In a short time the whole party arrived, and, as Florian had wounded the animal, his servant Richarn considered that he should give the coup de grace; but upon his advancing with his drawn knife, the boar charged desperately, and inflicted a serious wound across the palm of his hand, which was completely divided to the bone by a gash with the sharp tusk. Abou Do immediately rode to the rescue, and with a blow of his sword divided the spine behind the shoulder, and nearly cut the boar in half. By this accident Richarn was disabled for some days.

Upon our arrival at the camp, there were great rejoicings among our people at the result of the day's sport. Old Moosa, the half fortune-teller, half priest, of the Tokrooris, had in our absence employed himself in foretelling the number of elephants we should kill. His method of conjuring was rather perplexing, and, although a mystery beyond my understanding, it might be simple to an English spiritualist or spirit-rapper; he had nevertheless satisfied both himself and others, therefore the party had been anxiously waiting our return to hear the result. Of course, old Moosa was wrong, and of course he had a loop-hole for escape, and thereby preserved his reputation. The aggageers expected to find our wounded elephants on the following morning, if dead, by the flights of vultures. That night the lions again serenaded us with constant roaring, as they had still some bones to gnaw of the buffalo's remains.

At daybreak the next morning, the aggageers in high glee mounted their horses, and with a long retinue of camels, and men provided with axes and knives, together with large gum sacks to contain the flesh, they quitted the camp to cut up the numerous elephants. As I had no taste for this disgusting work, I took two of my Tokrooris, Hadji Ali and Hassan, and, accompanied by old Abou Do, the father of the sheik, with his harpoon, we started along the margin of the river in quest of hippopotami.

The harpoon for hippopotamus and crocodile hunting is a piece of soft steel about eleven inches long, with a narrow blade or point of about three-quarters of an inch in width, and a single but powerful barb. To this short, and apparently insignificant weapon, a strong rope is secured, about twenty feet in length, at the extremity of which is a buoy or float as large as a child's head formed of an extremely light wood called ambatch (Anemone mirabilis), that is about half the specific gravity of cork. The extreme end of the short harpoon is fixed in the point of a bamboo about ten feet long, around which the rope is twisted, while the buoy end is carried in the left hand.

The old Abou Do being resolved upon work, had divested himself of his tope or toga before starting, according to the general custom of the aggageers, who usually wear a simple piece of leather wound round the loins when hunting, but, I believe in respect for our party, they had provided themselves with a garment resembling bathing drawers, such as are worn in France, Germany, and other civilized countries; but the old Abou Do, like the English, had resisted any such innovation, and he accordingly appeared with nothing on but his harpoon; and a more superb old Neptune I never beheld. He carried this weapon in his hand, as the trident with which the old sea-god ruled the monsters of the deep; and as the tall Arab patriarch of threescore years and ten, with his long grey locks flowing over his brawny shoulders, stepped as lightly as a goat from rock to rock along the rough margin of the river, I followed him in admiration.

The country was very beautiful; we were within twenty miles of lofty mountains, while at a distance of about thirty-five or forty miles were the high peaks of the Abyssinian Alps. The entire land was richly wooded, although open, and adapted for hunting upon horseback. Through this wild and lovely country the river Settite flowed in an ever-changing course. At times the bed was several hundred yards wide, with the stream, contracted at this season, flowing gently over rounded pebbles; the water was as clear as glass; in other places huge masses of rock impeded the flow of water, and caused dangerous rapids; then, as the river passed through a range of hills, perpendicular cliffs of sandstone and of basalt walled it within a narrow channel, through which it rushed with great impetuosity; issuing from these straits it calmed its fury in a deep and broad pool, from which it again commenced a gentle course over sands and pebbles. At that season the river would have been perfection for salmon, being a series of rapids, shallows, deep and rocky gorges, and quiet silent pools of unknown depth; in the latter places of security the hippopotami retreated after their nocturnal rambles upon terra firma. The banks of this beautiful river were generally thickly clothed with bright green nabbuk trees, that formed a shelter for *innumerable* guinea-fowl, and the black francolin partridge. Herds of antelopes of many varieties were forced to the river to drink, as the only water within many miles; but these never remained long among the thick nabbuk, as the lions and leopards inhabited that covert expressly to spring upon the unwary animal whose thirst prompted a too heedless advance. Wherever there was a sand bank in the river, a crocodile basked in the morning sunshine: some of these were of enormous size.

Hippopotami had trodden a path along the margin of the river, as these animals came out to feed shortly after dark, and travelled from pool to pool. Wherever a plot of tangled and succulent herbage grew among the shady nabbuks, there were the marks of the harrow-like teeth, that had torn and rooted up the rank grass like an agricultural implement.

After walking about two miles, we noticed a herd of hippopotami in a pool below a rapid: this was surrounded by rocks, except upon one side, where the rush of water had thrown up a bank of pebbles and sand. Our old Neptune did not condescend to bestow the slightest attention when I pointed out these animals; they were too wide awake; but he immediately quitted the river's bed, and we followed him quietly behind the fringe of bushes upon the border, from which we carefully examined the water. About half a mile below this spot, as we clambered over the intervening rocks through a gorge which formed a powerful rapid, I observed, in a small pool just below the rapid, an immense head of a hippopotamus close to a perpendicular rock that formed a wall to the river, about six feet above the surface. I pointed out the hippo to old Abou Do, who had not seen it. At once the gravity of the old Arab disappeared, and the energy of the hunter was exhibited as he motioned us to remain, while he ran nimbly behind the thick screen of bushes for about a hundred and fifty yards below the spot where the hippo was unconsciously basking, with his ugly head above the surface. Plunging into the rapid torrent, the veteran hunter was carried some distance down the stream, but breasting the powerful current, he landed upon the rocks on the opposite side, and retiring to some distance from the river, he quickly advanced towards the spot beneath which the hippopotamus was lying. I had a fine view of the scene, as I was lying concealed exactly opposite the hippo, who had disappeared beneath the water. Abou Do now stealthily approached the ledge of rock beneath which he had expected to see the head of the animal; his long sinewy arm was raised, with the harpoon ready to strike, as he carefully advanced. At length he reached the edge of the perpendicular rock; the hippo had vanished, but, far from exhibiting surprise, the old Arab remained standing on the sharp ledge, unchanged in attitude. No figure of bronze could have been more rigid than that of the old river-king, as he stood erect upon the rock with the left foot advanced, and the harpoon poised in his ready right hand above his head, while in the left he held the loose coils of rope attached to the ambatch buoy. For about three minutes he stood like a statue, gazing intently into the clear and deep water beneath his feet. I watched eagerly for the reappearance of the hippo; the surface of the water was still barren, when suddenly the right arm of the statue descended like lightning, and the harpoon shot perpendicularly into the pool with the speed of an arrow. What river-fiend answered to the summons? In an instant an enormous pair of open jaws appeared, followed by the ungainly head and form of the furious hippopotamus, who, springing half out of the water, lashed the river into foam, and, disdaining the concealment of the deep pool, he charged straight up the violent rapids. With extraordinary power he breasted the descending stream; gaining a footing in the rapids, about five feet deep, he ploughed his way against the broken waves, sending them in showers of spray upon all sides, and upon gaining broader shallows he tore along through the water, with the buoyant float hopping behind him along the surface, until he landed from the river, started at full gallop along the dry shingly bed, and at length disappeared in the thorny nabbuk jungle.

I never could have imagined that so unwieldy an animal could have exhibited such speed; no man would have had a chance of escape, and it was fortunate for our old Neptune that he was secure upon the high ledge of rock, for if he had been in the path of the infuriated beast. there would have been an end of Abou Do. The old man plunged into the deep pool just quitted by the hippo, and landed upon our side; while in the enthusiasm of the moment I waved my cap above my head, and gave him a British cheer as he reached the shore. His usually stern features relaxed into a grim smile of delight: this was one of those moments when the gratified pride of the hunter rewards him for any risks. I congratulated him upon his dexterity: but much remained to be done. I proposed to cross the river, and to follow upon the tracks of the hippopotamus, as I imagined that the buoy and rope would catch in the thick jungle, and that we should find him entangled in the bush; but the old hunter gently laid his hand upon my arm, and pointed up the bed of the river, explaining that the hippo would certainly return to the water after a short interval.

In a few minutes later, at a distance of nearly half a mile, we observed the hippo emerge from the jungle, and descend at full trot to the bed of the river, making direct for the first rocky pool in which we had noticed the herd of hippopotami. Accompanied by the old howarti (hippo hunter), we walked quickly towards the spot: he explained to me that I must shoot the harpooned hippo, as we should not be able to secure him in the usual method by ropes, as nearly all our men were absent from camp, disposing of the dead elephants.

Upon reaching the pool, which was about a hundred and thirty yards in diameter, we were immediately greeted by the hippo, who snorted and roared as we approached, but quickly dived, and the buoyant float ran along the surface, directing his course in the same manner as the cork of a trimmer with a pike upon the hook. Several times he appeared, but, as he invariably faced us, I could not obtain a favourable shot; I therefore sent the old hunter round the pool, and he, swimming the river, advanced to the opposite side, and attracted the attention of the hippo who immediately turned towards him. This afforded me a good chance, and I fired a steady shot behind the ear, at about seventy yards, with a single-barrelled rifle. As usual with hippopotami, whether dead or alive, he disappeared beneath the water at the shot. The crack of the ball and the absence of any splash from the bullet told me that he was hit; the ambatch float remained perfectly stationary upon the surface. I watched it for some minutes – it never moved; several heads of hippopotami appeared and vanished in different directions, but the float was still; it marked the spot where the grand old bull lay dead beneath.

I shot another hippo, that I thought must be likewise dead; and, taking the time by my watch, I retired to the shade of a tree with Hassan, while Hadji Ali and the old hunter returned to camp for assistance in men and knives, &c.

In a little more than an hour and a half, two objects like the backs of turtles appeared above the surface: these were the flanks of the two hippos. A short time afterwards the men arrived, and, regardless of crocodiles, they swam towards the bodies. One was towed directly to the shore by the rope attached to the harpoon, the other was secured by a long line, and dragged to the bank of clean pebbles.

I measured the bull that was harpooned; it was fourteen feet two inches from the upper lip to the extremity of the tail; the head was three feet one inch from the front of the ear to the edge of the lip in a straight line. The harpoon was sticking in the nape of the neck, having penetrated about two and a half inches beneath the hide; this is about an inch and three-quarters thick upon the back of the neck of a bull hippopotamus. It was a magnificent specimen, with the largest tusks I have ever seen; the skull is now in my hall in England.

Although the hippopotamus is generally harmless, the solitary old bulls are sometimes extremely vicious, especially when in the water. I have frequently known them charge a boat, and I have myself narrowly escaped being upset in a canoe by the attack of one of these creatures, without the slightest provocation. The females are extremely shy and harmless, and they are most affectionate mothers: the only instances that I have known of the female attacking a man, have been those in which her calf had been stolen. To the Arabs they are extremely valuable, yielding, in addition to a large quantity of excellent flesh, about two hundred pounds of fat, and a hide that will produce about two hundred coorbatches, or camel whips. I have never shot these useful creatures to waste; every morsel of the flesh has been stored either by the natives or for our own use; and whenever we have had a good supply of antelope or giraffe meat, I have avoided firing a shot at the hippo. Elephant flesh is exceedingly strong and disagreeable, partaking highly of the peculiar smell of the animal. We had now a good supply of meat from the two hippopotami, which delighted our people. The old Abou Do claimed the bull that he had harpooned as his own private property, and he took the greatest pains in dividing the hide longitudinally, in strips of the width of three fingers, which he cut with great dexterity.

Although the hippopotamus is amphibious, he requires a large and constant supply of air; the lungs are of enormous size, and he invariably inflates them before diving. From five to eight minutes is the time that he usually remains under water; he then comes to the surface, and expends the air within his lungs by blowing; he again refills the lungs almost instantaneously, and if frightened, he sinks immediately. In places where they have become extremely shy from being hunted, or fired at, they seldom expose the head above the surface, but merely protrude the nose to breathe through the nostrils; it is then impossible to shoot them. Their food consists of aquatic plants, and grasses of many descriptions. Not only do they visit the margin of the river, but they wander at night to great distances from the water if attracted by good pasturage, and, although clumsy and ungainly in appearance, they clamber up steep banks and precipitous ravines with astonishing power and ease. In places where they are perfectly undisturbed, they not only enjoy themselves in the sunshine by basking half asleep upon the surface of the water, but they lie upon the shore beneath the shady trees, upon the river's bank; I have seen them, when disturbed by our sudden arrival during the march, take a leap from a bank about twenty feet perpendicular depth into the water below, with a splash that has created waves in the quiet pool, as though a paddle-steamer had passed by. The Arabs attach no value to the tusks; these are far more valuable than elephant ivory, and are used by dentists in Europe for the manufacture of false teeth, for which they are admirably adapted, as they do not change colour. Not wishing to destroy the remaining hippopotami that were still within the pool, I left my men and old Abou Do busily engaged in arranging the meat, and I walked quietly homeward.

Chapter XIV.

A Foreboding of Evil.

I had been for some hours in the camp, but none of the aggageers had returned, neither had we received any tidings of our people and camels that had left us at daybreak to search for the dead elephants. Fearing that some mishap might have occurred in a collision with the Base, I anxiously looked out for some sign of the party. At about 4 p.m. I observed far up the bed of the river several men, some mounted, and others upon foot, while one led a camel with a curious looking load. Upon a nearer approach I could distinguish some large object upon the camel's back, that was steadied by two men, one of whom walked on either side. I had a foreboding that something was wrong, and in a few minutes I clearly perceived a man lying upon a make-shift litter, carried by the camel, while the Sheik Abou Do and Suleiman accompanied the party upon horseback; a third led Jali's little grey mare.

They soon arrived beneath the high bank of the river upon which I stood. Poor little Jali, my plucky and active ally, lay, as I thought, dead upon the litter. We laid him gently upon my angarep, which I had raised by four men, so that we could lower him gradually from the kneeling camel, and we carried him to the camp, about thirty yards distant. He was faint, and I poured some essence of peppermint (the only spirit I possessed) down his throat, which quickly revived him. His thigh was broken about eight inches above the knee, but fortunately it was a simple fracture.

Abou Do now explained the cause of the accident. While the party of camel-men and others were engaged in cutting up the dead elephants, the three aggageers had found the track of a bull that had escaped wounded. In that country, where there was no drop of water upon the east bank of the Settite for a distance of sixty or seventy miles to the river Gash, an elephant if wounded was afraid to trust itself to the interior; one of our escaped elephants had therefore returned to the thick jungle, and was tracked by the aggageers to a position within two or three hundred yards of the dead elephants. As there were no guns, two of the aggageers, utterly reckless of consequences, resolved to ride through the narrow passages formed by the large game, and to take their chance with the elephant, sword in hand. Jali, as usual, was the first to lead, and upon his little grey mare he advanced with the greatest difficulty through the entangled thorns, broken by the passage of heavy game; to the right and left of the passage it was impossible to move. Abou Do had wisely dismounted, but Suleiman followed Jali. Upon arriving within a few yards of the elephant, which was invisible in the thick thorns, Abou Do crept forward on foot, and discovered it standing with ears cocked, evidently waiting for the attack. As Jali followed on his light grey mare, the elephant immediately perceived the white colour, and at once charged forward. Escape was next to impossible: Jali turned his mare sharp round, and she bounded off, but caught in the thorns, the mare fell, throwing her rider in the path of the elephant that was within a few feet behind, in full chase. The mare recovered herself in an instant, and rushed away; the elephant, occupied by the white colour of the animal, neglected the man, upon whom he trod in the pursuit, thus breaking his thigh. Abou Do, who had been between the elephant and Jali, had wisely jumped into the thick thorns, and, as the elephant passed him, he again sprang out behind, and followed with his drawn sword, but too late to save Jali, as it was the affair of an instant. Jumping over Jali's body, he was just in time to deliver a tremendous cut at the hind leg of the elephant, that must otherwise have killed both horses and probably Suleiman also, as the three were caught in a cul de sac in a passage that had no outlet, and were at the elephant's mercy.

Abou Do seldom failed; it was a difficult feat to strike correctly in the narrow jungle passage with the elephant in full speed, but the blow was fairly given, and the back sinew was divided. Not content with the success of the cut, he immediately repeated the stroke upon the other leg, as he feared that the elephant, although disabled from rapid motion, might turn and trample Jali. The extraordinary dexterity and courage required to effect this can hardly be appreciated by those who have never hunted a wild elephant; but the extreme agility, pluck, and audacity of these Hamran sword-hunters surpass all feats that I have ever witnessed.

I set Jali's broken thigh, and employed myself in making splints; fortunately, my tool-chest was at hand, and I selected some pieces of dry wood that had been left on the bank by the retiring river. I made two splints, one with a crutch to fit beneath the arm; this I carried to about three inches beyond the foot, and cut a V-shaped notch to secure the bandage; the other was a common short splint about eighteen inches long. My wife quickly made about sixty yards of bandages, while Barrak, the maid, prepared thick gum water, from gum arabic, that the mimosas produced in unlimited quantity. Fixing the long splint under the arm, and keeping it upon the outside of the thigh, with the leg perfectly straight, I lashed the foot and ankle securely to the V-shaped notch: I then strapped the upper portion of the splint with bandages passed around the patient's chest, until he was swathed from beneath the arms to the hips, thus securing the splint to his body. The thigh, and entire leg from the fork to the ankle, I carefully secured to the long splint with three rows of bandages, the first plain, and the last two layers were soaked in thick gum-water. When these became dry and hard, they formed a case like an armour of paste-board: previous to bandaging the limb in splints, I had bathed it for some hours with cold applications.

On the following morning I expected to find my patient in great pain; but, on the contrary, he complained very little. His pulse was good, and there was very little swelling or heat. I gave him some cooling medicine; and the only anxiety that he expressed was the wish to get well immediately, so as to continue the expedition.

The Arabs thought that I could mend the leg of a man as though it were the broken stock of a gun, that would be serviceable immediately when repaired. As these people never use spirituous liquors, they are very little subject to inflammation, and they recover quickly from wounds that would be serious to Europeans. I attended to Jali for four days. He was a very grateful, but unruly patient, as he had never been accustomed to remain quiet. At the end of that time we arranged an angarep comfortably upon a camel, upon which he was transported to Geera, in company with a long string of camels, heavily laden with dried meat and squares of hide for shields, with large bundles of hippopotamus skin for whip making, together with the various spoils of the chase. Last, but not least, were numerous leathern pots of fat that had been boiled down from elephants and hippopotami.

The camels were to return as soon as possible with supplies of corn for onr people and horses. Another elephant-hunter was to be sent to us in the place of Jali; but I felt that we had lost our best man.[8]

Although my people had been in the highest spirits up to this time, a gloom had been thrown over the party by two causes – Jali's accident, and the fresh footmarks of the Base that had been discovered upon the sand by the margin of the river. The aggageers feared nothing, and if the Base had been legions of demons they would have faced them, sword in hand, with the greatest pleasure. But my Tokrooris, who were brave in some respects,

---

8   I heard from Jali six weeks later; he was then well, and offered to rejoin us shortly, but I declined to risk the strength of his leg.

had been so cowed by the horrible stories recounted of these common enemies at the nightly camp-fires by the Hamran Arabs, that they were seized with a panic, and resolved to desert en masse, and return to Katariff, where I had originally engaged them, and at which place they had left their families.

This desertion having been planned, they came to me in a body, just as the camels and Jali were about to depart, and commenced a series of absurd excuses for their intended desertion. The old grey-headed Moosa, by whose fortune-telling and sorcery the party were invariably guided, had foretold evil. This had confirmed them in their determination to return home. They were not a bad set of fellows, but, like most of their class, they required peculiar management. If natives are driven, they invariably hate their master, and turn sulky; if you give in to them, they lose respect, and will never obey. They are exceedingly subject to sudden impulses, under the influence of which they are utterly unreasonable. As the expedition depends for success entirely upon the union of the party, it is highly necessary to obtain so complete a control over every individual, that the leader shall be regarded with positive reverence, and his authority in all matters accepted as supreme. To gain such a complete ascendancy is a work of time, and is no easy matter, as an extreme amount of tact and judgment is necessary, combined with great kindness and common sense, with, at times, great severity. The latter should be avoided as long as possible.

In this instance, the desertion of my Tokrooris would have been a great blow to my expedition, as it was necessary to have a division of parties. I had now Tokrooris, Jaleens, and Hamran Arabs. Thus they would never unite together, and I was certain to have some upon my side in a difficulty. Should I lose the Tokrooris, the Hamran Arabs would have the entire preponderance.

The whole of my Tokrooris formed in line before me and my wife, just as the camels were about to leave; each man had his little bundle prepared for starting on a journey. Old Moosa was the spokesman, – he said that they were all very sorry: that they regretted exceedingly the necessity of leaving us, but some of them were sick, and they would only be a burden to the expedition; that one of them was bound upon a pilgrimage to Mecca, and that God would punish him should he neglect this great duty; others had not left any money with their families in Katariff, that would starve in their absence. (I had given them an advance of wages, when they engaged at Katariff, to provide against this difficulty.) I replied, "My good fellows, I am very sorry to hear all this, especially as it comes upon me so suddenly; those who are sick, stand upon one side" (several invalids, who looked remarkably healthy, stepped to the left). "Who wishes to go to Mecca?" Abderachman stepped forward (a huge specimen of a Tokroori, who went by the nickname of "El Jamoos," or the buffalo.) "Who wishes to remit money to his family, as I will send it and deduct it from his wages?" No one came forward. During the pause, I called for pen and paper, which Mahomet brought. I immediately commenced writing, and placed the note within an envelope, which I addressed, and gave to one of the camel-drivers. I then called for my medicine chest, and having weighed several three-grain doses of tartar emetic, I called the invalids, and insisted upon their taking the medicine before they started, or they might become seriously ill upon the road, which for three days' march was uninhabited. Mixed with a little water, the doses were swallowed, and I knew that the invalids were safe for that day, and that the others would not start without them.

I now again addressed my would-be deserters: "Now, my good fellows, there shall be no misunderstanding between us, and I will explain to you how the case stands. You engaged yourselves to me for the whole journey, and you received an advance of wages to provide for your families during your absence. You have lately filled yourselves with meat, and you have become lazy; you have been frightened by the footprints of the Base; thus you wish to leave the country. To save yourselves from imaginary danger, you would forsake my wife and myself and leave us to a fate which you yourselves would avoid. This is your gratitude for kindness; this is the return for my confidence, when without hesitation I advanced you money. Go! Return to Katariff to your families! I know that all the excuses you have made are false. Those who declare themselves to be sick, Inshallah (please God) shall be sick. You will all be welcomed upon your arrival at Katariff. In the letter I have written to the Governor, inclosing your names, I have requested him to give each man upon his appearance *five hundred lashes with the coorbatch, for desertion;* and to imprison him until my return."

Check-mate! My poor Tokrooris were in a corner, and in their great dilemma they could not answer a word. Taking advantage of this moment of confusion, I called forward "the buffalo" Abdcrachman, as I had heard that he really had contemplated a pilgrimage to Mecca. "Abderachman," I continued, "you are the only man who has spoken the truth. Go to Mecca! and may God protect you on the journey; I should not wish to prevent you from performing your duty as a Mahometan."

Never were people more dumbfounded with surprise; they retreated, and formed a knot in consultation, and in about ten minutes they returned to me, old Moosa and Hadji Ali both leading the pilgrim Abderachman by the hands. They had given in; and Abderachman, the buffalo of the party, thanked me for my permission, and with tears in his eyes, as the camels were about to start, he at once said good-bye. "Embrace him!" cried old

Moosa and Hadji Ali; and in an instant, as I had formerly succumbed to the maid Barrake, I was actually kissed by the thick lips of Abderachman the unwashed! Poor fellow! this was sincere gratitude without the slightest humbug; therefore, although he was an odoriferous savage, I could not help shaking him by the hand and wishing him a prosperous journey, assuring him that I would watch over his comrades like a father, while in my service. In a few instants these curious people were led by a sudden and new impulse; my farewell had perfectly delighted old Moosa and Hadji Ali, whose hearts were won. "Say good-bye to the Sit!" (the lady) they shouted to Abderachman; but I assured them that it was not necessary to go through the whole operation to which I had been subjected, and that she would be contented if he only kissed her hand. This he did with the natural grace of a savage, and was led away crying by his companions, who embraced him with tears, and they parted with the affection of brothers.

Now to hard-hearted and civilized people, who often school themselves to feel nothing, or as little as they can, for anybody, it may appear absurd to say that the scene was affecting, but somehow or other it was; and in the course of half-an-hour, those who would have deserted had become staunch friends, and we were all, black and white, Mahometans and Christians, wishing the pilgrim God speed upon his perilous journey to Mecca.

The camels started, and, if the scene was affecting, the invalids began to be more affected by the tartar emetic; this was the third act of the comedy. The plot had been thoroughly ventilated: the last act exhibited the perfect fidelity of my Tokrooris, in whom I subsequently reposed much confidence.

In the afternoon of that day, the brothers Sheriff arrived; these were the most renowned of all the sword-hunters of the Hamrans, of whom I have already spoken; they were well mounted, and, having met our caravan of camels on the route, heavily laden with dried flesh, and thus seen proofs of our success, they now offered to join our party. I am sorry to be obliged to confess, that my ally, Abou Do, although a perfect Nimrod in sport, an Apollo in personal appearance, and a gentleman in manner, was a mean, covetous, and grasping fellow, and withal absurdly jealous. Taher Sheriff was a more celebrated hunter, having had the experience of at least twenty years in excess of Abou Do, and although the latter was as brave and dexterous as Taher and his brothers, he wanted the cool judgment that is essential to a first-rate sportsman. He was himself aware of his inferiority to Taher Sheriff, though too proud to admit it; but, to avoid competition he declined to allow the Sheriffs to join our party, declaring that if I insisted upon the fresh alliance, he and his comrade Suleiman would return home. Notwithstanding his objections, I arranged for the present that, as Jali was hors de combat, Taher Sheriff's party should join us until the arrival of a fresh hunter in his place, otherwise our party would be incomplete. To prevent complications, the greedy Abou Do selected his share of the ivory, carefully choosing the best and most perfect tusks, and he presented Taher's party with a small quantity of meat that would render them independent of his hospitality. I at once ordered my people to give them a large supply of both meat and corn from my own store, and they encamped in a quarter of our circle.

The following day was the new year, January 1st, 1862; and, with the four brothers Sheriff and our party, we formed a powerful body of hunters: six aggageers and myself, all well mounted. With four gun-bearers, and two camels, both of which carried water, we started in search of elephants. Florian was unwell, and remained in camp.

In this dry climate it was only necessary to ride along the margin of the river to look for fresh tracks, as the animals were compelled to visit the Settite to drink, and of course there was no difficulty in discovering their traces. It appeared, however, that the elephants had been frightened away from the neighbourhood by the recent attack, as we rode for about ten miles without seeing any fresh marks. We therefore struck inland, on the east bank of the river, intending to return home by a circuit. The country was exactly like an English park, with no larger timber than thorn trees. Every now and then there was an exception in a gigantic homera (Adansonia digitata), or baobab; these, towering over the heads of the low mimosas, could be seen from a great distance. Having steered direct for one, we halted, and dismounted to rest the horses beneath the shade. This tree was about forty feet in circumference, and the spongy trunk was formed into a ladder by pegs of hard wood driven into its side by the Base hunters, who had thus ascended the slippery stem in search of honey. Bees are very fond of these trees, as they are generally more or less hollow, and well adapted for hives. The Adansonia digitata, although a tree, always reminds me of a gigantic fungus; the stem is disproportioned in its immense thickness to its height, and its branches are few in number, and as massive in character as the stem. The wood is not much firmer in substance than cork, and is as succulent as a carrot. In Kordofan, where water is exceedingly scarce, the Adansonia is frequently used as a reservoir; one of these huge hollow trees is cleaned out and filled with water during the short rainy season. The fruit was ripe at the time we halted, and after many attempts, by throwing sticks, we succeeded in procuring a considerable number. The sub-acid flavour of the seeds, enveloped in a dry yellow powder within the large shell, was exceedingly refreshing.

The immediate neighbourhood was a perfect exhibition of gum-arabic-bearing mimosas. At this season the gum was in perfection, and the finest quality was now before us in beautiful amber-coloured masses upon the stems and branches, varying from the size of a nutmeg to that of an orange. So great was the quantity, and so excellent were the specimens, that, leaving our horses tied to trees, both the Arabs and myself gathered a large collection. This gum, although as hard as ice on the exterior, was limpid in the centre, resembling melted amber, and as clear as though refined by some artificial process. The trees were perfectly denuded of leaves from the extreme drought, and the beautiful balls of frosted yellow gum recalled the idea of the precious jewels upon the trees in the garden of the wonderful lamp of the "Arabian nights." This gum was exceedingly sweet and pleasant to the taste; but, although of the most valuable quality, there was no hand to gather it in this forsaken, although beautiful country; it either dissolved during the rainy season, or was consumed by the baboons and antelopes. The aggageers took off from their saddles the skins of tanned antelope leather that formed the only covering to the wooden seats, and with these they made bundles of gum. When we remounted, every man was well laden.

We were thus leisurely returning home through alternate plains and low open forest of mimosa, when Taher Sheriff, who was leading the party, suddenly reined up his horse, and pointed to a thick bush, beneath which was a large grey, but shapeless, mass. He whispered, as I drew near, "Oom gurrin" (mother of the horn), their name for the rhinoceros. I immediately dismounted, and, with the short No. 10 Tatham rifle I advanced as near as I could, followed by Suleiman, as I had sent all my gun-bearers direct home by the river when we had commenced our circuit. As I drew near, I discovered two rhinoceros asleep beneath a thick mass of bushes; they were lying like pigs, close together, so that at a distance I had been unable to distinguish any exact form. It was an awkward place; if I were to take the wind fairly, I should have to fire through the thick bush, which would be useless; therefore I was compelled to advance with the wind direct from me to them. The aggageers remained about a hundred yards distant, while I told Suleiman to return, and hold my horse in readiness with his own. I then walked quietly to within about thirty yards of the rhinoceros, but so curiously were they lying that it was useless to attempt a shot. In their happy dreams they must have been suddenly disturbed by the scent of an enemy, for, without the least warning, they suddenly sprang to their feet with astonishing quickness, and with a loud and sharp whiff, whiff, whiff! one of them charged straight at me. I fired my right-hand barrel in his throat, as it was useless to aim at the head protected by two horns at the nose. This turned him, but had no other effect, and the two animals thundered off together at a tremendous pace.

Now for a "tally ho!" Our stock of gum was scattered on the ground, and away went the aggageers in full speed after the two rhinoceros. Without waiting to reload, I quickly remounted my horse Tetel, and, with Suleiman in company, I spurred hard to overtake the flying Arabs. Tetel was a good strong cob, but not very fast; however, I believe he never went so well as upon that day, for, although an Abyssinian horse, I had a pair of English spurs, which worked like missionaries, but with a more decided result. The ground was awkward for riding at full speed, as it was an open forest of mimosas, which, although wide apart, were very difficult to avoid, owing to the low crowns of spreading branches; these, being armed with fish-hook thorns, would have been serious on a collision. I kept the party in view, until in about a mile we arrived upon open ground. Here I again applied the spur, and by degrees I crept up, always gaining, until I at length joined the aggageers.

Here was a sight to drive a hunter wild! The two rhinoceros were running neck and neck, like a pair of horses in harness, but bounding along at tremendous speed within ten yards of the leading Hamran. This was Taher Sheriff, who, with his sword drawn, and his long hair flying wildly behind him, urged his horse forward in the race, amidst a cloud of dust raised by the two huge but active beasts, that tried every sinew of the horses. Roder Sheriff, with the withered arm, was second; with the reins hung upon the hawk-like claw that was all that remained of a hand, but with his naked sword grasped in his right, he kept close to his brother, ready to second his blow. Abou Do was third; his hair flying in the wind – his heels dashing against the flanks of his horse, to which he shouted in his excitement to urge him to the front, while he leant forward with his long sword, in the wild energy of the moment, as though hoping to reach the game against all possibility. Now for the spurs! and as these, vigorously applied, screwed an extra stride out of Tetel, I soon found myself in the ruck of men, horses, and drawn swords. There were seven of us, – and passing Abou Do, whose face wore an expression of agony at finding that his horse was failing, I quickly obtained a place between the two brothers, Taher and Roder Sheriff. There had been a jealousy between the two parties of aggageers, and each was striving to outdo the other; thus Abou Do was driven almost to madness at the superiority of Taher's horse, while the latter, who was the renowned hunter of the tribe, was determined that his sword should be the first to taste blood. I tried to pass the rhinoceros on my left, so as to fire close into the shoulder my remaining barrel with my right hand, but it was impossible to overtake the animals, who bounded along with undiminished speed. With the greatest exertion of men and horses we could only retain our position within about three or four yards of their tails – just out of reach of the swords. The only chance in the race was to hold the pace until the rhinoceros should begin to flag. The horses were pressed to the utmost; but we had already run about two miles, and the game showed no signs of giving in. On they flew, – sometimes over open ground, then through low bush, which tried the horses severely; then through strips of open forest, until at length the party began to tail off, and only a select few kept their places. We arrived at the summit of a ridge, from which the ground sloped in a gentle inclination for about a mile towards the river; at the foot of this incline was thick thorny nabbuk jungle, for which impenetrable covert the rhinoceros pressed at their utmost speed. Never was there better ground for the finish of a race; the earth was sandy, but firm, and as we saw the winning-post in the jungle that must terminate the hunt, we redoubled our exertions to close with the unflagging game. Suleiman's horse gave in – we had been for about twenty minutes at a killing pace. Tetel, although not a fast horse, was good for a distance, and he now proved his power of endurance, as I was riding at least two stone heavier than any of the party. Only four of the seven remained; and we swept down the incline, Taher Sheriff still leading, and Abou Do the last! His horse was done, but not the rider; for, springing to the ground while at full speed, sword in hand, he forsook his tired horse, and, preferring his own legs, he ran like an antelope, and, for the first hundred yards, I thought he would really pass us, and win the honour of first blow. It was of no use, the pace was too severe, and, although running wonderfully, he was obliged to give way to the horses. Only three now followed the rhinoceros – Taher Sheriff, his brother Roder, and myself. I had been obliged to give the second place to Roder, as he was a mere monkey in weight; but I was a close third. The excitement was intense – we neared the jungle, and the rhinoceros began to show signs of flagging, as the dust puffed up before their nostrils, and, with noses close to the ground, they snorted as they still galloped on. Oh for a fresh horse! "A horse ! a horse! my kingdom for a horse!" We were within two hundred yards of the jungle; but the horses were all done. Tetel reeled as I urged him forward, Roder pushed ahead; we were close to the dense thorns, and the rhinoceros broke into a trot; they were done! "Now, Taher, for-r-a-a-r-r-d! for-r-r-a-a-r-d, Taher!!!" Away he went – he was close to the very heels of the beasts; but his horse could do no more than his present pace; still he gained upon the nearest; he leaned forward with his sword raised for the blow – another moment, and the jungle would be reached! One effort more, and the sword flashed in the sunshine, as the rearmost rhinoceros disappeared in the thick screen of thorns, with a gash about a foot long upon his hind-quarters. Taher Sheriff shook his bloody sword in triumph above his head; but the rhinoceros was gone. We were fairly beaten, regularly outpaced; but I believe another two hundred yards would have given us the victory. "Bravo, Taher," I shouted. He had ridden splendidly, and his b]ow had been marvellously delivered at an extremely long reach, as he was nearly out of his saddle when he sprang forward to enable the blade to obtain a cut at the last moment. He could not reach the hamstring, as his horse could not gain the proper position.

We all immediately dismounted; the horses were thoroughly done, and I at once loosened the girths and contemplated my steed Tetel, who with head lowered, and legs wide apart, was a tolerable example of the effects of pace. The other aggageers shortly arrived, and as the rival Abou Do joined us, Taher Sheriff quietly wiped the blood off his sword without making a remark; this was a bitter moment for the discomfited Abou Do.

Although we had failed, I never enjoyed a hunt so much either before or since; it was a magnificent run, and still more magnificent was the idea that a man, with no weapon but a sword, could attack and generally vanquish every huge animal of creation. I felt inclined to discard all my rifles, and to adopt the sabre, with a first-class horse instead of the common horses of this country, that were totally unfit for such a style of hunting, when carrying nearly fifteen stone.

Taher Sheriff explained that at all times the rhinoceros was the most difficult animal to sabre, on account of his extraordinary swiftness, and, although he had killed many with the sword, it was always after a long and fatiguing hunt: at the close of which, the animal becoming tired, generally turned to bay, in which case one hunter occupied his attention, while another galloped up behind, and severed the hamstring. The rhinoceros, unlike the elephant, can go very well upon three legs, which enhances the danger, as one cut will not utterly disable him.

There is only one species of this animal in Abyssinia; this is the two-horned black rhinoceros, known in South Africa as the keitloa. This animal is generally five feet six inches to five feet eight inches high at the shoulder, and, although so bulky and heavily built, it is extremely active, as our long and fruitless hunt had exemplified. The skin is about half the thickness of that of the hippopotamus, but of extreme toughness and closeness of texture; when dried and polished it resembles horn. Unlike the Indian species of rhinoceros, the black variety of Africa is free from folds, and the hide fits smoothly on the body like that of the buffalo. This two-horned black species is exceedingly vicious; it is one of the very few animals that will generally assume the offensive; it considers all creatures to be enemies, and, although it is not acute in either sight or hearing, it possesses so wonderful a power of scent, that it will detect a stranger at a distance of five or six hundred yards should the wind be favourable.

I have observed that a rhinoceros will generally charge down upon the object that it smells, but does not see; thus when the animal is concealed either in high grass or thick jungle, should it scent a man who may be passing unseen to windward, it will rush down furiously upon the object it has winded, with three loud whiffs, resembling a jet of steam from a safety-valve. As it is most difficult and next to impossible to kill a rhinoceros when charging, on account of the protection to the brain afforded by the horns, an unexpected charge in thick jungle is particularly unpleasant; especially when on horseback, as there is no means of escape but to rush headlong through all obstacles, when the rider will most likely share the fate that befell the unfortunate Jali.

The horns of the black Abyssinian species seldom exceed two feet in length, and are generally much shorter; they are not fitted upon the bone like the horns of all other animals, but are merely rooted upon the thick skin, of which they appear to be a continuation. Although the horn of a rhinoceros is a weapon of immense power, it has no solid foundation, but when the animal is killed, it can be separated from its hold upon the second day after death, by a slight blow with a cane. The base forms an exceedingly shallow cup, and much resembles the heart of an artichoke when the leaves have been picked off. The teeth are very peculiar, as the molars have a projecting cutting edge on the exterior side; thus the jaws when closed form a pair of shears, as the projecting edges of the upper and lower rows overlap: this makes a favourable arrangement of nature to enable the animal to clip off twigs and the branches upon which it feeds, as, although it does not absolutely refuse grass, the rhinoceros is decidedly a wood eater. There are particular bushes which form a great attraction, among these is a dwarf mimosa with a reddish bark: this tree grows in thick masses, which the rhinoceros clips so closely that it frequently resembles a quickset hedge that has been cut by the woodman's shears. These animals are generally seen in pairs, or the male, female, and calf; the mother is very affectionate, and exceedingly watchful and savage. Although so large an animal, the cry is very insignificant, and is not unlike the harsh shrill sound of a penny trumpet. The drinking hour is about 8 P.M. or two hours after sunset, at which time the rhinoceros arrives at the river from his daily retreat, which is usually about four miles in the interior. He approaches the water by regular paths made by himself, but not always by the same route; and, after drinking, he generally retires to a particular spot beneath a tree that has been visited upon regular occasions; in such places large heaps of dung accumulate. The hunters take advantage of this peculiarity of the rhinoceros, and they set traps in the path to his private retreat; but he is so extremely wary, and so acute is the animal's power of scent, that the greatest art is necessary in setting the snare. A circular hole about two feet deep and fifteen inches in diameter is dug in the middle of his run, near to the tree that has been daily visited; upon this hole is placed a hoop of tough wood arranged with a vast number of sharp spikes of a strong elastic wood, which, fastened to the rim, meet in the centre, and overlap each other as would the spokes of a wheel in the absence of the nave, if lengthened sufficiently. We will simplify the hoop by calling it a wheel without a centre, the spokes sharpened and overlapping the middle. The instrument being fitted neatly above the hole, a running noose of the strongest rope is laid in the circle upon the wheel; the other extremity of the rope is fastened to the trunk of a tree that has been felled for that purpose, and deeply notched at one end to prevent the rope from slipping. This log, which weighs about five or six hundredweight, is then buried horizontally in the ground, and the entire trap is covered with earth and carefully concealed; the surface is smoothed over with a branch instead of the hand, as the scent of a human touch would at once be detected by the rhinoceros. When completed, a quantity of the animal's dung is swept from the heap upon the snare. If the trap is undiscovered, the rhinoceros steps upon the hoop, through which his leg sinks into the hole, and upon his attempt to extricate his foot, the noose draws tight over the legs; as the spiked hoop fixing tightly into the skin prevents the noose from slipping over the foot. Once caught, his first effort to escape drags the heavy log from the trench, and as the animal rushes furiously away, this acts as a drag, and by catching in the jungle and the protruding roots of trees, it quickly fatigues him. On the following morning the hunters discover the rhinoceros by the track of the log that has ploughed along the ground, and the animal is killed by lances, or by the sword. The hide of a rhinoceros will produce seven shields; these are worth about two dollars each, as simple hide before manufacture; the horn is sold in Abyssinia for about two dollars per pound, for the manufacture of sword-hilts, which are much esteemed if of this material.

Upon our return to camp, I found that the woman Barrake was ill. She had insisted upon eating a large quantity of the fruit of the hegleek tree (Balanites Aegyptiaca), which abounded in this neighbourhood. This tree is larger than the generality in that country, being about thirty feet in height and eighteen inches in diameter; the ashes of the burnt wood are extremely rich in potash, and the fruit, which is about the size and shape of a date, is sometimes pounded and used by the Arabs in lieu of soap for washing their clothes. This fruit is exceedingly pleasant, but in a raw state it has an irritating effect upon the bowels, and should be used in small quantities. Barrake had been cautioned by the Arabs and ourselves, but she had taken a fancy that she was determined to gratify; therefore she had eaten the forbidden fruit from morning until night, and a grievous attack of diarrhoea was the consequence. My wife had boiled the fruit with wild honey, and had made a most delicious preserve; in this state it was not unwholesome. She had likewise preserved the fruit of the nabbuk in a similar manner: the latter resembles minute apples in appearance, with something of the medlar in flavour; enormous quantities were produced upon the banks of the river, which, falling when ripe, were greedily eaten by guinea-fowl, wild hogs, antelopes, and monkeys. Elephants are particularly fond of the fruit of the hegleek, which, although apparently too insignificant for the attention of such mighty animals, they nevertheless enjoy beyond any other food, and they industriously gather them one by one. At the season when the fruit is ripe, the hegleek tree is a certain attraction to elephants, who shake the branches and pick up the fallen berries with their trunks; frequently they overturn the tree itself, as a more direct manner of feeding.

Florian was quite incapable of hunting, as he was in a weak state of health, and had for some months been suffering from chronic dysentery. I had several times cured him, but, as Barrake insisted upon eating fruit, so he had a weakness for the strongest black coffee, which, instead of drinking, like the natives, in minute cups, he swallowed wholesale in large basins, several times a day; this was actual poison with his complaint, and he was completely ruined in health. He had excellent servants, – Richarn, whom I subsequently engaged, who was my only faithful man in my journey up the White Nile, and two good Dongalowas.

At this time, his old companion, Johann Schmidt, the carpenter, arrived, having undertaken a contract to provide, for the Italian Zoological Gardens, a number of animals. I therefore proposed that the two old friends should continue together, while I would hunt by myself, with the aggageers, towards the east and south.

This arrangement was agreed to, and we parted. In the following season, I engaged this excellent man, Johann Schmidt, as my lieutenant for the White Nile expedition, on the banks of which fatal river he now lies, with the cross that I erected over his grave.

Poor Florian at length recovered from his complaint, but was killed by a lion. He had wounded an elephant, which on the following morning he found dead; a lion had eaten a portion during the night. While he was engaged with his men in extracting the tusks, one of his hunters (a Tokroori) followed the track of the lion on the sand, and found the animal lying beneath a bush; he fired a single-barrelled rifle, and wounded it in the thigh.

He at once returned to his master, who accompanied him to the spot, and the lion was found lying under the same bush, licking the wound. Florian fired and missed; the lion immediately crouched for a spring; Florian fired his remaining barrel, the ball merely grazed the lion, who almost in the same instant bounded forward, and struck him upon the head with a fearful blow of the paw, at the same time it seized him by the throat.

The Tokroori hunter, instead of flying from the danger, placed the muzzle of his rifle to the lion's ear, and blew its brains out on the body of his master. The unfortunate Florian had been struck dead, and great difficulty was found in extracting the claws of the lion, which had penetrated the skull. Florian, although a determined hunter, was an exceedingly bad shot, and withal badly armed for encounters with dangerous game; I had frequently prophesied some calamity from the experience I had had in a few days' shooting in his society, and most unhappily my gloomy prediction was fulfilled.

This was the fate of two good and sterling Germans, who had been my companions in this wild country, where degrees of rank are entirely forgotten, provided a man be honest and true. I constantly look back to the European acquaintances and friends that I made during my sojourn in Africa, nearly all of whom are dead: a merciful Providence guided us through many dangers and difficulties, and shielded us from all harm, during nearly five years of constant exposure. Thanks be to God.

Our camels returned from Geera with corn, accompanied by an Abyssinian hunter, who was declared by Abou Do to be a good man, and dexterous with the sword. We accordingly moved our camp, said adieu to Florian and Johann, and penetrated still deeper into the Base.

Chapter XV.

Antelopes on the Settite.

OUR course lay as usual along the banks of the river, which we several times forded to avoid the bends. Great numbers of antelopes were upon the river's bed, having descended to drink; by making a circuit, I cut off one party upon their retreat, and made two good shots with the Fletcher No. 24, bagging two tetel (Antelopus Bubalis), at considerable ranges. I also shot an ariel (G. Dama), and, upon arriving at a deep pool in the river, I shot a bull hippopotamus, as a present for Taher Sheriff and his brothers. We decided upon encamping at a spot known to the Arabs as Delladilla; this was the forest upon the margin of the river where I had first shot the bull elephant, when the aggageers fought with him upon foot. The trees were larger in this locality than elsewhere, as a great portion of the country was flooded by the river dnring the rainy season, and much rich soil had been deposited; this, with excessive moisture, had produced a forest of fine timber, with an undergrowth of thick nabbuk. We fixed upon a charming spot for a camp, beneath a large tree that bore a peculiar fruit, suspended from the branches by a strong but single fibre, like a cord; each fruit was about eighteen inches in length, by six in diameter; it was perfectly worthless, but extremely ornamental. We had arrived beneath this tree, and were still on horseback; my wife had just suggested that it would be unpleasant should one of the large fruit fall upon our heads if we camped under the branches, when suddenly a lioness glided by us, within three yards of the horses, and almost immediately disappeared in the thick thorns; unfortunately, I had the moment before given my rifle to a servant, prior to dismounting. I searched the bushes in every direction, but to no purpose.

This spot was so favourably situated that I determined to remain for some time, as I could explore the country on horseback to a great distance upon all sides. We immediately set to work to construct our new camp, and by the evening our people had cleared a circle of fifty yards diameter; this was swept perfectly clean, and the ground being hard, though free from stones, the surface was as even as a paved floor. The entire circle was well protected with a strong fence of thorn bushes, for which the kittar is admirably adapted; the head being mushroom-shaped, the entire tree is cut down, and the stem being drawn towards the inside of the camp, the thick and wide-spreading thorny crest covers about twelve feet of the exterior frontage; a fence thus arranged is quickly constructed, and is quite impervious. Two or three large trees grew within the camp; beneath the shade of this our tent was pitched. This we never inhabited, but it served as an ordinary room, and a protection to the luggage, guns, &c. The horses were well secured within a double circle of thorns, and the goats wandered about at liberty, as they were too afraid of wild animals to venture from the camp: altogether this was the most agreeable spot we had ever occupied; even the night-fires would be perfectly concealed within the dense shade of the nabbuk jungle, thus neither man nor beast would be aware of our presence. We were about a hundred paces distant from the margin of the river; late in the evening I took my rod, and fished in the deep bend beneath a cliff of conglomerate pebbles. I caught only one fish, a baggar, about twelve pounds, but I landed three large turtles; these creatures were most determined in taking the bait; they varied in size from fifty to about ninety pounds, and were the same species as that which inhabits the Nile (Trionis Nilotica). From one of them we took upwards of a hundred eggs which we converted into omelettes, but they were rather strong in flavour.

Although this species of turtle is unprepossessing in appearance, having a head very like that of a snake, with a dark green shell spotted with yellow, it produces excellent soup; the body is exceedingly flat, and the projecting edges of the shell are soft; it runs extremely fast upon the shore, and is suggestive of the tortoise that beat the hare in the well-known race. Throughout the Nile and its tributaries there are varieties of fish and reptiles closely connected, and the link can be distinctly traced in the progression of development. There is a fish with a hard bony frame, or shell, that includes the head, and extends over more than half the body; this has two long and moveable spikes beneath the fore fins, upon which it can raise itself as upon legs when upon the land; when first caught, this fish makes a noise something like the mewing of a cat: this appears to be closely linked to the tortoise. The Lepidosiren Annectens, found in the White Nile, is a link between the fish and the frog; and certain varieties of mud fish that remain alive throughout a dry season in the sun-baked earth, and reappear with the following rains exhibit a close affinity to reptiles.

On the morning after our arrival, I started to explore the country with the aggageers, and rode about forty miles, From this point, hills of basalt and granite commenced, connected by rugged undulations of white quartz, huge blocks of which were scattered upon the surface; in many of these I found thin veins of galena.

All the rocks were igneous; we had left the sandstone that had marked the course of the Atbara and the valley of the Settite as far as Ombrega, and I was extremely puzzled to account for the presence of the pure white and rose-coloured limestone that we had found only in one place – Geera. As we were now among the hills and mountains, the country was extremely beautiful; at the farthest point of that day's excursion we were close to the high range from which, in the rainy season, innumerable torrents pour into the Settite; some of these gorges were ornamented with the dark foliage of large tamarind trees, while upon rocks that did not appear to offer any sustenance, the unsightly yet mighty baobab[9] grasped with its gnarled roots the blocks of granite, and formed a peculiar object in the wild and rugged scenery.

Through this romantic wilderness, the Settite flowed in a clear and beautiful stream, sometimes contracted between cliffs to a width of a hundred yards, at others stretching to three times that distance. The hippopotami were in great numbers; many were lying beneath the shady trees upon the banks, and splashed into the water as we appeared; others were basking in large herds upon the shallows; while the young calves, supported upon the backs of their mothers, sailed about upon their animated rafts in perfect security. The Base had been here recently, as we discovered their footprints upon the sand, and we arrived at some tobacco plantations that they had formed upon the sandbanks of the river. The aggageers expressed their determination to sabre them should we happen to meet, and were much displeased at my immediately placing a veto upon their bloody intentions, with a reservation for necessity in self-defence.

The Base were far too wide awake, and, although seen once during the day by my people, they disappeared like monkeys; their spies had doubtless reported our movements ever since we had entered their country, and, fearing the firearms, they had retreated to their fastnesses among the mountains.

During the day's march we had seen a large quantity of game, but I had not wished to shoot until on our return towards the camp. We were about four miles from home, when a nellut (A. Strepsiceros) bounded away from a ravine. I was riding Tetel, whom I had taught to stand fire, in which he was remarkably steady. I made a quick shot with the little Fletcher from the saddlle; but, as the nellut ran straight before me, the bullet struck the

---

9   The largest baobab (Adansonia digitata) that I have measured was fifty-one feet and one inch in circumference.

haunch: away went the aggageers after the wounded animal, like greyhounds, and in a few hundred yards the sword finished the hunt.

The Nellut is the handsomest of all the large antelopes; the male is about thirteen hands high, and carries a pair of beautiful spiral horns, upwards of three feet in length; the colour of the hide is a dark mouse-grey, ornamented with white stripes down the flanks, and a white line along the back from the shoulder to the tail. The female is without horns, but is in other respects similar to the male. These beautiful animals do not inhabit the plains like the other varieties of antelopes, but are generally found in deep-wooded ravines. In South Africa it is known as the koodoo.

The aggageers quickly flayed and quartered the game, which was arranged upon the horses, and thus it was carried to our camp, at which we arrived late in the evening.

On the following morning, at my usual hour of starting, a little before sunrise, we crossed a deep portion of the river, through which the horses were obliged to swim; on this occasion I rode Aggahr, who was my best hunter. In that very charming and useful book by Mr. Francis Galton, "The Art of Travel," advice is given for crossing a deep river, by holding to the tail of the swimming horse. In this I cannot agree; the safety of the man is much endangered by the heels of the horse, and his security depends upon the length of the animal's tail. In rivers abounding in crocodiles, which generally follow an animal before they seize, the man hanging on to the tail of the horse is a most alluring bait, and he would certainly be taken, should one of these horrible monsters be attracted to the party. I have always found great comfort in crossing a river by simply holding to the mane, just in front of the saddle, with my left hand, with the bridle grasped as loosely as possible, so that the horse does not feel the bit; in this position, on the off side, the animal does not feel any hindrance; the man not only can direct his horse, but his presence gives it confidence, as he can speak to it coaxingly while swimming with one arm by its side. Upon landing, he at once controls the horse by the reins within his left grasp.

Many horses become exceedingly scared in swimming a rapid river, and will frequently lose their presence of mind, and swim with the current, in which case they may miss the favourable landing place; if the man holds by the tail, he has no control over the horse upon landing, and, if wild or vicious, the animal will probably kick up its heels and bolt away, leaving the unfortunate proprietor helpless. In swimming a river with the horse, the powder, &c. should be made into a parcel with your outer garment, and tied upon the head; then lead your horse gently into the water, and for a moment allow it to drink, to prevent all shyness; continue to lead it until you lose your depth, when, by holding with your left hand to the mane, both horse and man will cross with perfect ease.

We had crossed the river, and, as we passed through an opening in the belt of jungle on the banks, and entered upon a plain interspersed with clumps of bush, we perceived, at about two hundred yards distance, a magnificent lion, whose shaggy yellow mane gave him a colossal appearance, as he stalked quietly along the flat sandy ground towards the place of his daily retreat. The aggageers whispered, "El Assut!" (the lion), and instinctively the swords flashed from their sheaths. In an instant, the horses were at full speed sweeping over the level ground. The lion had not observed us; but, upon hearing the sound of the hoofs, he halted and raised his head, regarding us for a moment with wonder, as we rapidly decreased our distance, when, thinking retreat advisable, he bounded off, followed by the excited hunters, as hard as the horses could be pressed. Having obtained a good start, we had gained upon him, and we kept up the pace until we at length arrived within about eighty yards of the lion, who, although he appeared to fly easily along like a cat, did not equal the speed of the horses. It was a beautiful sight. Aggahr was an exceedingly fast horse, and, having formerly belonged to one of the Hamran hunters, he thoroughly understood his work. His gallop was perfection, and his long steady stride was as easy to himself as to his rider; there was no necessity to guide him, as he followed an animal like a greyhound, and sailed between the stems of the numerous trees, carefully avoiding their trunks, and choosing his route where the branches allowed ample room for the rider to pass beneath. In about five minutes we had run the lion straight across the plain, through several open strips of mimosas, and we were now within a few yards, hut unfortunately, just as Taher and Abou Do dashed forward in the endeavour to ride upon either flank, he sprang down a precipitous ravine, and disappeared in the thick thorns.

The ravine formed a broad bottom, which, covered with dense green nabbuk, continued for a great distance, and effectually saved the lion. I was much disappointed, as we should have had a glorious fight, and I had long sought for an opportunity of witnessing an attack upon the lion with the sword. The aggageers were equally annoyed, and they explained that they should have been certain to kill him. Their plan was to ride upon either flank, at a few yards' distance, when he would have charged one man, who would have dashed away, while the other hunter would have slashed the lion through the back with his sword. They declared that a good hunter should be able to protect himself by a back-handed blow with his sword, should the lion attack the horse from behind; but that the great danger in a lion hunt arose when the animal took refuge in a solitary bush, and turned to bay. In such instances the hunters surrounded the bush, and rode direct towards him, when he generally sprang out upon some man or horse; he was then cut down immediately by the sabre of the next hunter. The aggageers declared that, in the event of an actual fight, the death of the lion was certain, although one or more men or horses might be wounded, or perhaps killed.

The morning gallop had warmed our nags after their bath in the cool river, and we now continued leisurely towards the stream, upon the margin of which we rode for several miles. We had determined to set fire to the grass, as, although upon poorer soil it had almost disappeared through the withering of the roots, upon fertile ground it was almost nine feet high, and not only concealed the game, but prevented us from riding. We accordingly rode towards a spot where bright yellow herbage invited the fire-stick; but hardly had we arrived, when we noticed a solitary bull buffalo (Bos Caffer), feeding within about a hundred and fifty yards. I immediately dismounted, and, creeping towards him to within fifty paces, I shot him through the neck with one of my Reilly No. 10 rifles. I had hoped to drop him dead by the shot, instead of which he galloped off, of course followed by the aggageers, with the exception of one, who held my horse. Quickly mounted, we joined in the hunt, and in about three minutes we ran the buffalo to bay in a thicket of thorns on the margin of the river. These thorns were just thick enough to conceal him at times, but to afford us a glance of his figure as he moved from his position. There was a glade which cut through and divided the jungle, and I wished the aggageers to drive him, if possible, across this, when I should have a good opportunity of shooting. To my astonishment, one of the most daring hunters jumped off his horse with his drawn sword, and, telling me to look out, he coolly entered the jungle alone to court the attack of the buffalo. I would not allow him to risk his life for an animal that I had been the first to wound, therefore I insisted upon his return, and begging Abou Do to hold my bridle when I should fire, I rode with him carefully along the skirts of the jungle along the glade, keeping a good look-out among the thorns for the buffalo. Presently I heard a short grunt within twenty yards of us, and I quickly perceived the buffalo standing broadside on, with his head to the wind, that brought down the scent of the people on the other side.

I had my little Fletcher No. 24 in my hand – that handy little weapon that almost formed an extra bone of myself, and, whispering to Abou Do to hold my bridle close to the bit, as Aggahr was not very steady under fire, I took a clean shot direct at the centre of the shoulder. The ball smacked as though it had struck an iron target. Aggahr gave a start, and for the moment both Abou Do and myself were prepared for a rush; but the buffalo had never flinched, and he remained standing as though immoveable. Abon Do whispered, "You missed him, I heard the bullet strike the tree;" I shook my head, and quickly re-loaded – it was impossible to miss at that distance, and I knew that I had fired steadily. Hardly had I rammed the bullet down, when, with a sudden thump, down fell the buffalo upon his side, and, rolling over upon his back, he gave a few tremendous struggles, and lay dead.

Great caution should be invariably used in approaching a fallen buffalo and all other dangerous animals, as they are apt to recover sufficiently, upon seeing the enemy, to make a last effort to attack, which is generally more serious than any other phase of the hunt. We accordingly pitched a few large stones at him to test the reality of death, and then walked up and examined him. The Reilly No. 10 had gone quite through the neck, but had missed a vital part. The little Fletcher had made a clean and minute hole exactly through the shoulder, and upon opening the body we found the ball sticking in the ribs on the opposite side, having passed through the very centre of the lungs.

The aggageers now carefully flayed it, and divided the tough hide into portions accurately measured for shields. One man galloped back to direct the two water-camels that were following in our tracks, while others cut up the buffalo, and prepared the usual disgusting feast by cutting up the reeking paunch, over which they squeezed the contents of the gall-bladder, and consumed the whole, raw and steaming.[10] On the arrival of the camels they were quickly loaded, and we proceeded to fire the grass on our return to camp. The Arabs always obtained their fire by the friction of two pieces of wood; accordingly, they set to work. A piece of dry nabbuk was selected, about as thick as the little finger. A notch was cut in this, and it was laid horizontally upon the ground, with the notch uppermost; into this was fixed the sharp point of a similar piece of wood, about eighteen inches long, which, being held perpendicularly with both hands, was worked between the palms like a drill, with as great a pressure as possible, from the top to the bottom, as the hands descended with the motion of rubbing or rolling the stick. After about two minutes of great labour, the notch began to smoke, a brown dust, like ground coffee, fell from the singed wood, and this charred substance, after increased friction, emitted a still denser smoke, and commenced smouldering; the fire was produced. A rag was torn from the thorn-brushed drawers of one of the party, in which the fire was carefully wrapped and fanned with the breath; it was then placed in a wisp of dry grass, and rapidly turned in the air until the flame burst

---

10   All these Arabs, in like manner with the Abyssinians, are subject to the attacks of intestinal worms, induced by their habit of eating raw flesh.

forth. A burning-glass should be always carried in these countries, where a cloudless sky ensures an effect. Although in Arab hands the making of fire appears exceedingly simple, I have never been able to effect it. I have worked at the two sticks until they have been smoking and I have been steaming, with my hands blistered, but I have never got beyond the smoke; there is a peculiar knack which, like playing the fiddle, must be acquired, although it looks very easy. It is not every wood that will produce fire by this method; those most inflammable are the cotton-tree and the nabbuk. We now descended to the river, and fired the grass; the north wind was brisk, and the flames extended over miles of country within an hour.

We returned towards the camp. On the way we saw numerous antelopes; and, dismounting, I ordered one of the hunters to lead my horse while I attempted to stalk a fine buck mehedehet (Redunca Ellipsyprimna). There were several in the herd, but there was a buck with a fine head a few yards in advance; they were standing upon an undulation on open ground backed by high grass. I had marked a small bush as my point of cover, and creeping unobserved towards this, I arrived unseen within about a hundred and twenty yards of the buck. With the Fletcher 24 I made a good shoulder-shot; the buck gave a few bounds and fell dead; the does looked on in astonishment, and I made an equally lucky shot with the left-hand barrel, bringing down what I at first had mistaken to be a doe, but I discovered it to be a young buck.

The Mehedehet is an antelope of great beauty; it resembles the red deer in colour, but the coat is still rougher; it stands about thirteen hands in height, with a pair of long slightly-curved annulated horns. The live weight of the male would be about five hundred pounds; the female, like the nellut (Tragelaphus Strepsiceros), is devoid of horns, and much resembles the female of the Sambur deer of India. This antelope is the "water-buck" of South Africa.

On arrival at the camp, I resolved to fire the entire country on the following day, and to push still farther up the course of the Settite to the foot of the mountains, and to return to this camp in about a fortnight, by which time the animals that had been scared away by the fire would have returned. Accordingly, on the following morning, accompanied by a few of the aggageers, I started upon the south bank of the river, and rode for some distance into the interior, to the ground that was entirely covered with high withered grass. We were passing through a mass of kittar and thorn-bush, almost hidden by the immensely high grass, when, as I was ahead of the party, I came suddenly upon the tracks of a rhinoceros; these were so unmistakeably recent that I felt sure we were not far from the animals themselves. As I had wished to fire the grass, I was accompanied by my Tokrooris, and my horse-keeper, Mahomet No. 2. It was difficult ground for the men, and still more unfavourable for the horses, as large disjointed masses of stone were concealed in the high grass.

We were just speculating as to the position of the rhinoceros, and thinking how uncommonly unpleasant it would be should he obtain our wind, when whiff! whiff! whiff! We heard the sharp whistling snort, with a tremendous rush through the high grass and thorns close to us; and at the same moment two of these determined brutes were upon us in full charge. I never saw such a scrimmage; sauve qui peut! There was no time for more than one look behind. I dug the spurs into Aggahr's flanks, and clasping him round the neck, I ducked my head down to his shoulder, well protected with my strong hunting-cap, and I kept the spurs going as hard as I could ply them, blindly trusting to Providence and my good horse, over big rocks, fallen trees, thick kittar thorns, and grass ten feet high, with the two infernal animals in full chase only a few feet behind me. I heard their abominable whiffing close to me, but so did good horse also, and the good old hunter flew over obstacles that I should have thought impossible, and he dashed straight under the hooked thorn bushes and doubled like a hare. The aggageers were all scattered; Mahomet No. 2 was knocked over by a rhinoceros; all the men were sprawling upon the rocks with their guns, and the party was entirely discomfited. Having passed the kittar thorn, I turned, and, seeing that the beasts had gone straight on, I brought Aggahr's head round, and tried to give chase, but it was perfectly impossible; it was only a wonder that the horse had escaped in ground so difficult for riding. Although my clothes were of the strongest and coarsest Arab cotton cloth, which seldom tore, but simply lost a thread when caught in a thorn, I was nearly naked. My blouse was reduced to shreds; as I wore sleeves only half way from the shoulder to the elbow, my naked arms were streaming with blood; fortunately my hunting cap was secured with a chin strap, and still more fortunately I had grasped the horse's neck, otherwise I must have been dragged out of the saddle by the hooked thorns. All the men were cut and bruised, some having fallen upon their heads among the rocks, and others had hurt their legs in falling in their endeavours to escape. Mahomet No. 2, the horse-keeper, was more frightened than hurt, as he had been knocked down by the shoulder and not by the horn of the rhinoceros, as the animal had not noticed him; its attention was absorbed by the horse.

I determined to set fire to the whole country immediately, and descending the hill towards the river to obtain a favourable wind, I put my men in a line, extending over about a mile along the river's bed, and they fired the grass in different places. With a loud roar, the flame leapt high in air and rushed forward with astonishing velocity; the grass was as inflammable as tinder, and the strong north wind drove the long line of fire spreading in every direction through the country.

We now crossed to the other side of the river to avoid the flames, and we returned towards the camp. On the way, I made a long shot and badly wounded a tetel, but lost it in thick thorns; shortly after, I stalked a nellut (A. Strepsiceros), and bagged it with the Fletcher rifle.

We arrived early in camp, and on the following day we moved sixteen miles farther up stream, and camped under a tamarind tree by the side of the river. No European had ever been farther than our last camp, Delladilla, and that spot had only been visited by Johann Schmidt and Florian. In the previous year, my aggageers had sabred some of the Base at this very camping-place; they accordingly requested me to keep a vigilant watch during the night, as they would be very likely to attack us in revenge, unless they had been scared by the rifles and by the size of our party. They advised me not to remain long in this spot, as it would be very dangerous for my wife to be left almost alone during the day, when we were hunting, and that the Base would be certain to espy us from the mountains, and would most probably attack and carry her off when they were assured of our departure. She was not very nervous about this, but she immediately called the dragoman, Mahomet, who knew the use of a gun, and she asked him if he would stand by her in case they were attacked in my absence; the faithful servant replied, "Mahomet fight the Base? No, Missus; Mahomet not fight; if the Base come, Missus fight; Mahomet run away; Mahomet not come all the way from Cairo to get him killed by black fellers; Mahomet will run – Inshallah!" (please God).

This frank avowal of his military tactics was very reassuring. There was a high hill of basalt, something resembling a pyramid, within a quarter of a mile of us; I accordingly ordered some of my men every day to ascend this look-out station, and I resolved to burn the high grass at once, so as to destroy all cover for the concealment of an enemy. That evening I very nearly burnt our camp; I had several times ordered the men to clear away the dry grass for about thirty yards from our resting-place; this they had neglected to obey. We had been joined a few days before by a party of about a dozen Hamran Arabs, who were hippopotami hunters; thus we mustered very strong, and it would have been the work of about half an hour to have cleared away the grass as I had desired.

The wind was brisk, and blew directly towards our camp, which was backed by the river. I accordingly took a fire-stick, and I told my people to look sharp, as they would not clear away the grass. I walked to the foot of the basalt hill, and fired the grass in several places. In an instant the wind swept the flame and smoke towards the camp. All was confusion; the Arabs had piled the camel-saddles and all their corn and effects in the high grass about twenty yards from the tent; there was no time to remove all these things; therefore, unless they could clear away the grass so as to stop the fire before it should reach the spot, they would be punished for their laziness by losing their property. The fire travelled quicker than I had expected, and, by the time I had hastened to the tent, I found the entire party working frantically; the Arabs were slashing down the grass with their swords, and sweeping it away with their shields, while my Tokrooris were beating it down with long sticks and tearing it from its withered and fortunately tinder-rotten roots, in desperate haste. The flames rushed on, and we already felt the heat, as volumes of smoke enveloped us; I thought it advisable to carry the gunpowder (about 20 lbs.), down to the river, together with the rifles; while my wife and Mahomet dragged the various articles of luggage to the same place of safety. The fire now approached within about sixty yards, and dragging out the iron pins, I let the tent fall to the ground. The Arabs had swept a line like a highroad perfectly clean, and they were still tearing away the grass, when they were suddenly obliged to rush back as the flames arrived.

Almost instantaneously the smoke blew over us, but the fire had expired upon meeting the cleared ground. I now gave them a little lecture upon obedience to orders; and from that day, their first act upon halting for the night was to clear away the grass, lest I should repeat the entertainment. In countries that are covered with dry grass, it should be an invariable rule to clear the ground around the camp before night; hostile natives will frequently fire the grass to windward of a party, or careless servants may leave their pipes upon the ground, which fanned by the wind would quickly create a blaze. That night the mountain afforded a beautiful appearance as the flames ascended the steep sides, and ran flickering up the deep gullies with a brilliant light.

We were standing outside the tent admiring the scene, which perfectly illuminated the neighbourhood, when suddenly an apparition of a lion and lioness stood for an instant before us at about fifteen yards distance, and then disappeared over the blackened ground before I had time to snatch a rifle from the tent. No doubt they had been disturbed from the mountain by the fire, and had mistaken their way in the country so recently changed from high grass to black ashes. In this locality I considered it advisable to keep a vigilant watch during the night, and the Arabs were told off for that purpose.

A little before sunrise I accompanied the howartis, or hippopotamus hunters, for a day's sport. There were numbers of hippos in this part of the river, and we were not long before we found a herd. The hunters failed in several attempts to harpoon them, but they succeeded in stalking a crocodile after a most peculiar fashion. This large beast was lying upon a sandbank on the opposite margin of the river, close to a bed of rushes.

The howartis, having studied the wind, ascended for about a quarter of a mile, and then swam across the river, harpoon in hand. The two men reached the opposite bank, beneath which they alternately waded or swam down the stream towards the spot upon which the crocodile was lying. Thus advancing under cover of the steep bank, or floating with the stream in deep places, and crawling like crocodiles across the shallows, the two hunters at length arrived at the bank of rushes, on the other side of which the monster was basking asleep upon the sand. They were now about waist-deep, and they kept close to the rushes with their harpoons raised, ready to cast the moment they should pass the rush bed and come in view of the crocodile. Thus steadily advancing, they had just arrived at the corner within about eight yards of the crocodile, when the creature either saw them, or obtained their wind; in an inatant it rushed to the water; at the same moment, the two harpoons were launched with great rapidity by the hunters. One glanced obliquely from the scales; the other stuck fairly in the tough hide, and the iron, detached from the bamboo, held fast, while the ambatch float, running on the surface of the water, marked the course of the reptile beneath.

The hunters chose a convenient place, and recrossed the stream to our side, apparently not heeding the crocodiles more than we should fear pike when bathing in England. They would not waste their time by securing the crocodile at present, as they wished to kill a hippopotamus; the float would mark the position, and they would be certain to find it later. We accordingly continued our search for hippopotami; these animals appeared to be on the qui vive, and, as the hunters once more failed in an attempt, I made a clean shot behind the ear of one, and killed it dead. At length we arrived at a large pool in which were several sandbanks covered with rushes, and many rocky islands. Among these rocks was a herd of hippopotami, consisting of an old bull and several cows; a young hippo was standing, like an ugly little statue, on a protruding rock, while another infant stood upon its mother's back that listlessly floated on the water.

This was an admirable place for the hunters. They desired me to lie down, and they crept into the jungle out of view of the river; I presently observed them stealthily descending the dry bed about two hundred paces above the spot where the hippos were basking behind the rocks. They entered the river, and swam down the centre of the stream towards the rock. This was highly exciting: – the hippos were quite unconscious of the approaching danger, as, steadily and rapidly, the hunters floated down the strong current; they neared the rock, and both heads disappeared as they purposely sunk out of view; in a few seconds later they reappeared at the edge of the rock upon which the young hippo stood. It would be difficult to say which started first, the astonished young hippo into the water, or the harpoons from the hands of the howartis! It was the affair of a moment; the hunters dived directly they had hurled their harpoons, and, swimming for some distance under water, they came to the surface, and hastened to the shore lest an infuriated hippopotamus should follow them. One harpoon had missed; the other had fixed the bull of the herd, at which it had been surely aimed. This was grand sport! The bull was in the greatest fury, and rose to the surface, snorting and blowing in his impotent rage; but as the ambatch float was exceedingly large, and this naturally accompanied his movements, he tried to escape from his imaginary persecutor, and dived constantly, only to find his pertinacious attendant close to him upon regaining the surface. This was not to last long; the howartis were in earnest, and they at once called their party, who, with two of the aggageers, Abou Do and Suleiman, were near at hand; these men arrived with the long ropes that form a portion of the outfit for hippo hunting.

The whole party now halted on the edge of the river, while two men swam across with one end of the long rope. Upon gaining the opposite bank, I observed that a second rope was made fast to the middle of the main line; thus upon our side we held the ends of two ropes, while on the opposite side they had only one; accordingly, the point of junction of the two ropes in the centre formed an acute angle. The object of this was soon practically explained. Two men upon our side now each held a rope, and one of these walked about ten yards before the other. Upon both sides of the river the people now advanced, dragging the rope on the surface of the water until they reached the ambatch float that was swimming to and fro, according to the movements of the hippopotamus below. By a dexterous jerk of the main line, the float was now placed between the two ropes, and it was immediately secured in the acute angle by bringing together the ends of these ropes on our side.

The men on the opposite bank now dropped their line, and our men hauled in upon the ambatch float that was held fast between the ropes. Thus cleverly made sure, we quickly brought a strain upon the hippo, and, although I have had some experience in handling big fish, I never knew one pull so lustily as the amphibious animal that we now alternately coaxed and bullied. He sprang out of the water, gnashed his huge jaws, snorted with tremendous rage, and lashed the river into foam; he then dived, and foolishly approached us beneath the water. We quickly gathered in the slack line, and took a round turn upon a large rock, within a few feet of the river. The hippo now rose to the surface, about ten yards from the hunters, and, jumping half out of the water, he snapped his great jaws together, endeavouring to catch the rope, but at the same instant two harpoons were launched into his side. Disdaining retreat, and maddened with rage, the furious animal charged from the depths of the river, and, gaining a footing, he reared his bulky form from the surface, came boldly upon the sandbank, and attacked the hunters open-mouthed. He little knew his enemy; they were not the men to fear a pair of gaping jaws, armed with a deadly array of tusks, but half a dozen lances were hurled at him, some entering his mouth from a distance of five or six paces, at the same time several men threw handfuls of sand into his enormous eyes. This baffled him more than the lances; he crunched the shafts between his powerful jaws like straws, but he was beaten by the sand, and, shaking his huge head, he retreated to the river. During his sally upon the shore, two of the hunters had secured the ropes of the harpoons that had been fastened in his body just before his charge; he was now fixed by three of these deadly instruments, but suddenly one rope gave way, having been bitten through by the enraged beast, who was still beneath the water. Immediately after this he appeared on the surface, and, without a moment's hesitation, he once more charged furiously from the water straight at the hunters, with his huge mouth open to such an extent that he could have accommodated two inside passengers. Suleiman was wild with delight, and springing forward lance in hand, he drove it against the head of the formidable animal, but without effect. At the same time, Abou Do met the hippo sword in hand, reminding me of Perseus slaying the sea-monster that would devour Andromeda, but the sword made a harmless gash, and the lance, already blunted against the rocks, refused to penetrate the tough hide; once more handfuls of sand were pelted upon his face, and, again repulsed by this blinding attack, he was forced to retire to his deep hole and wash it from his eyes. Six times during the fight the valiant bull hippo quitted his watery fortress, and charged resolutely at his pursuers; he had broken several of their lances in his jaws, other lances had been hurled, and, falling upon the rocks, they were blunted, and would not penetrate. The fight had continued for three hours, and the sun was about to set, accordingly the hunters begged me to give him the coup de grace, as they had hauled him close to the shore, and they feared he would sever the rope with his teeth. I waited for a good opportunity, when he boldly raised his head from water about three yards from the rifle, and a bullet from the little Fletcher between the eyes closed the last act. This spot was not far from the pyramidical hill beneath which I had fixed our camp, to which I returned after an amusing day's sport.

The next morning, I started to the mountains to explore the limit that I had proposed for my expedition on the Settite. The Arabs had informed me that a river of some importance descended from the mountains, and joined the main stream about twelve miles from our camp. The aggageers were seriously expecting an attack from the Base, and they advised me not to remain much longer in this spot. The route was highly interesting: about five miles to the south-east of the camp we entered the hilly and mountainous country; to the east rose the peaked head of Allatakoora, about seven thousand feet from the base, while s.s.e. was the lofty table-mountain, known by the Arabs as Boorkotan. We rode through fertile valleys, all of which were free from grass, as the various fires had spread throughout the country; at times we entered deep gorges between the hills, which were either granite, quartz, or basalt, the latter predominating. In about three hours and a half we arrived at Hor Mehetape, the stream that the Arabs had reported. Although a powerful torrent during the rains, it was insignificant as one of the tributaries to the Settite, as the breadth did not exceed twenty-five yards. At this season it was nearly dry, and at no time did it appear to exceed a depth of ten or twelve feet. As we had arrived at this point, some distance above the junction, we continued along the margin of the stream for about two miles until we reached the Settite. The Hor (a ravine) Mehetape was the limit of my exploration; it was merely a rapid mountain torrent, the individual effect of which would be trifling; but we were now among the mountains whose drainage caused the sudden rise of the Atbara river and the Nile. Far as the eye could reach to the south and east, the range extended in a confused mass of peaks of great altitude, from the sharp granite head of one thousand, to flat-topped basalt hills of five or six thousand feet, and other conical points far exceeding, and perhaps double, that altitude.

The Settite was very beautiful in this spot, as it emerged from the gorge between the mountains, and it lay in a rough stony valley about two hundred feet below our path as we ascended from the junction of the Hor to better riding ground. In many places, our route lay over broken stones, which sloped at an inclination of about thirty degrees throughout the entire distance of the river below; these were formed of decomposed basalt rocks that had apparently been washed from decaying hills by the torrents of the rainy season. At other parts of the route, we crossed above similar debris of basalt that lay at an angle of about sixty degrees, from a height of perhaps two hundred feet to the water's edge, and reminded me of the rubbish shot from the side of a mountain when boring a tunnel. The whole of the basalt in this portion of the country was a dark slate colour; in some places it was almost black; upon breaking a great number of pieces I found small crystals of olivine. Much of the granite was a deep red, but the exterior coating was in all cases decomposed, and crumbled at a blow; exhibiting a marked contrast to the hard-faced granite blocks in the rainless climate of Lower Egypt. We saw but little game during the march – a few nellut and tetel, and the smaller antelopes, but no larger animals.

We returned to camp late in the evening, and I found the howartis had secured the crocodile of yesterday, but the whole party was anxious to return to the camp at Delladilla, as unpleasant reports were brought into camp by our spies, who had seen parties of the Base in several directions.

Chapter XVI.

Abou Do is Greedy.

Abou Do and Suleiman had lately given me some trouble, especially the former, whose covetous nature had induced him to take much more than his share of the hides of buffaloes and other animals that I had shot; all of which I had given to my head camel-man and tracker, Taher Noor, to divide among his people and the Tokrooris. This conduct was more improper, since the aggageers had become perfectly useless as elephant-hunters; they had ridden so recklessly upon unnecessary occasions, that all their horses were lamed, and, with the exception of Abou Do's, they were incapable of hunting. My three, having been well cared for, were in excellent condition. Abou Do coolly proposed that I should lend him my horses, which I of course refused, as I had a long journey before me; this led to disagreement, and I ordered him and his people to leave my camp, and return to Geera. During the time they had been with me, I had shot great numbers of animals, including large antelopes, buffaloes, elephants, &c.; and about twenty camel-loads of dried flesh, hides, fat, &c. had been transported to Geera as the Arabs' share of the spoils. They had also the largest share of ivory, and altogether they had never made so successful a hunting expedition. It was time to part; their horses being used up, they began to be discontented, therefore I had concluded that it would be advisable to separate, to avoid a graver misunderstanding.

I warned them not to disturb my hunting-grounds by attempting to hunt during their journey, but they were to. ride straight home, which they could accomplish in four days, without baggage camels. This they promised to do, and we parted.

I was now without aggageers, as Taher Sheriff's party had disagreed with Abou Do some time before, and they were hunting on their own account on the banks of the river Royan, which I intended to visit after I should have thoroughly explored the Settite. I made up my mind to have one more day in the neighbourhood of my present camp, and then to return to our old quarters at Delladilla, previous to our journey to the Royan junction.

Within three hundred yards of the camp was a regular game path, by which the animals arrived at the river to drink every morning from seven to nine. I had shot several tetel and ariel by simply waiting behind a rock at this place, and, as this was my last day, I once more concealed myself, and was shortly rewarded by the arrival of several herds, including nellut (A. Strepsiceros), tetel (A. Bubalis), ariel (G. Dama), the black-striped gazelle (G. Dorcas), the small oterop (Calotragus Montanus); and, among these, two ostriches. I had seen very few ostriches in this country. I now had a good chance, as the herd of animals returned from drinking by charging at full speed up the steep bank from the water, and they passed about ninety yards from my hiding-place, headed by the ostriches. Having the little Fletcher, I was suddenly tempted to fire a right and left, so as to bag an ostrich with one barrel, and a tetel with the other. Both fell for an instant; the tetel dead, shot through the neck; but my ostrich, that was a fine cock bird, immediately recovered, and went off with his wife as hard as their long legs could carry them. I was exceedingly disgusted; I had evidently fired too far behind, not having allowed sufficiently for the rapidity of their speed. However, to make amends, I snatched a spare single-rifle from Hassan, and knocked over another tetel that was the last of the herd. For about an hour I attempted to follow up the tracks of the ostrich, but among the rocky hills this was impossible. I therefore mounted Aggahr, and with my tracker, Taher Noor, and the Tokrooris as gun-bearers, I crossed the river and rode straight into the interior of the country. This was now thoroughly clear, as the fire had consumed the grass, and had left the surface perfectly black. Upon the ashes, the track of every animal could be seen distinctly.

I had ridden about four miles, followed, as usual, by two camels, with water, ropes, &c. when we observed in a perfectly open place, about three hundred yards from us, a rhinoceros standing alone. Fortunately, there was little or no wind, or, as we were to windward of him, he would instantly have perceived us. The moment that I saw him, I backed my horse and motioned to my people to retreat out of sight, which they did immediately. Dismounting, I gave them the horse, and, accompanied only by Taher Noor, who carried one of my spare rifles, I took a Reilly No. 10, and we made a circuit so as to obtain the wind, and to arrive upon the lee side of the rhinoceros. This was quickly accomplished, but upon arrival at the spot, he was gone. The black ashes of the recent fire showed his, foot-marks as clearly as though printed in ink, and as these were very close together, I knew that he had walked slowly off, and that he had not been disturbed, otherwise he would have started quickly. He had gone down wind; it would, therefore, be impossible to follow upon his tracks. Our only resource was to make another circuit, when, should his tracks not have crossed the arc, we should be sure that he was to windward. Accordingly, we described half a circle of about five hundred yards. No tracks had crossed our path; the ground was stony and full of hollows, in which grew a few scattered mimosas, while the surface of the earth was covered in many places with dark brown masses of basalt rock. We carefully stepped over this uneven ground, lest some falling stone might give the alarm, and we momentarily expected to be in view of the enemy as we arrived at the edge of each successive hollow. Sure enough, as I glanced down a sudden inclination covered with scorched mimosas, I perceived him standing on the slope beneath a tree within five-and-thirty paces; this was close enough, and I took a steady shot behind the shoulder. The instant that I fired, he whisked sharply round, and looked upon all sides for the cause of his wound. I had taken the precaution to kneel down immediately after firing, and I now crouched close to a rock about two feet high, with which my brown blouse matched exactly, as well as my skin-covered hunting-cap. For a few moments he sought upon all sides for an enemy, during which I remained like a block of stone, but with my finger on the trigger ready for the left-hand barrel should he charge. Taher Noor was lying on the ground behind a stone about five yards from me, and the rhinoceros, having failed to discover us, walked slowly past me within less than ten yards, and gained the summit of the inclination, where the ground was level. As he passed, I reloaded quickly, and followed behind him. I saw that he was grievously wounded, as he walked slowly, and upon arrival at a thickly-spreading mimosa he lay down. We now advanced towards the tree, and I sent Taher Noor round to the other side in order to divert his attention should he be able to rise. This he quickly proved by springing up as I advanced; accordingly, I halted until Taher Noor had taken his stand about eighty paces beyond the tree. The rhinoceros now turned and faced him; this gave me the opportunity that I had expected, and I ran quickly to within thirty yards, just in time to obtain a good shoulder shot, as hearing my footsteps he turned towards me. Whiff! whiff! and he charged vigorously upon the shot; but just as I prepared to fire the remaining barrel, he ran round and round in a narrow circle, uttering a short, shrill cry, and fell heavily upon his side. I threw a stone at him, but he was already dead. Taher Noor returned for the people, who shortly arrived with the camels. I found that the last bullet of quicksilver and lead from my Reilly No. 10 had passed completely through the body, just behind the shoulder. The first shot was also a mortal wound, having broken one rib upon either side, and passed through the posterior portion of the lungs; the bullet was sticking under the skin on the opposite flank. The hide of the rhinoceros is exceedingly easy to detach from the body, as the quality is so hard and stiff that it separates from the flesh like the peel of a ripe orange.

In a couple of hours, the hide had been detached in sections for shields, and sufficient flesh was loaded upon the camel, together with the vicious-looking head, which was secured by ropes upon the saddle. We were en route for the camp, when we suddenly came upon fresh elephant tracks, upon following which, we discovered, after about an hour's march, the spoor of horses on the same path. At once the truth flashed upon me that, although Abou Do had promised to return direct home, he was somewhere in the neighbourhood, and he and his two companions were disturbing the country by hunting. I at once gave up the idea of following the elephants, as, in all probability, these aggageers had pursued them some hours ago. In a very bad humour I turned my horse's head and took the direction for the Settite river. As we descended from the hilly ground, after the ride of about four miles, we arrived upon an extensive plain, upon which I noticed a number of antelopes galloping as though disturbed; a few moments later I observed three horsemen, a camel, and several men on foot, steering in the same direction as ourselves for the river, but arriving from the high ground upon which we had seen the elephants. These were soon distinguished, and I rode towards them with my people; they were the aggageers, with some of the hippopotami hunters.

Upon our arrival among them, they looked exceedingly sheepish, as they were caught in the act. Suspended most carefully upon one side of the camel, in a network of ropes, was a fine young rhinoceros which they had caught, having hunted the mother until she forsook the calf. Johann Schmidt had offered forty dollars for any young animal of this species, for the Italian menageries, therefore to the aggageers this was a prize of great value. I had hardly directed my attention to the calf, when I noticed a rope that was forcibly placed under the throat to support the heavy head, the weight of which bearing upon the cord was evidently producing strangulation. The tongue of the animal was protruding, and the tail stiffened and curled convulsively above the back, while a twitching of the hind legs, that presently stretched to their full extent, persuaded me that the rhinoceros was in his last gasp. As I looked intently at the animal, while my Tokrooris abused Abou Do for having deceived us, I told the aggageers that they had not gained much by their hunt, as the rhinoceros was dead. For a moment Abou Do smiled grimly, and, quite unconscious of the real fact, Suleiman replied, "It is worth forty dollars to us." "Forty dollars for a dead rhinoceros calf!" I exclaimed; "who is fool enough to give it?"

Abou Do glanced at the rhinoceros; his expression changed; he jumped from his horse, and, assisted by the other aggageers, he made the camel kneel as quickly as possible, and they hastened to unstrap the unfortunate little beast, which, upon being released and laid upon its side, convulsively stretched out its limbs, and lay a strangled rhinoceros. The aggageers gazed with dismay at their departed prize, and, with superstitious fear, they remounted their horses without uttering a word, and rode away; they attributed the sudden death of the animal to the effect of my "evil eye." We turned towards our camp. My Tokrooris were delighted, and I heard them talking and laughing together upon the subject, and remarking upon the extremely "bad eye" of their master.

On the rising of the sun next day we had struck our camp, and were upon the march to Delladilla. On the way I shot a splendid buck mehedehet (R. Ellipsyprimna), and we arrived at our old quarters, finding no change except that elephants had visited them in our absence, and our cleanly swept circus was covered with the dung of a large herd. As this spot generally abounded with game, I took a single-barrelled small rifle, while the men were engaged in pitching the tent and arranging the camp, and with Taher Noor as my only companion, I strolled through the forest, expecting to obtain a shot at a nellut within a quarter of a mile. I had walked about that distance, and had just entered upon a small green glade, when I perceived, lying at full length upon the sand, a large lion, who almost immediately sprang up, and at the same moment received a bullet from my rifle as he bounded beneath a bush and crouched among some withered grass. I was unloaded, when, to my astonishment, Taher Noor immediately drew his sword, and, with his shield in his left hand, he advanced boldly towards the wounded lion. I reloaded as quickly as possible, just as this reckless Hamran had arrived within springing distance of the lion, who positively slunk away and declined the fight; retreating into the thick thorns, it disappeared before I could obtain a shot. Taher Noor explained, that his object in advancing towards the lion was to attract its attention; he had expected that it would have remained in a crouching position until I should have reloaded; but he ran the extreme risk of a charge, in which case he would have fared badly with simple sword and shield. Being close to the tent, I returned, and, in addition to my single-barrelled rifle, I took my two Reillys No. 10, with Hassan and Hadji Ali. In company with Taher Noor we searched throughout the bushes for the wounded lion, but without success. I now determined to make a cast, hoping that we might succeed in starting some other animal that would give us a better chance. The ground was sandy but firm, therefore we made no sound in walking, and, as the forest was bounded upon two sides by the river, and separated from the main land by a ravine, the fire that had cleared the country of grass had spared this portion, which was an asylum for all kinds of game, as it afforded pasturage and cover. We had not continued our stroll for five minutes beyond the spot lately occupied by the lion, when we suddenly came upon two bull buffaloes, who were lying beneath a thick bush on the edge of a small glade: they sprang up as we arrived, and started off. I made a quick shot as they galloped across the narrow space, and dropped one apparently dead with a Reilly No. 10. My Tokrooris were just preparing to run in and cut the throat, as good Mussulmans, when the buffalo, that was not twenty yards distant, suddenly sprang to his feet and faced us. In another moment, with a short grunt, he determined upon a charge, but hardly was he in his first bound, when I fired the remaining barrel aimed at the point of the nose, as this was elevated to such a degree that it would have been useless to have fired at the forehead. He fell stone dead at the shot; we threw some clods of earth at him, but this time there was no mistake. Upon an examination of the body, we could only find the marks of the first bullet that had passed through the neck; there was no other hole in the skin, neither was there a sign upon the head or horns that he had been shot; at length I noticed blood issuing from the nose, and we found that the bullet had entered the nostril; I inserted a ramrod as a probe, and we cut to the extremity and found the bullet imbedded in the spine, which was shattered to pieces in a portion of the neck. As a souvenir of this very curious shot, I preserved the skull. My men now flayed the buffalo and took a portion of the meat, but I ordered them to leave the carcase as a bait for lions, with which this neighbourhood abounded, although it was exceedingly difficult to see them, as they were concealed in the dense covert of nabbuk bush. I left the buffalo, and strolled through the jungle towards the river. As I was leisurely walking through alternate narrow glades and thick jungle, I heard a noise that sounded like the deep snort of the hippopotamus. I approached the steep bank of the river, and crept carefully to the edge, expecting to see the hippo as I peered over the brink. Instead of the hippopotamus, a fine lion and lioness were lying on the sand about sixty yards to my left, at the foot of the bank. At the same instant they obtained our wind, and sprang up the high bank into the thick jungle, without giving me a better chance than a quick shot through a bush as they were disappearing.

I now returned home, determined to circumvent the lions if possible in this very difficult country. That night we were serenaded by the roaring of these animals in all directions, one of them having visited our camp, around which we discovered his footprints on the following morning. I accordingly took Taher Noor, with Hadji Ali and Hassan, two of my trusty Tokrooris, and went straight to the spot where I had left the carcase of the buffalo. As I had expected, nothing remained – not even a bone: the ground was much trampled, and tracks of lions were upon the sand; but the body of the buffalo had been dragged into the thorny jungle. I was determined, if possible, to get a shot, therefore I followed carefully the track left by the carcase, which had formed a path in the withered grass. Unfortunately the lions had dragged the buffalo down wind; therefore, after I had arrived within the thick nabbuk and high grass, I came to the conclusion that my only chance would be to make a long circuit, and to creep up wind through the thorns, until I should be advised by my nose of the position of the carcase, which would by this time lie in a state of putrefaction, and the lions would most probably be with the body. Accordingly, I struck off to my left, and continuing straight forward for some hundred yards, I again struck into the thick jungle, and came round to the wind. Success depended on extreme caution, therefore I advised my three men to keep close behind me with the spare rifles, as I carried my single-barrelled Beattie. This rifle was extremely accurate, therefore I had chosen it for this close work, when I expected to get a shot at the eye or forehead of a lion crouching in the bush. Softly and with difficulty I crept forward, followed closely by my men; through the high withered grass, beneath the dense green nabbuk bushes; peering through the thick covert, with the nerves turned up to full pitch, and the finger on the trigger ready for any emergency. We had thus advanced for about half an hour, during which I frequently applied my nose to within a foot of the ground to catch the scent, when a sudden puff of wind brought the unmistakeable smell of decomposing flesh. For the moment I halted, and, looking round to my men, I made a sign that we were near to the carcase, and that they were to be ready with the rifles. Again I crept gently forward, bending, and sometimes crawling, beneath the thorns to avoid the slightest noise. As I approached, the scent became stronger, until I at length felt that I must be close to the cause. This was highly exciting. Fully prepared for a quick shot, I stealthily crept on. A tremendous roar in the dense thorns within a few feet of me suddenly brought my rifle to the shoulder: almost in the same instant I observed the three-quarter figure of either a lion or a lioness within three yards of me, on the other side of the bush, under which I had been creeping – the foliage concealed the head, but I could almost have touched the shoulder with my rifle. Much depended upon the bullet; and I fired exactly through the shoulder. Another tremendous roar! and a crash in the bushes as the animal made a bound forward, was succeeded immediately by a similar roar, as another lion took the exact position of the last, and stood wondering at the report of the rifle, and seeking for the cause of the intrusion. This was a grand lion with a shaggy mane; but I was unloaded, keeping my eyes fixed on the beast, while I stretched my hand back for a spare rifle; the lion remained standing, but gazing up wind with his head raised, snuffing in the air for a scent of the enemy. No rifle was put in my hand. I looked back for an instant, and saw my Tokrooris faltering about five yards behind me. I looked daggers at them, gnashing my teeth and shaking my fist. They saw the lion, and Taher Noor snatching a rifle from Hadji Ali, was just about to bring it, when Hassan, ashamed, ran forward – the lion disappeared at the same moment! Never was such a fine chance lost through the indecision of the gun-bearers! I made a vow never to carry a single-barrelled rifle again when hunting large game. If I had had my dear little Fletcher 24, I should have nailed the lion to a certainty.

However, there was not much time for reflection – where was the first lion? Some remains of the buffalo lay upon my right, and I expected to find the lion most probably crouching in the thorns somewhere near us. Having reloaded, I took one of my Reilly No. 10 rifles and listened attentively for a sound. Presently I heard within a few yards a low growl. Taher Noor drew his sword, and, with his shield before him, he searched for the lion, while I crept forward towards the sound, which was again repeated. A low roar, accompanied by a rush in the jungle, showed us a glimpse of the lion, as he bounded off within ten or twelve yards: but I had no chance to fire. Again the low growl was repeated, and upon quietly creeping towards the spot, I saw a splendid animal crouched upon the ground among the withered and broken grass. The lioness lay dying with the bullet wound in the shoulder. Occasionally, in her rage, she bit her own paw violently, and then struck and clawed the ground. A pool of blood lay by her side. She was about ten yards from us, and I instructed my men to throw a clod of earth at her (there were no stones), to prove whether she could rise, while I stood ready with the rifle. She merely replied with a dull roar, and I terminated her misery by a ball through the head. She was a beautiful animal; the patch of the bullet was sticking in the wound; she was shot through both shoulders, and as we were not far from the tent, I determined to have her brought to camp upon a camel as an offering to my wife. Accordingly I left my Tokrooris, while I went with Taher Noor to fetch a camel.

On our road through the thick jungle, I was startled by a rush close to me: for the moment I thought it was a lion, but almost at the same instant I saw a fine nellut dashing away before me, and I killed it immediately with a bullet through the back of the neck. This was great luck, and we now required two camels, as in two shots I had killed a lioness and a nellut (A. Strepsiceros).

We remained for some time at our delightful camp at Delladilla. Every day, from sunrise to sunset, I was either on foot or in the saddle, without rest, except upon Sundays, which I generally passed at home, with the relaxation of fishing in the beautiful river Settite. There was an immense quantity of large game, and I had made a mixed bag of elephants, hippopotami, buffaloes, rhinoceros, giraffes, and great numbers of the large antelopes. Lions, although numerous, were exceedingly difficult to bag; there was no chance but the extreme risk of creeping through the thickest jungle. Upon two or three occasions I had shot them by crawling into their very dens, where they had dragged their prey; and I must acknowledge that they were much more frightened of me than I was of them. I had generally obtained a most difficult and unsatisfactory shot at close quarters; sometimes I rolled them over with a mortal wound, and they disappeared to die in impenetrable jungle; but at all times fortune was on my side. On moonlight nights I generally lay in wait for these animals with great patience; sometimes I shot hippopotami, and used a hind-quarter as a bait for lions, while I watched in ambush at about twenty yards distance; but the hyaenas generally appeared like evil spirits, and dragged away the bait before the lions had a chance. I never fired at these scavengers, as they are most useful creatures, and are contemptible as game. My Arabs had made their fortune, as I had given them all the meat of the various animals, which they dried and transported to Geera, together with fat, hides, &c. It would be wearying to enumerate the happy hunting-days passed throughout this country. We were never ill for a moment; although the thermometer was seldom below 88 degrees during the day, the country was healthy, as it was intensely dry, and therefore free from malaria: at night the thermometer averaged 70 degrees, which was a delightful temperature for those who exist in the open air.

As our camp was full of meat, either dried or in the process of drying in festoons upon the trees, we had been a great attraction to the beasts of prey, who constantly prowled around our thorn fence during the night. One night in particular a lion attempted to enter, but had been repulsed by the Tokroris, who pelted him with firebrands; my people woke me up and begged me to shoot him, but, as it was perfectly impossible to fire correctly through the hedge of thorns, I refused to be disturbed, but I promised to hunt for him on the following day. Throughout the entire night the lion prowled around the camp, growling and uttering his peculiar guttural sigh. Not one of my people slept, as they declared he would bound into the camp and take somebody, unless they kept up the watch-fires and drove him away with brands. The next day, before sunrise, I called Hassan and Hadji Ali, whom I lectured severely upon their cowardice on a former occasion, and I received their promise to follow me to death. I entrusted them with my two Reillys No. 10; and with my little Fletcher in hand, I determined to spend the whole day in searching every thicket of the forest for lions, as I felt convinced that the animal that had disturbed us during the night was concealed somewhere within the neighbouring jungle.

The whole day passed fruitlessly; I had crept through the thickest thorns in vain; having abundance of meat, I had refused the most tempting shots at buffaloes and large antelopes, as I had devoted myself exclusively to lions. I was much disappointed, as the evening had arrived without a shot having been fired, and as the sun had nearly set, I wandered slowly towards home. Passing through alternate open glades of a few yards width, hemmed in on all sides by thick jungle, I was carelessly carrying my rifle upon my shoulder, as I pushed my way through the opposing thorns, when a sudden roar, just before me, at once brought the rifle upon full cock, and I saw a magnificent lion standing in the middle of the glade, about ten yards from me: he had been lying on the ground, and had started to his feet upon hearing me approach through the jungle. For an instant he stood in an attitude of attention, as we were hardly visible; but at the same moment I took a quick but sure shot with the little Fletcher. He gave a convulsive bound, but rolled over backwards: before he could recover himself, I fired the left-hand barrel. It was a glorious sight. I had advanced a few steps into the glade, and Hassan had quickly handed me a spare rifle, while Taher Noor stood by me sword in hand. The lion in the greatest fury, with his shaggy mane bristled in the air, roared with deathlike growls, as open-mouthed he endeavoured to charge upon us; but he dragged his hind-quarters upon the ground, and I saw immediately that the little Fletcher had broken his spine. In his tremendous exertions to attack, he rolled over and over, gnashing his horrible jaws, and tearing holes in the sandy ground at each blow of his tremendous paws, that would have crushed a man's skull like an egg-shell. Seeing that he was hors de combat, I took it coolly, as it was already dusk, and the lion having rolled into a dark and thick bush, I thought it would be advisable to defer the final attack, as he would be dead before morning. We were not ten minutes' walk from the camp, at which we quickly arrived, and my men greatly rejoiced at the discomfiture of their enemy, as they were convinced that he was the same lion that had attempted to enter the zareeba.

On the following morning, before sunrise, I started with nearly all my people and a powerful camel, with the intention of bringing the lion home entire. I rode my horse Tetel, who had frequently shown great courage, and I wished to prove whether he would advance to the body of a lion.

Upon arrival near the spot which we supposed to have been the scene of the encounter, we were rather puzzled, as there was nothing to distinguish the locality; one place exactly resembled another, as the country was flat and sandy, interspersed with thick jungle of green nabbuk; we accordingly spread out to beat for the lion. Presently Hadji Ali cried out: "There he lies dead!" and I immediately rode to the spot, together with the people. A tremendous roar greeted us, as the lion started to his fore-feet, and with his beautiful mane erect, and his great hazel eyes flashing fire, he gave a succession of deep short roars, and challenged us to fight. This was a grand picture; he looked like a true lord of the forest, but I pitied the poor brute, as he was helpless, and, although his spirit was game to the last, his strength was paralysed by a broken back.

It was a glorious opportunity for the horse. At the first unexpected roar, the camel had bolted with its rider; the horse had for a moment started on one side, and the men had scattered; but in an instant I had reined Tetel up, and I now rode straight towards the lion, who courted the encounter about twenty paces distant. I halted exactly opposite the noble-looking beast, who, seeing me in advance of the party, increased his rage, and growled deeply, fixing his glance upon the horse. I now patted Tetel on the neck, and spoke to him coaxingly; he gazed intently at the lion, erected his mane, and snorted, but showed no signs of retreat. "Bravo! old boy!" I said, and, encouraging him by caressing his neck with my hand, I touched his flank gently with my heel; I let him just feel my hand upon the rein, and with a "Come along, old lad," Tetel slowly but resolutely advanced step by step towards the infuriated lion, that greeted him with continued growls. The horse several times snorted loudly, and stared fixedly at the terrible face before him; but as I constantly patted and coaxed him, he did not refuse to advance. I checked him when within about six yards from the lion. This would have made a magnificent picture, as the horse, with astounding courage, faced the lion at bay; both animals kept their eyes fixed upon each other, the one beaming with rage, the other with cool determination. This was enough – I dropped the reins upon his neck; it was a signal that Tetel perfectly understood, and he stood firm as a rock; for he knew that I was about to fire. I took aim at the head of the glorious but distressed lion, and a bullet from the little Fletcher dropped him dead. Tetel never flinched at a shot. I now dismounted, and having patted and coaxed the horse, I led him up to the body of the lion, which I also patted, and then gave my hand to the horse to smell. He snorted once or twice, and as I released my hold of the reins, and left him entirely free, he slowly lowered his head, and sniffed the mane of the dead lion: he then turned a few paces upon one side, and commenced eating the withered grass beneath the nabbuk bushes. My Arabs were perfectly delighted with this extraordinary instance of courage exhibited by the horse. I had known that the beast was disabled, but Tetel had advanced boldly towards the angry jaws of a lion that appeared about to spring. The camel was now brought to the spot and blindfolded, while we endeavoured to secure the lion upon its back. As the camel knelt, it required the united exertions of eight men, including myself, to raise the ponderous animal, and to secure it across the saddle.

Although so active and cat-like in its movements, a full-grown lion weighs about five hundred and fifty pounds. Having secured it, we shortly arrived in camp; the coup d'oeil was beautiful, as the camel entered the inclosure with the shaggy head and massive paws of the dead lion hanging upon one flank, while the tail nearly descended to the ground upon the opposite side. It was laid at full length before my wife, to whom the claws were dedicated as a trophy to be worn around the neck as a talisman. Not only are the claws prized by the Arabs, but the moustache of the lion is carefully preserved and sewn in a leather envelope, to be worn as an amulet; such a charm is supposed to protect the wearer from the attacks of wild animals.

In all probability, this was the lion that was in the habit of visiting our camp, as from that date, although the roars of such animals were our nightly music, we were never afterwards visited so closely.

As game was plentiful, the lions were exceedingly fat, and we preserved a large quantity of this for our lamps. When it was boiled down it was well adapted for burning, as it remained nearly liquid.

We had a large supply of various kinds of fat, including that of elephants, hippopotami, lions, and rhinoceros; but our stock of soap was exhausted, therefore I determined to convert a quantity of our grease into that very necessary article.

Soap-boiling is not so easy as may be imagined; it requires not only much attention, but the quality is dependent upon the proper mixture of the alkalis. Sixty parts of potash and forty of lime are, I believe, the proportions for common soap. I had neither lime nor potash, but I shortly procured both. The hegleek tree (Balanites Egyptiaca) was extremely rich in potash; therefore I burned a large quantity, and made a strong ley with the ashes; this I concentrated by boiling. There was no limestone; but the river produced a plentiful supply of large oyster-shells, that, if burned, would yield excellent lime. Accordingly I constructed a kiln, with the assistance of the white ants. The country was infested with these creatures, which had erected their dwellings in all directions; these were cones from six to ten feet high, formed of clay so thoroughly cemented by a glutinous preparation of the insects, that it was harder than sun-baked brick. I selected an egg-shaped hill, and cut off the top, exactly as we take off the slice from an egg. My Tokrooris then worked hard, and with a hoe and their lances, hollowed it out to the base, in spite of the attacks of the ants, which punished the legs of the intruders considerably. I now made a draught-hole from the outside base, at right angles with the bottom of the hollow cone. My kiln was perfect. I loaded it with wood, upon which I piled about six bushels of oyster-shells, which I then covered with fuel, and kept it burning for twenty-four hours. This produced excellent lime, and I commenced my soap-boiling. We possessed an immense copper pot of Egyptian manufacture, in addition to a large and deep copper basin called a "teshti." These would contain about ten gallons. The ley having been boiled down to great strength, I added a quantity of lime, and the necessary fat. It required ten hours' boiling, combined with careful management of the fire, as it would frequently ascend like foam, and overflow the edge of the utensils. However, at length, having been constantly stirred, it turned to soap. Before it became cold, I formed it into cakes and balls with my hands, and the result of the manufacture was a weight of about forty pounds of most excellent soap, of a very sporting description, "Savon a la bete feroce." We thus washed with rhinoceros soap; our lamp was trimmed with oil of lions; our butter for cooking purposes was the fat of hippopotami, while our pomade was made from the marrow of buffaloes and antelopes, scented with the blossoms of mimosas. We were entirely independent, as our whole party had subsisted upon the produce of the rod and the rifle.

We were now destined to be deprived of two members of the party. Mahomet had become simply unbearable, and he was so impertinent that I was obliged to take a thin cane from one of the Arabs and administer a little physical advice. An evil spirit possessed the man, and he bolted off with some of the camel men who were returning to Geera with dried meat.[11]

Our great loss was Barrake. She had persisted in eating the fruit of the hegleek, although she had suffered from dysentery upon several occasions. She was at length attacked with congestion of the liver. My wife took the greatest care of her, and for weeks she had given her the entire produce of the goats, hoping that milk would keep up her strength; but she died after great suffering, and we buried the poor creature, and moved our camp.

---

11   Some months afterwards he found his way to Khartoum, where he was imprisoned by the Governor for having deserted. He subsequently engaged himself as a soldier in a slave-hunting expedition on the White Nile; and some years later, on our return from the Albert N'yanza, we met him in Shooa, on 3 degrees north latitude. He had repented – hardships and discipline had effected a change – and, like the prodigal son, he returned. I forgave him, and took him with us to Khartoum, where we left him a sadder but a wiser man. He had many near relations during his long journey, all of whom had stolen some souvenir of their cousin, and left him almost naked. He also met Achmet, his "mothers brother's cousin's sister's mother's son," who turned up after some years at Gondokoro as a slave-hunter; he had joined an expedition, and, like all other blackguards, he had chosen the White Nile regions for his career. He was the proprietor of twenty slaves, he had assisted in the murder of a number of unfortunate negroes, and he was a prosperous and respectable individual.

Chapter XVII.

We Reach the Royan.

Having explored the Settite into the gorge of the mountain chain of Abyssinia, we now turned due south from our camp of Delladilla, and at a distance of twelve miles we reached the river Royan. The intervening country was the high and flat table-land of rich soil, that characterises the course of the Settite and Atbara rivers; this land was covered with hegleek trees of considerable size, and the descent to the Royan was through a valley, torn and washed by the rains, similar in appearance to that of the Settite, but upon a small scale, as the entire width did not exceed a mile.

Descending the rugged ground, we arrived at the margin of the river. At this season (February) the bed was perfectly dry sand, about ninety yards from bank to bank, and the high-water mark upon the perpendicular sides was a little above nine feet deep. The inclination was extremely rapid: thus the Royan during the rainy season must be a most frightful torrent, that supplies a large body of water to the Settite, but which runs dry almost immediately upon the cessation of the rains.

We descended the bank in a spot that had been broken down by elephants, and continued our course up stream along the sandy bed, which formed an excellent road. The surface was imprinted with the footsteps of every variety of game, and numerous holes about two feet deep had been dug in the sand by the antelopes and baboons to procure water. Great numbers of the oterop, a small reddish-brown antelope without horns (Calotragus Montanus) were drinking at these little watering-places, and did not appear to heed us. We disturbed many nellut and tetel upon the banks, and after having marched about four miles along the river's bed, we halted at a beautiful open forest of large trees at the junction of Hor Mai Gubba. This was a considerable torrent, which is tributary to the Royan; at this spot it had cut through a white sandstone cliff, about eighty feet perpendicular: thus upon either side it was walled in. The word Gubba is Abyssinian for the nabbuk, therefore the torrent was the Nabbuk River: this flowed past the village of Mai Gubba, which is the head-quarters of Mek Nimmur, from which we were not twenty-five miles distant. We camped in a forest of the largest trees that we had as yet seen in Africa, and as we had observed the fresh tracks of horses, on the sand, some of my Arabs went in search of the aggageers of Taher Sheriff's party, whom they had expected to meet at this point. While they were gone, I took a few men to beat the low jungle within the forest for francolin partridge, numbers of which I had seen running through the covert. I went up the dry bed of the river at the junction of the Hor Gubba, while they drove towards me, and I was compelled to fire as fast as I could load, as these beautiful birds flew across the ravine. I shot five brace almost immediately. There is no better game bird than the francolin: the flesh is white, and of a most delicate and rich flavour. My shots had attracted the aggageers, and shortly after my return to camp they arrived with my Arabs, as they had been stationed on the opposite side of the Royan in a forest within a quarter of a mile of us. Taher Sheriff was delighted to see us free from the company of Abou Do. His party had killed several elephants, and had captured two young ones; also, two young rhinoceroses, three giraffes, and several young antelopes; these were to be sold to Johann Schmidt, who contracted to supply the Italian agent at Cassala. I agreed to have a long day's hunt with Taher Sheriff; we were to start before sunrise, as he wished to ride to a spot about twenty-five miles distant, up the course of the Royan, that was a favourite resort for elephants.

That evening we had a delicious dinner of francolin partridges. This species is rather larger than the French partridge: it is dark brown, mottled with black feathers, with a red mark around the eye, and double spurs.

There was a small but deep pool of water in the bed of the river, beneath the high bank about two hundred paces from our camp; this was a mere hole of about twenty feet square, and I expected that large game might come to drink during the night. Accordingly, I determined to watch for elephants, as their tracks were numerous throughout the bed of the river. My wife and two gun-bearers accompanied me, and we sat behind an immense tree that grew on the bank, exactly about the drinking place. I watched for hours, until I fell asleep, as did my men likewise: my wife alone was awake, and a sudden tug at my sleeve attracted my attention. The moon was bright, and she had heard a noise upon the branches of the tree above us: there were no leaves, therefore I quickly observed some large animal upon a thick bough. My Tokrooris had awoke, and they declared it to be a baboon. I knew this to be impossible, as the baboon is never solitary, and I was just preparing to fire, when down jumped a large leopard within a few feet of us, and vanished before I had time to shoot. It must have winded our party, and quietly ascended the tree to reconnoitre. Nothing but hyaenas came to the pool, therefore we returned to camp.

According to my agreement, I went to the aggageers' camp at 5 A.M. with Hadji Ali and Hassan, both mounted on my two horses, Aggahr and Gazelle, while I rode Tetel. Taher Sheriff requested me not to shoot at anything, as the shots might alarm and scare away elephants; therefore I merely carried my little Fletcher, in case of meeting the Base, who hunted in this country. The aggageers mounted their horses; each man carried an empty water-skin slung to his saddle, to be filled at the river should it be necessary to quit its banks. We started along the upward course of the Royan.

For seven hours we rode, sometimes along the bed of the river between lofty overhanging rocks, or through borders of fine forest-trees; at other times we cut off a bend of the stream, and rode for some miles through beautiful country diversified with hills, and abounding in enormous baobab-trees (Adansonia digitata). At length we entered the mountains at the foot of the great chain. Here the views were superb. The Royan was no longer a stream of ninety or a hundred yards in width, but it was reduced to a simple mountain torrent about forty yards across, blocked in many places by masses of rock, while at others it had formed broad pools, all of which were now perfectly dry, and exhibited a bed of glaring sand. Numerous mountain ravines joined the main channel, and as the inclination was extremely rapid, there could be little doubt that the violent storms of the rainy season, descending from the great chain of mountains, would, by concentrating in the Royan, suddenly give birth to an impetuous torrent, that would materially affect the volume of the Settite. The entire country bore witness to the effect of violent rains, as the surface was torn and water-worn.

We had ridden nearly thirty miles, having seen large quantities of game, including antelopes, buffaloes, giraffes, and rhinoceroses, none of which we had hunted, as we were in search of elephants. This was the country where the aggageers had expected, without fail, to find their game.

They now turned away from the Royan, and descended a sandy valley at the foot of the mountains, the bottom of which appeared to have been overflowed during the wet season. Here were large strips of forest, and numerous sandy watercourses, along the dry bed of which we quickly discovered the deep tracks of elephants. They had been digging fresh holes in the sand in search of water, in which welcome basins we found a good supply; we dismounted, and rested the horses for half an hour, while the hunters followed up the tracks on the bed of the stream. Upon their return, they reported the elephants as having wandered off upon the rocky ground, that rendered further tracking impossible. We accordingly remounted, and, upon arrival at the spot where they had lost the tracks, we continued along the bed of the stream. We had ridden about a mile, and were beginning to despair, when suddenly we turned a sharp angle in the watercourse, and Taher Sheriff, who was leading, immediately reined in his horse, and backed him towards the party. I followed his example, and we were at once concealed by the sharp bend of the river. He now whispered, that a bull elephant was drinking from a hole it had scooped in the sand, not far round the corner. Without the slightest confusion, the hunters at once fell quietly into their respective places, Taher Sheriff leading, while I followed closely in the line, with my Tokrooris bringing up the rear; we were a party of seven horses.

Upon turning the corner, we at once perceived the elephant, that was still drinking. It was a fine bull; the enormous ears were thrown forward, as the head was lowered in the act of drawing up the water through the trunk; these shaded the eyes, and, with the wind favourable, we advanced noiselessly upon the sand to within twenty yards before we were perceived. The elephant then threw up its head, and, with the ears flapping forward, it raised its trunk for an instant, and then slowly, but easily, ascended the steep bank, and retreated. The aggageers now halted for about a minute to confer together, and then followed in their original order up the crumbled bank. We were now on most unfavourable ground; the fire that had cleared the country we had hitherto traversed had been stopped by the bed of the torrent. We were thus plunged at once into withered grass above our heads, unless we stood in the stirrups; the ground was strewed with fragments of rock, and altogether it was ill-adapted for riding. However, Taher Sheriff broke into a trot, followed by the entire party, as the elephant was not in sight. We ascended a hill, and when near the summit, we perceived the elephant about eighty yards ahead. It was looking behind during its retreat, by swinging its huge head from side to side, and upon seeing us approach, it turned suddenly round and halted. "Be ready, and take care of the rocks!" said Taher Sheriff, as I rode forward by his side. Hardly had he uttered these words of caution, when the bull gave a vicious jerk with its head, and with a shrill scream it charged down upon us with the greatest fury. Away we all went, helter skelter, through the dry grass, which whistled in my ears, over the hidden rocks, at full gallop, with the elephant tearing after us for about a hundred and eighty yards at a tremendous pace. Tetel was a surefooted horse, and, being unshod, he never slipped upon the stones. Thus, as we all scattered in different directions, the elephant became confused, and relinquished the chase; it had been very near me at one time, and in such ground I was not sorry when it gave up the hunt. We now quickly united, and again followed the elephant, that had once more retreated. Advancing at a canter, we shortly came in view. Upon seeing the horses, the bull deliberately entered a stronghold composed of rocky and uneven ground, in the clefts of which grew thinly a few leafless trees, the thickness of a man's leg. It then turned boldly towards us, and stood determinedly at bay.

Now came the tug of war! Taher Sheriff came close to me and said, "You had better shoot the elephant, as we shall have great difficulty in this rocky ground:" this I declined, as I wished to end the fight as it had been commenced, with the sword; and I proposed that he should endeavour to drive the animal to more favourable ground. "Never mind," replied Taher, "Inshallah (please God) he shall not beat us." He now advised me to keep as close to him as possible, and to look sharp for a charge.

The elephant stood facing us like a statue; it did not move a muscle beyond a quick and restless action of the eyes, that were watching all sides. Taher Sheriff and his youngest brother Ibrahim now separated, and each took opposite sides of the elephant, and then joined each other about twenty yards behind it; I accompanied them, until Taher advised me to keep about the same distance upon the left flank. My Tokrooris kept apart from the scene, as they were not required. In front of the elephant were two aggageers, one of whom was the renowned Roder Sheriff, with the withered arm. All being ready for action, Roder now rode slowly towards the head of the cunning old bull, who was quietly awaiting an opportunity to make certain of some one who might give him a good chance.

Roder Sheriff rode a bay mare, that, having been thoroughly trained to these encounters, was perfect at her work. Slowly and coolly she advanced towards her wary antagonist, until within about eight or nine yards of the elephant's head; the creature never moved, and the mise en scene was beautiful; not a word was spoken, and we kept our places amidst utter stillness, which was at length broken by a snort from the mare, who gazed intently at the elephant, as though watching for the moment of attack.

One more pace forward, and Roder sat coolly upon his mare, with his eyes fixed upon those of the elephant. For an instant I saw the white of the eye nearest to me "Look out, Roder! he's coming!" I exclaimed. With a shrill scream, the elephant dashed upon him like an avalanche!

Round went the mare as though upon a pivot, and away, over rocks and stones, flying like a gazelle, with the monkey-like form of little Roder Sheriff leaning forward, and looking over his left shoulder as the elephant rushed after him.

For a moment I thought he must be caught. Had the mare stumbled, all were lost; but she gained in the race after a few quick bounding strides, and Roder, still looking behind him, kept his distance so close to the elephant, that its outstretched trunk was within a few feet of the mare's tail.

Taher Sheriff and his brother Ibrahim swept down like falcons in the rear. In full speed they dexterously avoided the trees, until they arrived upon open ground, when they dashed up close to the hind-quarters of the furious elephant, who, maddened with the excitement, heeded nothing but Roder and his mare, that were almost within its grasp. When close to the tail of the elephant, Taher Sheriff's sword flashed from its sheath, as grasping his trusty blade he leapt nimbly to the ground, while Ibrahim caught the reins of his horse; two or three bounds on foot, with the sword clutched in both hands, and he was close behind the elephant; a bright glance shone like lightning, as the sun struck upon the descending steel; this was followed by a dull crack, as the sword cut through skin and sinews, and settled deep in the bone, about twelve inches above the foot. At the next stride, the elephant halted dead short in the midst of its tremendous charge. Taher had jumped quickly on one side, and had vaulted into the saddle with his naked sword in hand. At the same moment, Roder, who had led the chase, turned sharp round, and again faced the elephant as before; stooping quickly from the saddle, he picked up from the ground a handful of dirt, which he threw into the face of the vicious-looking animal, that once more attempted to rush upon him. It was impossible! the foot was dislocated, and turned up in front like an old shoe. In an instant Taher was once more on foot, and again the sharp sword slashed the remaining leg. The great bull elephant could not move! the first cut with the sword had utterly disabled it; the second was its death blow; the arteries of the leg were divided, and the blood spouted in jets from the wounds. I wished to terminate its misery by a bullet behind the ear, but Taher Sheriff begged me not to fire, as the elephant would quickly bleed to death without pain, and an unnecessary shot might attract the Base, who would steal the flesh and ivory during our absence. We were obliged to return immediately to our far distant camp, and the hunters resolved to accompany their camels to the spot upon the following day. We turned our horses' heads, and rode direct towards home, which we did not reach until nearly midnight, having ridden upwards of sixty miles during the day.

The hunting of Taher Sheriff and his brothers was superlatively beautiful; with an immense amount of dash, there was a cool, sportsman-like manner in their mode of attack, that far excelled the impetuous and reckless onset of Abou Do; it was difficult to decide which to admire the most, whether the coolness and courage of him who led the elephant, or the extraordinary skill and activity of the aggahr who dealt the fatal blow.

On the following day, the hunters started to the dead elephant with camels and sacks, but they returned at night thoroughly disgusted; the nimble Base had been before them, most probably attracted to the carcase by the cloud of vultures that had gathered in the air. Nothing remained but the bones and skull of the elephant, the flesh and the ivory had been stolen. The tracks of a great number of men were left upon the ground, and the aggageers were fortunate to return without an attack from overwhelming numbers.

After hunting and exploring for some days in this neighbourhood, I determined to follow the bed of the Royan to its junction with the Settite. We started at daybreak, and after a long march along the sandy bed, hemmed in by high banks, or by precipitous cliffs of sandstone, we arrived at the junction; this was a curious and frightful spot during the rainy season. The entire course of the Royan was extremely rapid, but at this extremity it entered a rocky pass between two hills, and leapt in a succession of grand falls into a circular basin of about four hundred yards diameter. This peculiar basin was surrounded by high cliffs, covered with trees; to the left was an island formed by a rock about sixty feet high; at the foot was a deep and narrow gorge through which the Settite river made its exit from the circle. This large river entered the basin through a rocky gap, at right angles with the rush of water from the great falls of the Royan, and as both streams issued from gorges which accelerated their velocity to the highest degree, their junction formed a tremendous whirlpool: thus, the basin which was now dry, with the exception of the single contracted stream of the Settite, was in the rainy season a most frightful scene of giddy waters. The sides of this basin were, for about fifty feet from the bottom, sheeted with white sand that had been left there by the centrifugal force of the revolving waters; the funnel-shaped reservoir had its greatest depth beneath the mass of rock that formed a barrier before the mouth of the exit. From the appearance of the high-water mark upon the rock, it was easy to ascertain the approximate depth when the flood was at its maximum. We pitched our camp on the slope above the basin, and for several days I explored the bed of the river, which was exceedingly interesting at this dry season, when all the secrets of its depths were exposed. In many places, the rocks that choked its bed for a depth of thirty and forty feet in the narrow passes, had been worked into caverns by the constant attrition of the rolling pebbles. In one portion of the river, the bottom was almost smooth, as though it had been paved with flagstones; this was formed by a calcareous sediment from the water, which had hardened into stone; in some places this natural pavement had been broken up into large slabs by the force of the current, where it had been undermined. This cement appeared to be the same that had formed the banks of conglomerate, which in some places walled in the river for a depth of ten or fifteen feet, with a concrete of rounded pebbles of all sizes from a nutmeg to a thirty-two pound shot.

I fired the grass on the west bank of the Royan, and the blaze extended with such rapidity, that in a few hours many miles of country were entirely cleared. On the following morning, the country looked as though covered with a pall of black velvet.

To my astonishment there were the fresh tracks of a rhinoceros within a quarter of a mile of the camp: this animal must have concealed itself in the bed of the Royan during the fire, and had wandered forth when it had passed. I followed up the tracks with Bacheet and two of my Tookroris. In less than half a mile from the spot, I found it lying down behind a bush, and creeping under cover of an ant-hill, I shot it through the shoulder with a Reilly No. 10; it immediately galloped off, but after a run of a couple of hundred yards it lay down on the edge of thick thorny jungle that bordered the margin of the Royan. I waited, in the expectation that it would shortly die, but it suddenly rose, and walked slowly into the thorns. Determined to cut off its retreat, I pushed through the bushes, intending to reach the dry bed of the Royan and shoot the rhinoceros as it crossed from the narrow belt of the jungle, into which it had retreated; but I had hardly reached half way, when I heard a sound in the bush upon my right, and I saw the wounded beast coming straight for our position, but evidently unconscious of our presence, as we were to leeward. I immediately crouched down, as did my men likewise, lest the animal should observe us. Slowly, but surely, it came on exactly towards us, until it was at last so near as to be unpleasant: I looked behind me, and I saw by the expression of my men that they were thinking of retreat. I merely shook my fist, and frowned at them to give them confidence, and I waited patiently for my opportunity. It was becoming too ridiculous; the rhinoceros was within five or six yards, and was slowly but steadily advancing direct upon us. At the next step that he made, I raised my rifle gently to my shoulder, and whistled sharply: in an instant it tossed its head up, and seeing nothing in front, as my clothes matched with the leafless bushes, it turned its head to the left, and I immediately pulled the trigger. It fell as though smitten by a sledge hammer, and it lay struggling on the ground. Bacheet sprang forward, and with an Arab sword he cut the hamstring of one leg. To the astonishment of us all, the rhinoceros jumped up, and on three legs it sprang quickly round and charged Bacheet, who skipped into the bushes, while I ran alongside the rhinoceros as it attempted to follow him, and, with Fletcher No. 24, I fired through the shoulder, by placing the muzzle within a yard of the animal. It fell dead to this shot, which was another feather in the cap of the good little rifle. The skull of the rhinoceros is very curiously shaped; I had fired for the temple, and had struck the exact point at which I had aimed, but, instead of hitting the brain, the bullet had smashed the joint of the jaw, in which it stuck fast. I never have been able to understand why that powerful rifle was thus baffled, unless there had been some error in the charge of powder. This rhinoceros had no ears, they had been bitten off close to the head by another of the same species, while fighting; this mutilation is by no means uncommon.

From this point I traversed the country in all directions; upon one occasion I took a large supply of water, and penetrated into the very heart of the Base, half way between the Settite and the river Gash or Mareb, near the base of the mountain chain; but, although the redoubtable natives were occasionally seen, they were as shy as wild animals, and we could not approach them.

Having explored the entire country, and enjoyed myself thoroughly, I was now determined to pay our promised visit to Mek Nimmur. Since our departure from the Egyptian territory, his country had been invaded by a large force, according to orders sent from the Governor-General of the Soudan. Mek Nimmur as usual retreated to the mountains, but Mai Gubba and a number of his villages were utterly destroyed by the Egyptians. He would, under these circumstances, be doubly suspicious of strangers.

My camel-men had constantly brought me the news on their return from Geera with corn,[12] and they considered that it was unsafe to visit Mek Nimmur after his defeat, as he might believe me to be a spy from the Egyptians; he was a great friend of Theodorus, king of Abyssinia, and as at that time he was on good terms with the English, I saw no reason to avoid his country.

We arrived at Ombrega, but, instead of camping among the thick jungle as formerly, we bivouacked under four splendid tamarind trees that formed a clump among the rocks on the left bank of the river, and which shaded a portion of its sandy bed; this was a delightful resting-place. We were now only one day from Geera, and we sent a messenger to the sheik of the Hamrans, who shortly returned with a young girl of about seventeen as a corn-grinder in the place of Barrake; she was hired from her owner at a dollar per month.

My camel-men had determined not to proceed to Mek Nimmur's country, as they were afraid that their camels might be stolen by his people; they therefore came to me one evening, and coolly declared that they should return to Geera, as it would be folly to tempt Mek Nimmur. It was in vain that I protested, and reminded them that I had engaged them to accompany me throughout the exploration. They were afraid of losing their camels, and nothing would satisfy them; they declared that they

---

12   Among other news I was glad to hear that my patient Jali could walk without difficulty.

required no wages, as the meat and hide, &c. they had received were sufficient for their services, but through Mek Nimmur's country they were determined not to go. Taher Noor was the only man who was willing, but he had no camel. We had constructed a fence of thorns around our camp, in which the camels were now reposing, and, as the argument had become hot, the Arabs expressed their determination of starting homewards that very instant, and we were to be left alone, unless they could persuade other men of their tribe to join us with their animals. Accordingly, they at once proceeded to saddle their camels for an immediate start. Without saying another word, I quietly took my little Fletcher rifle, and cocked both barrels as I sat within ten yards of the exit from the camp. The men were just ready to depart, and several had mounted their camels. "Good bye," I said; "give my salaams to the sheik when you arrive at Geera; but the first camel that passes the zareeba (camp) I shall shoot through the head." They had heard the sharp click of the locks, and they remembered the firing of the grass on a former occasion when I had nearly burnt the camp; – not a camel moved. My Tokrooris and Taher Noor now came forward as mediators, and begged me not to shoot the camels. As I had the rifle pointed, I replied to this demand conditionally, that the Arabs should dismount and unsaddle immediately: this led to a parley, and I agreed to become responsible for the value of the camels should they be stolen in Mek Nimmur's country. The affair was settled.

On March 16th, the day following this argument, as we were sitting in the evening beneath our trees in the river's bed, I suddenly heard the rattle of loose stones, and immediately after, a man on a white hygeen appeared from the jungle on our side of the river, followed quickly by a string of Arabs, all well mounted, who silently followed in single file towards the ford. They had not noticed us, as we were close to the high rocky bank upon their left, in the deep shade of the tamarind trees. I counted twenty-three; their shields and swords were slung upon their hygeens, and, as their clothes were beautifully clean, they had evidently started that morning from their homes.

The leader had reached the ford without observing us, as in this wild spot he had expected no one, and the whole party were astonished and startled when I suddenly addressed them with a loud "Salaam aleikum" (peace be with you). At first they did not reply, but as I advanced alone, their leader also advanced from his party, and we met half way. These were a troop of Mek Nimmur's people on a foray. I quickly explained who I was, and I invited him to come and drink coffee beneath the shade in our camp. Taher Noor now joined us, and confidence having been established, the leader ordered his party to cross the ford and to unsaddle on the opposite side of the river, while he accompanied me to our camp. At first he was rather suspicious, but a present of a new tarboosh (cap), and a few articles of trifling value, quickly reassured him, and he promised to be our guide to Mek Nimmur in about a couple of days, upon his return from a marauding expedition on the frontier; his party had appointed to unite with a stronger force, and to make a razzia upon the cattle of the Dabaina Arabs.

During the night, the marauding party and their leader departed.

There was no game at Ombrega, therefore I employed the interval of two days in cleaning all the rifles, and in preparing for a fresh expedition, as that of the Settite and Royan had been completed. The short Tatham No.10 rifle carried a heavy cylinder, instead of the original spherical ball. I had only fired two shots with this rifle, and the recoil had been so tremendous, owing to the heavy weight of the projectile, that I had mistrusted the weapon; therefore, when the moment arrived to fire off all the guns preparatory to cleaning, my good angel whispered a providential warning, and I agreed to fire this particular rifle by a long fishing-line attached to the trigger, while the gun should be fastened to a tree. It blew all to pieces! The locks were blown entirely away, and the stock was shattered into fragments: nothing remained but the thick end near the shoulder-plate. I had received a mysterious presentiment of this; had I fired that rifle in the usual manner, I must have been killed on the spot. The charge was five drachms, which was small in proportion to the weight of the cylindrical projectile. This may be a warning to such sportsmen who adopt new-fashioned projectiles to old-fashioned rifles, that were proved with the spherical bullet, which in weight and friction bears no proportion to the heavy cylinder; nevertheless, this rifle should not have burst, and the metal showed great inferiority, by blowing into fragments instead of splitting.

The leader of Mek Nimmur's party returned, as he had promised, to be our guide. I extract from my journal, verbatim, my notes upon that date.

"March 19, 1862. – Started at 1.30 P.M., and halted at 5 P.M. There is no water for about thirty miles; thus we had watered all the animals at the usual hour (noon), and they will accordingly endure until to-morrow evening. Upon ascending the slope of the Settite valley, the country is an immense plain of fertile soil, about two hundred feet above the river. While on the march, I espied a camel wandering without an owner; this was inmmediately secured as a lawful prize by our guide. This fellow's name is Mahomet; he is, doubtlessly, an out-and-out scoundrel; he is about five feet ten inches in height, and as thin as a live man can be; he is so crafty-looking, and so wiry and eel-like, that if I were to lock him up I should secure the key-hole, as he looks capable of squeezing through anything. We slept on the plain.

"March 20. – Started at 5 A.M., and in three hours we reached the chain of lofty wooded hills that bound the plain. In a march of four hours from this point, we arrived at a hor, or ravine, when we halted beneath a large tamarind tree, and pitched the tent according to the instructions of our guide. The plain from the Settite to the base of the hilly range that we had crossed, is about twenty-two miles wide by forty in length, and, like all the table-land in this country, it is well adapted for cotton cultivation. Were the route secure through the Base country, loaded camels might reach Cassala in six days and from thence to Souakim. All this country is uninhabited. On arrival at the base of the first bill, a grove of tamarinds shades a spring, at which we watered our horses, but the water is impregnated with natron, which is common throughout this country, and appears in many places as an efflorescence on the surface of the ground. From the spring at the eastern base of the hills, we ascended a rugged pass, winding for some miles among ravines, and crossing elevated shoulders of the range. Upon the summit we passed a rich mass of both rose-coloured and white limestone, similar to that we had seen at Geera; this was surrounded by basalt, and the presence of limestone entirely mystifies my ideas of geology. Immense quantities of very beautiful spar lay upon the surface in all directions; some of this was perfectly white, and veined like an agate – I believe it was white cornelian; other fragments, of sizes equalling sixty or seventy pounds weight, were beautifully green, suggesting the presence of copper. Large masses of exquisite bloodstone, the size of a man's head, were exceedingly numerous. Having crossed the hills, we descended to a rich and park-like valley, covered with grass, and ornamented with fine timber. Much dhurra was cultivated, and several villages were passed, that had been plundered by the Egyptians during the recent attack. This country must be exceedingly unhealthy during the rainy season, as the soil is extremely rich, and the valleys, surrounded by hills, would become swamps. From the Settite river, at Ombrega, to our halting-place beneath the tamarind-tree, at this spot, is about thirty-five miles south, 10 degrees east."

Our camp was in a favourable locality, well shaded by large trees, on the margin of a small stream; this was nearly dry at this season, and the water was extremely bad, having a strong taste of copper. I had remarked throughout the neighbourhood unmistakeable evidences of the presence of this metal – the surface of the rocks was in many places bright green, like malachite, and, upon an exploration of the bed of the stream, I found veins of a green substance in the perpendicular cliffs that had been cut through by the torrent. These green veins passed through a bed of reddish, hard rock, glistening with minute crystals, which I believe to have been copper.

There is no doubt that much might be done were the mineral wealth of this country thoroughly investigated.

The day following our arrival was passed in receiving visits from a number of Abyssinians, and the head men of Mek Nimmur. There was a mixture of people, as many of the Jaleen Arabs who had committed some crime in the Egyptian territory, had fled across the country and joined the exiled chief of their tribe. Altogether, the society in this district was not creme de la creme, as Mek Nimmur's territory was an asylum for all the blackguards of the adjoining countries, who were attracted by the excitement and lawlessness of continual border warfare. The troop that we had seen at Ombrega returned with a hundred and two head of camels, that they had stolen from the west bank of the Atbara. Mounted upon hygeens, Mek Nimmur's irregulars thought nothing of marching sixty miles in one day; thus their attack and retreat were equally sudden and unexpected.

I had a quantity of rhinoceros hide in pieces of the size required for shields; these were much prized in this fighting country, and I presented them to a number of head men who had honoured us with a visit. I begged them to guide two of my people to the presence of Mek Nimmur, with a preliminary message. This they promised to perform. Accordingly, I sent Taher Noor and Bacheet on horseback, with a most polite message, accompanied with my card in an envelope, and a small parcel, carefully wrapped in four or five different papers; this contained a very beautiful Persian lance-head, of polished steel inlaid with gold, that I had formerly purchased at Constantinople.

During their absence, we were inundated with visitors, the Abyssinians, in their tight pantaloons, contrasting strongly with the loosely-clad Arabs. In about an hour, my messengers returned, accompanied by two men on horseback, with a hospitable message fronm Mek Nimmur, and an invitation to pay him a visit at his own residence. I had some trifling present ready for everybody of note, and, as Taher Noor and my people had already explained all they knew concerning us, Mek Nimmur's suspicions had entirely vanished.

As we were conversing with Mek Nimmur's messengers through the medium of Taher Noor, who knew their language, our attention was attracted by the arrival of a tremendous swell who at a distance I thought must be Mek Nimmur himself. A snow-white mule carried an equally snow-white person, whose tight white pantaloons looked as though he had forgotten his trousers, and had mounted in his drawers. He carried a large umbrella to shade his complexion; a pair of handsome silver-mounted pistols were arranged upon his saddle, and a silver-hilted curved sword, of the peculiar Abyssinian form, hung by his side. This grand personage was followed by an attendant, also mounted upon a mule, while several men on foot accompanied them, one of whom carried his lance and shield. Upon a near approach, he immediately dismounted, and advanced towards us, bowing in a most foppish manner, while his attendant followed him on foot with an enormous violin, which he immediately handed to him. This fiddle was very peculiar in shape, being a square, with an exceedingly long neck extending from one corner; upon this was stretched a solitary string, and the bow was very short and much bent. This was an Abyssinian Paganini. He was a professional minstrel of the highest grade, who had been sent by Mek Nimmur to welcome us on our arrival.

These musicians are very similar to the minstrels of ancient times; they attend at public rejoicings, and at births, deaths, and marriages of great personages, upon which occasions they extemporize their songs according to circumstances. My hunting in the Base country formed his theme, and for at least an hour he sang of my deeds, in an extremely loud and disagreeable voice, while he accompanied himself upon his fiddle, which he held downwards like a violoncello: during the whole of his song he continued in movement, marching with a sliding step to the front, and gliding to the right and left in a manner that, if intended to be graceful, was extremely comic. The substance of this minstrelsy was explained to me by Taher Noor, who listened eagerly to the words, which he translated with evident satisfaction. Of course, like all minstrels, he was an absurd flatterer, and, having gathered a few facts for his theme, he wandered slightly from the truth in his poetical description of my deeds.

He sang of me as though I had been Richard Coeur de Lion, and recounted, before an admiring throng of listeners, how "I had wandered with a young wife from my own distant country to fight the terrible Base; how I had slain them in single combat; and how elephants and lions were struck down like lambs and kids by my hands; that during my absence in the hunt, my wife had been carried off by the Base; that I had, on my return to my pillaged camp, galloped off in chase, and, overtaking the enemy, hundreds had fallen by my rifle and sword, and I had liberated and recovered the lady, who now had arrived safe with her lord in the country of the great Mek Nimmur," &c. &c. &c.

This was all very pretty, no doubt, and as true as most poetical and musical descriptions, but I felt certain that there must be something to pay for this flattering entertainment; if you are considered to be a great man, a present is invariably expected in proportion to your importance. I suggested to Taher Noor that I must give him a couple of dollars. "What!" said Taher Noor, "a couple of dollars! Impossible! a musician of his standing it accustomed to receive thirty and forty dollars from great people for so beautiful and honourable a song."

This was somewhat startling; I began to reflect upon the price of a box at Her Majesty's Theatre in London; but there I was not the hero of the opera; this minstrel combined the whole affair in a most simple manner; he was Verdi, Costa, and orchestra all in one; he was a thorough Macaulay as historian, therefore I had to pay the composer as well as the fiddler. I compromised the matter, and gave him a few dollars, as I understood that he was Mek Nimmur's private minstrel, but I never parted with my dear Maria Theresa[13] with so much regret as upon that occasion, and I begged him not to incommode himself by paying us another visit, or, should he be obliged to do so, I trusted he would not think it necessary to bring his violin.

The minstrel retired in the same order that he had arrived, and I watched his retreating figure with unpleasant reflections, that were suggested by doubts as to whether I had paid him too little or too much; Taher Noor thought that he was underpaid; my own opinion was, that I had brought a curse upon myself equal to a succession of London organ-grinders, as I fully expected that other minstrels, upon hearing of the Austrian dollars, would pay us a visit, and sing of my great deeds.

In the afternoon, we were sitting beneath the shade of our tamarind tree when we thought we could perceive our musical friend returning. As he drew near, we were convinced that it was the identical minstrel, who had most probably been sent with a message from Mek Nimmur: there he was, in snow-white raiment, on the snow-white mule, with the mounted attendant and the violin as before. He dismounted upon arrival opposite the camp, and approached with his usual foppish bow; but we looked on in astonishment: it was not our Paganini, it was *another minstrel!* who was determined to sing an ode in our praise. I felt that this was an indirect appeal to Maria Theresa, and I at once declared against music. I begged him not to sing; "my wife had a headache – I disliked the fiddle – could he play anything else instead?" and I expressed a variety of polite excuses, but to no purpose; he insisted upon singing; if I "disliked the fiddle, he would sing without an accompaniment, but he could not think of insulting so great a man as myself by returning without an ode to commemorate our arrival."

I was determined that he should *not* sing; he was determined that he *would*, therefore I desired him to leave my camp; this he agreed to do, provided I would allow him to cross the stream, and sing to my Tokrooris, in my praise, beneath a neighbouring tree about fifty yards distant.

---

13   The Austrian dollar, that is the only large current coin in that country.

He remounted his mule with his violin, to ford the muddy stream, and he descended the steep bank, followed by his attendant on foot, who drove the unwilling mule. Upon arrival at the brink of the dirty brook, that was about three feet deep, the mule positively refused to enter the water, and stood firm with its fore feet sunk deep in the mud. The attendant attempted to push it on behind, at the same time he gave it a sharp blow with his sheathed sword; this changed the scene to the "opera comique." In one instant the mule gave so vigorous and unexpected a kick into the bowels of the attendant, that he fell upon his back, heels uppermost, while at the same moment the minstrel, in his snow-white garments, was precipitated head foremost into the muddy brook, and for the moment disappearing, the violin alone could be seen floating on the surface. A second later, a wretched-looking object, covered with slime and filth, emerged from the slough; this was Paganini the second! who, after securing his fiddle, that had stranded on a mud-bank, scrambled up the steep slope, amidst the roars of laughter of my people and of ourselves; while the perverse mule, having turned harmony into discord, kicked up its heels and galloped off, braying an ode in praise of liberty, as the "Lay of the last Minstrel." The discomfited fiddler was wiped down by my Tokrooris, who occasionally burst into renewed fits of laughter during the operation; the mule was caught, and the minstrel remounted, and returned home completely out of tune.

On the following morning, at sunrise, I mounted my horse, and, accompanied by Taher Noor and Bacheet, I rode to pay my respects to Mek Nimmur. Our route lay parallel to the stream, and, after a ride of about two miles through a fine, park-like country, bounded by the Abyssinian Alps about fifteen miles distant, I observed a crowd of people round a large tamarind tree, near which were standing a number of horses, mules, and dromedaries. This was the spot upon which I was to meet Mek Nimmur. Upon my approach the crowd opened, and, having dismounted, I was introduced by Taher Noor to the great chief. He was a man of about fifty, and exceedingly dirty in appearance. He sat upon an angarep, surrounded by his people; lying on either side upon his seat were two brace of pistols, and within a few yards stood his horse ready saddled. He was prepared for fight or flight, as were also his ruffianly-looking followers, who were composed of Abyssinians and Jaleens.

I commenced the conversation by referring to the hospitality shown by his father to my countryman, Mr. Mansfield Parkyns, and I assured him that such kind attentions were never forgotten by an Englishman, therefore I had determined to visit him, although the Egyptian authorities had cautioned me not to trust myself within his territory. I explained that I was bound towards an unknown point, in search of the sources of the White Nile, which might occupy some years, but that I wished to perfect the exploration by the examination of all the Abyssinian Nile affluents: and I concluded by asking for his assistance in my journey to the Bahr Angrab and the Salaam. He replied very politely, and gave me much local information; he said that the Egyptians gave him no peace, that he was obliged to fight in self-defence; but that, if I could make overtures on his part to the Egyptian authorities, he would engage never to cross the Atbara, provided they observed a similar condition. I promised to represent his offer to the Governor-General on my arrival at Khartoum. He agreed to give me a guide to the rivers Angrab and Salaam, that were not far distant, and he at once pointed out to me the two dark gorges, about twelve and sixteen miles distant, in the chain of precipitous mountains from which they flowed. He described the country upon the other side of the mountains to be the elevated plateau of Abyssinia, and he advised me to visit the king before my departure from his territory; this I could not conveniently accomplish, as my route lay in an opposite direction. He begged me for a telescope, so that he should be able to see the approach of the Turks (Egyptians) from a great distance, as he explained that he had spies upon all the mountain tops, so that no stranger could enter his country without his knowledge. He confessed that my movements while in the Base country had been watched by his spies, until he had felt assured that I had no sinister motive. I laughed at the idea; he replied, that we were most fortunate to have escaped an attack from the natives, as they were far worse than wild beasts, and he immediately pointed out several Base slaves who were present in the crowd, who had been captured when children; they appeared to be the same as the woolly-headed natives of the south bank of the Blue Nile, and not at all peculiar in appearance. He cautioned me against bathing in the stream, or drinking the water in the neighbourhood of our camp, as it was extremely poisonous, and would produce an irritation of the skin. I told him that I had discovered copper, and that I attributed the poisonous quality of the water to the presence of that mineral. This announcement was received with a general expression of approbation. "That is very curious," he said, "that we who live in this country are ignorant, and that you, a stranger, should at once explain the cause of the poison." He at once agreed to the suggestion, as he said, that during the rains, when the torrents were full, the water was not unwholesome, but in the dry weather, when the supply was scanty, and the stream feeble, the strength of the poison was necessarily increased. He assured me that, although the pasturage was excellent, all cattle that drank in that hor or stream became as thin as skeletons.

Mek Nimmur had been ignorant of the existence of copper, but he informed me that gold dust was common in the sand of most of the ravines, and that, if I would remain in his country, I might discover considerable quantities. I informed him that I had already discovered the existence of both gold and lead. He requested me to give him every information respecting the lead, as he should prefer it to gold, as he could manufacture bullets to shoot the Turks (as the Egyptians are called by the neighbouring tribes). After a long and satisfactory conversation, I made my salaam, and retired. Immediately on my arrival at the camp, I despatched Wat Gamma on horseback with Taher Noor, in charge of a pair of beautiful double-barrelled pistols, with the name of Tatham as the manufacturer; these were loaded, and I sent a polite message, begging Mek Nimmur's acceptance of the present; they were accompanied by a supply of ammunition.

In the evening Wat Gamma returned with the pistols; – they had *burst!* Mek Nimmur had requested him to fire at a mark, and one barrel of each pistol had given way; thus, the double rifle and the pistols of the same name "Tatham" had all failed; fortunately no one was injured. I was afraid that this would lead to some complication, and I was much annoyed; I had never used these pistols, but I had considered that they were first rate; thus I had given them to Mek Nimmur as a valuable present, and they had proved their utter worthlessness. I immediately mounted my horse, and with my revolver in my belt, and my beautiful single Beattie rifle in my hand, I galloped off to Mek Nimmur; he was seated in the same spot, watching the harvest of dhurra, enormous piles of which were being thrashed by a number of Abyssinians. The instant that I arrived, I went straight to him, and explained my regret and disappointment at the failure of the pistols, and I begged him to take his choice between my rifle and revolver. He behaved remarkably well; he had begged my messenger to leave the broken pistols with him, and not to mention the circumstance to me, as he felt sure that I should feel even more annoyed than himself; he now declined my offer, as he said I should require the weapons during my proposed journey up the White Nile, and he could not deprive me of their use. He was afraid of the revolver, as it was too complicated, but I tore from my note-book a small piece of paper, which I requested one of his people to stick upon a rock about ninety yards distant. I took a steady shot with the single rifle, and was fortunate enough to hit the paper exactly. This elicited general applause, and Mek Nimmur called one of his people, an Abyssinian, who he declared to be a celebrated shot, and he requested that he might be allowed to fire the rifle. I placed a similar mark upon the rock, and the Abyssinian fired from a rest, and struck the stone, in a good line, about six inches below the paper. The crowd were in raptures with the rifle, which I at once insisted upon Mek Nimmur accepting. I then made my salaam, and mounted my horse amidst general expressions of approval.

On the following morning, Mek Nimmur sent us two camel-loads of corn; a large gourd of honey, weighing about fifty pounds; and four cows that must have been a detachment of Pharaoh's lean kine, with a polite message that I was to select the *fattest*. These cattle were specimens of the poisonous qualities of the water; but, although disappointed in the substance of the present, my people were delighted with the acquisition, and they immediately selected a cow; but just as they were licking their lips at the prospect of fresh meat, which they had not tasted for some days, the cow broke away and made off across country. In despair at the loss, my men followed in hot pursuit, and two of the Tokrooris overtook her, and held on to her tail like bull-dogs, although dragged for some distance, at full gallop through thorns and ruts, until the other men arrived and overpowered the thin, but wiry animal. When slaughtered, there was a great squabble between my men and the Abyssinians, who endeavoured to steal the meat.

Chapter XVIII.

A Camel Falls, and Dies.

I extract a few notes from my journal: –

"March 25, 1862. – Mai Gubba is about twelve miles E.N.E. of our camp. Mek Nimmur's stronghold is upon a lofty table-mountain, due south of this spot, from which great elevation (about 5,000 feet) the granite mountain of Cassala is said to be plainly visible.

"March 27. – We started for the Bahr Salaam, and said good-bye to Mek Nimmur, as we passed his position on our march; he had given us a guide; an awful-looking scoundrel.

"We had hardly marched two miles, when one of the baggage-camels suddenly fell down to die; the Arabs immediately cut its throat with a sword, and Bacheet, having detached one ear as a witness of its death, galloped back to borrow a fresh camel of Mek Nimmur, which he very kindly sent without delay. We were obliged to bivouac on the spot for the night, as the Arabs required the flesh of their camel, which was cut into thin strips. As they were employed in skinning it, they ate large quantities raw and quivering. The stream, or hor, that flows through this country, parallel with our route, is the Ma Serdi; all this district is rich in copper.

"March 28. – Started at 5 A.M. course S.W. We crossed two hors, flowing from N.N.W. and joining the Ma Serdi; also a beautiful running stream of deep and clear water twelve miles from our bivouac of last evening: this stream is never dry; it springs from a range of hills about ten miles distant. The whole of this country is well watered by mountain streams, the trees are no longer the thorny mimosas, but as the land is not only fertile, but sufficiently moist, it gives birth to a different kind of vegetation, and the trees are mostly free from thorns, although at this season devoid of foliage. The country is ornamented by extensive cultivation, and numerous villages. We halted at 5 P.M. having marched twenty-one miles. The fertile soil of this country is thoroughly melted by rain during the wet season, and in the intense heat of the drought it becomes a mass of gaping crevices many feet deep, that render hunting on horseback most dangerous. Fortunately, as we halted, I observed a herd of tetel, and three ostriches: the latter made off immediately, but I succeeded in stalking the tetel, and shot two, right and left, one of which escaped, but the other became the prize of my Tokrooris.

"March 29. – Started at 5.30 A.M. and reached the river Salaam at 8 A.M.; the total distance from our camp in Mek Nimmur's country is thirty-five miles s.w. The Bahr Salaam is precisely similar in character to the Settite, but smaller; it has scooped through the rich lands a deep valley, like the latter river, and has transported the fertile loam to the Atbara, to increase the rich store of mud which that river delivers to the Nile. The Salaam is about two hundred yards wide; it flows through perpendicular cliffs that form walls of rock, in many places from eighty to a hundred and fifty feet above its bed; the water is as clear as crystal, and of excellent quality; even now, a strong though contracted stream is running over the rounded pebbles that form its bed, similar to that of the Settite. We descended a difficult path, and continued along the dry portion of the river's bed up the stream. While we were searching for a spot to encamp, I saw a fine bull mehedehet (A. Redunca Ellipsiprymna) by the water side; I stalked him carefully from behind a bed of high rushes, and shot him across the river with the Fletcher rifle; he went on, although crippled, but the left-hand barrel settled him by a bullet through the neck. We camped on the bank of the river.

"March 30. – I went out to explore the country, and, steering due east, I arrived at the river Angrab or Angarep, three miles from the Salaam; from a high rock I could trace its course from the mountain gorge to this spot, the stream flowing N.W. This noble river or mountain torrent is about a hundred and fifty yards wide, although the breadth varies according to the character of the country through which it passes; in most places it rushes through frightful precipices; sometimes it is walled within a channel of only forty or fifty yards, and in such places the cliffs, although at least a hundred feet perpendicular height, bear the marks of floods that have actually overtopped the rocks, and have torn away the earth, and left masses of bamboos and withered reeds clinging to the branches of trees, which, growing on still higher rocks, have dipped in the swollen torrent. I followed the circuitous course of the river for some miles, until, after a most fatiguing exploration among precipices and deep ravines, I arrived at the junction of the Salaam river. On the way, I came upon a fine bull nellut (A. Strepsiceros) beneath a shady nabbuk by the river's side; I could only obtain an oblique shot, as his hind quarters were towards me; the bullet passed through the ribs, and reached the shoulder upon the opposite side. This nellut had the finest horns that I had yet obtained; they measured four feet in the curve, three feet one inch and a half in a straight line, with a spread of two feet seven inches from point to point. I found tracks of hippopotami upon the high grassy hills; these animals climb up the most difficult places during the night, when they ascend from the river to seek for pasturage. I was not far from the tent when I arrived at the junction of the Angrab with the Bahr Salaam, but the rivers were both sunk in stupendous precipices, so that it was impossible to descend. The mouth of the river Angrab was an extraordinary sight; it was not wider than about fifteen yards, although the river averaged a width of at least a hundred and fifty yards. The exit of the water was between two lofty walls of basalt rock, which overhung the stream, which in the rainy season not only forced its way for about a hundred yards through this narrow cleft, but it had left proof of inundations that had leapt over the summit of the obstruction, when the rush of water had been too great for the area of the contracted passage. Altogether, the two rivers Sahaam and Angrab are interesting examples of the destructive effect of water, that has during the course of ages cut through, and hollowed out in the solid rock, a succession of the most horrible precipices and caverns, in which the maddened torrents, rushing from the lofty chain of mountains, boil along until they meet the Atbara, and assist to flood the Nile. No one could explore these tremendous torrents, the Settite, Royan, Angrab, Salaam, and Atbara, without at once comprehending their effect upon the waters of the Nile. The magnificent chain of mountains from which they flow, is not a simple line of abrupt sides, but the precipitous slopes are the walls of a vast plateau, that receives a prodigious rainfall in June, July, August, until the middle of September, the entire drainage of which is carried away by the above-named channels to inundate Lower Egypt."

Not being able to cross the river at the point of junction with the Salaam, I continued along the margin of the precipice that overhangs the latter river, until I should find a place by which we could descend with the camel, as this animal had made a great circuit to avoid the difficulties of the Angrab. We were at length united, and were continuing our route parallel with the river, over undulations of withered grass about three feet high, interspersed with trees, when I perceived above the surface the long horns of a mehedehet (R. Ellipsiprymna). I knew that he must be lying down, and, as he was about a hundred and fifty yards distant, I stalked him carefully from tree to tree; presently I observed three other pairs of horns at various distances; two were extremely large; but, unfortunately, an animal with smaller horns was lying between me and the largest. I could do no more than creep quietly from point to point, until the smaller animal should start and alarm the larger. This it did when I was about a hundred yards from the large bull, and both mehedehets sprang up, and, as is usual with this species, they stood for a few moments seeking for the danger. My clothes and hunting cap matched so well with the bark of the tree behind which I was kneeling, that I was unobserved, and, taking a rest against the stem with the little Fletcher, I fired both barrels, the right at the most distant bull. Both animals simply sprang for an instant upon their hind legs, and fell. This was capital; but at the report of the rifle, up jumped two other mehedehets, which appeared the facsimiles of those I had just shot; having missed their companions, and seeing no one, they stood motionless and gazed in all directions.

I had left my people far behind when I had commenced the stalk, therefore I had no spare rifle. I reloaded behind the tree with all haste. I had capped the nipples, and, as I looked out from my covering point, I saw them still in the same spot; the larger, with superb horns, was about a hundred and twenty yards distant. Again I took a rest, and fired. He sprang away as though untouched for the first three or four bounds, when he leapt convulsively in the air, and fell backwards. This was too much for the remaining animal, that was standing about a hundred yards distant – he bounded off; but the last barrel of the little Fletcher caught him through the neck at full gallop, and he fell all of a heap, stone dead.

These were the prettiest shots I ever recollect to have made, in a very long experience; I had bagged four with the same rifle in as many shots, as quickly as I could load and fire.

My Tokroori, Abdoolahi, who had been intently watching the shots from a distance, came rushing up in hot excitement with one of my sharp hunting knives, and, springing forward to hamstring one of the animals, that was still struggling, he foolishly made a downward cut, and, missing his blow, he cut his own leg terribly across the shin, the knife flying out of his hand as it struck against the bone: he was rendered helpless immediately. I tied up the wound with my handkerchief, and, having at length loaded the camel with as much meat as we could cut off the animals, Abdoolahi was assisted upon its back; my men carried the two finest heads. It was very late, and we now sought for a path by which we could descend to the river.

At length we discovered a dangerous antelope-track, that descended obliquely, by skirting an exceedingly steep side of a hill, with a perpendicular precipice immediately below, that fell for about seventy feet sheer to the river. My horse Tetel was as sure-footed as a goat, therefore, having taken off my shoes to avoid slipping, I led him to the bottom safely. Taher Noor called to the camel-driver not to attempt to follow. Although warned, this fellow persisted in leading the heavily-laden animal down the slippery and dangerous path. Hardly had he gone a few paces, when the camel's feet slipped, and it shot down the rapid incline, and disappeared over the edge of the precipice. I heard the camel roar, and, hastening up the path, I looked over the cliff, holding to a rope that Taher Noor fastened to a tree. I perceived that the animal was fortunately caught upon a narrow ledge of rock, and was prevented from falling to the bottom by a tough bush that grew from a cleft; this alone supported it in mid-air. My Arabs were wild and stupid. Abdoolahi had held on like a leech, and, as we were well provided with strong ropes, we soon hauled him up, but the Arabs declared their camel to be dead, as no power on earth could save it. Having examined the cliff, I felt sure that we could assist the camel, unless it had already broken some bones by the fall; accordingly, I gave orders to the Arabs, who obeyed implicitly, as they were so heart-broken at the idea of losing their animal, that they had lost all confidence in themselves. We lowered down Taher Noor by a rope to the bush, and after some difficulty, he unfastened the load of flesh, which he threw piece by piece to a platform of rock below, about ten feet square, which formed a shelf a few inches above the level of the water. The camel being relieved of both the load and its saddle, I ordered the Arabs to fasten together all their ropes; these, being made of twisted antelope's hide, were immensely strong, and, as I had established a rule that seven extra bundles should invariably accompany the water-camel, we had a large supply. The camel was now secured by a rope passed round the body beneath the forelegs, and the cloths of the Arabs were wrapped around the cord to prevent it from cutting the skin. This being arranged, I took a double turn of the rope round a tree, as thick as a man's thigh, that grew in a cleft of the rock where we stood, and throwing the honey axe to Taher Noor, I told him to cut away the bushes that supported the camel, and I would lower it gently down to the shelf by the water's edge. In a few minutes the bushes were cut away, and the camel, roaring with fright, swung in mid-air. Taher Noor held on to the rope, while I slacked off the line from the tree, and lowered both man and beast safely to the shelf, about seventy feet below. The camel was unhurt, and the Arabs were delighted; two other men now descended. We threw them down a quantity of dry wood to make a fire, and, as they were well off for meat, we left them prisoners upon the ledge of rock with the profoundly deep river before them, walled in by abrupt precipices upon either side.[14] It was nearly dark, and, having to find my way to the camp among dangerous ravines, I rode fast ahead of my men

---

14   On the following morning the camel was safely floated across the river, supported by the inflated skins of the mehedehets.

to discover a ford, and to reach home before complete darkness should increase the danger. Tetel was as sure-footed and as nimble as a cat, but we very nearly ended our days together, as the bank of a precipice gave way while we were skirting the edge. I felt it sinking, but the horse sprang forward and saved himself, as I heard the mass fall beneath.

That night we received a very audacious visit. I was asleep in my tent, when I was suddenly awakened by a slight pull at my sleeve, which was the signal always given by my wife if anything was wrong; on such occasions, I never replied until I had gently grasped my little Fletcher, which always slept with me beneath my mat. She now whispered that a hyaena had been within the tent, but that it had just bolted out, as these animals are so wary that they detect the slightest movement or noise. As a rule, I never shot at hyaenas, but, as I feared it might eat our saddles, I lay in bed with the rifle to my shoulder, pointed towards the tent door through which the moon was shining brightly. In a few minutes, a grey-looking object stood like an apparition at the entrance, peering into the tent to see if all were right before it entered. I touched the trigger, and the hyaena fell dead, with the bullet through its head. This was a regular veteran, as his body was covered with old scars from continual conflicts with other hyaenas. This was the first time that one of these animals had taken such a liberty; they were generally contented with eating the bones that were left from our dinner outside the tent door, which they cleared away regularly every night.

We remained in this beautiful country from March 29th until April 14th, during which time I seldom remained for an hour in camp, from sunrise to sunset; I was always in the saddle or on foot. Two of my best Tokrooris, Hadji Ali and Hassan, usually accompanied me on horseback, while Taher Noor and a couple of Arabs rode upon camels with a good supply of water. In this manner I traversed the entire country, into the base of the great mountain chain, and thence down the course of the river towards the Atbara junction. This district was entirely composed of the most fertile soil, through which the great rivers Angrab and Salaam had cut their way in a similar manner to the Atbara and Settite. The Salaam, after the junction of the Angrab, was equal in appearance to the Atbara, but the inclination of this great mountain torrent is so rapid, that it quickly becomes exhausted at the cessation of rain in the lofty mountains that form its source. Both the Angrab and the Salaam are short rivers, but, as they are the two main channels for the reception of the entire drainage of a vast mountain area, they bring down most violent floods, that materially affect the volume of the main artery.

The whole of this country abounded in game beyond any that I had hitherto seen, and I had most glorious sport. Among the varieties of antelopes, was a new species that I had seen upon several occasions on the Settite, where it was extremely rare. On the high open plains above the valley of the Salaam, this antelope was very numerous, but so wild and wary that it was impossible to approach nearer than from 350 to 500 yards. This magnificent animal, the largest of all the antelopes of Abyssinia and Central Africa, is known to the Arabs as the Maarif (Hippotragus Bakerii). It is a variety of the sable antelope of South Africa (Hippotragus Niger). The colour is mouse-grey, with a black stripe across the shoulders, and black and white lines across the nose and cheeks. The height at the shoulder would exceed fourteen hands, and the neck is ornamented with a thick and stiff black mane. The shoulders are peculiarly massive, and are extremely high at the withers; the horns are very powerful, and, like those of the roan and the sable antelope, they are annulated, and bend gracefully backwards. Both the male and female are provided with horns; those of the former are exceedingly thick, and the points frequently extend so far as to reach the shoulders.

The Maarif invariably inhabits open plains, upon which it can see an enemy at a great distance, thus it is the most difficult of all animals to stalk. Nothing can be more beautiful than a herd of these superb animals, but the only successful method of hunting would be to course them with greyhounds; my dogs were dead, thus I depended entirely upon the rifle. I was also deprived of the assistance of the aggageers, whom I had left at the Royan.

Rhinoceros and giraffes were very numerous throughout this country; but the ground was most unfavourable for riding. The surface resembled a beautiful park, composed of a succession of undulations, interspersed with thornless trees, and watered by streamlets at intervals of five or eight miles, while the magnificent Alps of Abyssinia bounded the view to the south; but there was no enjoyment in this country on horseback. The rainy season converted this rich loam into a pudding, and the dry season baked it into a pie-crust. The entire surface was loose, flaky, and hollow; there was not a yard of ground that was not split into deep crevices, that were regular pitfalls; and so unsound was the general character of the country, that a horse sank above his fetlocks at every footstep. I usually rode during the day when exploring; but whenever I shot, it was necessary to dismount, as it was impossible to follow an animal successfully on horseback. I had on several occasions attempted to ride down a giraffe, but upon such ground I had not the slightest chance; thus the aggageers, who invariably hunt the giraffe by riding at full speed until they can hamstring it with the sword, never visit this country. This accounted for the presence of so large a number of animals, as they were never disturbed by these untiring hunters.

Our camp was pitched at the junction of a torrent, which, flowing from the higher ground, joined the river Salaam in a succession of waterfalls. At this season, a gentle stream, as clear as glass, rippled over a rocky bed about twenty yards wide, and the holes in the flat surface above the fall formed natural basins of the purest water. I frequently strolled for some miles along the bed of the stream, that afforded excellent pasturage for the horses in a sweet, green grass, that was not only an attraction to antelopes and buffaloes (Bos Caffer), but formed a covert for incredible numbers of the beautiful francolin partridge, which might have been shot in hundreds as they rose from the cool herbage that afforded both food and concealment. I was returning late one evening along the bed of the stream, after a day's shooting, during which I had bagged several antelopes and wild boar, when I observed at a distance a dark mass in the bright yellow grass, which I quickly distinguished as a herd of elephants. It was just dusk, and having endeavoured to meet them as they came to drink, but without success, I determined to track them up on the following morning. I started at daybreak, with all my horses and gun-bearers. For about sixteen miles we tracked up the herd to within a short distance of the base of the mountain range. During the march, we had seen large quantities of giraffes, and all the varieties of large antelopes. The country, that had consisted of a vast plain, now changed to rapid undulations; the trees were generally small, and, at this season of intense dryness, were devoid of leaves. At the bottom of one of these undulations, among a number of skeleton trees, that afforded no shade, we discovered the elephants, standing in the high withered grass, that entirely concealed all but the upper portion of their heads; they were amusing themselves by tearing up the trees, and feeding upon the succulent roots. I ordered Taher Noor and Bacheet each to take a horse and rifle, and to lead them, together with my hunter Aggahr, about a hundred yards behind me, while I advanced towards the elephants on foot. At the sound of the first shot they were to mount, and to bring my horse and spare guns as rapidly as possible. Unfortunately, the herd was alarmed by a large bull giraffe that was asleep in the grass, which started up within thirty yards of us, and dashed off in terror through the mass of elephants. Their attention was roused, and they moved off to my left, which change of position immediately gave them our wind. There was no time to lose, as the herd was in retreat; and, as they were passing across my path, at about two hundred paces distance, I ran at my best speed, stumbling through the broken pie-crust, and sinking in the yawning crevices, the sides of which were perfectly rotten, until I arrived within shot of about twenty-five elephants. I was just on the point of firing at the temple of a large animal that was within about ten yards, when it suddenly turned, and charged straight at me. With the right-hand barrel of a Reilly No. 10, I was fortunate enough to turn it by a forehead shot, when so close that it was nearly upon me. As it swerved, I fired the remaining barrel exactly through the centre of the shoulder; this dropped and killed the elephant as though it had been shot through the brain.

The difficulties of the ground were such, that the horses were not led as quickly as I had expected; thus I had to reload, which I had just completed when Aggahr was brought by Taher Noor. Springing into the saddle I at once gave chase. The gallant old horse flew along through the high grass, regardless of the crevices and rotten ground. The herd was about three hundred yards ahead, but the long steady stride of Aggahr quickly shortened the distance, and in a few minutes I was riding alongside the elephants, that were shambling along at a great pace. I determined to head them, and drive them back towards my people, in which case I expected that we might be able to surround them. I touched Aggahr with the spur, and he shot ahead of the leading elephants, when I turned sharp to the right exactly before their path, and gave a shout to check their advance; in the same instant, Aggahr turned a complete somersault within a few yards of their feet, having put his fore-leg into a deep crevice, and I rolled over almost beneath the elephants with the heavy rifle in my hand. The horse recovered quicker than I, and, galloping off, he vanished in the high grass, leaving me rather confused from the fall upon my head. The herd, instead of crushing me as they ought to have done, took fright, and bolted off at their best pace. My eyes were dancing with the fall; the mounted gun-bearers were nowhere, as Gazelle would not face the elephants, and Tetel was far behind. My English saddle had vanished with Aggahr, and, as the stirrups of the Arab saddles were simple rings for the accommodation of the big toe, they were unserviceable. Had the aggageers been with me, I should have had great sport with this herd; but, with the exception of Taher Noor, the men were bad horsemen, and even he was afraid of the ground, which was frightfully dangerous.

We discovered that the bullet had passed through the great artery of the heart, which had caused the instantaneous death of the elephant I had shot.

We were now at least seventeen miles from camp, and I feared that Aggahr would be lost, and would most likely be devoured by a lion during the night: thus I should lose not only my good old hunter, but my English saddle. I passed several hours in searching for him in all directions, and, in order to prevent him from straying to the south, we fired the grass in all directions; we thus had a line of fire between the camp and ourselves; this burnt slowly, as the north wind had carried the blaze rapidly in the other direction. We rode along the bottom of a watercourse and reached the Salaam river, thus avoiding the fire; but, some hours before we neared the camp, night had set in. We had beaten the fire, as we had got to windward, and slowly and tediously we toiled along the crumbling soil, stumbling among the crevices, that were nearly invisible in the moonlight.

Thus we crept onwards; I had found riding impracticable, therefore the horses were led, with much difficulty, as they constantly slipped up to their knees in the numerous fissures. It was difficult to recognise our position in the moonlight, and we were doubtful whether we had not missed our route to the camp. My watch told me that it was past nine o'clock, and we had been sixteen hours in hard work without the slightest rest. We halted to confer about the direction of the camp, when suddenly I heard the report of a gun to our right; we immediately turned, and hastened towards the welcome sound; presently I heard a distant shout. As we approached, this was repeated, and as I hurried forward, I recognised my own name shouted in an agonised voice. I ran on alone at my best speed, after giving a loud shrill whistle upon my fingers. This was quickly replied to, and I repeated the well-known signal, until in about ten minutes I met my wife, who had been wandering about the country half distracted for hours, searching for me in every direction, as my horse Aggahr had returned to the camp with the bridle broken, and the empty saddle scratched by the boughs of trees; she had naturally concluded that some accident had happened. She had immediately armed herself with the little Fletcher that had been left in the camp, being too small for elephants; with this, and several of the Arabs armed with swords and lances, she had been hunting throughout this wild country during the night in a state of terrible anxiety. It was fortunate that she had fired the shot to direct our attention, otherwise we might have passed each other without being seen. "All's well that ends well:" we were about three miles from camp, but the distance appeared short to everybody, as we now knew the true direction, and we at length perceived the glare of a large fire that our people had lighted as a beacon.

The horse, Aggahr, must have found his way without difficulty, as he had arrived a little before sunset. This curious instinct, that enables a horse to find the direction to its last halting-place in a wild and pathless country, was thoroughly appreciated by the Arabs, who had comforted me with the assurance, that no Abyssinian horse would lose his way to the spot where he had last passed the night, if separated from his rider.

Chapter XIX.

Send a Party to Reconnoitre.

I had thoroughly explored the beautiful country of the Salaam and Angrab; it was the 11th of April, and I intended to push on to Gallabat, the frontier market-town of Abyssinia. We had no guide, as the fellow that had been supplied by Mek Nimmur had absconded the day after our arrival at the Salaam, but during the march he had pointed out a blue outline of a distant mountain in the south, that was called Nahoot Guddabi, or the Saddle of Guddabi. This was an unmistakeable landmark, as it exactly resembled an Arab saddle; at the foot of this mountain was the Tokroori village of Guddabi, the first habitation, at a distance of about fifty miles from the Bahr Salaam. Although, from the experience I had had in this neighbourhood, I had little doubt of the supply of water on the road, I sent three of my Tokrooris upon as many camels with water-skins, to reconnoitre before I should move the camp.

On the second day they returned, and reported the existence of several small streams, all of which produced excellent water.

We started on the following afternoon, and, with Hassan as our guide, and Taher Noor upon a camel, my wife and I cantered ahead of the main body, over a high ridge of stony, and accordingly firm ground. Upon arrival at the summit, we had a lovely view of the surrounding country, and we commenced a gentle descent into a vast plain sparsely covered with small trees. In the extensive prospect before us, the dark green veins of foliage in the otherwise yellow surface of withered grass marked out distinctly the course of small rivulets. We hurried on, sometimes over blackened ashes, where the fire had swept all before it, at other times through withered grass, that had been saved from destruction through the intervention of some ravine. At 7.30 P.M. we arrived at an excellent halting place, by a beautiful but small stream of water, shaded by a fringe of dome palms; this was by dead reckoning seventeen miles from our last camp. It had been pleasant travelling, as the moon was full;

we had ridden fast, therefore it was useless to expect the camels for some hours; we accordingly spread the carpet on the ground, and lay down to sleep, with the stocks of the rifles for pillows, as we had frequently done on former occasions.

On the following morning I sent a couple of men on camels to reconnoitre the country in advance, towards Guddabi, and to return with the report of the supply of water. This country abounded with large game, especially with the beautiful antelope already described, the maarif; they were as usual extremely wild, but I succeeded in breaking the hip of a fine bull at a long range; and, separating him from the herd, I ran the wounded antelope until I was thoroughly exhausted in the intense heat of the sun, but I lost it in the thick bush not far from our camp. That night we heard a lion roaring close to us, and, upon searching at daybreak I found the remains of a maarif, which I imagine must have been my wounded bull.

I mounted my horse Tetel, and, with Taher Noor and two of my Tokroories, Hadji Ali and Hassan, I rode towards a pyramidical hill about three miles distant, which I intended to ascend in order to obtain a panoramic view of the country. This hill was about three hundred feet high, and, as the fire had swept away a portion of the grass for several miles around, I should obtain a clear view of all living animals that might be in the neighbourhood. Upon arrival at the base of the hill I dismounted, and led my horse up the steep inclination of broken basalt that had fallen from the summit. From the top of the peak I had a superb panorama of the country, the mountain Nahoot Guddabi bearing s.w. about thirty miles distant. I had a complete bird's-eye view of great extent, and I immediately distinguished, in various positions, giraffes, buffaloes, tetel, and boars. At this season the trees were leafless, thus any animal upon the low ground would be at once discovered from this elevated point. I extract from my journal the account of this day's hunt, as it was written immediately upon my return to camp.

"I had been observing the country for some time from my high station, when I suddenly perceived two rhinoceros emerge from a ravine; they walked slowly through a patch of high grass, and skirted the base of the hill upon which we were standing: presently they winded something, and they trotted back and stood concealed in the patch of grass. Although I had a good view of them from my present position, I knew that I should not be able to see them in their covert, if on the same level; I therefore determined to send to the tent for my other horses, and to ride them down, if I could not shoot them on foot; accordingly, I sent a man off, directing him to lead Tetel from the peak, and to secure him to a tree at the foot of the hill, as I was afraid the rhinoceros might observe the horse upon the sky line. This he did, and we saw him tie the horse by the bridle to the branch of a tree below us, while he ran quickly towards the camp. In the mean time I watched the rhinoceros; both animals lay down in the yellow grass, resembling masses of stone. They had not been long in this position, before we noticed two pigs wandering through the grass directly to windward, towards the sleeping rhinoceros; in an instant these animals winded the intruders, and starting up, they looked in all directions, but could not see them, as they were concealed by the high grass. Having been thus disturbed, the rhinoceros moved their quarters, and walked slowly forward, occasionally halting, and listening; one was about a hundred yards in advance of the other. They were taking a direction at the base of the hill that would lead them directly upon the spot where Tetel was tied to the tree. I observed this to Taher Noor, as I feared they would kill the horse. 'Oh, no,' he replied, 'they will lie down and sleep beneath the first tree, as they are seeking for shade – the sun is like fire.' However, they still continued their advance, and, upon reaching some rising ground, the leading rhinoceros halted, and I felt sure that he had a clear view of the horse, that was now about five hundred yards distant, tied to the tree. A ridge descended from the hill, parallel with the course the animals were taking; upon this, I ran as quickly as the stony slope permitted, keeping my eye fixed upon the leading rhinoceros, who, with his head raised, was advancing directly towards the horse. I now felt convinced that he intended to attack it. Tetel did not observe the rhinoceros, but was quietly standing beneath the tree. I ran as fast as I was able, and reached the bottom of the hill just as the wilful brute was within fifty yards of the horse, which now for the first time saw the approaching danger; the rhinoceros had been advancing steadily at a walk, but he now lowered his head, and charged at the horse at full speed.

"I was about two hundred yards distant, and for the moment I was afraid of shooting the horse, but I fired one of the Reilly No. 10 rifles; the bullet, missing the rhinoceros, dashed the sand and stones into his face, as it struck the ground exactly before his nose, when he appeared to be just into the unfortunate Tetel. The horse in the same instant reared, and, breaking the bridle, it dashed away in the direction of the camp, while the rhinoceros, astonished at the shot, and most likely half blinded by the sand and splinters of rock, threw up his head, turned round, and trotted back upon the track by which he had arrived. He passed me at about a hundred yards distance, as I had run forward to a bush, by which he trotted with his head raised, seeking for the cause of his discomfiture.

Crack! went a bullet against his hide, as I fired my remaining barrel at his shoulder; he cocked his tail, and for a few yards he charged towards the shot; but he suddenly changed his course, and ran round several times in a small circle; he then halted, and reeling to and fro, he retreated very slowly, and lay down about a hundred yards off. Well done, Reilly! I knew that he had his quietus, but I was determined to bag his companion, who in alarm had now joined him, and stood looking in all quarters for the source of danger; but we were well concealed behind the bush. Presently, the wounded rhinoceros stood up, and walking very slowly, followed by his comrade, he crossed a portion of rising ground at the base of the hill, and both animals disappeared. I at once started off Hassan, who could run like an antelope, in search of Tetel, while I despatched another man to the summit of the peak to see if the rhinoceros were in view; if not, I knew they must be among the small trees and bushes at the foot of the hill. I thus waited for a long time, until at length the two greys, Aggahr and Gazelle, arrived with my messenger from the camp. I tightened the girths of the Arab saddle upon Aggahr, and I had just mounted, cursing all Arab stirrups, that are only made for the naked big toe, when my eyes were gladdened by the sight of Hassan cantering towards me upon Tetel, but from the exact direction the rhinoceros had taken. 'Quick! quick!' he cried, 'come along! One rhinoceros is lying dead close by, and the other is standing beneath a tree not far off.'

"I immediately jumped on Tetel, and, taking the little Fletcher rifle, as lighter and handier than the heavy No. 10, I ordered Taher Noor and Hassan to mount the other horses, and to follow me with spare rifles. I found the rhinoceros lying dead about two hundred yards from the spot where he had received the shot, and I immediately perceived the companion, that was standing beneath a small tree. The ground was firm and stony, all the grass had been burnt off, except in a few small patches; the trees were not so thick together as to form a regular jungle.

"The rhinoceros saw us directly, and he valiantly stood and faced me as I rode up within fifty yards of him. Tetel is worth his weight in gold as a shooting horse: he stands like a rock, and would face the devil. I was unable to take a shot in this position, therefore I ordered the men to ride round a half-circle, as I knew the rhinoceros would turn towards the white horses, and thus expose his flank; this he did immediately, aud firing well, exactly at the shoulder, I dropped him as though stone dead. Taher Noor shouted, 'Samme durrupto!' (well shot); the rhinoceros lay kicking upon the ground, and I thought he was bagged. Not a bit of it! the No. 24 bullet had not force to break the massive shoulder bone, but had merely paralysed it for the moment; up he jumped and started off in full gallop. Now for a hunt! up the hill he started, then obliquely he chose a regular rhinoceros path, and scudded away, Tetel answering to the spur and closing with him; through the trees; now down the hill over the loose rocks, where he gained considerably upon the horse. 'Easy down the hill, gently over the stones, Tetel,' and I took a pull at the reins until I reached the level ground beneath, which was firm and first-rate. I saw the rhinoceros pelting away about a hundred and twenty yards ahead, and spurring hard, I shot up to him at full speed until within twenty yards, when round he came with astonishing quickness and charged straight at the horse. I was prepared for this, as was my horse also; we avoided him by a quick turn, and again renewed the chase, and regained our position within a few yards of the game. Thus the hunt continued for about a mile and a half, the rhinoceros occasionally charging, but always cleverly avoided by the horse. Tetel seemed to enjoy the fun, and hunted like a greyhound. Nevertheless I had not been able to pass the rhinoceros, who had thundered along at a tremendous pace whenever I had attempted to close; however, the pace began to tell upon his wounded shoulder; he evidently went lame, and, as I observed at some distance before us the commencement of the dark-coloured rotten ground I felt sure that it would shortly be a case of 'stand still.' In this I was correct, and, upon reaching the deep and crumbling soil, he turned sharp round, made a clumsy charge that I easily avoided, and he stood panting at bay. Taher Noor was riding Gazelle; this was a very timid horse and was utterly useless as a hunter, but, as it reared and plunged upon seeing the rhinoceros, that animal immediately turned towards it with the intention of charging. Riding Tetel close to his flank, I fired both barrels of the little Fletcher into the shoulder; he fell to the shots, and, stretching out his legs convulsively, he died immediately."

This was a capital termination to the hunt; as I had expected the death of my good horse Tetel, when the first rhinoceros had so nearly horned him. The sun was like a furnace, therefore I rode straight to camp, and sent men and camels for the hides and flesh. As I passed the body of the first rhinoceros, I found a regiment of vultures already collected around it, while fresh arrivals took place every minute, as they gathered from all quarters; they had already torn out the eyes, and dragged a portion of flesh from the bullet-wound in the shoulder; but the tough hide of the rhinoceros was proof against their greedy beaks. A number of Marabou storks had also arrived, and were standing proudly among the crowd of vultures, preparing to perform the duty of sextons, when the skin should become sufficiently decomposed. Throughout all the countries that I had traversed, these birds were in enormous numbers. The question has been frequently discussed whether the vulture is directed to his prey by the sense of smell, or by keenness of vision; I have paid much attention to their habits, and, although there can be no question that their power of scent is great, I feel convinced that all birds of prey are attracted to their food principally by their acuteness of sight. If a vulture were blind, it would starve; but were the nostrils plugged up with some foreign substance to destroy its power of smell, it would not materially interfere with its usual mode of hunting. Scent is always stronger near the surface of the ground; thus hyaenas, lions, and other beasts of prey will scent a carcase from a great distance, provided they are to leeward; but the same animals would be unaware of the presence of the body if they were but a short distance to windward.

If birds of prey trusted to their nostrils, they would keep as near the ground as possible, like the carrion crow, which I believe is the exception that proves the rule. It is an astonishing sight to witness the sudden arrival of vultures at the death of an animal, when a few moments before not a bird has been in sight in the cloudless sky. I have frequently laid down beneath a bush after having shot an animal, to watch the arrival of the various species of birds in regular succession; they invariably appear in the following order: –

> No. 1, the black and white crow: this knowing individual is most industrious in seeking for his food, and is generally to be seen either perched upon rocks or upon trees; I believe he trusts much to his sense of smell, as he is never far from the ground, at the same time he keeps a vigilant look-out with a very sharp pair of eyes.
> No. 2 is the common buzzard: this bird, so well known for its extreme daring, is omnipresent, and trusts generally to sight, as it will stoop at a piece of red cloth in mistake for flesh; thus proving that it depends more upon vision than smell.
> No. 3 is the red-faced small vulture.
> No. 4 is the large bare-throated vulture.
> No. 5, the Marabou stork, sometimes accompanied by the adjutant.

When employed in watching the habits of these birds, it is interesting to make the experiment of concealing a dead animal beneath a dense bush. This I have frequently done; in which case the vultures never find it unless they have witnessed its death; if so, they will already have pounced in their descent while you have been engaged in concealing the body: they will then upon near approach discover it by the smell. But, if an animal is killed in thick grass, eight or ten feet high, the vultures will seldom discover it. I have frequently known the bodies of large animals, such as elephants and buffaloes, to lie for days beneath the shade of the dense nabbuk bushes, unattended by a single vulture; whereas, if visible, they would have been visited by these birds in thousands.

Vultures and the Marabou stork fly at enormous altitudes. I believe that every species keeps to its own particular elevation, and that the atmosphere contains regular strata of birds of prey, who, invisible to the human eye at their enormous height, are constantly resting upon their wide-spread wings, and soaring in circles, watching with telescopic sight the world beneath. At that great elevation they are in an exceedingly cool temperature, therefore they require no water; but some birds that make long flights over arid deserts, such as the Marabou stork, and the buzzard, are provided with water-sacks; the former in an external bag a little below the throat, the latter in an internal sack, both of which carry a large supply. As the birds of prey that I have enumerated, invariably appear at a carcase in their regular succession, I can only suggest that they travel from different distances or altitudes. Thus, the Marabou stork would be farthest from the earth; the large bare-necked vulture would be the next below him, followed by the red-faced vulture, the buzzard, and the crow that is generally about the surface. From their immense elevation, the birds of prey possess an extraordinary field of vision; and, although they are invisible from the earth, there can be no doubt that they are perpetually hunting in circles within sight of each other. Thus, should one bird discover some object upon the surface of the earth below, his sudden pounce would be at once observed and imitated by every vulture in succession. Should one vulture nearest the earth perceive a body, or even should he notice the buzzards collecting at a given point, he would at once become aware of a prey; his rush towards the spot would act like a telegraphic signal to others, that would be rapidly communicated to every vulture at successive airy stations.

If any animal be skinned, the red surface will attract the vultures in an instant; this proves that their sight, and not their scent, has been attracted by an object that suggests blood. I have frequently watched them when I have shot an animal, and my people have commenced the process of skinning. At first, not a bird has been in sight, as I have lain on my back and gazed into the spotless blue sky; but hardly has the skin been half withdrawn, than specks have appeared in the heavens, rapidly increasing. "Caw, caw," has been heard several times from the neighbouring bushes; the buzzards have swept down close to my people, and have snatched a morsel of clotted blood from the ground. The specks have increased to winged creatures, at the great height resembling flies, when presently a rushing sound behind me, like a whirlwind, has been followed by the pounce of a red-faced vulture, that has fallen from the heavens in haste with closed wings to the bloody feast, followed quickly by many of his brethren. The sky has become alive with black specks in the far-distant blue, with wings hurrying from all quarters. At length a coronet of steady, soaring vultures, forms a wide circle far above, as they hesitate to descend, but continue to revolve around the object of attraction. The great bare-necked vulture suddenly appears. The animal has been skinned, and the required flesh secured by the men; we withdraw a hundred paces from the scene. A general rush and descent takes place; hundreds of hungry beaks are tearing at the offal. The great bare-necked vulture claims respect among the crowd; but another form has appeared in the blue sky, and rapidly descends. A pair of long, ungainly legs, hanging down beneath the enormous wings, now touch the ground, and Abou Seen (father of the teeth or beak, the Arab name for the Marabou) has arrived, and he stalks proudly towards the crowds, pecking his way with his long bill through the struggling vultures, and swallowing the lion's share of the repast. Abou Seen, last but not least, had arrived from the highest region, while others had the advantage of the start. This bird is very numerous through the Nile tributaries of Abyssinia, and may generally be seen perched upon the rocks of the water-side, watching for small fish, or any reptile that may chance to come within his reach. The well-known feathers are situated in a plume beneath the tail.

On 14th April we left our camp in the afternoon, and, after marching nine miles, during which we passed two small streams, flowing, like all others, from this point, west to the Atbara, we slept by a large pool in a third stream of considerable size. A waterfall flowed over a row of perpendicular basalt columns that surrounded a deep basin, resembling piles of ebony artificially arranged. On the following morning we started before sunrise, and rode over the usual pathless burnt prairies, until we reached the base of Nahoot Guddabi, the mountain for which we had been steering. Eight miles farther, we arrived at Metemma, a Tokroori village, in the heart of the mountains, twenty-seven miles from our last resting-place, and fifty-one miles from our camp on the Salaam river. From this point to the river Salaam, the entire country slopes perceptibly to the west – the drainage being carried to the Atbara by numerous streams. The country that we had now entered, was inhabited exclusively by Tokroris, although belonging to Abyssinia. They came out to meet us upon our arrival at the village, and immediately fraternised with those of our people that belonged to their tribe, from whom they quickly learnt all about us.

They brought us a he-goat, together with milk and honey. The latter we had revelled in for some months past, as the countries through which we travelled abounded with a supply in the rocks and hollow trees; but the milk was a luxury, as our goats were nearly dry. The he-goat was a regular old patriarch of the flock, and, for those who are fond of savoury food, it might have been a temptation, but as it exhaled a perfume that rendered its presence unbearable, we were obliged to hand it over as a present to our Tokrooris – even they turned up their noses at the offer. A crowd of natives surrounded us, and the account of our travels was related with the usual excitement, amidst the ejaculations of the hearers, when they heard that we had been in the country of the Base, and had trusted ourselves in the power of Mek Nimmur.

On the following morning we were off before sunrise, and marched rapidly over a good path through low forest, at the foot of a range of hills; and after a journey of twenty miles, during which we had passed several small villages, and many brooks that flowed from the mountains, we arrived at our old friend, the Atbara river, at the sharp angle as it issues from the mountains. At this place it was in its infancy. The noble Atbara whose course we had tracked for hundreds of weary miles, and whose tributaries we had so carefully examined, was a second-class mountam torrent, about equal to the Royan, and not to be named in comparison with the Salaam or Angrab. The power of the Atbara depended entirely upon the western drainage of the Abyssinian Alps: of itself it was insignificant, until aided by the great arteries of the mountain chain. The junction of the Salaam at once changed its character; and the Settite or Taccazzy completed its importance as the great river of Abyssinia, that has washed down the fertile soil of those regions to create the Delta of Lower Egypt; and to perpetuate that Delta by annual deposits, that *are now forming a new egypt beneath the waters of the mediterranean.* We had seen the Atbara a bed of glaring sand – a mere continuation of the burning desert that surrounded its course, fringed by a belt of withered trees, like a monument sacred to the memory of a dead river. We had seen the sudden rush of waters when, in the still night, the mysterious stream had invaded the dry bed, and swept all before it like an awakened giant; we knew at that moment "the rains were falling in Abyssinia," although the sky above us was without a cloud. We had subsequently witnessed that tremendous rainfall, and seen the Atbara at its grandest flood. We had traced each river, and crossed each tiny stream, that fed the mighty Atbara from the mountain chain, and we now, after our long journey, forded the Atlara in its infancy, hardly knee deep, over its rocky bed of about sixty yards width, and camped in the little village of Toganai, on the rising ground upon the opposite side. It was evening, and we sat upon an angarep among the lovely hills that surrounded us, and looked down upon the Atbara for the last time, as the sun sank behind the rugged mountain of Ras el Feel (the elephant's head). Once more I thought of that wonderful river Nile, that could flow for ever through the exhausting deserts of sand, while the Atbara, during the summer months, shrank to a dry skeleton, although the powerful affluents, the Salaam and the Settite, never ceased to flow, every drop of their waters was evaporated by the air and absorbed by the desert sand in the bed of the Atbara, two hundred miles above its junction with the Nile!

The Atbara exploration was completed; and I looked forward to the fresh enterprise of new rivers and lower latitudes, that should unravel the mystery of the Nile!

Chapter XX.

Arrival at Metemma, or Gallabat.

We left the village of Toganai at 5 a.m. and, after a rapid march of sixteen miles, we came in view of Metemma, or Gallabat, in the bottom of a valley surrounded by hills, and backed on the east by the range of mountains of which Nahoot Guddabi formed the extremity of a spur. As we descended the valley, we perceived great crowds of people in and about the town, which, in appearance, was merely a repetition of Katariff. It was market-day, and as we descended the hill and arrived in the scene below, with our nine camels heavily laden with the heads and horns of a multitude of different beasts, from the gaping jaws of hippopotami to the vicious-looking heads of rhinoceros and buffalo, while the skins of lions and various antelopes were piled above masses of the much-prized hide of the rhinoceros, we were beset by crowds of people who were curious to know whence so strange a party had appeared. We formed a regular procession through the market, our Tokrooris feeling quite at home among so many of their brethren. Upon our arrival at the extremity of the valley, we were horribly disgusted at the appearance of the water. A trifling stream of about two inches in depth trickled over a bed of sand, shaded by a grove of trees. The putrefying bodies of about half a dozen donkeys, three or four camels, and the remains of a number of horses, lay in and about the margin of the water. Nevertheless, the natives had scraped small holes in the sand, as filters, and thus they were satisfied with this poisonous fluid; in some of these holes, the women were washing their filthy clothes. I immediately determined to follow up stream, until I should arrive at some clear spot above these horrible impurities, that were sufficient to create a pestilence. Ascending the rising ground, I found on the summit, at about half a mile distant, an immense sycamore (Ficus sycamorus), whose green and wide-spreading branches afforded a tempting shade. Not far from this spot, I found the bed of a dry torrent that flowed into the poisoned stream of Gallabat. I ordered my men to dig a deep hole in the sand, which fortunately discovered clear and good-flavoured water. We immediately pitched tents close to the sycamore. From this elevation, about a hundred and fifty feet above Gallabat, we had a beautiful view of the amphitheatre of hills and mountains, while the crowded town lay below, as in the bottom of a basin. The Atbara was not far distant in the ravine between the hill ranges, as it had made a sharp angle at Toganai, and altered its direction to the north.

Our arrival had made some stir in Gallabat, and many people had followed us, and stared with much curiosity at the collection of hunting trophies. Among our visitors was an Abyssinian merchant, Jusef, whose acquaintance I had formerly made at Cassala; he was an agreeable and well-informed man, who had been in Paris and London and spoke French and English tolerably. I accompanied him for a stroll through the market, and was introduced by him to a number of the principal Abyssinian merchants. The principal trade of Gallabat, which is the market-place for all commerce between Abyssinia and the Egyptian provinces, is in cotton, coffee, bees'-wax, and hides. Coffee is brought in large quantities by the Abyssinian merchants, who buy cotton in exchange, for the manufacture of clothes according to their own fashion. I bought a quantity of excellent coffee at the rate of two dollars for thirty-five pounds, equal to about two and three-quarters pence a pound. Sheds were arranged in lines; these were occupied by the coffee merchants with their stores, while a great stock of cotton in bales, to the number of some thousand, were piled in rows in an open space. Not far from the mass of goods was a confusion of camels, asses, and mules that had formed the means of transport. I now met an Italian merchant, with whom I subsequently became intimately acquainted, Signor Angelo Bolognesi – he had arrived from Khartoum to purchase coffee and bees'-wax. We were delighted to meet a civilized European after so long an absence. For some months we had had little intercourse with any human beings beyond the hunters that had composed our party, in countries that were so wild and savage, that the print of a naked foot upon the sand had instinctively brought the rifle upon full cock. Our European society was quickly increased: two German missionaries had arrived, en ronte for an establishment that had been set on foot in the heart of Abyssinia, under the very nose of the King Theodore, who regarded missionaries as an unsavoury odour. Both were suffering from fever, having foolishly located themselves in a hut close to the foul stench of dead animals on the margin of the polluted stream, the water of which they drank. One of these preachers was a blacksmith, whose iron constitution had entirely given way, and the little strength that remained, he exhausted in endless quotations of texts from the Bible, which he considered applicable to every trifling event or expression. I regretted that

I could not agree with him in the propriety of invading Abyssinia with Bible extracts, as the natives attached as great importance to their own particular form of Christianity, as any other of the numerous sects that unhappily divide that beautiful religion into schisms; any fresh dogma introduced by strangers might destroy the union of the Abyssinian Church, and would be not only a source of annoyance to the priesthood, but would most probably influence them and the king against all Europeans.

The blacksmith assured me that the special mission upon which he was employed was the conversion of the Abyssinian Jews. I suggested that we had a few Jews in England, that might offer a fair field for an experiment at home, before we commenced at so distant a country as Abyssinia; but I could not persuade the blacksmith, whose head was as hard as his anvil; he had fully persuaded himself that the word of God (according to *his own* translation of it) was the hammer with which, selon son metier, he was to drive his views of the truth into the thick skulls of the people. If he could twist iron, and hammer a ploughshare into a sword, or reverse the form, why should he be unable to effect a change in their opinions? It was perfectly useless to continue the argument; but I prophesied trouble, as the king was already discontented, and an influx of missionaries would not improve his humour. I advised him to stick to his trade, which would obtain for him far more respect than preaching. He replied, that "the word of God must be preached in all countries; that the Apostle Paul had encountered dangers and difficulties, but, nevertheless, he preached to, and converted the heathen," &c.

Whenever I have met an exceedingly ignorant missionary, he has invariably compared himself to the Apostle Paul. In half an hour I found, that I was conversing with St. Paul in the person of the blacksmith. Whether this excellent apostle is among the captives in Abyssinia at the present moment, I do not know; but, if so, their memory of the Bible will be continually refreshed by quotations, which fly from the tongue of the smith like sparks from his anvil. His companion was very ill, and incapable of moving. I went to see the poor fellow upon several occasions, and found him suffering from dysentery and diseased liver. These excellent but misguided people had a first-rate medicine chest, filled with useful drugs and deadly poisons, that had been provided for them cheaply, by the agent for their society at Cairo, who had purchased the stock in trade of a defunct doctor. This had been given to the missionaries, together with the caution that many of the bottles were not labelled, and that some contained poison. Thus provided with a medicine chest that they did not comprehend, and with a number of Bibles printed in the Tigre language which they did not understand, they were prepared to convert the Jews, who could not read.

The Bibles were to be distributed as the word of God, like "seed thrown upon the wayside;" and the medicines, I trust, were to be kept locked up in the chest, as their distribution might have been fatal to the poor Jews. These worthy and well-meaning missionaries were prepared to operate mentally and physically upon the Abyssinians, to open their minds as well as their bowels; but as their own (not their minds) were out of order, I was obliged to assist them by an examination of their medicine-chest, which they had regarded with such dread and suspicion that, although dangerously ill, they had not dared to attempt a dose. This medicine-chest accompanied them like a pet dog suspected of hydrophobia, which they did not like to part with, and were yet afraid to touch. I labelled the poisons, and weighed out some doses, that in a few days considerably relieved them; at the same time I advised the missionaries to move to a healthier locality, and to avoid the putrid water.

On the day following our arrival, I paid a visit to the Sheik of Gallabat – Jemma. He was ill, as were most people. They were too much accustomed to the use of the filthy water to trouble themselves about a pure supply; thus a frightful amount of sickness was prevalent among all classes.

The Sheik Jemma was a Tokroori; and as these people hate the Turks or Egyptians, although fanatical Mussulmans, he was exceedingly cold when he read my firman, that I had produced as a passport. He replied to my demand for assistance in men and camels, that "this was Abyssinia, and the firman of the Viceroy of Egypt was a bad introduction, as the Egyptians forced them to pay tribute at the point of the bayonet, although they had no right to enter this country;" they paid taxes willingly to the King of Abyssinia, as he had a right to exact them. I explained that I was an Englishman, and no Turk, but that, as I had travelled through the dominions of the Viceroy, I had been favoured with the sign-manual of his Excellency Said Pasha, and I narrated in a few words the object of our expedition. He paid very little attention, and merely asked me if I could send him some goat's milk, as he was very ill. I was astonished at such a request, as there were great numbers of these animals in the neighbourhood; but he explained that his doctor had ordered him to drink the milk of a black goat, and he had heard that I had two of that colour. I promised him a supply, and he agreed to assist me in engaging camels and fresh men, as I had formerly arranged with my people that their term of service should expire upon our arrival at Gallabat or Metemma. The latter name merely signifies "the capital:" as many places are designated by the same word, it creates much confusion.

The Sheik Jemma was the successor of Hamed, who formerly governed the Tokrooris. The Egyptians had captured Hamed three years previously, during which time he had been imprisoned in Cairo. Upon his release, he wrote to Jemma (who had governed pro tempore) to prepare for his arrival; but Jemma had no intention of vacating his seat, and he replied by an impertinent message. Hamed immediately applied to the Governor-General of the Soudan for assistance, declaring himself to be the subject of Egypt. Having obtained a powerful force, he advanced upon Gallabat, and attacked Jemma, who came out to meet him. This happened about three months before our arrival. In a pitched battle, the Tokroris were defeated with great loss, and Jemma, with the greater portion of the population, sought the assistance of Theodore, the king of Abyssinia. Theodore summoned the rival chiefs before him, and decided that, as Hamed had appealed to Egypt for assistance, he should lose his seat, and remain a prisoner in Abyssinia. Accordingly, Jemma was declared to be the governor of the town of Gallabat, and the sheik over all Tokroris.

The Tokroris are natives of Darfur, who were converted to Mahometanism after the conquest of Northern Africa by the Arabs. They are governed by a sultan in their own country, who strictly prohibits the entrance of white men; thus Darfur remains impenetrable to civilization. That country is extremely arid and unfruitful; thus, as the pilgrims journeyed towards Mecca from their own inhospitable soil, they passed through a land flowing with milk and honey, with excellent pasturage and fertile soil, in the district of Gallabat. As first settlements of men have always been caused by some local attraction and advantage, so the Tokroori pilgrims, on their return from Mecca, originally rested from the fatigues of their journey in the neighbourhood of Gallabat, as a country preferable to their own. The establishment of a few settlers formed a nucleus, and, as successive pilgrimages to Mecca were annually undertaken from Darfur, the colony rapidly increased by the settlement of the returned pilgrims. Thus commenced the establishment of a new tribe upon foreign soil, and, as the numbers of settlers increased to an important amount, permission was granted by the King of Abyssinia that they should occupy this portion of his territory, upon payment of taxes as his subjects. The Tokroris are a fine, powerful race, exceedingly black, and of the negro type, but differing from all negroes that I have hitherto known, as they are particularly industrious. They are great drunkards, very quarrelsome, and are bad servants, as, although they will work hard for themselves, they will do as little as they can for their master. They are seldom unemployed; and, while the Arab may be seen lazily stretched under the shade of a tree, the Tokroori will be spinning cotton, or working at something that will earn a few piastres.

Even during the march, I have frequently seen my men gather the cotton from some deserted bush, and immediately improvise a spindle, by sticking a reed through a piece of camel-dung, with which they would spin the wool into thread, as they walked with the caravan. My Tokrooris had never been idle during the time they had been in my service, but they were at work in the camp during every spare minute, either employed in making sandals from elephant's or buffalo's hide, or whips and bracelets from the rhinoceros' skin, which they cleverly polished. Upon our arrival at Gallabat, they had at least a camel-load of all kinds of articles they had manufactured. On the following morning I found them sitting in the market-place, having established stalls, at which they were selling all the various trophies of their expedition – fat, hides, whips, sandals, bracelets, &c.

The district inhabited by the Tokrooris is about forty miles in length, including a population of about twenty thousand. Throughout the country, they have cultivated cotton to a considerable extent, notwithstanding the double taxes enforced by both Abyssinians and Egyptians, and their gardens are kept with extreme neatness. Although of the negro type, the Tokrooris have not the flat nose; the lips are full, but not to be compared with those of the negroes of West Africa; neither is the jaw prognathous. The men are extremely independent in manner. They are armed with lances of various patterns; their favourite weapon is a horrible instrument barbed with a diabolical intention, as it can neither be withdrawn nor pushed completely through the body, but, if once in the flesh, there it must remain. This is called the chimbane; it is usually carried with two other lances with plain heads. The Tokrooris despise shields; therefore, in spite of their superior personal strength, they would be no match for the Arabs.

There is a curious weapon, the trombash, that is used by these people, somewhat resembling the Australian boomerang; it is a piece of flat, hard wood, about two feet in length, the end of which turns sharply at an angle of about 30 degrees. They throw this with great dexterity, and inflict severe wounds with the hard and sharp edge; but, unlike the boomerang, the weapon does not return to the thrower.

The women are very powerful, but exceedingly plain. They are good workers, and may be constantly seen either spinning or weaving; they keep their huts remarkably clean, and are rarely idle.

The greater portion of the cotton exhibited in the market of Gallabat is produced by the Tokrooris; it is uncleaned, and simply packed in mat bales of a hundred pounds weight, which at that date (April 1862) sold for one dollar each.

Much might be done to improve these peculiar people. Were the frontiers of Abyssinia positively determined, and security insured to the new settlers, the whole of that magnificent country through which we had travelled between the Settite and Gallabat might be peopled and cultivated. In many countries, both soil and climate may be favourable for the cultivation of cotton; but such natural advantages may be neutralized either by the absence of population, or by the indolence of the natives. The Tokroori is a most industrious labourer; and, were he assured of protection and moderate taxation, he would quickly change the character of these fertile lands, that are now uninhabited, except by wild animals. If the emigration of Tokroris from Darfur were encouraged, and advantages offered to settlers, by grants of land for a short term exempt from taxation, at a future time to bear a certain rate per acre, a multitude of emigrants would quit their own inhospitable country, and would people the beautiful waste lands of the Settite and the Salaam. These countries would produce an important supply of cotton, that might be delivered at Souakim at an exceedingly low rate, and find a market in England. Not only would the Tokrooris benefit by the change, but, should it be decided that the Abyssinian frontier, instead of extending to the Atbara river, should be confined to the ridge of the great mountain chain, the revenues of Upper Egypt might be enormously increased by the establishment of a Tokroori colony, as proposed.

I paid all my Tokrooris their wages, and I gave them an entertainment after their own taste, by purchasing several enormous bowls of honey wine. The Abyssinians are celebrated for this drink, which is known as "tetch." It is made of various strengths; that of good quality should contain, in ten parts, two of honey and eight of water; but, for a light wine, one of honey and nine of water is very agreeable. There is a plant of an intoxicating quality known by the Abyssinians as "jershooa," the leaves of which are added to the tetch while in a state of fermentation; a strong infusion of these leaves will render the tetch exceedingly heady, but without this admixture the honey wine is by no means powerful. In our subsequent journey in Central Africa, I frequently made the tetch by a mixture of honey and water, flavoured with wild thyme and powdered ginger; fermentation was quickly produced by the addition of yeast from the native beer, and the wine, after six or eight days, became excellent, but never very strong, as we could not procure the leaves of the jershooa.

My Arabs and Tokrooris enjoyed themselves amazingly, and until late at night they were playing rababas (guitars) and howling in thorough happiness; but on the following morning at sunrise I was disturbed by Wat Gamma, who complained that during the night some person had stolen three dollars, that had for some months been carefully sewn up in his clothes; he exhibited the garment that bore the unmistakeable impression of the dollars, and the freshly-cut ends of the thread proved that it had been ripped open very recently. Of course I was magistrate, and in all cases I was guided by my own code of laws, being at some thousand miles from an Act of Parliament.

Wat Gamma had no suspicion of any person in particular, but his money had evidently been stolen.

"Who was drunk last night?" I inquired. "We were all drunk," replied the plaintiff. "Who was very drunk, and who was the least drunk?" I inquired. This entailed a discussion among the people who had now assembled. It appeared that most of them had been "very drunk;" others only a little drunk; and one old white-headed Arab camel-driver had been perfectly sober, as he never drank anything but water. This was old Mini, a splendid specimen of a fine patriarchal Arab; he declared that he had not even joined the party. Wat Gamma had left his garment rolled up in the mat upon which he usually slept; this was in the same spot where the camel-drivers lived, and where old Mini declared he was fast asleep during the drinking bout.

I had my suspicions, but to express them would have defeated the chance of discovery. I therefore adopted my usual rule in cases of theft. I counted my people: nine camel-men, five Tokrooris, Taher Noor, and Bacheet; in all sixteen, without Wat Gamma. Three dollars were sixty piastres, – sixty divided by sixteen equalled three piastres and thirty paras. Thus I condemned the whole party to make up the loss, by each paying his share of the amount stolen, unless the thief could be discovered.

This plan was generally successful, as the thief was the only man contented with the arrangement. Every innocent man became a detective, as he was determined not to pay a fine for another's theft. A tremendous row took place, every one was talking and no one listening, and the crowd went away from my court of justice, determined to search the affair to the bottom.

In about half an hour they all returned, with the exception of old Mini; they had searched everywhere, and had found three dollars concealed in the stuffing of a camel's saddle, that belonged to Mini. He was the sober man, who had been asleep while the others were drinking. I considered the case proved; and Mini, having confessed, requested that I would flog him rather than deliver him to the Tokroori authorities, who wonld imprison him and take away his camel. I told him that I would not disgrace his tribe by flogging one of their oldest men, but that I should take him before the Sheik of Gallabat, and fine him the amount that he had stolen. This I immediately did, and Mini handed over to Jemma, with reluctance, three dollars for the poor-box of Gallabat, or the private pocket of the sheik, as the case may be.

On my return to camp I visited the establishments of the various slave merchants: these were arranged under large tents formed of matting, and contained many young girls of extreme beauty, ranging from nine to seventeen years of age. These lovely captives, of a rich brown tint, with delicately-formed features, and eyes like those of the gazelle, were natives of the Galla, on the borders of Abyssinia, from which country they were brought by the Abyssinian traders to be sold for the Turkish harems. Although beautiful, these girls are useless for hard labour; they quickly fade away and die unless kindly treated. They are the Venuses of that country, and not only are their faces and figures perfection, but they become extremely attached to those who show them kindness, and they make good and faithful wives. There is something peculiarly captivating in the natural grace and softness of these young beauties, whose hearts quickly respond to those warmer feelings of love that are seldom known among the sterner and coarser tribes. Their forms are peculiarly elegant and graceful – the hands and feet are exquisitely delicate; the nose is generally slightly aquiline, the nostrils large and finely shaped; the hair is black and glossy, reaching to about the middle of the back, but rather coarse in texture. These girls, although natives of Galla, invariably call themselves Abyssinians, and are generally known under that denomination. They are exceedingly proud and high-spirited, and are remarkably quick at learning. At Khartoum, several of the Europeans of high standing have married these charming ladies, who have invariably rewarded their husbands by great affection and devotion. The price of one of these beauties of nature at Gallabat was from twenty-five to forty dollars.

On the 24th April we were refreshed by a shower of rain, and in a few days the grass sprang from the ground several inches high. There was an unpleasant dampness in the air, and, although the rainy season would not commence until June, showers would occasionally fall among the mountains throughout the month of May. I accordingly purchased a number of large tanned ox-hides, that are rendered waterproof by a preparation with milk. These skins cost the trifling sum of nine piastres each (not two shillings), and were subsequently of great value during our White Nile expedition, as coverlets during the night's bivouac, &c.

The horse-fair was a disappointment. At this season the entire country in the neighbourhood of Gallabat was subject to an epidemic, fatal to these animals; therefore there were no good horses present. I had nothing to detain me at this place, after having procured fresh camels, therefore I paid all my people, and we parted excellent friends. To the Arabs and Tokrooris I gave all the hides of rhinoceros, elephants, &c. that I did not require, and, with our loads considerably lightened, we started from Gallabat, 12.30 P.M., 28th April, 1862, and marched due west towards the river Rahad. The country was hilly and wooded, the rocks were generally sandstone, and after a march of three hours we halted at a Tokroori village. I never witnessed more unprovoked insolence than was exhibited by these people. They considered me to be a Turk, to whom their natural hatred had been increased by the chastisement they had lately received from the Egyptians. It was in vain that my two lads, Wat Gamma and Bacheet, assured them that I was an Englishman: they had never heard of such a country as England; in their opinion, a white man must be a Turk. Not contented with refusing all supplies, they assembled in large numbers and commenced a quarrel with my men, several of whom were Tokrooris that I had hired to accompany us to Khartoum. These men, being newly engaged and entirely strange, were of little service; but, having joined in the quarrel like true Tokrooris, who are always ready for a row, the altercation grew so hot that it became rather serious. The natives determined that we should not remain in their village, and, having expressed a threat to turn us out, they assembled around us in a large crowd with their lances and trombashes. My wife was sitting by me upon an angarep, when the people closed around my men, and one very tall specimen of a Tokroori came forward, and, snatching a knife from its sheath that was worn upon the arm of my servant, he challenged him to fight. As Tokrooris are always more or less under the influence of drink, their fights are generally the effect of some sudden impulse. It was necessary to do something, as the crowd were determined upon a row; this was now commenced by their leader, who was eyeing me from head to foot with the most determined insolence, holding the knife in his hand that he had taken from my man. I therefore rose quietly from my seat, and, approaching him to within a convenient distance for striking, if necessary, I begged him very politely to leave my people to themselves, as we should depart on the following morning. He replied with great impertinence, and insisted upon fighting one or all of our party. I accommodated him without a moment's delay, as, stepping half a pace backwards, I came in with a left and right as fast as a rapid double-hit could be delivered, with both blows upon his impudent mouth. In an instant he was on his back, with his heels in the air; and, as I prepared to operate upon his backer, or upon any bystander who might have a penchant for fighting, the crowd gave way, and immediately devoted themselves to their companion, who lay upon the ground in stupid astonishment, with his fingers down his throat searching for a tooth; his eyes were fixed upon my hands to discover the weapon with which he had been wounded. His friends began to wipe the blood from his face and clothes, and at this juncture the sheik of the village appeared for the first time.

To my astonishment he was extremely civil; a sudden reaction had taken place, the Tokrooris had had their row, and were apparently satisfied. The sheik begged me not to kill his people by hitting them, "as they were mere chickens, who would at once die if I were to strike them with my fist." I begged him to keep his "chickens" in better order, and at once to order them away from our immediate neighbourhood. In a few minutes the sheik drove the crowd away, who picked up their man and led him off. The sheik then begged us to accept a hut for the night, and he paid us every attention.

On the following morning, we left shortly after sunrise; the natives very civilly assisted to load our camels, and among the most active was my fighting friend of yesterday, who, with his nose and mouth all swollen into one, had been rapidly converted from a well-featured Tokroori into a real thick-lipped, flat-nosed African nigger, with prognathous jaw, that would have delighted the Ethnological Society.

"April 29. – It rained hard during the night. Our course was due west, along the banks of a hor, from which the natives procure water by sinking wells about twelve feet deep in the sandy bed, which is dry in the hot season. Throughout this country the water is bad. At 11 A.M. we reached Roumele; this is the last village between Gallabat and the river Rahad. The natives say that there is no water on the road, and their accounts of the distance are so vague and contradictory that I cannot rely upon the information.

"I could procure only one water-skin, and none of my old stock were serviceable; I therefore arranged to water all the animals, and push on throughout the night, by which plan I hoped to arrive by a forced march at the Rahad on the following morning, without exhausting both men and beasts by a long journey through an unknown distance in the heat of the sun. Hardly were the horses watered at a well in the dry bed of the stream, when Aggahr was taken ill with inflammation. I left two men to attend upon him, with orders to bring him on if better on the following day: we started on our journey, but we had not proceeded a quarter of a mile when Gazelle, that I was riding, was also seized with illness, and fell down; with the greatest difficulty I led the horse back again to the village. My good old hunter Aggahr died in great agony a few minutes after our return, and Gazelle died during the night; the natives declared this to be the horse sickness that was annually prevalent at this season. The disease appeared to be inflammation of the bowels, which I attributed to the sudden change of food; for months past they had lived principally upon dry grass, but within the past few days they had greedily eaten the young herbage that had appeared after a few showers; with this, may have been poisonous plants that they had swallowed unawares. We had now only one horse, Tetel, that was ridden by my wife; I therefore determined to start on foot on the following morning, and to set the pace at four miles an hour, so as to reach the Rahad by a forced march in one rapid stretch, and thus to eke out our scanty supply of water. Accordingly we started, and marched at that rate for ten hours, including a halt when half-way, to rest for one hour and a half. Throughout the distance, the country was a dead flat of the usual rich soil, covered with mimosa forest. We marched thirty-four miles, steering due west for a distant hill, which in the morning had been a faint blue streak upon the horizon.

"Upon our arrival at the hill, we found that the river was some miles beyond, while a fine rugged mountain that we had seen for two days previous rose about fifteen miles south of this point, and formed an unmistakeable landmark; the name of this mountain is Hallowa. We had marched with such rapidity across this stretch of thirty-four miles, that our men were completely exhausted from thirst, as they had foolishly drunk their share of water at the middle of the journey, instead of reserving it for the moment of distress. Upon arrival at the Rahad they rushed down the steep bank, and plunged into the clear water of the river.

"The Rahad does not exceed eighty or ninety yards in breadth. The rain that had recently fallen in the mountain had sent a considerable stream down the hitherto dry bed, although the bottom was not entirely covered. By dead reckoning, this point of the river is fifty-five miles due west from Gallabat or Metemma; throughout this distance we had seen no game, neither the tracks of any animals except giraffes. We were rather hard up for provisions, therefore I took my rod, and tried for a fish in a deep pool below the spot where we had pitched the tent. I only had one run, but I fortunately landed a handsome little baggar about twelve pounds weight, which afforded us a good dinner. The river Dinder is between fifty and sixty miles from the Rahad at this point, but towards the north the two rivers approximate closely, and keep a course almost parallel. The banks of the Rahad are in many places perpendicular, and are about forty-five feet above the bed. This river flows through rich alluvial soil; the country is a vast level plane, with so trifling a fall that the current of the river is gentle; the course is extremely circuitous, and although, when bank full, the Rahad possesses a considerable volume, it is very inferior as a Nile tributary to any river that I have visited to the east of Gallabat."

Chapter XXI.

Fertility of the Country on the Banks of the Rahad.

We daily followed the banks of the Rahad, the monotony of which I will not inflict upon the public. This country was a vast tract of wonderfully fertile prairie, that nearly formed an island, surrounded by the Rahad, Blue Nile, Great Nile, and Atbara; it was peopled by various tribes of Arabs, who cultivated a considerable extent upon the banks of the Rahad, which for upwards of a hundred miles to the north were bordered with villages at short intervals. Cotton and tobacco were produced largely, and we daily met droves of camels laden with these goods, en route for the Abyssinian market. We had now fairly quitted Abyssinian territory, and upon our arrival at the Rahad we were upon the soil of Upper Egypt. I was much struck with the extraordinary size and condition of the cattle. Corn (dhurra) was so plentiful that it was to be purchased in any quantity for eight piastres the rachel, or about 1s. 8d. for 500 pounds; pumpkins were in great quantities, with a description of gourd with an exceedingly strong shell, which is grown especially for bowls and other utensils; camel-loads of these gourd-basins packed in conical crates were also journeying on the road towards Gallabat. Throughout the course of the Rahad the banks are high, and, when full, the river would average forty feet in depth, with a gentle stream, the course free from rocks and shoals, and admirably adapted for small steamers.

The entire country would be a mine of wealth were it planted with cotton, which could be transported by camels to Katariff, and thence direct to Souakim. We travelled for upwards of a hundred miles along the river, through the unvarying scene of flat alluvial soil; the south bank was generally covered with low jungle. The Arabs were always civil, and formed a marked contrast to the Tokrooris; they were mostly of the Roofar tribe. Although there had been a considerable volume of water in the river at the point where we had first met it, the bed was perfectly dry about fifty miles farther north, proving the great power of absorption by the sand. The Arabs obtained water from deep pools in the river, similar to those in the Atbara, but on a small scale, of not sufficient importance to contain hippopotami, which at this season retired to the river Dinder. Wherever we slept we were besieged by gaping crowds of Arabs: these people were quite unaccustomed to strangers, as the route we had chosen along the banks of the Rahad was entirely out of the line adopted by the native merchants and traders of Khartoum, who travelled via Abou Harraz and Katariff to Gallabat. These Arabs were, as usual, perfectly wild, and ignorant of everything that did not immediately concern them. My compass had always been a source of wonder to the natives, and I was asked whether by looking into it I rould distinguish the "market days" of the different villages. My own Tokroris continually referred to me for information on various topics, and, if I declined to reply, they invariably begged me to examine my moondera (mirror), as they termed the compass, and see what it would say. This country swarmed with Arabs, and abounded in supplies: superb fat oxen were seven dollars each; large fowls were a penny; and eggs were at the rate of nine for a penny farthing.

We arrived at a large village, Sherrem, on May 11, having marched 118 miles in a straight line along the course of the Rahad. The heat was extreme, but I had become so thoroughly accustomed to the sun that I did not feel it so much as my men, whose heads were covered with a thin cap of cotton (the tageea). My camel-men had expected to find their families at a village that we had passed about six miles from Sherrem, and they had been rejoicing in anticipation, but on arrival we found it deserted, – "family out of town;" the men were quite dejected; but upon arrival at Sherrem they found all their people, who had migrated for water, as the river was dry. We waited at Sherrem for a couple of days to rest the men, whose feet were much swollen with marching on the burning soil. Although frequent showers had fallen at Gallabat, we had quickly entered the dry country upon steering north, where neither dew nor rain had moistened the ground for many months. The country was treeless on the north bank of the Rahad, and the rich alluvial soil was free from a single stone or pebble for many miles. Although for 118 miles we had travelled along the course of the Rahad, throughout this distance only one small brook furrowed the level surface and added its waters during the rainy season to the river; the earth absorbed the entire rainfall. Our camels were nearly driven mad by the flies which swarmed throughout the fertile districts.

On the 15th of May we arrived at Kook, a small village on the banks of the Rahad, and on the following morning we started to the west for the river Dinder. The country was the usual rich soil, but covered with high grass and bush; it was uninhabited, except by wandering Arabs and their flocks, that migrate at the commencement of the rainy season, when this land becomes a mere swamp, and swarms with the seroot fly. At 6.30 we halted, and slept on the road. This was the main route to Sennaar, from which place strings of camels were passing to the Rahad, to purchase corn. On the 16th of May, we started by moonlight at 4.30 A.M. due west, and at 7.30 A.M. we arrived at the river Dinder, which, at this point, was eighteen miles from the village of Kook, on the Rahad.

We joined a camp of the Kunana Arabs, who at this season throng the banks of the Dinder. This river is similar in character to the Rahad, but larger: the average breadth is about a hundred and ten yards: the banks are about fifty feet high, and the immediate vicinity is covered with thick jungle of nabbuk and thorny acacias, with a great quantity of the Acacia Arabica, that produces the garra, already described as valuable for tanning leather. I made ink with this fruit, pounded and boiled, to which I added a few rusty nails, and allowed it to stand for about twenty-four hours. The Dinder was exceedingly deep in many places, although in others the bed was dry, with the exception of a most trifling stream that flowed through a narrow channel in the sand, about an inch in depth. The Arabs assured me that the crocodiles in this river were more dangerous than in any other, and their flocks of goats and sheep were attended by a great number of boys, to prevent the animals from descending to the water to drink, except in such places as had been prepared for them by digging small holes in the sand. I saw many of these creatures, of very large size; and, as I strolled along the banks of the river, I found a herd of hippopotami, of which I shot two, to the great delight of my people, who had been much disappointed at the absence of game throughout our journey from Gallabat. We had travelled upwards of 200 miles without having seen so much as a gazelle, neither had we passed any tracks of large game, except, upon one occasion, those of a few giraffes. I had been told that the Dinder country was rich in game, but, at this season, it was swarming with Arabs, and was so much disturbed that everything had left the country, and the elephants merely drank during the night, and retreated to distant and impenetrable jungles. At night we heard a lion roar, but this, instead of being our constant nightingale, as upon the Settite river, was now an uncommon sound. The maneless lion is found on the banks of the Dinder; all that I saw, in the shape of game, in the neighbourhood of that river and the Rahad, were a few hippopotami and crocodiles. The stream of the Dinder is obstructed with many snags and trunks of fallen trees that would be serious obstacles to rapid navigation: these are the large stems of the soont (Acacia Arabica), that, growing close to the edge, have fallen into the river when the banks have given way. I was astonished at the absence of elephants in such favourable ground; for some miles I walked along the margin of the river without seeing a track of any date. Throughout this country, these animals are so continually hunted that they have become exceedingly wary, and there can be little doubt that their numbers are much reduced. Even in the beautiful shooting country comprised between the river Gash and Gallabat, although we had excellent sport, I had been disappointed at the number of elephants, which I had expected to find in herds of many hundreds, instead of forty or fifty, which was the largest number that I had seen together. The habits of all animals generally depend upon the nature of the localities they inhabit. Thus, as these countries were subject to long drought and scarcity of water, the elephants were, in some places, contented with drinking every alternate day. Where they were much hunted by the aggageers, they would seldom drink twice consecutively in the same river; but, after a long draught in the Settite, they would march from twenty-five to thirty miles, and remain for a day between that river and the Mareb or Gash, to which they would hurry on the following night. At other times, these wily animals would drink in the Settite, and retire to the south; feeding upon Mek Nimmur's corn-fields, they would hurry forward to the river Salaam, about thirty miles distant, and from thence, in a similar manner, either to the Atbara on one side, or into the Abyssinian mountains, where, at all times, they could procure a supply of water. I have frequently discovered fresh grains of dhurra in their dung, at a great distance from the nearest corn-field; when the rapid digestion of the elephant is considered, it must be allowed that the fresh dung found in the morning bore witness to the theft of corn during the past night; thus the elephant had marched many miles after feeding. In the "Rifle and Hound in Ceylon," published in 1854, I gave a detailed description of the elephants of that country, which, although peculiar in the general absence of tusks, are the same as the Indian species.

Although the elephant is found throughout many countries, extending over an enormous area, there are only two species at present in existence, – the Indian and African; these are totally different in their habits, and are distinguished by peculiarities of form. The most striking difference is in the shape of the head and spine. The head of the Indian species is perfectly distinct; the forehead, when held in the natural position of inaction, is perpendicular; and above the slight convexity at the root of the trunk there is a depression, in shape like a herald's shield: a bullet in the lower portion of that shield would reach the brain in a direct line. The head of the African elephant is completely convex from the commencement of the trunk to the back of the skull, and the brain is situated much lower than in that of the Indian species; the bone is of a denser quality, and the cases for the reception of the tusks are so closely parallel, that there is barely room for a bullet to find a chance of penetrating to the brain; it must be delivered in the exact centre, and extremely low, in the very root of the trunk; even then it will frequently pass above the brain, as the animal generally carries his head high, and thrown slightly back. The teeth of the African elephant differ materially from those of the Indian, by containing a lesser number of laminae or plates, the surfaces of which, instead of exhibiting straight and parallel lines like those of the Indian, are shaped in slight curves, which increase the power of grinding. The ears of the African species are enormous, and when thrown back they completely cover the shoulders; they are also entirely different in shape from those of the Indian species. When an African bull elephant advances in full charge with his ears cocked, his head measures about fourteen feet from the tip of one ear to that of the other, in a direct line across the forehead. I have frequently cut off the ear to form a mat, upon which I have slept beneath the shade of a tree, while my people divided the animal.

The back of the Indian elephant is exceedingly convex; that of the African is exactly the reverse, and the concavity behind the shoulders is succeeded by a peculiarity in the sudden rise of the spine above the hips. The two species are not only distinct in certain peculiarities of form, but they differ in their habits. The Indian elephant dislikes the sun, and invariably retreats to thick shady forests at sunrise; but I have constantly found the African species enjoying themselves in the burning sun in the hottest hours of the day, among plains of withered grass, many miles from a jungle. The African is more active than the Indian, and not only is faster in his movements, but is more capable of enduring long marches, as proved by the great distances through which it travels to seek its food in the native's corn-fields. In all countries, the bulls are fiercer than the females. I cannot see much difference in character between the Indian and the African species; it is the fashion for some people to assert that the elephant is an innocent and harmless creature, that, like the giraffe it is almost a sin to destroy. I can only say that, during eight years' experience in Ceylon, and nearly five years' in Africa, I have found that elephants are the most formidable animals with which a sportsman has to contend. The African species is far more dangerous than the Indian, as the forehead shot can never be trusted; therefore the hunter must await the charge with a conviction that his bullet will fail to kill.

The African elephant is about a foot higher than the average of the Indian species. The bulls of the former are about ten feet six inches at the shoulder; the females are between nine feet and nine feet six. Of course there are many bulls that exceed this height, and I have seen some few of both species that might equal twelve feet, but those are the exceptional Goliaths.

The tusks of elephants vary considerably, and there appears to be no rule to determine a reason for their size and quality. In Abyssinia and Taka, a single tusk of a bull elephant seldom exceeds forty pounds, nor do they average more than twenty-five, but in Central Africa they average about forty, and I have seen them upwards of one hundred and fifty pounds. The largest that I have had the good fortune to bag was eighty pounds; the fellow-tusk was slightly below seventy. Elephants invariably use one tusk in preference, as we use the right hand; thus it is difficult to obtain an exact pair, as the Hadam (or servant), as the Arabs call the working tusk, is generally much worn. The African elephant is a more decided tree-feeder than the Indian, and the destruction committed by a large herd of such animals when feeding in a mimosa forest is extraordinary; they deliberately march forward, and uproot or break down every tree that excites their appetite. The mimosas are generally from sixteen to twenty feet high, and, having no tap-root, they are easily overturned by the tusks of the elephants, which are driven like crowbars beneath the roots, and used as levers, in which rough labour they are frequently broken. Upon the overthrow of a tree, the elephants eat the roots and leaves, and strip the bark from the branches by grasping them with their rough trunks.

The African elephant is equally docile as the Indian, when domesticated, but we have no account of a negro tribe that has ever tamed one of these sagacious animals: their only maxim is "kill and eat." Although the flesh of the elephant is extremely coarse, the foot and trunk are excellent, if properly cooked. A hole should be dug in the earth, about four feet deep, and two feet six inches in diameter, the sides of which should be perpendicular; in this a large fire should be lighted, and kept burning for four or five hours with a continual supply of wood, so that the walls become red hot. At the expiration of the blaze, the foot should be laid upon the glowing embers, and the hole covered closely with thick pieces of green wood laid parallel together to form a ceiling; this should be covered with wet grass, and the whole plastered with mud, and stamped tightly down to retain the heat. Upon the mud, a quantity of earth should be heaped, and the oven should not be opened for thirty hours, or more. At the expiration of that time, the foot will be perfectly baked, and the sole will separate like a shoe, and expose a delicate substance that, with a little oil and vinegar, together with an allowance of pepper and salt, is a delicious dish that will feed about fifty men.

The Arabs are particularly fond of elephant's flesh, as it is generally fat and juicy. I have frequently used the fat of the animal for cooking, but it should be taken from the body without delay; as, if left for a few hours, it partakes of the peculiar smell of the elephant, which no amount of boiling will overcome. The boiling of fat for preservation requires much care, as it should attain so great a heat that a few drops of water thrown upon the surface will hiss and evaporate as though cast upon molten metal; it should then be strained, and, when tolerably cool, be poured into vessels, and secured. No salt is necessary, provided it is thoroughly boiled. When an animal is killed, the flesh should be properly dried, before boiling down, otherwise the fat will not melt thoroughly, as it will be combined with the water contained in the body. The fat should be separated as well as possible from the meat; it should then be hung in long strips upon a line and exposed in the sun to dry; when nearly dried, it should be cut into pieces of about two inches in length, and placed in a large vessel over a brisk fire, and kept constantly stirred. As the fat boils out from the meat, the residue should be taken out with a pierced ladle; this, when cool, should be carefully preserved in leathern bags. This is called by the Arabs "reveet," a supply of which is most valuable, as a quantity can be served out to each man during a long march when there is no time to halt; it can be eaten without bread, and it is extremely nourishing. With a good supply of reveet in store, the traveller need not be nervous about his dinner. Dried meat should also be kept in large quantities; the best is that of the giraffe and hippopotamus, but there is some care required in preparing the first quality. It should be cut from portions of the animals as free as possible from sinews, and should be arranged in long thin strips of the diameter of about an inch and a quarter; these ribbon-like morsels should be hung in the shade. When nearly dry, they should be taken down, and laid upon a flat rock, upon which they should be well beaten with a stone, or club of hard wood; this breaks the fibre; after which they should be hung up and thoroughly dried, care being taken that the flesh is not exposed to the sun. If many flies are present, the flesh should be protected by the smoke of fires lighted to windward.

When meat is thus carefully prepared, it can be used in various ways, and is exceedingly palatable; if pounded into small pieces like coarse sawdust, it forms an admirable material for curry and rice. The Arabs make a first-class dish of melach, by mixing a quantity of pounded dried meat with a thick porridge of dhurra meal, floating in a soup of barmian (waker), with onions, salt, and red peppers; this is an admirable thing if the party is pressed for time (if not too hot, as a large quantity can be eaten with great expedition. As the Arabs are nomadic, they have a few simple but effective arrangements for food during the journey. For a fortnight preparatory to an expedition, the women are busily engaged in manufacturing a supply of abrey. This is made in several methods: there is the sour, and the sweet abrey; the former is made of highly-fermented dhurra paste that has turned intensely acid; this is formed into thin wafers, about sixteen inches in diameter, upon the doka or hearth, and dried in the sun until the abrey has become perfectly crisp; the wafers are then broken up with the hands, and packed in bags. There is no drink more refreshing than water poured over a handful of sour abrey, and allowed to stand for half an hour; it becomes pleasantly acid, and is superior to lemonade. The residue is eaten by the Arabs: thus the abrey supplies both meat and drink. The finest quality of sweet abrey is a very delicate affair; the flour of dhurra must be well sifted; it is then mixed with milk instead of water, and, without fermenting, it is formed into thin wafers similar to those eaten with ice-creams in this country, but extremely large; these are dried in the sun, and crushed like the sour abrey; they will keep for months if kept dry in a leathern bag. A handful of sweet abrey steeped in a bowl of hot milk, with a little honey, is a luxurious breakfast; nothing can be more delicious, and it can be prepared in a few minutes during the short halt upon a journey. With a good supply of abrey and dried meat, the commissariat arrangements are wonderfully simplified, and a party can march a great distance without much heavy baggage to impede their movements.

The flesh that is the least adapted for drying is that of the buffalo (Bos Caffer), which is exceedingly tough and coarse. There are two species of the Bos Caffer in Abyssinia and Central Africa, which, similar in general appearance, differ in the horns; that which resembles the true Bos Caffer of South Africa has very massive convex horns that unite in front, and completely cover the forehead as with a shield; the other variety has massive, but perfectly flat horns of great breadth, that do not quite unite over the os frontis, although nearly so; the flatness of the horns continues in a rough surface, somewhat resembling the bark of a tree, for about twelve inches; the horns then become round, and curve gracefully inwards, like those of the convex species. Buffaloes are very dangerous and determined animals; but, although more accidents occur in hunting these than any other variety of game, I cannot admit that they are such formidable opponents as the elephant and black rhinoceros; they are so much more numerous than the latter, that they are more frequently encountered: hence the casualties.

A buffalo can always be killed with a No. 10 rifle and six drachms of powder when charging, if the hunter will only wait coolly until it is so close that he cannot miss the forehead; but the same rifle will fail against an African elephant, or a black rhinoceros, as the horns of the latter animal effectually protect the brain from a front shot. I have killed some hundreds of buffaloes, and, although in many cases they have been unpleasantly near, the rifle has always won the day. There cannot be a more convenient size than No. 10 for a double rifle, for large game. This will throw a conical projectile of three ounces, with seven drachms of powder. Although a breechloader is a luxury, I would not have more than a pair of such rifles in an expedition in a wild country, as they would require more care in a damp climate than the servants would be likely to bestow upon them, and the ammunition would be a great drawback. This should be divided into packets of ten cartridges each, which should be rolled up in flannel and hermetically sealed in separate tin canisters. Thus arranged, they would be impervious to damp, and might be carried conveniently. But I should decidedly provide myself with four double-barrelled muzzle-loading No. 10's as my regular battery; that, if first class, would never get out of order. Nothing gives such confidence to the gun-bearers as the fact of their rifles being good slayers, and they quickly learn to take a pride in their weapons, and to strive in the race to hand the spare rifles. Dust storms, such as I have constantly witnessed in Africa, would be terrible enemies to breech-loaders, as the hard sand, by grating in the joints, would wear away the metal, and destroy the exactness of the fittings.

A small handy double rifle, such as my little Fletcher 24, not exceeding eight pounds and a half, is very necessary, as it should seldom be out of the hand. Such a rifle should be a breech-loader, as the advantage of loading quickly while on horseback is incalculable. Hunting-knives should be of soft steel, similar to butchers' knives; but one principal knife to be worn daily should be of harder steel, with the back of the blade roughed and case-hardened like a butcher's steel, for sharpening other knives when required.

All boxes for rough travelling should be made of strong metal, japanned. These are a great comfort, as they are proof both against insects and weather, and can be towed with their contents across a river.

Travelling is now so generally understood, that it is hardly necessary to give any instructions for the exploration of wild countries; but a few hints may be acceptable upon points that, although not absolutely essential, tend much to the comfort of the traveller. A couple of large carriage umbrellas with double lining, with small rings fixed to the extremities of the ribs, and a spike similar to that of a fishing-rod to screw into the handle, will form an instantaneous shelter from sun or rain during a halt on the march, as a few strings from the rings will secure it from the wind, if pegged to the ground. Waterproof calico sheeting should be taken in large quantities, and a tarpaulin to protect the baggage during the night's bivouac. No vulcanised India-rubber should be employed in tropical climates; it rots, and becomes useless. A quart syringe for injecting brine into fresh meat is very necessary. In hot climates, the centre of the joint will decompose before the salt can penetrate to the interior, but an injecting syringe will thoroughly preserve the meat in a few minutes. A few powerful fox-traps are useful for catching night-game in countries where there is no large game for the rifle: also wire is useful for making springs.

Several sticks of Indian-ink are convenient, as sufficient can be rubbed up in a few moments to write up the note-book during the march. All journals and note-books should be of tinted paper, green, as the glare of white paper in the intense sunlight of the open sky is most trying to the eyes. Burning glasses and flint and steels are very necessary. Lucifer matches are dangerous, as they may ignite and destroy your baggage in dry weather, and become utterly useless in the damp.

A large supply of quicksilver should be taken for the admixture with lead for hardening bullets, in addition to that required for the artificial horizon; the effect of this metal is far greater than a mixture of tin, as the specific gravity of the bullet is increased.

Throughout a long experience in wild sports, although I admire the velocity of conical projectiles, I always have retained my opinion that, in jungle countries, where in the absence of dogs you require either to disable your game on the spot, or to produce a distinct blood-track that is easily followed, the old-fashioned two-groove belted ball will bag more game than modern bullets; but, on the other hand, the facility of loading a conical bullet already formed into a cartridge is a great advantage. The shock produced by a pointed projectile is nothing compared to that of the old belted ball, unless it is on the principle of Purday's high velocity expanding bullet, which, although perfection for deer-shooting, would be useless against thick-skinned animals, such as buffalo and rhinoceros. In Africa, the variety of game is such, that it is impossible to tell, when loading, at what animal the bullet will be fired; therefore, it is necessary to be armed with a rifle suitable for all comers. My little Fletcher was the Enfield bore, No. 24, and, although a most trusty weapon, the bullets generally failed to penetrate the skull of hippopotami, except in places where the bone was thin, such as behind the ear, and beneath the eyes. Although I killed great numbers of animals with the Enfield bullet, the success was due to tolerably correct shooting, as I generally lost the larger antelopes if wounded by that projectile in any place but the neck, head, or shoulder; the wound did not bleed freely, therefore it was next to impossible to follow up the blood-track; thus a large proportion of wounded animals escaped.

I saw, and shot, thirteen varieties of antelopes while in Africa. Upon arrival at Khartoum, I met Herr von Heuglin, who commanded the expedition in search of Dr. Vogel; he was an industrious naturalist, who had been many years in the Soudan and in Abyssinia. We compared notes of all we had seen and done, and he very kindly supplied me with a list of all the antelopes that he had been able to trace as existing in Abyssinia and the Soudan; he now included my maarif, which he had never met with, and which he agreed was a new species. In the following list, which is an exact copy of that which he had arranged, those marked with an asterisk are species that I have myself shot: –

Catalogue des especes du genre **"Antilope,"** observees en Egypte, dans la Nubie, au Soudan orientale et en Abissinie.

A. – **Gazella,** Blains.
    1. – Spec. G. Dorcas.* Arab. Ghasal.
    2. – G. Arabica,* Ehr. A la cote de la Mer rouge.
    3. – G. Loevipes, Sund. Arab. Abou Horabet? Nubie, Taka, Sennaar, Kordofan.
    4. – G. spec. (?) en Tigreh Choquen (Bogos).
    5. – G. Dama,* Licht. Arab. Adra, Ledra. Riel, Bajouda, Berber, Sennaar, Kordofan.
    6. – G. Soemmeringii, Rupp. Arab. Om Oreba. Tigreh, Arab. Taka, Massowa, Gedaref, Berber, Sennaar.
    7. – G. Leptoceros. Arab. Abou Harab. Gazelle a longues cornes, minces et paralleles. Bajouda, Berber, Taka, Sennaar, Kordofan.

B. – **Calotragus,** Luad.
    8. – C. montanus,* Rupp. Arab. Otrab and El Mor. Amhar, Fiego, Sennaar, Abissinie, Taka, Galabat.
    9. – C. Saltatrix, Forst. Amhar. Sasa. Abissinie.

C. – **Nanotragus,** Wagn.
    10. – N. Hemprichianus, Ehr. Arab. Om dig dig. Abissinie orie tale et occidentale, Taka, Kordofan.

D. – **Cephalolophus,** H. Smith.
    11. – C. Madaqua. Amhar. Midakoua. Galabat, Barka, Abissinie.
    12, 13. – Deux especes inconnues du Fleuve blanc, nominees par les Djenkes, "Amok."

E. – **Redunca.**
    14. – R. Eleotragus, Schrb. Djenke, Bor. Bahr el Abiad.
    15. – R. Behor, Rupp. Amhar. Behor. Abissinie centrale, Kordofan.

16. – R. Kull, nov. spec. Djenke, Koul. Bahr el Abiad.
17. – R. leucotis, Peters et Licht. Djenke, Adjel. Bahr el Abiad, Saubat.
18. – R. Wuil, nov. spec. Djenke, Ouil. Bahr el Abiad, Saubat.
19. – R. Lechee,* Gray. Bahr el Abiad.
20. – R. megcerosa,* Heuglin. Kobus Maria, Gray. Djenke, Abok, Saubat, Bahr el Abiad et Bahr Ghazal.
21. – R. Defassa,* Rupp. Arab. Om Hetehet. Amhar. Dofasa. Djenke, Bor. Bahr el Salame, Galabat, Kordofan, Bahr el Abiad, Dender, Abissinie occidentale et centrale.
22. – R. ellipsiprymna, Ogilby. Djenke, Bor. Bahr el Abiad.

F. – HIPPOTRAGUS, Sund.
23. – H. niger, Harris. Arab. Abou Maarif. Kordofan meridionale, fleuve Blanc (Chilouk).
24. – H. nov. spec. Arab. Abou Maarif.* – Bakerii.* Bahr el Salaam, Galabat Dender, fleuve BIeu, Sennaar meridionale.
25. – H. Beisa, Rupp. Arab. Beisa et Damma. Souakim, Massowa, Danakil, Somauli, Kordofan.
26. – H. ensicornis, Ehr. Arab. Ouahoh el bagr. Nubie, Berber, Kordofan.
27. – H. Addax, Licht. Arab. Akach. Bajouda, Egypte occidentale (Oasis de Siouah).

G. – TAUROTRAGUS, Wagn.
28. – T. Orcas, Pall. (Antilope Canna). Djenke, Goualgonal. Bahr el Abiad.
29. – T. gigas, nov. spec. Chez les pleuplades Atoats, au Bahr el Abiad.

H. – TRAGELAPHUS, Blains.
30. – Tr. strepsiceros (Pallas). Arab. Nellet, Miremreh. Tigreh, Garona. Ambar. Agazen. Abissinie, Sennaar, Homran, Galabat, Kordofan.
31. – Tr. sylvaticus, Spaerm. Bahr el Abiad.
32. – Tr. Dekula, Rupp. Amhar. Dekoula. Arab. Houch. Djenke, Ber. Taka, Abissinie, Bahr el Abiad.

I. – BUBALIS.
33. – B. Mauritanica, Sund. (Antilope Bubalis, Cuvier). Arab. Tetel; Tigreh, Tori. Taka, Homran, Barka, Galabat, Kordofan, Bahr el Abiad.

34. – B. Caama, Cuv. Arab. Tetel. Djenke, Awalwon. Bahr el Abiad, Kordofan meridionale.
35. – B. Senegalensis, H. Smith. Bahr el Abiad.
36. – B. Tiang, nov. spec. Djenke, Tian. Bahr el Abiad, Bahr Ghazal.
37. – B. Tian-riel, nov. spec. Bahr el Abiad.

Species Incertae

- "Soada," au Oualkait et Mareb (Taurotragus?).
- "Uorobo," au Godjam, Agow (Hippotragus).
- "Ouoadembi." March, Oualkait (Hippotragus).
- "El Mor." Sennaar, Fazogle (Nanotragus?).
- "El Khondieh." Kordofan (Redunca?).
- "Om Khat." Kordofan (Gazella?).
- "El Hamra." Kordofan, Bajouda (Gazella?).

Chapter XXII.

We Leave the Dinder.

For some days we continued our journey along the banks of the Dinder, and as the monotonous river turned towards the junction with the Blue Nile, a few miles distant, we made a direct cut across the flat country, to cross the Rahad and arrive at Abou Harraz on the Blue Nile. We passed numerous villages and extensive plantations of dhurra that were deserted by the Arabs, as the soldiers had arrived to collect the taxes. I measured the depths of the wells, seventy-five feet and a half, from the surface to the bottom; the alluvial soil appeared to continue the whole distance, until the water was discovered resting upon hard sand, full of small particles of mica. During the march over a portion of the country that had been cleared by burning, we met a remarkably curious hunting-party. A number of the common black and white stork were hunting for grasshoppers and other insects, but mounted upon the back of each stork was a large copper-coloured flycatcher, which, perched like a rider on his horse, kept a bright look-out for insects, which from its elevated position it could easily discover upon the ground. I watched them for some time: whenever the storks perceived a grasshopper or other winged insect, they chased it on foot, but if they missed their game, the flycatchers darted from their backs and flew after the insects like falcons, catching them in their beaks, and then returning to their steeds to look out for another opportunity.

On the evening of the 23d May we arrived at the Rahad close to its junction with the Blue Nile: it was still dry, although the Dinder was rising. I accounted for this, from the fact of the extreme length of the Rahad's bed, which, from its extraordinary tortuous course, must absorb a vast amount of water in the dry sand, before the advancing stream can reach the Nile. Both the Rahad and Dinder rise in the mountains of Abyssinia, at no great distance from each other, and during the rains they convey a large volume of water to the Blue Nile. Upon arrival at Abou Harraz, four miles to the north of the Rahad junction, we had marched, by careful dead reckoning, two hundred and eighty miles from Gallabat. We were now about a hundred and fifteen miles from Khartoum, and we stood upon the banks of the magnificent Blue Nile, the last of the Abyssinian affluents.

About six miles above this spot, on the south bank of the river, is the large town of Wat Medene, which is the principal trading-place upon the river. Abou Harraz was a miserable spot, and was only important as the turning point upon the road to Katariff from Khartoum. The entire country upon both sides of the river is one vast unbroken level of rich soil, wlich on the north and east sides is bounded by the Atbara. The entire surface of this fertile country might be cultivated with cotton. All that is required to insure productiveness, is a regular supply of water, which might be artificially arranged without much difficulty. The character of all the Abyssinian rivers is to rise and fall suddenly; thus at one season there is an abundance of water, to be followed by a scarcity: but in all the fertile provinces adjacent to the Settite and the upper portion of the Atbara, the periodical rains can be absolutely depended upon, from June to the middle of September; thus, they are peculiarly adapted for cotton, as a dry season is insured for gathering the crop. As we advance to the north, and reach Abou Harraz, we leave the rainy zone. When we had left Gallabat, the grass had sprung several inches, owing to the recent showers; but as we had proceeded rapidly towards the north, we had entered upon vast dusty plains devoid of a green blade; the rainy season between Abou Harraz and Khartoum consisted of mere occasional storms, that, descending with great violence, quickly passed away. Nothing would be more simple than to form a succession of weirs across the Rahad and Dinder, that would enable the entire country to be irrigated at any season of the year, but there is not an engineering work of any description throughout Upper Egypt, beyond the sageer or water-wheel of the Nile. Opposite Abou Harraz, the Blue Nile was a grand river, about five hundred yards in width; the banks upon the north side were the usual perpendicular cliffs of alluvial soil, but perfectly bare of trees; while, on the south, the banks were ornamented with nabbuk bushes and beautiful palms. The latter are a peculiar species known by the Arabs as "dolape" (Borassus AEthiopicus): the stem is long, and of considerable thickness, but in about the centre of its length it swells to nearly half its diameter in excess, and after a few feet of extra thickness it continues its original size to the summit, which is crowned by a handsome crest of leaves shaped like those of the palmyra. The fruit of this palm is about the size of a cocoa-nut, and when ripe it is of a bright yellow, with an exceedingly rich perfume of apricots; it is very stringy, and, although eaten by the natives, it is beyond the teeth of a European. The Arabs cut it into slices, and boil it with water until they obtain a strong syrup. Subsequently I found this palm in great quantities near the equator.

At Abou Harraz I discharged my camels, and endeavoured to engage a boat to convey us to Khartoum, thus to avoid the dusty and uninteresting ride of upwards of a hundred miles along its flat and melancholy banks; but there was not a vessel of any kind to be seen upon the river, except one miserable, dirty affair, for which the owner demanded fourteen hundred piastres for a passage. We accordingly procured camels, and started, intending to march as rapidly as possible.

"June 2, 1862. – We packed the camels in the morning and started them off to Rufaar. We followed at 2.30 P.M. as the natives declared it was half a day's journey; but we did not arrive until 8.30 P.M. having marched about twenty-one miles. The town is considerable, and is the head-quarters of our old friend, the great Sheik Achmet Abou Sinn; he is now absent, but his son Ali is at home. He received us very kindly, and lodged us in his own house within a large inclosed court, with a well of good water in the centre. Having read my firman, be paid us the usual compliments, but he lacked the calm dignity and ease of manner of his grand old father. He sat stiffly upon the divan, occasionally relieving the monotony of his position by lifting up the cover of the cushions, and spitting beneath it. Not having a handkerchief, but only the limited natural advantages of a finger and thumb, a cold in the head gave him much trouble, and unpleasant marks upon the wall exhibited hieroglyphics of recent date, that were ill adapted to the reception-room of an Arab chieftain. In about an hour he departed, and shortly after, a dinner of four dishes was brought. No. 1 was an Arab Irish stew, but alas! *minus* the potatoes; it was very good, nevertheless, as the mutton was fat. No. 2 was an Arab stew, with no Irish element; it was very hot with red pepper, and rather dry. No. 3 was a good quick fry of small pieces of mutton in butter and garlic (very good); and No. 4 was an excellent dish of the usual melach, already described.

The wind had within the last few days changed to south, and we had been subjected to dust storms and sudden whirlwinds similar to those we had experienced at this season in the preceding year, when about to start from Berber. We left Rufaar, and continued our march along the banks of the Blue Nile, towards Khartoum. It was intensely hot; whenever we felt a breeze it was accompanied with a suffocating dust, but the sight of the broad river was cool and refreshing. During the dry season the water of the Blue Nile is clear, as its broad surface reflects the colour of the blue sky; hence the appellation, but at that time it was extremely shallow, and in many places it is fordable at a depth of about three feet, which renders it unnavigable for large boats, which, laden with corn, supply Khartoum from the fertile provinces of the south. The river had now begun to rise, although it was still low, and the water was muddy, as the swelling torrents of Abyssinia brought impurities into the main channel. It was at this same time last year, when at Berber, that we had noticed the sudden increase and equally sudden fall of the Nile, that was influenced by the fluctuations of the Blue Nile, at a time when the Atbara was dry.

From Abou Harraz throughout the route to Khartoum there is no object of interest; it is the same vast flat, decreasing rapidly in fertility until it mingles with the desert; and once more, as we journey to the north, we leave the fertile lands behind, and enter upon sterility. The glare of barren plains and the heat of the summer's sun were fearful. Bacheet had a slight coup de soleil; my Tokrooris, whose woolly heads were shaved, and simply covered with a thin skull-cap, suffered severely, as we marched throughout the burning hours of the day. The Arabs were generally very inhospitable, as this was the route frequented by all native merchants, where strangers were of daily occurrence; but towards evening we arrived at a village inhabited by a large body of Fakeers, or priests. As we entered, we were met by the principal Faky, who received us with marked attention, and with a charming courtesy of manner that quite won our hearts; he expressed himself as delighted at our arrival, hoped we were not fatigued by the heat, and trusted that we would rest for a few minutes before we departed to the enchanting village "just beyond those trees," as he pointed to a clump of green nabbuk on the yellow plain, about a mile distant; there, he assured us, we could obtain all kinds of supplies, together with shade, and a lovely view of the river. We were delighted with this very gentlemanly Faky, and, saying adieu with regret, we hurried on to the promised village "just beyond those trees."

For fourteen miles we travelled, hungry and tired, beyond the alluring clump of trees, along the wild desert of hot sand without a habitation; the only portion of truth in the Faky's description was the "lovely view of the river," that certainly accompanied us throughout our journey. We were regularly "sold" by the cunning Faky, who, not wishing to be incommoded by our party, had got rid of us in a most gentlemanly manner. At length we arrived at a village, where we had much difficulty in procuring provisions for ourselves and people.

On the 11th June, having slept at the village of Abou Dome, we started at sunrise, and at 9 A.M. we reached the bank of the river, opposite to Khartoum. We were delighted with the view, as the morning sun shone upon the capital of the Soudan provinces; the grove of date trees shaded the numerous buildings, their dark green foliage contrasting exquisitely with the many coloured houses on the extreme margin of the beautiful river; long lines of vessels and masts gave life to the scene, and we felt that once more, after twelve months of utterly wild life, we had arrived in civilization. We had outridden our camels, therefore we rode through a shallow arm of the river, and arrived upon an extensive sandbank that had been converted into a garden of melons; from this point a large ferry-boat plied regularly to the town on the south bank. In a few minutes we found ourselves on board, with our sole remaining horse, Tetel, also the donkeys that we had purchased in Berber before our expedition, and our attendants. As we gained the centre of the river, that was about 800 yards broad, we were greeted by the snort of three of our old friends, the hippopotami, who had been attracted to the neighbourhood by the garden of water-melons. We landed at Khartoum, and, having climbed up the steep bank, we inquired the way to the British Consulate.

The difference between the view of Khartoum at the distance of a mile, with the sun shining upon the bright river Nile in the foreground, to the appearance of the town upon close inspection, was about equal to the scenery of a theatre as regarded from the boxes or from the stage; even that painful exposure of an optical illusion would be trifling compared with the imposture of Khartoum; the sense of sight had been deceived by distance, but the sense of smell was outraged by innumerable nuisances, when we set foot within the filthy and miserable town. After winding through some narrow dusty lanes, hemmed in by high walls of sun-baked bricks, that had fallen in gaps in several places, exposing gardens of prickly pears and date palms, we at length arrived at a large open place, that, if possible, smelt more strongly than the landing spot. Around this square, which was full of holes where the mud had been excavated for brickmaking, were the better class of houses; this was the Belgravia of Khartoum. In the centre of a long mud wall, ventilated by certain attempts at frameless windows, guarded by rough wooden bars, we perceived a large archway with closed doors; above this entrance was a shield, with a device that gladdened my English eyes: there was the British lion and the unicorn! Not such a lion as I had been accustomed to meet in his native jungles, a yellow cowardly fellow, that had often slunk away from the very prey from which I had driven him, but a real red British lion, that, although thin and ragged in the unhealthy climate of Khartoum, looked as though he was pluck to the backbone.

This was the English Consulate. I regarded our lion and unicorn for a few moments with feelings of veneration; and as Mr. Petherick, the consul, who was then absent on the White Nile in search of Speke and Grant, had very kindly begged me to occupy some rooms in the Consulate, we entered a large courtyard, and were immediately received by two ostriches that came to meet us; these birds entertained us by an impromptu race as hard as they could go round the courtyard, as though performing in a circus. When this little divertissement was finished, we turned to the right, and were shown by a servant up a flight of steps into a large airy room that was to be our residence, which, being well protected from the sun, was cool and agreeable. Mr. Petherick had started from Khartoum in the preceding March, and had expected to meet Speke and Grant in the upper portion of the Nile regions, on their road from Zanzibar; but there are insurmountable difficulties in those wild countries, and his expedition met with unforeseen accidents, that, in spite of the exertions of both himself, his very devoted wife, Dr. Murie, and two or three Europeans, drove them from their intended path. Shortly after our arrival at the Consulate, a vessel returned from his party with unfavourable accounts; they had started too late in the season, owing to some difficulties in procuring boats, and the change of wind to the south, with violent rain, had caused great suffering, and had retarded their progress. This same boat had brought two leopards that were to be sent to England: these animals were led into the courtyard, and, having been secured by chains, they formed a valuable addition to the menagerie, which consisted of two wild boars, two leopards, one hyaena, two ostriches, and a cynocephalus or dog-faced baboon, who won my heart by taking an especial fancy to me, because I had a beard like his master.

Although I take a great interest in wild animals, I confess to have an objection to sleep in the Zoological Gardens should all the wild beasts be turned loose. I do not believe that even the Secretary of that learned Society would volunteer to sleep with the lions; but as the leopards at the Khartoum Consulate constantly broke their chains, and attacked the dogs and a cow, and as the hyaena occasionally got loose, and the wild boars destroyed their mud wall, and nearly killed one of my Tokrooris during the night, by carving him like a scored leg of pork with their tusks, the fact of sleeping in the open air in the verandah, with the simple protection of a mosquito-netting, was full of pleasant excitement, and was a piquante entertainment that prevented a reaction of ennui after twelve months passed in constant watchfulness. The shield over the Consulate door, with the lion and the unicorn, was but a sign of the life within; as the grand picture outside the showman's wagon may exemplify the nature of his exhibition. I enjoyed myself extremely with these creatures, especially when the ostriches invited themselves to tea, and swallowed our slices of water-melons and the greater portion of the bread from the table a few moments before we were seated. These birds appeared to enjoy life amazingly; one kind of food was as sweet as another; they attacked a basket of white porcelain beads that had been returned by Mr. Petherick's men, and swallowed them in great numbers in mistake for dhurra, until they were driven off; they were the scavengers of the courtyard, that consumed the dung of the camels and horses, together with all other impurities.

For some months we resided at Khartoum, as it was necessary to make extensive preparations for the White Nile expedition, and to await the arrival of the north wind, which would enable us to start early in December. Although the north and south winds blow alternately for six months, and the former commences in October, it does not extend many degrees southward until the beginning of December. This is a great drawback to White Nile exploration, as when near the north side of the equator, the dry season commences in November, and closes in February; thus, the departure from Khartoum should take place by a steamer in the latter part of September; that would enable the traveller to leave Gondokoro, lat. N. 4 degrees 54 minutes, shortly before November; he would then secure three months of favourable weather for an advance inland.

Having promised Mek Nimmur that I would lay his proposals for peace before the Governor-General of the Soudan, I called upon Moosa Pasha at the public divan, and delivered the message; but he would not listen to any intercession, as he assured me that Mek Nimmur was incorrigible, and there would be no real peace until his death, which would be very speedy should he chance to fall into his hands. He expressed great surprise at our having escaped from his territory, and he declared his intention of attacking him after he should have given the Abyssinians a lesson, for whom he was preparing an expedition in reply to an insolent letter that he had received from King Theodore. The King of Abyssinia had written to him upon a question of frontier. The substance of the document was a declaration that the Egyptians had no right to Khartoum, and that the natural boundary of Abyssinia was the junction of the Blue and White Niles as far north as Shendy (Mek Nimmur's original country); and from that point, in a direct line, to the Atbara; but that, as the desert afforded no landmark, he should send his people to dig a ditch from the Nile to the Atbara, and he requested that the Egyptians would keep upon the north border. Moosa Pasha declared that the king was mad, and that, were it not for the protection given to Abyssinia by the English, the Egyptians would have eaten it up long ago, but that the Christian powers would certainly interfere should they attempt to annex the country.

The Egyptians seldom had less than twenty thousand troops in the Soudan provinces; the principal stations were Khartoum, Cassala, and Dongola. Cassala was close to the Abyssinian frontier, and within from fifteen to twenty days' march of Souakim, on the Red Sea, to which reinforcements could be despatched in five days from Cairo. Khartoum had the advantage of the Blue Nile, that was navigable for steamers and sailing vessels as far south as Fazogle, from which spot, as well as from Gallabat, Abyssinia could be invaded; while swarms of Arabs, including the celebrated Hamrans, the Beni Amer, Hallongas, Hadendowas, Shookeriahs, and Dabainas, could be slipped like greyhounds across the frontier. Abyssinia is entirely at the mercy of Egypt.

Moosa Pasha subsequently started with several thousand men to drive the Abyssinians from Gallabat, which position they had occupied in force with the avowed intention of marching upon Khartoum; but upon the approach of the Egyptians they fell back rapidly across the mountains, without a sign of showing fight. The Egyptians would not follow them, as they feared the intervention of the European powers.

Upon our first arrival in Khartoum, from 11th June until early in October, the heat was very oppressive, the thermometer seldom below 95 degrees Fahr. in the shade, and frequently 100 degrees, while the nights were 82 degrees Fahr. In the winter, the temperature was agreeable, the shade 80 degrees, the night 62 degrees Fahr. But the chilliness of the north wind was exceedingly dangerous, as the sudden gusts checked the perspiration, and produced various maladies, more especially fever. I had been extremely fortunate, as, although exposed to hard work for more than a year in the burning sun, I had remarkably good health, as had my wife likewise, with the exception of one severe attack while at Sofi. Throughout the countries we had visited, the temperature was high, averaging about 90 degrees in the shade from May until the end of September; but the nights were generally about 70 degrees, with the exception of the winter months, from November until February, when the thermometer generally fell to 85 degrees Fahr. in the day, and sometimes as low as 58 degrees at between 2 and 5 a.m.

I shall not repeat a minute description of Khartoum that has already been given in the "Albert N'yanza;" it is a wretchedly unhealthy town, containing about thirty thousand inhabitants, exclusive of troops. In spite of its unhealthiness and low situation, on a level with the river at the junction of the Blue and White Niles, it is the general emporium for the trade of the Soudan, from which the productions of the country are transported to Lower Egypt, i.e. ivory, hides, senna, gum arabic, and bees'-wax. During my experience of Khartoum it was the hotbed of the slave-trade. It will be remarked that the exports from the Soudan are all natural productions. There is nothing to exhibit the industry or capacity of the natives; the ivory is the produce of violence and robbery; the hides are the simple sun-dried skins of oxen; the senna grows wild upon the desert; the gum arabic exudes spontaneously from the bushes of the jungle; and the bees'-wax is the produce of the only industrious creatures in that detestable country.

When we regard the general aspect of the Soudan, it is extreme wretchedness; the rainfall is uncertain and scanty, thus the country is a desert, dependent entirely upon irrigation. Although cultivation is simply impossible without a supply of water, one of the most onerous taxes is that upon the sageer or water-wheel, with which the fields are irrigated on the borders of the Nile. It would appear natural that, instead of a tax, a premium should be offered for the erection of such means of irrigation, which would increase the revenue by extending cultivation, the produce of which might bear an impost. With all the talent and industry of the native Egyptians, who must naturally depend upon the waters of the Nile for their existence, it is extraordinary that for thousands of years they have adhered to their original simple form of mechanical irrigation, without improvement.

If any one will take the trouble to watch the action of the sageer or water-wheel, it must strike him as a most puny effort to obtain a great result, that would at once suggest an extension of the principle. The sageer is merely a wheel of about twenty feet diameter, which is furnished with numerous earthenware jars upon its exterior circumference, that upon revolving perform the action of a dredger, but draw to the surface water instead of mud. The wheel, being turned by oxen, delivers the water into a trough which passes into a reservoir, roughly fashioned with clay, from which, small channels of about ten inches in width radiate through the plantation. The fields, divided into squares like a chess-board, are thus irrigated by a succession of minute aqueducts. The root of this principle is the reservoir. A certain steady volume of water is required, from which the arteries shall flow throughout a large area of dry ground; thus, the reservoir insures a regular supply to each separate channel.

In any civilized country, the existence of which depended upon the artificial supply of water in the absence of rain, the first engineering principle would suggest a saving of labour in irrigation: that, instead of raising the water in small quantities into reservoirs, the river should raise its own waters to the required level.

Having visited every tributary of the Nile during the explorations of nearly five years, I have been struck with the extraordinary fact that, although an enormous amount of wealth is conveyed to Egypt by the annual inundations of the river, the force of the stream is entirely uncontrolled. From time immemorial, the rise of the Nile has been watched with intense interest at the usual season, but no attempt has been made to insure a supply of water to Egypt during all seasons.

The mystery of the Nile has been dispelled; we have proved that the equatorial lakes supply the main stream, but that the inundations are caused by the sudden rush of waters from the torrents of Abyssinia in July, August, and September; and that the soil washed down by the floods of the Atbara is at the present moment silting up the mouths of the Nile, and thus slowly, but steadily, forming a delta beneath the waters of the Mediterranean, on the same principle that created the fertile Delta of Egypt. Both the water and the mud of the Nile have duties to perform, – the water to irrigate; the deposit to fertilize; but these duties are not regularly performed: sometimes the rush of the inundation is overwhelming, at others it is insufficient; while at all times an immense proportion of the fertilizing mud is not only wasted by a deposit beneath the sea, but navigation is impeded by the silt. The Nile is a powerful horse without harness, but, with a bridle in its mouth, the fertility of Egypt might be increased to a vast extent.

As the supply of water raised by the sageer is received in a reservoir, from which the irrigating channels radiate through the plantations, so should great reservoirs be formed throughout the varying levels of Egypt, from Khartoum to the Mediterranean, comprising a distance of sixteen degrees of latitude, with a fall of fifteen hundred feet. The advantage of this great difference in altitude between the Nile in latitude 15 degrees 30 minutes and the sea, would enable any amount of irrigation, by the establishment of a series of dams or weirs across the Nile, that would raise its level to the required degree, at certain points, from which the water would be led by canals into natural depressions; these would form reservoirs, from which the water might be led upon a vast scale, in a similar manner to the insignificant mud basins that at the present day form the reservoirs for the feeble water-wheels. The increase of the river's level would depend upon the height of the dams; but, as stone is plentiful throughout the Nile, the engineering difficulties would be trifling.

Mehemet Ali Pasha acknowledged the principle, by the erection of the barrage between Cairo and Alexandria, which, by simply raising the level of the river, enabled the people to extend their channels for irrigation; but this was the crude idea, that has not been carried out upon a scale commensurate with the requirements of Egypt. The ancient Egyptians made use of the lake Mareotis as a reservoir for the Nile waters for the irrigation of a large extent of Lower Egypt, by taking advantage of a high Nile to secure a supply for the remainder of the year; but, great as were the works of those industrious people, they appear to have ignored the first principle of irrigation, by neglecting to raise the level of the river.

Egypt remains in the same position that Nature originally allotted to her; the life-giving stream that flows through a thousand miles of burning sands suddenly rises in July, and floods the Delta which it has formed by a deposit, during perhaps hundreds of thousands of inundations; and it wastes a superabundance of fertilizing mud in the waters of the Mediterranean. As Nature has thus formed, and is still forming a delta, why should not Science create a delta, with the powerful means at our disposal? Why should not the mud of the Nile that now silts up the Mediterranean be directed to the barren but vast area of deserts, that by such a deposit would become a fertile portion of Egypt? This work might be accomplished by simple means: the waters of the Nile, that now rush impetuously at certain seasons with overwhelming violence, while at other seasons they are exhausted, might be so controlled that they should never be in excess, neither would they be reduced to a minimum in the dry season; but the enormous volume of water heavily charged with soil, that now rushes uselessly into the sea, might be led throughout the deserts of Nubia and Libya, to transform them into cotton fields that would render England independent of America. There is no fiction in this idea; it is merely the simple and commonplace fact, that with a fall of fifteen hundred feet in a thousand miles, with a river that supplies an unlimited quantity of water and mud at a particular season, a supply could be afforded to a prodigious area, that would be fertilized not only by irrigation, but by the annual deposit of soil from the water, allowed to remain upon the surface. This suggestion might be carried out by gradations; the great work might be commenced by a single dam above the first cataract at Assouan, at a spot where the river is walled in by granite hills; at that place, the water could be raised to an exceedingly high level, that would command an immense tract of country. As the system became developed, similar dams might be constructed at convenient intervals that would not only bring into cultivation the neighbouring deserts, but would facilitate the navigation of the river, that is now impeded, and frequently closed, by the numerous cataracts. By raising the level of the Nile sixty feet at every dam, the cataracts would no longer exist, as the rocks which at present form the obstructions would be buried in the depths of the river. At the positions of the several dams, sluice gates and canals would conduct the shipping either up or down the stream. Were this principle carried out as far as the last cataracts, near Khartoum, the Soudan would no longer remain a desert; the Nile would become not only the cultivator of those immense tracts that are now utterly worthless, but it would be the navigable channel of Egypt for the extraordinary distance of twenty-seven degrees of latitude – direct from the Mediterranean to Gondokoro, N. lat. 4 degrees 54 minutes.

The benefits, not only to Egypt, but to civilization, would be incalculable; those remote countries in the interior of Africa are so difficult of access, that, although we cling to the hope that at some future time the inhabitants may become enlightened, it will be simply impossible to alter their present condition, unless we change the natural conditions under which they exist. From a combination of adverse circumstances, they are excluded from the civilized world: the geographical position of those desert-locked and remote countries shuts them out from personal communication with strangers: the hardy explorer and the missionary creep through the difficulties of distance in their onward paths, but seldom return: the European merchant is rarely seen, and trade resolves itself into robbery and piracy upon the White Nile, and other countries, where distance and difficulty of access have excluded all laws and political surveillance. Nevertheless, throughout that desert, and neglected wilderness, the Nile has flowed for ages, and the people upon its banks are as wild and uncivilized at the present day as they were when the Pyramids were raised in Lower Egypt. The Nile is a blessing only half appreciated; the time will arrive when people will look in amazement upon a mighty Egypt, whose waving crops shall extend, far beyond the horizon, upon those sandy and thirsty deserts where only the camel can contend with exhausted nature. Men will look down from some lofty point upon a network of canals and reservoirs, spreading throughout a land teeming with fertility, and wonder how it was that, for so many ages, the majesty of the Nile had been concealed. Not only the sources of that wonderful river had been a mystery from the earliest history of the world, but the resources and the power of the mighty Nile are still mysterious and misunderstood.

In all rainless countries, artificial irrigation is the first law of nature, it is self-preservation; but, even in countries where the rainfall can be depended upon with tolerable certainty, irrigation should never be neglected; one dry season in a tropical country may produce a famine, the results of which may be terrible, as instanced lately by the unfortunate calamity in Orissa. The remains of the beautiful system of artificial irrigation that was employed by the ancients in Ceylon, attest the degree of civilization to which they had attained; in that island the waters of various rivers were conducted into valleys that were converted into lakes, by dams of solid masonry that closed the extremity, from which the water was conducted by artificial channels throughout the land. In those days, Ceylon was the most fertile country of the East; her power equalled her prosperity; vast cities teeming with a dense population stood upon the borders of the great reservoirs, and the people revelled in wealth and plenty. The dams were destroyed in civil warfare; the wonderful works of irrigation shared in the destruction; the country dried up; famine swallowed up the population; and the grandeur and prosperity of that extraordinary country collapsed and withered in the scorching sun, when the supply of water was withdrawn.

At the present moment, ten thousand square miles lie desolate in thorny jungles, where formerly a sea of waving rice-crops floated on the surface; the people are dead, the glory is departed. This glory had been the fruit of irrigation. All this prosperity might be restored: but in Egypt there has been no annihilation of a people, and the Nile invites a renewal of the system formerly adopted in Ceylon; there is an industrious population crowded upon a limited space of fertile soil, and yearning for an increase of surface. At the commencement of this work, we saw the Egyptians boating the earth from the crumbling ruins, and transporting it with arduous labour to spread upon the barren sandbanks of the Nile, left by the retreating river; they were striving for every foot of land thus offered by the exhausted waters, and turning into gardens what in other countries would have been unworthy of cultivation. Were a system of irrigation established upon the principle that I have proposed, the advantages would be enormous. The silt deposited in the Mediterranean, that now chokes the mouths of the Nile, and blocks up harbours, would be precipitated upon the broad area of newly-irrigated lands, and by the time that the water arrived at the sea, it would have been filtered in its passage, and have become incapable of forming a fresh deposit. The great difficulty of the Suez canal will be the silting up of the entrance by the Nile; this would be prevented were the mud deposited in the upper country.

During the civil war in America, Egypt proved her capabilities by producing a large amount of cotton of most excellent quality, that assisted us materially in the great dearth of that article; but, although large fortunes were realized by the extension of this branch of agriculture, the Egyptians suffered considerably in consequence. The area of fertile soil was too limited, and, as an unusual surface was devoted to the growth of cotton, there was a deficiency in the production of corn; and Egypt, instead of exporting as heretofore, was forced to import large quantities of grain. Were the area of Egypt increased to a vast extent by the proposed system of irrigation, there would be space sufficient for both grain and cotton to any amount required. The desert soil, that is now utterly worthless, would become of great value; and the taxes upon the increased produce would not only cover the first outlay of the irrigation works, but would increase the revenue in the ratio proportionate to the increased surface of fertility. A dam across the Atbara would irrigate the entire country from Gozerajup to Berber, a distance of upwards of 200 miles; and the same system upon the Nile would carry the waters throughout the deserts between Khartoum and Dongola, and from thence to Lower Egypt. The

Nubian desert, from Korosko to Abou Hamed, would become a garden, the whole of that sterile country inclosed within the great western bend of the Nile towards Dongola would be embraced in the system of irrigation, and the barren sands that now give birth to the bitter melon of the desert (Cucumis colocynthis), would bring forth the water-melon, and heavy crops of grain.[15] The great Sahara is desert, simply because it receives no rainfall: give it only water, and the sand will combine with the richer soil beneath, and become productive. England would become a desert, could it be deprived of rain for three or four years; the vegetation would wither and be carried away by the wind, together with the lighter and more friable portions of the soil, which, reduced to dust, would leave the coarser and more sandy particles exposed upon the surface; but the renewal of rain would revivify the country. The deserts of Egypt have never known rain, except in the form of an unexpected shower, that has passed away as suddenly as it arrived; even that slight blessing awakens ever-ready Nature, and green things appear upon the yellow surface of the ground, that cause the traveller to wonder how their seeds could germinate after the exposure for so many months in the burning sand. Give water to these thirsty deserts, and they will reply with gratitude.

This is the way to civilize a country: the engineer will alter the hard conditions of nature, that have rendered man as barren of good works as the sterile soil upon which he lives. Let man have hope; improve the present, that his mind may look forward to a future; give him a horse that will answer to the spur, if he is to run in the race of life; give him a soil that will yield and tempt him to industry; give him the means of communication with his fellow-men, that he may see his own inferiority by comparison; provide channels for the transport of his produce, and for the receipt of foreign manufactures, that will engender commerce: and then, when he has advanced so far in the scale of humanity, you may endeavour to teach him the principles of Christianity. Then, and not till then, can we hope for moral progress. We must begin with the development of the physical capabilities of a country before we can expect from its inhabitants sufficient mental vigour to receive and understand the truths of our religion. I have met with many Christian missionaries, of various and conflicting creeds, who have fruitlessly sown the seed of Christianity upon the barren soil of

15   The great deserts of Northern Africa, to about the 17o N. lat., are supposed to have formed the bottom of the Mediterranean, but to have been upheaved to their present level. The volcanic bombs discovered in the Nubian Desert suggest, by their spherical form, that the molten lava ejected by active volcanoes had fallen from a great heigh into water, that had rapidly cooled them, in the same manner that lead shot is manufactured at the present day. It is therefore highly probable that the extinct craters now in existence in the Nubian Desert were active at a period when they formed volcanic islands in a sea – similar to Stromboli, &c. &c.

Africa; but their labours were ill-timed, they were too early in the field, the soil is unprepared; the missionary, however earnest, must wait until there be some foundation for a superstructure. Raise the level of the waters, and change the character of the surrounding deserts: this will also raise the intellectual condition of the inhabitants by an improvement in the natural conditions of their country. . . . .

The first portion of our task was completed. We had visited all the Nile tributaries of Abyssinia, including the great Blue Nile that had been traced to its source by Bruce. The difficult task still lay before us – to penetrate the unknown regions in the distant south, to discover the White Nile source.[16] Speke and Grant were on their road from Zanzibar, cutting their way upon untrodden ground towards Gondokoro. Petherick's expedition to assist them had met with misfortune, and we trusted to be able to reach the equator, and perhaps to meet our Zanzibar explorers somewhere about the sources of the Nile. Although we had worked hard throughout all seasons, over an immense extent of country, we were both strong and well, and the rest of some months at Khartoum had only served to inspire us with new vigour for the commencement of the work before us. By the 17th December, 1862, our preparations were completed; three vessels were laden with large quantities of stores – 400 bushels of corn, twenty-nine transport animals, including camels, donkeys, and horses (among the latter was my old hunter Tetel). Ninety-six souls formed my whole party, including forty well-armed men, with Johann Schmidt and Richarn. On the 18th December we sailed from Khartoum upon the White Nile towards its unknown sources, and bade farewell to the last vestige of law, government, and civilization. I find in my journal, the last words written at our departure upon this uncertain task, "God grant us success; if He guides, I have no fear."

---

16   The account of the White Nile voyage, with the happy meeting of captains Speke and Grant, and the subsequent discovery of the "Albert N'yanza," has been already given in the work of that title.

www.ingramcontent.com/pod-product-compliance
Lightning Source LLC
LaVergne TN
LVHW021559070426
835507LV00014B/1858